Reforming Institutions in Water Resource Management

Reforming Institutions in Water Resource Management

Policy and Performance for Sustainable Development

Edited by Lin Crase and Vasant P. Gandhi

First published by Earthscan in the UK and USA in 2009

For a full list of publications please contact:
Earthscan
2 Park Square, Milton Park, Abingdon, Oxfordshire OX14 4RN
711 Third Avenue, New York, NY 10017

First issued in paperback 2015

Earthscan is an imprint of the Taylor & Francis Group, an informa business

ISBN 13: 978-1-138-86692-8 (pbk)
ISBN 13: 978-1-8440-7755-7 (hbk)

Typeset by FiSH Books, Enfield
Cover design by Yvonne Booth

A catalogue record for this book is available from the British Library

Library of Congress Cataloging-in-Publication Data

Reforming institution in water resource management: policy performance for sustainable development/edited by Lin Crase and Vasant P. Gandhi.
p. cm.
Includes bibliographical references and index.
ISBN 978–1–84407–755–7 (hardback)
1. Water-supply–Government policy–Developing countries. 2. Water-supply–Government policy–India. 3. Water resources development–Government policy–Developing countries. 4. Sustainable development–Developing countries. 5. Rural poor–Services for–Developing countries. 6. Public institutions–Developing countries–Administration.
I. Crase, Lin. II. Gandhi, Vasant P.
TD327.R45 2009
363.6'1–dc22 2009001380

This manuscript is dedicated to Phillip Pagan in recognition of his wise insights into institutional analysis, his enthusiasm for research and thorough professionalism. His friendship and good humour are sadly missed by his colleagues.

Contents

List of Figures, Tables and Boxes

Figures

Tables

Boxes

List of Contributors

Dr Jayanath Ananda is a lecturer in economics and business at La Trobe University, Australia. His research interests centre on water policy and decision making, institutional economics and sustainability. Currently he is involved in several projects relating to enhancing the performance of water institutions.

Vaibhav Bhamoriya is a doctoral student at the Indian Institute of Management, Ahmedabad, India. His thesis focuses on adaptiveness of water management institutions. He holds a Masters in rural management and has worked with the International Water Management Institute on research projects focusing on waste-water irrigation, tribal community water use and livelihoods, and the adoption of micro-irrigation. He has several publications. His research interests include institutional economics, performance of water institutions, rural socio-economic development and livelihoods.

Dr Lin Crase is the executive director of La Trobe University's Albury-Wodonga campus and associate professor of economics. His research interests are primarily in the area of policy formulation and institutional economics, with a particular focus on water and regional communities. He has published widely on both topics including contributing to a recent volume dealing with policy and strategic behaviour in water resource management.

Dr Vasant P. Gandhi is professor of economics and agribusiness at the Indian Institute of Management, Ahmedabad, India. He holds a PhD from Stanford University and has worked with the World Bank and the International Food Policy Research Institute. He has published widely and represents India on the Council of the International Association of Agricultural Economists. His research interests include institutional economics, water resource management, investment behaviour in agriculture, technology in agriculture, food marketing and food policy.

Dr Gamini Herath is an associate professor of economics at the School of Accounting, Economics and Finance, Deakin University, Geelong Campus at Waurn Ponds, Australia. His work focuses mostly on water and forest resource management and he recently published a book on multicriteria decision analysis in natural resource management with Professor Tony Prato of Missouri University, USA.

William Keeton is an associate lecturer at La Trobe University, Victoria, Australia, where he lectures in management and logistics. He is a retired lieutenant colonel from the United States Army with over 20 years of leadership and logistics experience. His research interests centre on transformational leadership, communication and follower motivation.

Dr N. V. Namboodiri is a senior research associate at the Centre for Management in Agriculture, Indian Institute of Management, Ahmedabad, India. He holds a Masters in agricultural economics and a PhD in economics. He has been a visiting researcher with the International Food Policy Research Institute. He has authored many research articles and books. His major research interests include agricultural finance, agricultural resource management, and agricultural policy.

Phillip Pagan was an economist with the Department of Primary Industry in New South Wales. He had worked on a variety of resource management projects and was keenly interested in institutional arrangements circumscribing water resources, particularly in the Australian Capital Territory.

Dr Ashutosh Roy is currently assistant vice president in the Risk Analytics and Instruments division of Deutsche Bank in London. He works on methodological enhancements in the bank's risk management infrastructure. He recently completed his doctoral study at the Indian Institute of Management, Ahmedabad, India, working on the performance of grain commodity markets. His research work and interests include commodity derivatives, food marketing, institutions in water resource management, and advanced econometric analysis.

Suresh Sharma is a research associate with the Indian Institute of Management, Ahmedabad, India. He holds a Masters degree. He has substantial experience in rural studies, particularly those involving extensive primary data collection in the Indian rural and agricultural setting, including institutional studies. He has contributed to research in the fields of water institutions, food marketing, agricultural inputs, rural development and livelihoods.

Videh Upadhyay is an advocate and legal consultant for natural resources and development law based in Delhi. He has been an environment and development lawyer for ten years with substantial focuses on water law and institutions. He has co-authored a three-volume handbook on environmental law and two other books.

List of Acronyms and Abbreviations

ACIAR	Australian Centre for International Agricultural Research
ACT	Australian Capital Territory
ACTEW	ACT Electricity and Water
ANOVA	analysis of variance
ANRA	Australian National Resource Atlas
BDO	Block Development Officer
CAD	Command Area Development
CADAs	Command Area Development Authorities
CGWA	Central Ground Water Authority
CoAG	Council of Australian Governments
DC	Distributary Committee
DGA	District Ground Water Authorities
EPA	Environment Protection Act
ESD	environmentally sustainable development
FOs	farmer organizations
GL	gigalitres (i.e. one thousand million litres)
GNP	gross national product
GP	*Gram Panchayat*
GSDA	Ground Water Survey and Development Agency
GWA	Ground Water Act
IAD	institutional analysis and development
IDE	International Development Enterprises
IMT	irrigation management transfer
IWMI	International Water Management Institute
LWMU	local watershed management units
ML	megalitres (i.e. one million litres)
MoWR	Ministry of Water Resources
MWRRA	Maharashtra Water Resources Regulatory Authority
NIE	New Institutional Economics
NRM	natural resource management

NSS	National Sample Survey
NSW	New South Wales
NWI	National Water Initiative
O&M	operation and maintenance
PC	Project Committee
PRIs	*Panchayati Raj* institutions
PWD	Public Works Department
Qld	Queensland
RBOs	river basin organizations
SA	South Australia
Vic	Victoria
WA	Western Australia
WUAs	water user associations

Part 1
Theoretical Dimensions of Institutional Analysis

1 The Effectiveness of Water Institutions

Lin Crase and Vasant Gandhi

Introduction

The management of water resources is proving to be a major international challenge. In March 2007 international scientists and development workers responded to serious concerns about increasing water scarcity and the attendant implications for hunger and poverty by calling for an expansion of the goals embodied in the United Nations Millennium Declaration. More specifically, the *Vientiane Statement* espouses a vision that comprises 'a more water and food secure world, one where water management, innovative technologies and effective institutional arrangements work together towards eliminating hunger, poverty and disease, and where ecological services and resource quality are preserved'. Ambitiously, the authors of the *Statement* contended that 'such a world is within our reach' (CGIAR, 2007, p1).

And yet the problems emanating from injudicious water management are far from new. Almost a decade earlier Serageldin (1996, p50) observed that continued growth of world population alone had reduced per capita water supplies by one-third since 1970. In 1994 approximately 11.11 billion people in developing countries did not have access to safe drinking water and some 2.87 billion souls lacked adequate sanitation. While the World Health Organization (1996) was predicting an improvement in access to safe water supplies by the year 2000, the number of people without adequate sanitation was simultaneously expected to rise to 3.31 billion. A decade before the *Vientiane Statement* was produced pundits were predicting that population growth, accompanied by higher rates of industrialization, urbanization and the extension of agriculture would result in as many as 52 countries and 3 billion people having insufficient water supplies by 2025, largely dispelling much of the progress achieved during the International Drinking-Water and Sanitation Decade of 1981–90 (Serageldin, 1996, p50; Helmer, 1997, p40). By 2006, UN-Water (2008) optimistically reported that, overall, the world was on track to meet the Millennium Development Goals in the context of drinking water. However, many countries in sub-Saharan Africa and Oceania were expected to fall well short of the 2015 objective 'leaving significant portions of the population without access to improved drinking-water supplies' (UN-Water, 2008, p9). Needless to add, the global goal for access to sanitation is not expected to be met by the target date of 2015.

In 1994, global water withdrawal and in-stream requirements were estimated at 54 per cent of the geographically and temporally accessible water runoff (UN, 1996). Of the users of water, irrigation was by far the single largest consumer, accounting for around 87 per cent of global consumption (Helmer, 1997, p40). By 2006, the UN was reporting that global water withdrawals had increased sixfold since the 1990s, twice the rate of population growth. Against this background irrigated agriculture laid claim to about 70 per cent of all freshwater withdrawals and was accordingly coming under increased scrutiny (UN, 2006, p3).

Adding to the weight of this issue is the potential for the existing resource endowment to intensify inequalities within and between nations. Water resources are not distributed evenly. For example, in Israel per capita water consumption is three to four times higher than that of the Palestinians resident in the West Bank and Gaza Strip. Similarly, in Haiti, the poorest households spend almost 20 per cent of their income on water while the richer households spend only 10 per cent of their income to access water (Serageldin, 1996, pp51–52). In some cases these inequities reflect the incongruous definition of hydrological and political boundaries. The employment of water resources for the purpose of economic or environmental benefit in one state often occurs at the opportunity cost of other users in the same basin. Moreover, since most of the world's river basins are shared between nations, national growth spurred by 'water development' in one state can, in most instances, only be achieved at the expense of others. For example, the proposed development of large water storage and diversions in Turkey is expected to raise agricultural production in that nation by some 400 per cent. However, the same project implies restricted in-stream flows in the Tigris and Euphrates rivers to the downstream nations of Syria and Iraq (Serageldin, 1996, p51). It follows that there is potential for international conflict arising from a nationalist approach to global water resource management.

Changes to water quality have also sharpened international focus on the limited nature of water resources. Water supplies come under increasing pressure through the addition of pollutants by urban, industrial and agricultural users. The saturation and degradation of natural systems slows the rate of removal of pollutants and inhibits alternative users' access to potable water.

In spite of these difficulties, a convergence of opinion appeared to be emerging on the global management of water resources by the end of the 1990s. For example, three principles of consensus were specifically articulated in the *Dublin Statement* issued at the conclusion of the International Conference on Water and the Environment. Briscoe (1997, p34) describes these principles as the 'ecosystem principle', which recommends a more holistic approach to water management, and two important 'institutional principles'. The first of these hinges on the philosophy of a participatory approach to water resource management. The second institutional principle centres on an acceptance of water as an economic good.

The mere existence of the *Vientiane Statement* a decade after the pronouncements in the *Dublin Statement* is testament to the intractable difficulties associated with institutional change in the context of water. Arguably, these challenges are nowhere more acute than in India. Here water resource management is crucial for food production and rural incomes, as well as for the alleviation of poverty and hunger. In addition, the development of irrigation is a central feature of India's agricultural development strategy.

Water resource management is also critically important in India because of the growing demand for food and because the incomes and employment of 60–70 per cent of the population depend directly or indirectly on agriculture. Small-sized private farms dominate Indian agriculture and the problem of water management is becoming increasingly serious as development proceeds. Local scarcities are now common and frequent. In the context of the challenges of water resource management in India, standard neoclassical theories usually have little to offer in terms of practical and durable solutions. Determining the right price for water hardly solves the problem since imposing the price and achieving cost recovery are themselves formidable tasks – resolving such issues is primarily an institutional challenge, not a technical one (Reddy, 1998).

There are serious problems in the administration of surface water because of the substantial investments required. In addition there are attendant challenges associated with project implementation, maintenance, distribution, and the necessity to account for environmental impacts. There are also non-trivial problems in the management of ground water, where over-extraction and inadequate recharge is becoming commonplace. The technical and economic solutions to these problems are typically well known, but their institutional management in the political economy is becoming very difficult (Parthasarathy, 2000; Saleth, 1996; Gandhi and Namboodiri, 2002).

Researchers indicate that institutional deficiencies are at the root of many water resource management problems in India (Shah, 2000) with institutional development lagging well behind reforms in other countries, such as Australia. Innovations in institutional arrangements and management structures are a necessary precondition for tackling the problems of water management (Vaidyanathan, 1999). It is important to understand past weaknesses and existing arrangements while simultaneously searching for institutions that facilitate socially acceptable, efficient, equitable and sustainable uses of water.

This focus on comparisons between real-world alternatives is one of the defining characteristics of a strand of inquiry described as the New

Institutional Economics. While recognizing the difficulty of defining the new institutional paradigm with any precision, a number of common themes are apparent. For example, Alston et al (1996, p1) make the following observation:

> *An interdisciplinary research program that deals explicitly with the link between institutions, institutional change, and economic performance is now emerging. The new institutional analysis is a line of investigation that departs from but does not abandon neoclassical economics. Central to the research agenda is an emphasis on property rights, the transaction costs of measurement and enforcement, and incomplete information. The research program has been further enriched through cross-fertilization with law, political science, sociology, anthropology, and history.*

To gain an appreciation of the breadth and development of New Institutional Economics, we draw upon Rutherford's (1994) review of old and new institutionalism. Old institutionalism, although comprising a disparate number of theories, contains two main research programmes. First, a 'focus on investigating the effects of new technology on institutional schemes, and the ways in which established social conventions and vested interests resist such change' (Rutherford, 1994, p2). This programme of research is associated with Thornstein Veblen and the later work of Clarence Ayres. The second programme of research within old institutionalism centres on 'law, property rights and organisations, the evolution and impact on legal and economic power, economic transactions, and the distribution of income' (Rutherford, 1994, p2). Within this second programme the traditions established by John Commons, and later Samuels and Schmid, are important contributions. While acknowledging that the Commons tradition has links with the new institutionalism, Rutherford (1994, pp2–3) offers a broad taxonomy for defining themes within new institutional economics. These include work on property rights (Alchian and Demsetz, 1973), common law (Posner, 1977), rent-seeking and distributional coalitions (Olson, 1982; Mueller, 1989), agency theory (Jensen and Meckling, 1976), transaction costs economics (Coase, 1937; Williamson, 1975; 1985), game theory in institutional settings (Shubik, 1975) and institutional economic history (North, 1979; 1984). The preferred theoretical approach for considering water resource management and irrigation is given greater attention in Chapters 2 to 4.

Crase and Dollery (2008) suggest that academic enthusiasm for employing the New Institutional Economics to consider water allocation issues stems from several sources. First, institutional analysis allows the researcher to overtly acknowledge the bounded rationality of human decision making and thus shifts the focus to a comparison of real-world alternatives rather than idealized utopian solutions. Second, the institutional lens is sufficiently flexible to allow for contributions from multiple disciplines. In this regard the framework offered later in this book draws upon a range of social sciences including economics and management science. Third, 'institutional analysis provides an elegant means of dealing with the vexing policy debate over the relative merits of markets as a vehicle for allocating resources and State apportionment of water' (Crase and Dollery, 2008, p75). This is accomplished by focusing on the suite of costs that attend a given institutional setting rather than being distracted by the philosophical merits of markets over the state or vice versa. Fourth, the flexibility of institutional analysis implies that it is more conducive to dealing with a fugitive resource like water. Moreover, water can simultaneously display both private and public good attributes and the resulting common property regimes in some jurisdictions can only meaningfully be assessed using the tools of institutional analysis. Fifth, and as implied earlier, enthusiasm for institutional analysis in this context can be traced to the progressive acknowledgement that engineering solutions cannot resolve the problem of water scarcity in their own right. In this context Ostrom (1992) observed some time ago that even the most technically advanced irrigation systems are often beset by institutional failures. Sixth, institutional analysis is grounded in a consideration of both formal and informal rules. Accordingly, this approach is well placed to consider the role of water as societies' accepted norms evolve and change over time. Finally, the lessons that derive from institutional analysis are not bound to a particular society or timeframe; such lessons are likely to provide valuable insights into rule design, decision making and water policy formulation in a range of settings.

Scope of this book

This book owes its origins to a collaborative project undertaken by Indian and Australian researchers. The project aimed to use techniques derived from the New Institutional Economics literature to understand and comment upon the performance of various modes of governance in Indian irrigation. The project was sponsored by the Australian government, via the Australian Centre for International Agricultural Research, and commenced in earnest in 2003. Drawing insights from the various efforts to reform the management of water resources in Australia, the project specifically sought to apply empirical techniques to identify those elements of institutional design that were most conducive to the successful management of water resources in India.

Readers of this book might well query the rationale for exploring Indian irrigation institutions on the basis of information gleaned from Australian experiences. After all, the contrasts between the two settings appear remarkably stark.

On the one hand, Indian irrigation, and agriculture more generally, is the mainstay for a large proportion of the population. By way of contrast, agriculture, of which irrigation is a subset, contributes a relatively modest amount to the economic well-being of most Australians. Similarly, the factor endowments of the two nations vary markedly. Australia has long enjoyed a competitive advantage in dryland agriculture, as poignantly described by Davidson in the 1960s (see, for example, Davidson, 1969). Australia lacks the quantities of labour necessary to benefit from irrigated agriculture and is generally more suited to the land-intensive demands of dryland farming. Interestingly, this reality was largely ignored by Australian governments of all persuasions for many years and remains a contentious issue within irrigation communities presently calling for increased government support. On the other hand, India's factor endowment (tightly held land resources and ample labour) is more conducive to the requirements of intensive irrigated agriculture. Interestingly, the strong political influence of irrigated agriculture in both nations would appear to belie these substantial variations in economic endowments.

Australia also has a reputation for achieving considerable reform in the water sector. For instance, *The Economist* proclaimed in 2003 that Australia was 'the country that takes top prize for sensible water management'. This reputation should be adjudged against international standards which, by reference to recent outputs from the UN cited earlier, would appear to be modest at best. In contrast, India has arguably made relatively humble progress in this context. Importantly, this is not for lack of trying, as will be explored in later chapters. Rather, it seems to be a combination of the politically vexing nature of water allocations within such a populous democratic nation and the associated difficulties of designing and delivering adequate institutions.

Notwithstanding these differences, the two nations also have much in common. The hydrology and geography of both nations vary enormously within national borders. Thus, while both countries occupy similar latitudes, a diversity of landscapes is common to both settings. Accordingly, the role and prominence of irrigated agriculture is far from homogeneous across each nation and different states and regions will have varying degrees of interest in an irrigation reform agenda.

India and Australia also share the legacy of British rule. As a result, both nations have state jurisdictions that hold substantial power over water and federal governments that battle to attain a coordinated approach where resources straddle state borders. The legal implications of these arrangements are profound and the impact on water institutions is given special attention in later chapters.

Perhaps most significantly in the context of this project, both countries face substantial contemporary challenges in the management and allocation of water resources. In Australia's case the institutional responses to these problems can be considered against a less pressing backdrop – the relative per capita wealth of Australia implies that failed irrigation reform is unlikely to directly lead to increased hunger and malnutrition of a large portion of the citizenry. In this context the lessons from reform can be considered in a more sanguine fashion before reflecting on their potential in the Indian context.

In order to gain an appreciation of the two settings for this work a synoptic overview of important water and irrigation policy issues is provided to establish the context for subsequent chapters.

Australia's water challenges[1]

Australia is frequently cited as the driest inhabited continent on Earth. In practice, it would be more accurate to describe Australia's water resources as highly variable in spatial and temporal terms (Letcher and Powell, 2008). Perhaps the most influential component of this variability on irrigation is the fact that the average Australian water storage needs to be twice as large as the 'average dam' in the world in order to deliver an equivalent reliability of supply (Smith, 1998). The upshot is that the economics of water are very different in Australia compared to most other places.

Notwithstanding the substantial economic challenges to shoring up Australia's water supplies, these constraints were no match for the engineering enthusiasm that typified most of the 19th and 20th centuries in this country. This was a time when European-derived attitudes that espoused the nobility of harnessing resources far outweighed the more conservative approaches to resource management employed by the indigenous population for millennia. Musgrave (2008) describes this period as a series of 'development' phases where the overriding ambition was to establish closer settlement of the interior and 'to make the desert bloom'.

Important institutional and legal traditions were established at this time. These included the conferring of water as a state resource (including all surface and ground water); the general abandonment of the riparian doctrine; an acceptance that powerful state bureaucracies were well placed to make water allocation decisions and, in some instances, agricultural production choices; and a willingness to absolve debts accumulated by irrigation trusts on the basis that such activities were akin to 'nation building' and therefore deserving of support from the public purse.

These attitudes persisted largely unchecked until the 1960s at which point governments began to seriously question the fiscal soundness of irrigation expansion and support. This anxiety was joined with environmental concerns that began to surface in the 1970s and 1980s. The mounting evidence on salinity and the deleterious impacts of excessive extraction was of particular concern, especially in the Murray-Darling Basin where the development ethos had been most enthusiastically embraced.

It was against this background that the shift towards 'sensible water management', as applauded by *The Economist* (2003), began to emerge. The changes in water management comprised five key policy reforms. First, the states that share the Murray-Darling Basin committed to a basin-wide cap on extractions. The management of the Murray-Darling Basin Cap is described in greater detail in Chapter 5 but, importantly, this policy decision signalled a substantial movement away from increased 'development' towards a system premised on the view that the Australian water economy had reached 'maturity' (Randall, 1981). Second, reform of Australia's water institutions became bound up with a series of wider economic reforms under the National Competition Policy Framework. This manifested itself in the formation of the Council of Australian Governments (CoAG) which then became the vehicle by which successive federal governments exercised their persuasive fiscal powers over water policy and suppressed long-standing state rivalries over water. Initially, this was in the form of the Water Reform Framework of 1994, which sought to ensure that pricing structures were in place to recover costs and reflect usage. These reforms also established volumetric and tradable water entitlements that were separated from land. In addition, the 1994 agenda sought to separate government regulation, service delivery and resource management functions, introduced two-part tariffs for urban water users, and established economic and environmental hurdles that were to be passed in order to justify future infrastructure investments.

The 1994 reforms were heralded by many as a major achievement, particularly in economic circles. However, substantial flaws soon became evident. Among these was the apparent conflict between compliance with the Murray-Darling Basin Cap and the decision to sanction water markets. This arose from the activation of what were euphemistically termed 'sleeper' and 'dozer' water rights. In simple terms, many water rights had been issued by government agencies but not all had been fully used. Once a market was established for virtually all water rights, and since it was a requirement of the Cap that 'new' irrigation works should be achieved by purchasing rights from existing right holders, there was a clear incentive to sell underused water rights. The collective impact of these events was to threaten the Cap that was put in place primarily to keep extraction in check.

Problems with the adequate definition of water rights was the primary focus of the third major reform episode. This was articulated in the 'National Water Initiative' and advocated that all water rights be described in a similar form – as perpetual but variable shares of a defined consumptive pool. This process required that environmental benefits be accounted for in water planning and that this should be based on the best available science. The National Water Initiative also began to recognize in legislation the difficulties of dealing with uncertainty and risk by specifying the manner by which rights would be adjusted over time and the compensation attracted by different forms of adjustment.

The fourth and fifth episodes represent a major departure from the general thrust evident in the 1994 and 2004 policy programmes. In 2007, the then Howard government announced its 'National Plan for Water Security'. This was an ambitious programme that, in many respects, was reminiscent of the enthusiasm for publicly funded water engineering 'solutions' of earlier generations. The plan proposed to spend $A10 billion with most being spent on infrastructure that would purportedly modernize irrigation and 'save' water for environmental purposes. The proposal was 'prepared in haste, well away from the troublesome gaze of Treasury and Finance officials and the experienced eye of the Murray-Darling Basin Commission' (Watson, 2007, p1), but nevertheless also allocated $A3 billion to buy back water rights in over-allocated systems.

The most recent episode largely replicates the direction of the National Plan for Water Security and is embodied in the Rudd government's 'Water for the Future' manifesto. Again there are two main elements to this approach: (i) substantial investment of public funds in irrigation infrastructure under the guise that such investments will deliver additional water to over-allocated systems and free up water for environmental purposes, and (ii) use of the public purse to buy back water access rights from willing sellers.

Both of these reform approaches have attracted substantial criticism, albeit from different quarters. On the one hand, agricultural lobbyists have bemoaned the purchase of water rights, citing the third-party impacts that would attend a contraction of agriculture (see, e.g., Cawood, 2008). On the other hand, many economists have been critical of the apparent policy U-turn that seems likely to result in large sums of public money again being invested in irrigation infrastructure (see, e.g., Crase et al, 2007; Watson, 2007; Quiggin, 2006). There is also considerable angst about the accuracy of purported water savings and the difficulty of accounting for such expenditure where organizations have previously insisted on the principle of cost recovery (Crase and O'Keefe, 2009).

There is one enduring and poignant message from these episodes: modifying the rules by which water is managed and allocated is no simple task, even in a relatively wealthy nation where agriculture plays only a modest role in the country's economic affairs.

India's water challenges

The contemporary challenges that attend water resource management in India share several themes in common with the episodes described in the earlier section. Certainly, the challenge of containing extractions at sustainable levels is a formidable one in India, as it is in Australia. However, the context in which these challenges are being considered also needs to be appreciated and we use this brief section to establish the scope of the book and to set the scene for more detailed analysis in subsequent chapters.

Irrigation has been among the most important strategic factors in the Green Revolution in India. It has played a major part in increasing food production, raising productivity and delivering food security. In the state of Punjab, agricultural productivity grew by around 6 per cent annually between 1960 and 1980 and by the end of the 1980s wheat and rice yields had trebled. Annual per capita income rose from US$60 in 1980–81 to US$440 in 1997–98, well above the national average.

However, the successes of the Green Revolution were largely limited to irrigated areas. In addition, poor water management and slowing productivity growth began to tarnish the image of Punjab as the 'bread basket' by the mid 1980s. Among the important factors in this context was the shift from water-prudent crops, such as millets and pulses, to wheat and rice. Ultimately, this resulted in a substantial increase in the demand for ground water and over-exploitation in areas such as north western India has substantially lowered ground-water levels and caused inadequate recharge of the water table. Many adverse environmental consequences such as soil erosion, waterlogging and depletion of local water resources are also now evident.

As noted earlier, India is far from a homogeneous landscape. In addition to the numerous geographical differences between regions there are strong social and cultural boundaries that have given rise to a range of water management regimes. These include the *Warabandi*, *Shejpali*, Land Class System and Assured Irrigation Area System (*Satta*). Some of these approaches are supported by government policy, including through law, although often these are not effective. *Warabandi* has legal sanction in the Northern India Irrigation and Drainage Act of 1873. This law, with amendments, is the basic irrigation law for the northern states of Punjab, Haryana, Rajasthan and Uttar Pradesh. Similarly, *Shejpali* has legal support in western India in the Bombay Irrigation Act of 1879. An amended version of this law is the basic irrigation law for the state of Gujarat. The relatively recent Maharashtra Irrigation Act of 1976 continues to recognize *Shejpali* as the basic approach to irrigation management, although it also authorizes alternatives. Similarly, the *Satta* system is based on the Bengal Irrigation Act of 1876. This Act, as amended, is the basic irrigation law for the eastern states of Bihar, West Bengal and Orissa. There is no comparable law from British time for southern India (Brewer et al, 1999; Mitra, 1992).

All surface water in India is legally under the control of the state governments. Ground water, however, is treated in most states as the private property of the person holding the overlying land. Local laws also result in some variations in property rights appertaining to the different types of water. Most states have government agencies concerned specifically with irrigation. These are commonly called irrigation departments or water resource departments and specialize in the construction, operation and maintenance of irrigation systems. Typically such organizations do not attempt to deliver water to each farm but deliver water to outlets serving more than one farmer. Below each outlet, farmers are collectively responsible for both water distribution and maintenance of the distribution system (Brewer et al, 1999).

A major national initiative emerged in 1973, when a coordinated approach to the development of irrigated agriculture was attempted through the creation of Command Area Development Authorities (CAD). An important objective here was to upgrade the outlet command with suitable on-farm development works so as to allow for the even distribution of water over the entire irrigation command (Singh, 1991). Most states created multi-departmental project organizations headed by senior officers of government to implement the CAD programme. However, CAD was seen as a government programme imposed from the top. There were innumerable cases of farmers wilfully destroying irrigation structures and measuring devices built to facilitate the orderly distribution of water.

In an attempt to improve farmers' acceptance of the CAD, some project administrators argued that farmers should be given more responsibility for irrigation management. Although this received only limited support from administrators initially, some took the opportunity to involve farmers in executing off-farm development works and irrigation management. Farmers receiving water from an outlet point were consulted and water user associations were formed. However, a common experience was that farmers' involvement in water management could not be sustained after construction works had been completed and once a system of water distribution had been introduced. Most irrigation committees established in this manner ultimately became defunct.

The above scenario indicates that water resource management in India is at a turning point. In which direction should it proceed? For over a decade, there has been a growing awareness among irrigation professionals that factors related to the management of irrigation are critically important in determining irrigation performance. These 'management factors' are quite broad and encapsulate things that are somehow different to those issues that reside in the 'technical' domain. Irrigation is not simply a process of design engineering but very much a socio-economic phenomenon. An approach that delineates the social relationships could provide a much richer interpretation of irrigation performance.

The argument for management change is premised, in part, on the notion that the structure of institutions creates an enduring set of rewards, incentives and penalties that subsequently influence patterns of behaviour. Accordingly, understanding institutions may be at least as critical to uncovering the key to poverty alleviation as the introduction of improved crops or agricultural techniques.

Objectives of this book

The overall aim of this book is to report on lessons for the design of better institutions and policies to overcome the problems attending water management in Indian agriculture. Initially, the task was conceived as studying selected formal and informal initiatives in India against the backdrop of the institutional knowledge accumulated from the Australian experience of water reform. While this approach has been largely maintained, some Indian initiatives have specifically evolved in response to the nuances of a particular environment or as a response to a unique problem. Nevertheless, the lens offered by New Institutional Economics is suitably broad to allow for the transposition of useful lessons drawn from Australia and application of them in other locales within India.

The research reported herein offers an intimate understanding of the different institutional situations that pertain to water. We specifically sought to test the hypothesis that successful institutions would lead to discernable changes in behaviour and that this would ultimately be manifest in sustainable water use practices, improved water distribution and, consequently, greater well-being and perceptions of equity.

Priorities of the research programme included the necessity to increase our depth of understanding around economic and social processes. This required knowledge about the forms of participation in institutions for water appropriation and use, understanding of distributional conflicts and conflict resolution processes. It was also anticipated that we would need to understand how rules combined with the particular physical, economic and cultural environments of India to produce incentives and outcomes, and what individuals and societies accept as adequate solutions.

The thrust of this research was to study extant water management institutions in order to draw lessons about factors affecting the success of different arrangements, related transactions costs, the efficiency in allocating resources, compliance issues and whether or not institutions were able to achieve what they initially set out to do.

Accordingly, the research was structured around five critical questions:

1 What are the generic characteristics of useful institutional analysis that can be used to explore irrigation?
2 What is the magnitude and contour of water resource management in India?
3 What empirical methods can be harnessed from the theoretical insights offered by New Institutional Economics and related disciplines and how might these assist in guiding policy and institutional reform?
4 What does empirical analysis tell us about institutional performance?
5 What lessons might be derived for policy makers?

Structure of the book

The structure of this book broadly follows these critical research questions. However, the book itself is organized into four main parts. Part 1 provides an overview of the theoretical dimensions of institutional analysis and how this relates to water resource management and irrigated agriculture generally. This section comprises the first four chapters. It covers the development of an institutional framework based on New Institutional Economics and provides a generic vehicle for contemplating the performance of water institutions. This section draws primarily on the experiences of Australian water reform. The rationale for developing the theoretical framework in this setting was described earlier but, in essence, it is a useful way of abstracting from the severe realities of India without abandoning all links with real-life dilemmas. The purpose of this section is to provide a foundation for considering a range of policy and institutional design issues.

In Chapter 2, Phil Pagan describes institutions as the humanly devised arrangements that guide the way people interact. These include the laws, customs, social conventions, regulations and rules that shape our behaviour. Pagan offers an institutional economics perspective on the role that institutions play in water management, and how the outcomes of water management may be able to be improved through better institutional design. Pagan identifies five generic characteristics that are conducive to good institutional outcomes: clear institutional objectives; connectedness between formal and informal institutions; adaptability; appropriateness of scale; and compliance capacity. He also proposes a framework for assessing alternative institutional arrangements, which incorporates these generic characteristics. The chapter is used by Pagan to include discussion of empirical approaches that might be used to evaluate the influence of various institutional features.

Chapter 3 provides substantive commentary on water institutions and the process of reform from an Australian perspective. This chapter is employed to reflect upon the processes that have driven institutional change in Australian water policy and offers insights into the mechanics of water policy formulation, political economy and institutional design generally. In this chapter Crase traces the water reform agenda against other trends within the Australian community as a mechanism for exposing the apparatus of adjustment. The transaction costs framework offered by Pagan (Chapter 2) is embellished and refined by Crase. This is done primarily to account for hierarchical decision making which is common in water resource management. In addition, the chapter is used to explore some of the interdependencies between transaction and transformation costs in such a hierarchy.

The final chapter in this section, Chapter 4, is used to highlight the power of internal organizational influences over the relative performance of institutions. More specifically, this chapter contains information that shows that even optimal institutions (i.e. a set of rules) can still result in suboptimal performance if organizational players are of a mind to subvert the intent of reform. This chapter uses information gleaned from the Australian milieu to illustrate the necessity to account for organizational variables in any measure of institutional performance. More specifically, Pagan, Crase and Gandhi argue that a comprehensive assessment of institutional performance should also take account of the technical rationality, organizational rationality and political rationality of organizations involved in water decisions.

Part 2 of the book is used to provide an overview of water resource development and management in India. This section includes a discussion of the experiences, constraints and initiatives of institutional development in this country. It also depicts the legal foundations of the environment and offers a macro review of the institutions in this setting. This section covers Chapters 5 to 8 inclusive.

In Chapter 5, Gamin Herath provides a survey of water institutions based on collective action, particularly those that have emerged in developing countries in Asia. Herath uses this chapter to explore a suite of empirical studies in this context and considers the deficiencies of the extant empirical work. He also highlights the success of institutions where social capital is strong and traces the relationship between environmental degradation and weak institutional performance. Accordingly, this chapter provides a useful introduction to the Indian milieu.

Jayanath Ananda uses Chapter 6 to provide a survey of various formal and informal water institutions that are currently operational in India. He also examines the design features of these institutions. The analysis indicates that crafting 'winning institutions' and the policy frameworks to strengthen them should take into account not only the proven criteria of institutional design but also changing socio-economic, political and cultural factors.

Water law is a complex area of study in most jurisdictions in the world and this is no less the case in India. As noted earlier, surface water is vested in state jurisdictions in India. However, ground water is commonly controlled by individuals who own overlying land. In some instances water resources are jointly/community-owned and managed. This has given rise to a range of legal instruments that seek to control water extractions such that they remain within sustainable limits. Chapter 7 is used by Upadhyay to review these measures with particular emphasis on the water law in Gujarat, Andhra Pradesh and Maharashtra. Accordingly, the chapter offers an additional important foundation for exploring institutional issues in water resource management.

In Chapter 8 Gandhi and Namboodiri provide an overview of Indian irrigation and water resource development. This chapter re-emphasizes the fact that the prosperity and well-being of the vast majority of India's population rests heavily upon the success of agriculture. Water resource management and governance in the agricultural sector thus play a crucial role in alleviating poverty. As noted earlier, many of the challenges of water management in India are institutional in nature but understanding these dynamics also requires an appreciation of the hydrological and agricultural factors that circumscribe irrigation management. This chapter traces the distribution and use of surface and ground water in India in order to buttress the institutional analysis in subsequent chapters.

Comprising Chapters 9 to 12, Part 3 is based on field research and provides an in-depth examination of water institutions and their relative performance in three states in India. Importantly, this section is grounded in the framework developed earlier in the book, and thus provides empirical lessons supported by the theoretical traditions established by New Institutional Economics and concepts from management science. The analysis includes perspectives relating to different sources of water, (e.g. ground water, surface water and rain water/check dam agriculture) and various institutional types. The section focuses primarily on the assembled empirical data, but nonetheless commences the process of honing in on important policy implications.

In Chapter 9 Vasant Gandhi, Lin Crase and Ashutosh Roy describe the development and analysis of the rich data developed from extensive interviews with farmers in three Indian states. These data are used to test and explore hypotheses arising from the institutional framework developed earlier in the book. The empirical analysis offered in this chapter also provides a broad overview of institutional performance and offers insights into the appropriate role of the state in the process of water reform.

N. V. Namboodiri and Vasant Gandhi specifically examine the performance of surface water institutions in Chapter 10. These institutions differ markedly from ground-water institutions inasmuch as they are heavily influenced by the activities of the state. The rapid development of water user associations (WUAs) to allow for greater decision-making power by farmers provides the backdrop to this chapter. The data assembled as part of this project are further scrutinized to provide preliminary insights into the impact of differing approaches to farmer management adopted by state governments.

Ground-water development and use has grown much more rapidly than surface water abstraction as a source of irrigation, particularly in the more arid regions of India. In part, this is due to innovative institutional arrangements such as tube-well cooperatives and tube-well partnerships. Vasant Gandhi and Ashutosh Roy use Chapter 11 to empirically analyse the institutional success of these arrangements. Importantly, the chapter also highlights the difficulty of constraining water extractions to sustainable levels, even though partnerships and cooperatives might prove successful in the narrow sense of the word or in the short term.

In Chapter 12 Vasant Gandhi and Suresh Sharma examine the phenomenon of check dams used for rain-water harvesting and their relationship to irrigated agriculture. Check dams have been deployed in Gujarat as a means of bolstering ground-water recharge. The relative success of these institutions is empirically analysed. In addition, caveats on the basin-wide implications of such initiatives are briefly developed.

Part 4 of the book synthesizes the observations from the empirical analysis to consider the implications for water resource and related policies in India. This section comprises the remaining four chapters and touches on the formidable challenges confronting policy makers.

The empirical data offered in Part 3 point to the benefits and limitations of devolving responsibility for irrigation to farmers and farmer groups. However, rights devolution is not always straightforward. Gamini Herath considers some of the procedural issues that are required to underpin successful devolution of decision making in Chapter 13.

The important role of information in decision making is given specific consideration in Chapter 14. Here, Jayanath Ananda, Lin Crase and William Keeton draw on the empirical work in India to explore the role of information and expertise in underpinning successful institutional design. This analysis provides some preliminary conclusions about the appropriateness of information at various points in the decision-making process.

The underlying motivation for improving irrigation performance is its direct link to agricultural livelihoods and the potential benefits bestowed upon the poor. Vasant Gandhi and Vaibhav Bhamoriya use Chapter 15 to consider the data presented in Part 3 and reflect upon the broader policy objective of poverty alleviation. The chapter offers some predictions on the distributional impacts of water reform and explores mechanisms for improving both the efficiency and equity of irrigation in India.

Finally, we return to the original questions raised in this chapter. Chapter 16 taps into the valued perspectives made by all contributors to briefly summarize responses to the five key questions posed earlier in this introductory chapter.

Note

1 This section borrows heavily from Crase (2009).

References

Alchian, A. and Demsetz, H. (1973) 'The property rights paradigm', *Journal of Economic History*, vol 33, pp16–27

Alston, L., Eggertsson, T. and North, D. (1996) *Empirical Studies in Institutional Change*, Cambridge University Press, New York

Brewer, J., Kolavalli, S., Kalro, A., Naik, G., Ramnarayan, S., Raju, K. and Sakthivadivel, R. (1999) *Irrigation Management Transfer in India: Policies, Processes and Performance*, Oxford & IBH, New Delhi

Briscoe, J. (1997) *Financing and Managing Water and Wastewater Services: A Global Perspective*, 17th Federal Convention of the Australian Water and Wastewater Association, Star Printery, Melbourne

Cawood, M. (2008) 'Darling water buyback causes ripples in Qld', *The Land*, Fairfax, Sydney

CGIAR (2007) *Vientiane Statement*, CGIAR, Vientiane, Laos

Coase, R. (1937) 'The nature of the firm', *Economica*, vol 4, pp386–405

Crase, L. (2009) 'Water policy in Australia: The impacts of change and uncertainty', in A. Dinar and J. Albiac (eds) *Policy and Strategic Behaviour in Water Resource Management*, Earthscan, London, pp91–108

Crase, L. and Dollery, B. (2008) 'The institutional setting', in L. Crase (ed) *Water Policy in Australia: The Impact of Change and Uncertainty*, Resources for the Future, Washington DC, pp74–89

Crase, L. and O'Keefe, S. (2009) 'The paradox of National Water Savings: Water use efficiency is not a solution', *Agenda,* forthcoming

Crase, L., Byrnes, J. and Dollery, B. (2007) 'The political economy of urban–rural water trade', *Public Policy*, vol 2, no 2, pp130–140

Davidson, B. R. (1969) *Australia, Wet or Dry? The Physical and Economic Limits to the Expansion of Irrigation*, Melbourne University Press, Melbourne

Gandhi, Vasant P. and Namboodiri, N. V. (2002) 'Water resource management in India: Institutions and development', in D. Brennan (ed) *Water Policy Reform: Lessons from Asia and Australia*, Australian Centre for International Agricultural Research (ACIAR), Canberra, pp106–130

Helmer, R. (1997) *Meeting the Challenge for Providing Potable Water*, 17th Federal Convention of the Australian Water and Wastewater Association, Star Printery, Melbourne

Jensen, M. and Meckling, W. (1976) 'Theory of the firm: Managerial behaviour, agency costs and ownership structure', *Journal of Financial Economics,* vol 3, no 3, pp305–360

Letcher, R. and Powell, S. (2008) 'The hydrological setting', in L. Crase (ed) *Water Policy in Australia: The Impact of Change and Uncertainty*, Resources for the Future, Washington, DC, pp17–27

Mitra, A. (1992) 'Joint management of irrigation systems in India: Relevance of Japanese experience', *Economic and Political Weekly,* 27 June

Mueller, D. (1989) *Public Choice II*, Cambridge University Press, Cambridge

Musgrave, W. (2008) 'Historical development of water resources in Australia: Irrigation policy in the Murray-Darling Basin', in L. Crase (ed) *Water Policy in Australia: The Impact of Change and Uncertainty*, Resources for the Future, Washington DC, pp28–43

North, D. (1979) 'A framework for analysing the state in economic history', *Explorations in Economic History,* vol 16, no 3, pp249–259

North, D. (1984) *Structure and Change in Economic History*, Norton, New York

Olson, M. (1982) *The Rise and Decline of Nations,* Yale University Press, New Haven

Ostrom, E. (1992) *Crafting Institutions for Self-Governing Irrigation Systems*, ICS Press, San Francisco

Parthasarathy, R. (2000) 'Participatory irrigation management program in Gujarat: Institutional and financial issues', *Economic and Political Weekly*, vol 35 (August)

Posner, R. (1977) *Economic Analysis of Law*, Little Brown, Boston

Quiggin, J. (2006) 'Urban water supply in Australia: The option of diverting water from irrigation', *Public Policy,* vol 1, no 1, pp14–22

Randall, A. (1981) 'Property entitlements and pricing policies for a mature water economy', *Australian Journal of Agricultural Economics,* vol 25, no 3, pp195–220

Reddy, Ratna V. (1998) 'Institutional imperatives and co-production strategies for large irrigation systems in India', *Indian Journal of Agricultural Economics,* vol 53, no 3

Rutherford, M. (1994) *Institutions in Economics: The Old and New Institutionalism*, Cambridge University Press, New York

Saleth, Maria R. (1996) *Water Institutions in India: Economics, Law and Policy*, Commonwealth Publishers, New Delhi

Serageldin, I. (1996) 'Surviving scarcity: Sustainable management of water resources', *Harvard International Review*, vol 18, no 3, pp50–53

Shah, A. (2000) 'Capacity building for participatory irrigation management', in J. A. Hooja (ed) *Participatory Irrigation Management Paradigm for the 21st Century*, Rawat Publications, New Delhi

Shubick, M. (1975) 'The general equilibrium model is not complete and not adequate for the reconciliation of micro and macroeconomic theory', *Kyklos,* vol 28, no 3, pp545–573

Singh, K. K. (1991) *Farmers in the Management of Irrigation Systems*, Sterling Publishers, New Delhi

Smith, D. (1998) *Water in Australia: Resources and Management*, Oxford University Press, Melbourne

The Economist (2003) 'Survey: Liquid assets', *The Economist*, vol 368, no 13

United Nations (1996) *Comprehensive Freshwater Assessment*, UN, New York

UN (2006) 'Water & Shared Responsibility: The United Nations World Water Development Report 2', available at http://unesdoc.unesco.org/images/0014/001454/145405E.pdf, accessed 20 December 2008

UN-Water (2008) *Global Annual Assessment of Sanitation and Drinking Water Pilot Report*, UN, New York

Vaidyanathan, A. (1999) *Water Resource Management: Institutions and Irrigation Development in India*, Oxford University Press, New Delhi

Watson, A. (2007) 'A national plan for water security: Pluses and minuses', *Connections – Farm, Food and Resources Issues*, vol 7, no 1

Williamson, O. (1975) *Markets and Hierarchies: Analysis and Antitrust Implications*, Free Press, New York

Williamson, O. (1985) *The Economic Institutions of Capitalism*, Free Press, New York

World Health Organization (1996) *Water Supply and Sanitation Sector Monitoring Report: Sector status as of 31 December 1994*. World Health Organization, Geneva, pp41–43

2

Laws, Customs and Rules: Identifying the Characteristics of Successful Water Institutions

Phillip Pagan

Introduction

Institutions are the humanly devised arrangements that guide the way people interact. They include the laws, customs, social conventions, regulations and rules that structure our behaviour. The role of institutions in water management has increased in importance over the last decade, in line with the claim by Ostrom (1993, p1907) that 'for the next several decades the most important question related to water resources development is that of institutional design rather than engineering design'. This is particularly true in India where institutional change in irrigation has dominated the reform agenda (see, e.g., Chapter 8). Similarly, in Australia institutional change in the water sector has been heavily promoted by the Council of Australian Governments (CoAG) after initial agreement on the reform agenda was reached across state jurisdictions in 1994.

Notwithstanding the multinational enthusiasm for institutional reform in this context, the relative merit of amending institutional arrangements can often prove contentious. Resolving questions of institutional performance is also complicated by the challenge of identifying empirical work with relevance to a specific context or policy issue. Thus, while Saleth and Dinar (2004, p56) contend that 'tremendous growth has occurred in the empirical literature on issues related to institutional structure, institutional change, and economic performance' there remains a dearth of empirical work in the field of institutions relative to other analytical frameworks.

This chapter discusses, from an institutional economics perspective, the role that institutions play in water management, and how the outcomes of water management may potentially be improved through better institutional design. The primary aim of the chapter is to establish the initial foundations for developing an institutional framework capable of empirically adjudging institutional performance in water management, particularly in irrigation. I propose a framework for assessing alternative institutional arrangements, based initially on the generic characteristics that are the key to achieving good institutional outcomes. The chapter also includes discussion of empirical approaches to evaluating institutional features within the framework.

The chapter itself is divided into four additional parts. The following section is used to discuss what institutions are, why they are important in the management of economic resources (and water in particular), and how alternative institutional designs might be usefully analysed. Subsequently, I focus on five generic characteristics that typify good institutional outcomes: clear institutional objectives; connectedness between formal and informal institutions; adaptability; appropriateness of scale; and compliance capacity. Empirical techniques appropriate for measuring these generic attributes are then discussed before offering some brief concluding remarks.

Institutional background

What are institutions?

Defining institutions with precision can often prove problematic, reflecting the different disciplinary perspectives and theoretical traditions that pervade institutional analysis (Saleth and Dinar, 2004, p23). Three conceptualizations of institutions are outlined by Aoki (2000). Aoki employs an analogy of the economic process as a game to demonstrate how institutions are thought of as (i) players of a game, (ii) the rules of a game, or (iii) the outcome of a game.

Organizations are often referred to as institutions, and in the analysis of economic processes particular government and non-government organizations are identified as the relevant institutional players (or the players of the game).

Others, such as North (1990; 1995), regard organizations and their political entrepreneurs as agents of institutional change (i.e., as rule makers), but the institutions themselves are the rules by which interactions between individuals, groups and organizations are governed. These institutions include both formal and informal rules. Formal institutions are determined in the 'political market' under pressures that are ultimately derived from changes in relative prices. Informal rules are socially derived and form part of the cultural heritage of a community. Consequently, they are relatively slow-changing, and their persistence effectively constrains changes in the politically determined formal rules.

Finally, the 'outcome of a game' perspective on institutions argues that they are determined endogenously as an equilibrium outcome from which agents are not motivated to depart, as long as others also do not modify their behaviour (e.g. Schotter, 1981; Greif, 1994; Young, 1998; Greif, 1999; Saleth and Dinar, 2004). This contrasts to the 'rules' formulation where institutions are consciously designed and imposed through political processes (subject to cultural constraints).

The conceptualization of institutions assumed in this chapter most closely aligns with the 'rules' perspective. I follow North's specific definition inasmuch as 'institutions are the rules of the game in a society or, more formally, are the humanly devised constraints that shape human interaction' (1990). Consistent with this definition are others such as that offered by Dovers (2001): 'Institutions are persistent, largely predictable arrangements, laws, processes, customs and organizations that structure aspects of political, social or economic transactions in society'; and by Neale (1994): '[Institution is the word used for] the regular, patterned behaviour of people in a society and for the ideas and values associated with these regularities.'

The theoretical case for the role of institutions

Recognition and incorporation of the importance of institutional arrangements in the analysis of economic activity is the key concern of the branch of economic theory known as New Institutional Economics (NIE). The views of three distinguished NIE economists (Richard North, Ronald Coase and Oliver Williamson) are useful in illustrating the importance of institutions.

North (2000) articulates the importance of institutions as arising from a recognition that laissez-faire markets do not exist. That is, there is no such thing as an efficient market that is not structured by the players to produce the particular results associated with a free market. North states that all social systems (including markets) are humanly devised and are a complex mix of rules, norms, conventions and behavioural beliefs. Together they shape the way in which we operate and determine how successful we are in achieving our goals.

In discussing the contribution that NIE could bring to the field of economics, Coase claims that the limitations of neoclassical approaches are borne from a disregard for what happens concretely in the real world. He contends that the key problem is one of economists studying how supply and demand determine prices, but not studying the factors that determine what goods and services are actually traded on markets (and therefore are priced). 'We study the circulation of the blood without a body' (Coase, 2000, p4).

Coase illustrates the key role of institutions through the following simple description of an economic system:

> *The welfare of a human society depends on the flow of goods and services, and this in turn depends on the productivity of the economic system. Adam Smith explained that the productivity of the economic system depends on specialization (he says the division of labour), but specialization is only possible if there is*

> *exchange – and the lower the costs of exchange (transaction costs if you will), the more specialization there will be and the greater the productivity of the system. But the costs of exchange depend on the institutions of a country: its legal system, its social system, its education system, its culture and so on. In effect it is the institutions that govern the performance of an economy, and it is this that gives the 'new institutional economics' its importance for economists.* (Coase, 2000, p4)

The above description by Coase introduces the concept of transaction costs. Crase (2000) identifies two distinct definitions of transaction costs. The first regards transaction costs as an actor's opportunity costs of establishing and maintaining internal control of resources. That is, they are the costs of measurement and enforcement incurred to protect values both in voluntary exchange, and against involuntary exchange (such as theft) (Alston et al, 1996). The second and broader conceptualization of transaction costs is that they include all costs associated with the creation, use and change of an institution or organization (Furubotn and Richter, 1992). Given the nature of the task at hand (i.e. understanding overall institutional performance in irrigation), I adopt the second of these definitions.

Transaction cost economics is an important component of the NIE approach, following the early work of Coase (1960) and others, who brought recognition that market failures are themselves derived from the existence of transaction cost. Williamson (1985) cites the common characteristic of NIE research being the conceptualization of the firm as a governance structure rather than (or in addition to) the conceptualization of the firm as a production function. Williamson clearly synthesizes the concepts of institutions, transaction costs, and their role in the economy with the following observations: 'The economic institutions of capitalism have the main purpose and effect of economizing on transaction costs' (1985, p17), and 'the underlying viewpoint that informs the comparative study of issues of economic organization is this: transaction costs are economized by assigning transactions (which differ in their attributes) to governance structures (the adaptive capacities and associated costs of which differ) in a discriminating way' (1985, p18). Put simply, superior economic performance is associated with transaction cost minimization.

Empirical evidence on the importance of institutions and transaction costs

The above discussion indicates that there is a strong theoretical case for the importance of institutions in the organization of economic activity. However, the supporting empirical case is not as complete, due to a range of issues that are discussed later in this chapter. Nevertheless, empirical analysis has and continues to be undertaken on institutional issues, including some broad empirical studies that indicate the role of institutions and transaction costs in influencing economic outcomes.

Keefer and Shirley (2000) report that World Bank (1998) research investigating different combinations of macroeconomic policy and institutional quality found that countries with high levels of institutional quality and poor macroeconomic policies grew twice as fast as countries with the reverse combination. Keefer and Shirley report corroborating results when they undertook additional analysis using panel data from 84 countries for the period 1982–94, and investigated whether the quality of institutions affected three policy variables (growth in government consumption, public investment and public debt).

In a broad study of the transaction sector in the US, Wallis and North (1986) found that transaction costs as a proportion of gross national product (GNP) had grown from 25 per cent in 1870 to 45 per cent of GNP in 1970. This increase was largely due to the changing institutional environment in which firms operated.

Transaction costs have also been measured at the micro scale in a number of settings pertinent to water and irrigation. Often these analyses have focused on the costs of using markets as a means of allocating water between competing users (see, e.g., Colby, 1998; Crase et al, 2000). Nevertheless, Crase (2000) observes that empirical analyses of water institutions and the enumeration of particular transaction costs remain relatively rare.

One of the few substantive pieces of empirical analysis of water institutions and transaction costs was developed by Saleth and Dinar (2004). Here the researchers focused primarily on formal institutions at the national scale and sourced the perceptions of experts to unbundle institution-performance interactions. Analysis of the assembled subjective and objective data was used to consider the role of transaction cost and political economy factors that were both endogenous and exogenous to the water sector. Notwithstanding the insights brought by this approach, the authors acknowledge that it is important to avoid 'stereotypical approaches' and to recognize the importance of 'location-specific aspects in reform design and implementation' (p328).

The conflict between the location specificity of some transaction costs and the desire for a transaction cost framework that can be used to buttress generalized analysis remains as one of the most substantial challenges of NIE.

Transaction and transformation costs

Notwithstanding the empirical challenges, it is clear from the preceding discussion that there is a palpable link between institutions and transaction costs. North (1990), however, brought forward the proposition that the simple relationship where institutions only determining transaction costs, and techniques only determining transformation costs, actually masked a more complex interaction. In particular, it can be demonstrated that given a desired level of output, institutions will be chosen that minimize the total transaction and transformation costs of production (North and Wallis, 1994).

Transaction costs

Transaction costs, as defined in the earlier section, refer to all costs associated with the creation, use and change of an institution (i.e. a set of informal and formal rules). But transaction costs can be further divided (see Table 2.1) according to whether they are incurred through operating within a particular institutional environment (static transaction costs), or during or because of changes in the institutional environment (dynamic transaction costs).

Static transaction costs involved in market exchanges, for example, include costs such as those associated with product search and comparison (in terms of price and quality information), and any fees or costs associated with transferring ownership – registration and the like. Alternatively, if resources are allocated by a state agency, costs might arise from agencies securing information about the resource, or the activities associated with declaring and monitoring a given allocation.

In contrast to the costs of dealing with the institutional status quo, dynamic transaction costs relate to changing that institutional environment. These costs can be further divided into categories of transition costs and intertemporal transaction costs (Challen and Schilizzi, 1999; Marshall, 2003). Institutional transition costs are those incurred in the current period and are associated with changing institutional arrangements. These include costs such as research and development costs, costs of deciding on new institutional rules and structures (e.g. lobbying, bureaucratic and political), and payments that may need to be made to those disadvantaged by the institutional changes.

Intertemporal transaction costs are the costs that chosen institutional structures can impose in the future, in the form of higher transition costs of change in those future periods. The link between current arrangements and the costs of future changes is because of 'path dependencies' (North, 1990). These arise from the interdependence that develops between institutions and organizations, and because of the subjective models of the world that people rely upon in making choices. Transaction costs in political and economic markets make for inefficient property rights, but these subjective models of individual perception often prevent people from recognizing preferred property rights arrangements.

Table 2.1 *Typology of transaction and transformation costs*

Costs	*Technology*	*Institutions*
Associated with operating under existing institutions (static)	Static transformation	Static transaction
Associated with changing institutions (dynamic)	Technological transition Intertemporal transformation	Institutional transition Intertemporal transaction

Transformation costs

A similar dichotomy of transformation costs (also see Table 2.1) can be outlined, based primarily on the work of Marshall (2003), who chose to describe technology costs in terms of pollution abatement technologies. Static transformation costs are bound up in the production technology and production process costs that are borne from operating in a particular institutional environment in the present state. In the context of motor vehicles this might include the costs related to producing cars that have additional abatement technologies designed to limit harmful emissions, in line with formal or informal rules. Technological transition costs accrue from institutional influences on modifying the choice of production technology and production process. They are the current costs of making changes to technology and process. Again, in the context of motor vehicles, these costs might include the costs of modifying production technologies to comply with more stringent rules on vehicle emissions.

Intertemporal transformation costs are the technological costs that may arise from future institutional (or related technological) changes. These are caused predominantly by current institutional choices. For instance, a motor vehicle manufacturer may opt to limit vehicle emissions by producing hybrid cars that draw on both conventional fossil fuels and electricity. If, in the future, new institutions impose limits on the way electricity is generated, there are likely to be costs that will subsequently flow from having to modify these motor vehicles yet again. Similar path dependency issues from institutional choice operate in relation to transformation costs as outlined above in relation to transaction costs – the choices of today impose potential costs on moving to preferred technologies in the future.

This dichotomy between transaction and transformation costs is central to the development of the framework developed in this chapter. These concepts are further developed in Chapter 4 with particular relevance to water institutions and technologies in Australia.

Generic institutional design features

To date I have attempted to provide an introduction to the nature and complexity of institutions, and to also illustrate their pervasive influence. North (2000) identifies the analysis of formal institutions (how they are formed through the aggregation of choices in political markets) and informal institutions as being of key importance to improving the management of economic resources and as a vehicle for improving economic performance. Institutions are critical to the way in which societies work, yet relatively little is known of how they work, how they evolve over time, or what makes them work well or poorly. This section of the chapter is used in an effort to shed some light on the latter of these issues – institutional performance – and aims to identify some of the characteristics that make for 'good' institutions.

Researchers in recent years have examined the specific institutional rules for a wide range of industries and different systems from within individual industries (e.g. Ostrom, 1993; Goodin, 1996; Ostrom et al, 1994 specifically for common property irrigation institutions). This type of analysis enables the identification of design characteristics that are consistently associated with successful management of resources (and therefore low transaction and transformation costs). Following an analysis of the literature, five generic institutional design characteristics have emerged as being of key importance: clear objectives; interconnection with other formal and informal institutions; adaptiveness; appropriateness of scale; and compliance capacity. Each of these is discussed in detail below.

Clear institutional objectives

The attributes of this characteristic that make it vital in determining the success of institutions include:

- clarity of institutional purpose; and
- transparency in the process of adjustment, where the purpose changes or evolves.

Clarity of institutional purpose

Institutions can have a wide range of objectives, such as efficiency, lack of bias, sustainability, equity and fairness (Loehman and Kilgour, 1998). The objective that is chosen as the principle aim of any institution will ultimately affect the welfare of those people influenced by it. Take, for example, an institution for the management and allocation of mineral exploration licences. If the institution pursues an equitable distribution across the community as its primary objective, this will provide for very different welfare outcomes to those associated with an objective founded on resource preservation. However, clearly articulating that objective is critical in an institutional design sense because clarity will facilitate the achievement of the objective in as efficient a manner as possible (i.e. at lowest transaction and transformation costs).

This straightforward aspect of good institutional design is regularly violated simply because there are multiple institutional objectives. Moreover, often it is not at all clear which of these objectives is the key focus of the institution and which of the others should be viewed as constraints on the pursuit of the main objective. The Tinbergen principle makes it clear that at least as many instruments are required as independent objectives (Tinbergen, 1950). An example of a possible dilemma of this type is the desire to use a single policy instrument, say water markets, to simultaneously pursue multiple and sometimes conflicting objectives.

It is worth noting at this point that a potentially perverse relationship exists between the desirability of having clear objectives, and another attractive feature discussed below, adaptiveness. Hence, while adaptive capacity is a highly valuable feature of institutions, this extends to adaptiveness in objectives as well, and this may itself make objectives less clear.

Transparency in the process of adjusting institutional objectives

A transparent process of adjusting institutional objectives is relevant because of the role that 'power' plays in establishing institutions. Transparency limits the exercise of power used by individuals and groups. In essence, transparency ensures that institutional objectives are modified in ways that are consistent with community objectives. To quote North (1990, p 16):

> *Institutions are not necessarily or even usually created to be socially efficient; rather they, or at least the formal rules, are created to serve the interests of those with the bargaining power to devise new rules. In a zero-transaction-cost world, bargaining strength does not affect the efficiency of outcomes, but in a world of positive transaction costs it does ...*

Transparency in the process mitigates the potential use of bargaining power to effect institutional change that is not in the interests of the broader group governed by the institution – it ensures that feedback is provided to the broader group. This lessens the incentives faced by political actors to make inconsistent changes in objectives. The role of informal institutions in constraining this whole process of formal institutional change is an issue pursued in the following section. There are also obvious links between this issue and the institutional characteristic of 'adaptiveness' discussed later.

Interconnection with other formal and informal institutions

It has been widely recognized for some time that bringing about change in the way a social system operates requires changes in the formal and informal institutions of society (e.g. Williamson, 1985; Ostrom, 1993; North, 2000; Dovers, 2001). However, the only group of rules over which there is direct control are the formal institutions. In addition, there are claims by some that informal institutions play a crucial role. For example, North (1990) claims that the relative success of the US economy through modern history, in comparison to countries with similar formal institutional structures, has been because the underlying informal institutional framework of the US has persistently reinforced incentives for organizations to engage in productive activity (whereas the informal institutional framework in some other countries has not). Therefore, the nature of the relationship between formal and informal institutions and the influence of each in determining overall institutional performance in the management of any system is of key interest.

The cultural values and governance system of a society to a large extent determine the internal values of organizations, and these in turn rule the organization (Ruys et al, 2000). Similarly, the informal institutions of society can be seen as determining or constraining the scope of actors with political power to alter the formal governing institutions (of society broadly or of some other social organization). This view is consistent with Challen's (2000) conceptual model of the process of institutional change and his application of this process to water institutions in Australia (see Figure 2.1 below).

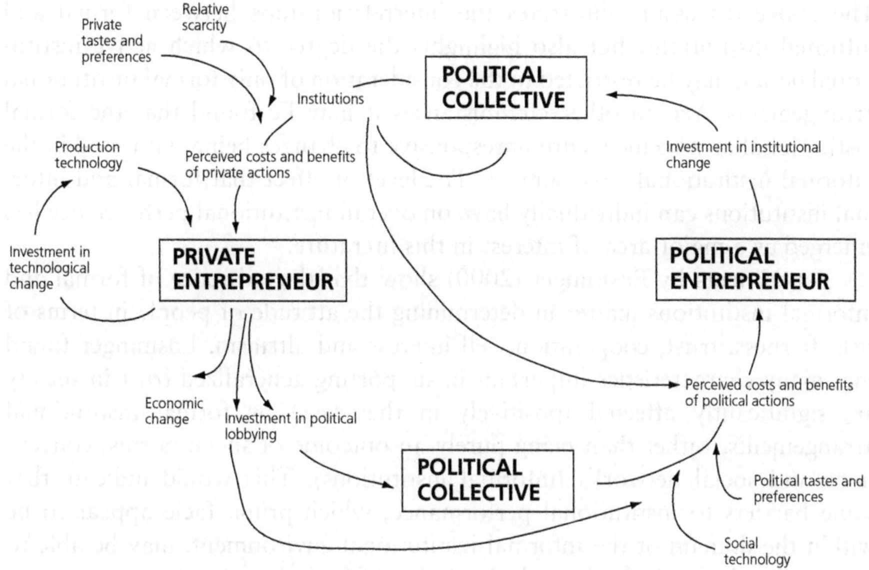

Figure 2.1 *Conceptual model of the process of institutional change*

This model stylizes the interactions between private entrepreneurs (who are the firms, households, producers and consumers typical of the actors in economic models), and political entrepreneurs (members of the polities that develop and implement formal institutions of social and economic change). It illustrates how:

- both sets of entrepreneurs react to changing incentives;
- the capacity of political entrepreneurs to bring about formal institutional change (through the political collective) is constrained by private tastes and preferences, political tastes and preferences, and states of social technology; and
- the resulting formal institutional arrangements affect future change (i.e. it is a cyclical process).

An example of the complexity of this relationship between formal and informal institutions and the relevant actors to their management, and the incremental pace of institutional change is provided in relation to water management by the following observation from Barr and Cary (1992, p206):

> *The salinization of irrigated lands seeped into the public consciousness in the 1980s. Bureaucrats, engineers, agricultural scientists and farmers knew of it earlier, there was plenty of evidence of failures of irrigated agriculture and horticulture in the 1950s when the last great irrigation engineering feats were being wrought.*

The above discussion illustrates the interrelationships between formal and informal institutions, but also highlights the degree to which active institutional design may be restricted to the consideration of only formal institutional arrangements. Yet, in other circumstances it may be found that the formal institutional arrangements are unresponsive to changes being witnessed in the informal institutional environment. The level of effect that formal and informal institutions can individually have on overall institutional performance has emerged as a major area of interest in this literature.

Experiments by Ensminger (2000) show that the existence of formal and informal institutions matter in determining the attitude of people in terms of risk, fairness, trust, cooperation, self-interest and altruism. Ensminger found that many characteristics important in supporting generalized trust in society are significantly affected (positively in this case) by formal institutional arrangements, rather than being purely an outcome of social norms, conventions and social networks (informal institutions). This would indicate that some barriers to institutional performance, which prima facie appear to be within the domain of the informal institutional environment, may be able to be influenced effectively through the design of formal institutions.

Conversely, there is also research evidence that informal institutions can substitute for formal institutions in particular circumstances (North, 1990; Ensminger, 1992; Greif, 1993; Greif, 1994). However, Keefer and Shirley (2000) caution that informal institutions do a relatively poor job of protecting against expropriation by private actors and government officials, and may not provide consistent support to all people with a stake in a particular issue.

Closer investigation by Keefer and Shirley (2000) indicated that a crucial ingredient is the complementarity of formal and informal institutions. Keefer and Shirley analysed differences in the growth in foreign investment throughout the 1990s in China and Ghana, and the proposition that high foreign investment in China (in the absence of strong formal institutions to protect investment capital) was due to the strength of Chinese informal institutions. This proposition becomes difficult to support in the face of similar formal and informal institutional capacities in Ghana, which has low growth in foreign investment. They found instead that a key difference was the extent of complementarity between formal and informal institutional arrangements in China compared to Ghana (due particularly to differences in political decentralization between the two countries).

Finally, all this would indicate the desirability of having as high a level of consistency as possible between formal and informal institutions. Others, however, such as Dovers (2001) and Goodin (1996), identify the need for an element of inconsistency, or poor fit, in order to generate a tension for institutional change.

In summary, the evidence suggests that:

- both formal and informal institutions are important to overall institutional performance;

- a balance of 'power' needs to exist between formal and informal institutional actors;
- political actors (responsible for formal institutional change) need to be accountable;
- informal institutions should be well connected to, but retain some independence from, political actors, and
- where there is a poor interconnection between the formal and informal institutional environment, there is some scope for cautious substitution.

Adaptiveness

Institutions associated with the management of natural resources need to be adaptive because of the inherent complexity of natural systems. This creates uncertainties in relation to the adequacy of management actions to address specific issues, and produces uncertainty with respect to the consequences of these actions on other parts of these complex dynamic systems. In addition, all institutions (even those where full knowledge of the consequence of actions is known) need adaptive capacity because changes in technology, and private and political tastes and preferences will generate pressures for institutional change. Dovers (2001) identifies the following principles for adaptive institutions: persistence, purposefulness, information-richness and sensitivity, inclusiveness, flexibility and scale appropriateness.

Adaptive management allows resource managers to continue to manage despite inherent complexity and uncertainty (Holling, 1995). It has increasingly been adopted as a guiding management principle by natural resource managers in Australia, particularly as the focus of resource management has moved from objectives of 'efficient exploitation' to 'sustainable use' (Allan and Curtis, 2003).

However, there is a range of different forms of adaptive management. Evolutionary adaptive management describes a trial-and-error approach to management. Passive adaptive management uses lessons from the past to develop a single best policy to adopt in practice. Active adaptive management is learning-focused and uses policy and its implementation as tools for learning. Active adaptive management is also participatory and uses policy implementation to test hypotheses. (For a comprehensive evaluation of the application of adaptive management philosophies in the context of Australian water resources see, e.g., Pagan, 2008.)

All this would appear to indicate that the increased experimentation and learning, which is a key to effective adaptive management, will necessarily have positive institutional and management performance outcomes. Unfortunately, the existence of dynamic costs of change, and specifically intertemporal transaction and transformation costs (outlined earlier), makes the adoption of broad scale institutional experimentation problematic. In discussing the history of water management in Australia and its implications for future management, Smith (1998, p138) quoted the following from social scientist George Kennan (1973):

> *Every mistake is in a sense a product of all that has gone before it, from which it derives a sort of cosmic forgiveness, and at the same time every mistake is in a sense the determinant of all the mistakes of the future from which it derives a sort of cosmic unforgiveableness.*

Challen (2000) concluded that these dynamic costs might in fact favour conservative decision making, which ensures that some institutional flexibility is maintained. This implies that caution is required with institutional experimentation. This may be particularly true with innovative, but risky institutional variations, because the long-term costs caused by path dependency outweigh the benefits. The opposing view to the cautious approach is that while the costs of poor institutional innovations may be magnified when viewed in the real (dynamic) environment, it is also true that the opportunity costs of not undertaking good institutional innovations are also magnified through path dependency. The key would appear to lie in maximizing the level and effectiveness of institutional learning, without compromising institutional flexibility. This requires the adoption of 'active' adaptive management approaches, and a thorough evaluation of the potential dynamic costs and benefits of institutional experimentation, not just the static benefits and costs.

Appropriateness of scale

The spatial and administrative scales upon which institutions are based are extremely important to their success (Dovers, 2001).

Spatial scale refers to the physical area over which the institution operates and to the basis by which the boundaries of this area are determined. For example, a spatial scale could be determined on the basis of a river catchment or habitat type (ecological), state, local government or electorate areas (political), the people living in a particular street or town, or who are members of a particular organization (social).

The boundaries of natural resource institutions are occasionally based on catchment areas. However, as institutions are the constraints that shape human interactions, it is also important that the social context is considered in the process of determining an appropriate scale over which to construct institutions. Curtis et al (2002) claim that the establishment of local groups using social boundaries is critical to sustaining water management groups over time. This is because of the effects on community cohesion and sense of purpose that are generated when groups are established on social and not just catchment boundaries. It could be argued that the potential for success of these groups is raised because they are based on a scale that reflects their shared informal institutional foundation.

The administrative scale of an institution refers to the group that is responsible for its implementation. This may be some level of government, a small or large social group, or the community in general. Challen (2000) illustrates the importance of scale through the analysis of institutional functions within hierarchies (e.g., defining the entitlements of potential water users). The administrative and spatial scale ascribed to a particular institution within an institutional hierarchy has been shown to dramatically affect the transaction costs associated with management decisions (Challen, 2000).

Compliance capacity

North (2000) identifies enforcement as a key issue in understanding how to develop better institutions, and claims that there is imperfection in the enforcement of all formal and informal institutions. The reasons for these differences in enforcement are not particularly well understood, although some theoretical perspectives in the context of water are emerging (see, e.g., Cooper, 2009). Ostrom (1993) also identifies compliance as being central to the design of enduring irrigation institutions.

The reason why compliance and enforcement are important is because there are costs involved in the making of a contract. These costs mean that contracts will rarely be comprehensive in covering all conceivable outcomes – they are incomplete. This incompleteness creates the incentive for parties to expend resources trying to capture the unallocated potential for benefit under the contract. In addition, compliance capacity is required to deal with the violations of contractual elements that are specified.

Menard (2000) cites previous research by Levy and Spiller (1994) and Shirley (1995), and reports strong links between the enforcement capacity specified in particular contracts and the success of particular institutional forms. Appropriate enforcement arrangements exhibit themselves through the persistence and success of particular contractual arrangements within the same sector and within the same institutional environment.

There are two forms that compliance mechanisms can take. Barzel (2000) refers to these compliance mechanisms as self-enforcement and third-party enforcement. These mechanisms are also referred to as internal and external compliance measures. The essence of both of these enforcement mechanisms is the ability to punish. The costs of punishment can be imposed in a variety of ways, falling into two broad categories:

- by third parties reducing the level of valuable long-term relations between the enforced and others (e.g., by tarnishing image); and
- when there is no enduring relationship between the enforcer and the enforced, by imposing harm, generally through violence. Violence is defined as an impersonal means of imposing costs. This includes the threat of physical violence, such as incarceration, and the confiscation of valuable assets. (Barzel, 2000)

While a range of individuals and groups can provide third-party enforcement, the state generally has a comparative advantage because of its ability to impose immediate large costs. Self-enforcement works well where there is a positive value for all parties associated with maintaining a contract. Where the value of a venture is believed likely to become negative to one party during the period of a contract, third-party enforcement is likely to be required. Significant differences exist in the transaction and transformation costs of different enforcement arrangements.

Empirical techniques for measuring institutional performance

Capacity to empirically estimate transaction costs

As discussed earlier, NIE provides a theoretical framework for the evaluation of alternative institutions through the assessment of transaction and transformation costs. This cost-effectiveness approach runs into problems in empirical analysis due to a lack of procedures and techniques for measuring and quantifying the different types of transaction costs (e.g., Coase, 2000). This is particularly the case with regard to the measurement of intertemporal transaction and transformation costs.

Benham and Benham (2000) outline a broader range of reasons why there are relatively few empirical studies undertaken of transaction costs, given the importance of transaction cost information in determining economic performance. These include:

- the lack of standard terminology defining transaction costs;
- estimation problems because production and transaction costs are jointly determined;
- an understanding of the opportunity costs of the full range of alternatives that determine choices of individuals is difficult when many kinds of transaction do not take place in open markets (if at all); and
- the law of one price does not apply, with different individuals facing very different transaction costs.

Overall, however, they reach a similar conclusion regarding the evaluation of transaction costs: 'The opportunity cost of measuring the opportunity costs of exchange is likely to be very high' (Benham and Benham, 2000, p372). Put simply, not tackling this task is likely to severely limit welfare enhancements in many contexts. In addition, they conclude that most attempts are in ex post analysis, which brings little assistance to the more pressing problem of ex ante evaluation of alternative institutional forms.

Nevertheless, while being ex post oriented, a range of empirical studies of transaction costs can be identified. The methods employed vary, but include hedonic pricing methods (and analyses of price dispersion that is not explained by product heterogeneity or imperfect information), and the evaluation of standard exchanges in alternative institutional settings (e.g., land title exchange, purchase of equipment).

As noted earlier, examples specifically concerning water management also exist, particularly relating to water transfers. In the investigation of water allocation issues, Colby (1998) identifies a small number of studies that attempt to quantify transaction costs in relation to water transfers. These include studies by Khoshakhlagh et al (1977), Anderson (1983) and Nunn (1989). Easter et al (1999) cites Archibald and Renwick (1998), Hearne and Easter (1997), Howe (1998) and Colby (1998), all in relation to research on transaction costs associated with water transfers. Australian studies which include discussion or estimation of transaction costs in water management include Challen (2000), Crase (2000), Crase et al (2000), Bjornlund and McKay (2001) and Young et al (2000), although enthusiasm for articulating transaction costs in an empirical form appears to have stalled.

Crase (2000) includes a review of empirical studies of institutional design issues related to water markets. Crase distinguishes between 'quasi-empirical' analyses (which employ observations from related input and output markets to infer behaviour under idealized water-trading scenarios) and 'pure-empirical' analyses (which have a clearer focus on the behaviour of genuine economic agents in water markets). A total of 25 quasi-empirical studies were reviewed, employing a wide range of simulation and optimization methods. There is little indication that considering transaction costs was anything more than a minor specification within these models. The group of 12 pure-empirical studies, which by the nature of Crase's delineation were ex post evaluations, placed much greater emphasis on transaction cost influences and their estimation. Nevertheless, Crase concludes that:

> *Explorations to date have employed a relatively narrow definition of transaction costs focussing on conventional market failures, third-party effects, infrastructure impediments, policy induced costs and administratively induced transaction costs. In most cases analyses have used empirical evidence to acknowledge the existence of transaction costs without quantifying the extent of specific costs.* (Crase, 2000, p191)

Criticism of the studies that have been undertaken of transaction costs associated with institutions for use of natural resources also comes from Challen (2000). Challen's concerns derive from two sources. First, there is a lack of a consistent conceptual approach to identifying, classifying and quantifying transaction costs. Second, there is a persistent failure to generalize research findings within a conceptual model of institutional choice. Without these attributes, Challen claims these studies are little more than data collection exercises.

Williamson (1985) and Marshall (2003) also agree that there are significant barriers to the empirical evaluation of transaction costs, but suggest that there may be alternative approaches to the appraisal of alternative institutional forms other than through direct measurement of transaction costs. Williamson (1985) proposes that as transaction costs are always assessed in a comparative institutional way, it is the difference between them rather than the absolute magnitude of transaction costs that matters. Further, Williamson claims that evaluative emphasis should be placed on determining the consistency of institutional form with the type of transactions:

> *Empirical research on transaction cost matters almost never attempts to measure such costs directly. Instead, the question is whether organizational relations (contracting practices; governance structures) line up with the attributes of transactions as predicted by transaction cost reasoning or not.* (Williamson, 1985, p22)

Marshall (2003) approaches the problem of transaction cost measurement from a similar perspective, proposing the use of inductive (rather than deductive) approaches to the analysis of institutions. This involves searching for regularities in the behaviour and performance of particular institutional forms in relation to associated transaction and transformation costs. Marshall's approach is outlined below, and forms the core of the measurement framework proposed herein.

Framework for assessing alternative institutional forms

The framework proposed links five elements that have been discussed above. First, it adopts North's (1990) recognition of the effects of institutions on both transaction and transformation costs. Second, it includes Challen's (2000) emphasis on the dynamically determined costs of institutions. Third, it incorporates Marshall's (2003) extension of these dynamic cost dimensions to transformation costs as well as transaction costs, and fourth, Marshall's (2003) proposed use of heuristics in assessing the transaction and transformation costs of alternative institutions. Finally, the framework employs the generic institutional design features to guide the comparison of alternative institutional structures.

Marshall builds on the framework for institutional choice developed by Challen (2000). Challen proposed that the criterion for institutional choice is cost-effectiveness in achieving a given policy objective. The relevant costs in his framework include static transaction costs, transition costs and intertemporal opportunity costs. Marshall augmented the framework by also including recognition of the effects that the institutional environment has on the technology employed. As we observed earlier, Marshall's extension was developed in the context of institutions for pollution control, and consequently refers to the technology effects as static abatement costs, technological transition costs and intertemporal abatement costs. For the purposes of this chapter we deploy the terminology developed in the earlier section. That is, optimal institutional structure can be analysed as the minimization of the sum of all transaction costs (static transaction costs, institutional transition costs and intertemporal transaction costs) and transformation costs (static transformation costs, technological transition costs and intertemporal transformation costs).

The next component of the framework involves the use of heuristics to replace some elements of empirical evaluation. Clearly, the sum of transaction and transformation costs is important in empirical comparisons of institutions. It is also clear that the complex web of transaction and transformation costs is unlikely to be comprehensively evaluated either because of evaluation resource constraints, or because of the inherent difficulty associated with evaluating some aspects (such as intertemporal transaction and transformation costs).

The final element of the framework is the use of the generic institutional features that have a demonstrated role in determining institutional performance. We anticipate that focusing empirical evaluation (either formally or through the use of heuristics) on those aspects known to be important in determining institutional performance (because they are the source of considerable variability in transaction and transformation costs) will generate much higher returns on the resources invested in institutional evaluation. This addresses the concerns of Benham and Benham (2000) in relation to the high opportunity costs of measuring transaction costs, and is also consistent with Williamson's (1985) position that it is the difference between rather than the absolute magnitude of transaction costs that matters.

Empirical measures relevant to the assessment of generic institutional design features

Having established a range of key institutional features, and the need to evaluate the transaction and transformation costs of different institutional options in relation to these features, I turn to the potential empirical analyses of these costs, which may be relevant in analysis of particular institutional problems. While the development of useful heuristics requires the consideration of a wide range of circumstances in order to determine reliable patterns, some potentially useful heuristics for the consideration of water institutions are proposed.

Institutional design feature 1: Clear objectives

Potential empirical measures

- non-monetary measures of consistency of water management legislative objectives between jurisdictions, and of community awareness and agreement with water management objectives;
- time and financial resources invested in altering legislative objectives (this is related to the dispersion of political power);
- cost of legal disputes centred on water management objectives;
- measures of price dispersion (which is not explained by imperfect information) as a measure of static transaction costs for heterogeneous resources for which there is a market.

Potential heuristics

- Institutions with clearly defined objectives will lower static and dynamic transaction costs (e.g. classification of sub-catchments according to principal management objective).
- Where political influence over the determination of institutions is

concentrated, transformation costs will be lower under conditions of clearly defined objectives in comparison to transformation costs where objectives are unclear (e.g. determination of bulk water pricing in New South Wales (NSW) and the resulting effect on agricultural production costs).

Institutional design feature 2: Interconnection with other formal and informal institutions

Potential empirical measures

- cost of creating formal institutions, which merely replicate institutions that, in other circumstances, could have existed as informal institutions;
- extent to which formal institutions reflect norms and values evident in the management of other resources/circumstances;
- difference in cost of collecting information, monitoring and decision making to support formal institutions, compared to operation in presence of supportive informal institutions;
- difference in welfare outcomes of similar formal institutions within different informal institutional environments.

Potential heuristics

- Formal institutional arrangements that are highly consistent with informal institutional norms and values have lower static transaction and transformation costs (but may not be highly adaptive).
- Where there is some ambiguity about the consistency of formal and informal institutions, informal institutional capacity can lower the static and dynamic transaction costs (e.g. management of water resources to meet aboriginal cultural needs).

Institutional design feature 3: Adaptiveness

Potential empirical measures

- estimation of costs of reversing institutional change;
- estimation of option values of learning from particular circumstances;
- salvage value of technology employed which is specific to institutional environment;
- static transaction and transformation costs of property right attenuation and transition cost caused by property right attenuation;
- trends in static transaction and transformation costs over time;
- measure of heterogeneity in management processes between management units;
- heterogeneity in transformation technologies between production units;
- analysis of extent to which evaluation and experimental evidence have previously been incorporated into future management principles for particular types of institutional arrangements. Pertinent characteristics include relevance, comprehensibility, validity and comprehensiveness.

Potential heuristics

- Institutions that facilitate experimentation and innovation are likely to induce lower transformation costs over time.
- Institutions that support clear monitoring and review processes are likely to have lower institutional transition and intertemporal transaction costs.
- Institutions that incorporate flexibility in how outcomes are achieved are likely to have lower transaction and transformation costs than institutions that prescribe processes (as learning is correlated to variation and experimentation).
- Experimentation and innovation will lower the intertemporal transaction costs of institutional change under conditions of uncertainty.
- Institutions with active adaptive management processes will have higher static transaction costs, in the short term at least.
- Institutions that incorporate evaluation as an integral component of operational process will have lower institutional transition and intertemporal transaction costs, and lower technological transition and intertemporal transformation costs.

Institutional design feature 4: Appropriateness of scale

Potential empirical measures

- analysis of information collection costs at different scales (to support particular water management decisions the institution is intended to guide);
- type and level of interest or stake (direct, indirect, public/private goods) that individuals and groups in the community have in water management outcomes as an indicator of institutional transition costs at different scales.

Potential heuristics

- Intertemporal transaction costs tend to be higher the more that property rights are decentralized (e.g. future costs of changing institutional rules over water access are higher when property rights to access by final users are fully specified).
- Natural resource management (NRM) institutions that have common social and ecological scales have lower static and dynamic transaction costs (e.g. local supply channel management).

Institutional design feature 5: Compliance capacity

Potential empirical measures

- measures of internal enforcement costs (relative to value of resource use);
- measures of external enforcement costs (relative to value of resource use);
- levels and cost of non-compliance.

Potential heuristics

- Institutions that have high levels of internal enforcement support will have lower static and dynamic transaction costs where maintaining a contract for its full duration is mutually beneficial (e.g. government and irrigators undertaking actions which both improve agricultural productivity and improve water quality in a river).
- Institutions that have high levels of external enforcement support will have lower static and dynamic transaction costs where maintaining a contract disadvantages any party at any time during the life of a contract (e.g. compliance with a water extraction cap).
- External compliance measures that monitor indirect attributes based on specified production technology or processes will have higher intertemporal transformation costs (e.g. compliance measures to monitor water use by stipulating production technologies and practices).

Undertaking these analyses or applying these heuristics in the assessment of alternative institutions is still no straightforward task. In particular, the aggregation of costs when heuristics are used remains problematic. Heuristics only provide an indication of the relative magnitude of a particular type of cost, and for particular features of institutional design. In addition, insights gained from the consideration of transaction and transformation costs in relation to specific design features may be invaluable, but a clear understanding of the interactions between institutional features is also required in the overall assessment of alternative institutions.

Concluding remarks

The theory developed as part of New Institutional Economics (NIE) points to the importance of transaction and transformation costs when considering institutional choices. Empirical approaches are available to either measure transaction and transformation costs in aggregate forms, or measure individual elements of these costs. The measurement of individual elements is required in order for the process to inform researchers and policy makers of relationships that are important in determining institutional performance in different circumstances. This is particularly important when considering the potential transfer of institutional arrangements from one context (industry, resource, region, country) to another. Crucially, it needs to be remembered that it is the lessons of successful institutions that need to be transferred, not the (apparent) institution itself.

A framework for assessing alternative institutions has been proposed in this chapter. Under this framework optimal institutional structure is analysed as the minimization of the sum of transaction costs (static transaction costs, institutional transition costs and intertemporal transaction costs) and transformation costs (static transformation costs, technological transition costs and intertemporal transformation costs). The framework focuses on these costs in relation to five particular institutional features, all of which have been shown to be important in explaining differences in institutional success. These five institutional features are:

- clear institutional objectives;
- connectedness between formal and informal institutions;
- adaptability;
- appropriateness of scale; and
- compliance capacity.

A range of empirical measures of static and dynamic transaction and transformation costs has been discussed in regard to these institutional features and potential heuristics have been proposed that, in certain circumstances, may act as proxies in the absence of comprehensive empirical techniques.

The usefulness of a framework such as this rests in its capacity to significantly increase the value of institutional analysis. First, the framework provides a means of gaining a better understanding of specific elements of institutional design (e.g., the static transaction costs associated with alternative compliance measures, as part of institutional arrangements for unregulated water allocation in a catchment). Importantly, it does so in a way that facilitates the integration of findings with other elements of institutional design critical to the management of that particular resource or situation (e.g., what effect the adoption of particular compliance rules may have on the costs of reallocation of the water, or of changing production practices or technologies in the future).

Second, the framework allows for the generalization of research findings about alternative institutional design to other contexts. This is because the findings are linked to specific institutional features, the nature of which can be compared to the features of the alternative setting.

Notwithstanding these advantages, the framework itself provides only a starting point for institutional analysis. It is expected that theoretical refinements and modifications will emerge in response to attempted applications. Moreover, the remainder of the book is based on the view that the application of institutional analysis yields both useful policy information and helps inform additional research in this field.

References

Allan, C. and Curtis, A. (2003) 'Learning to implement adaptive management', *Natural Resource Management*, vol 6, no 1, pp25–30

Alston, L., Eggertsson, T. and North, D. C. (1996) *Empirical Studies in Institutional Change*, Cambridge University Press, New York

Anderson, T. L. (1983) *Water Rights*, Pacific Institute for Public Policy, San Francisco

Aoki, M. (2000) 'Institutional evolution as punctuated equilibria', in C. Menard (ed)

Institutions, Contracts and Organizations: Perspectives from New Institutional Economics, Edward Elgar, Cheltenham, UK

Archibald, S. O. and Renwick, M. E. (1998) 'Expected transaction costs and incentives for water market development', in A. Dinar (ed), *Markets for Water: Potential and Performance*, Kluwer Academic Publishers, Boston

Barr, N. and Cary, J. (1992) *Greening a Brown Land: The Australian Search for Sustainable Land Use*, Macmillan Education Australia, Melbourne

Barzel, Y. (2000) 'The state and the diversity of third-party enforcers', in C. Menard (ed) *Institutions, Contracts and Organizations: Perspectives from New Institutional Economics,* Edward Elgar, Cheltenham, UK

Benham, A. and Benham, L. (2000) *Measuring the Costs of Exchange*, Edward Elgar, Cheltenham, UK

Bjornlund, H. and McKay, J. (2001) 'Operational mechanisms for the efficient working of water markets: Some Australian experiences', Joint Conference of the International Water and Resource Economics Consortium and the Seminar on Environmental and Resource Economics, Girona, Spain, unpublished paper

Challen, R. (2000) *Institutions, Transaction Costs and Environmental Policy: Institutional Reform for Water Resources*, Edward Elgar, Cheltenham, UK

Challen, R. and Schilizzi, S. (1999) 'History, statics and options: Transaction costs in institutional change for water resources', paper presented at the 43rd Annual Conference of the Australian Agricultural and Resource Economics Society, Christchurch, NZ, January

Coase, R. H. (1960) 'The problem of social cost', *The Journal of Law and Economics*, vol 3, pp1–44

Coase, R. H. (2000) 'The new institutional economics', in C. Menard (ed) *Institutions, Contracts and Organizations: Perspectives from New Institutional Economics*, Edward Elgar, Cheltenham, UK

Colby, B. G. (1998) 'Negotiated transaction costs as a conflict resolution mechanism: Bargaining over water in the American west', in A. Dinar (ed) *Markets for Water: Potential and Performance,* Kluwer Academic Publishers, Boston

Cooper, B. (2009) 'Factors influencing compliance with water restrictions', unpublished paper presented at the Australian Agricultural and Resource Economics Conference, Cairns, 15–19 February

Crase, L. (2000) 'Measuring transaction costs in the market for permanent water entitlements in NSW: An application of choice modelling', unpublished PhD thesis, La Trobe University, Melbourne

Crase, L., O'Reilly, L. and Dollery, B. (2000) 'Water markets as a vehicle for water reform: The case of New South Wales', *Australian Journal of Agricultural and Resource Economics*, vol 44, no 2, pp299–321

Curtis, A., Shindler, B. and Wright, A. (2002) 'Sustaining local watershed initiatives: Lessons from landcare and watershed councils', *Journal of the American Water Resources Association*, vol 38, no 5, pp1207–1223

Dovers, S. (2001) 'Institutions for sustainability', *TELA: Environment, Economy and Society*, no 7, April

Easter, K. W., Rosegrant, M. W. and Dinar, A. (1999) 'Formal and informal markets for water: Institutions, performance, and constraints', *World Bank Research Observer*, vol 14, no 1, pp99–116

Ensminger, J. (1992) *Making a Market: The Institutional Transformation of an African Society*, Cambridge University Press, New York

Ensminger, J. (2000) 'Experimental economics in the bush: Why institutions matter', in Menard, C. (ed) *Institutions, Contracts and Organizations: Perspectives from*

New Institutional Economics, Edward Elgar, Cheltenham, UK

Furubotn, E. G. and Richter, R. (1992) 'The new institutional economics: An assessment', in E. G. Furubotn (ed) *New Institutional Economics*, Edward Elgar Publishing, Cheltenham, UK

Goodin, R. E. (1996) 'Institutions and their design', in R. E. Goodin (ed) *The Theory of Institutional Design*, Cambridge University Press, Cambridge

Greif, A. (1993) 'Contract enforceability and economic institutions in early trade: The Maghribi traders' coalition', *American Economic Review*, vol 83, no 3, pp525–548

Greif, A. (1994) 'Cultural beliefs and the organization of society: A historical and theoretical reflection on collectivist and individualist societies', *Journal of Political Economy*, vol 102, pp912–950

Greif, A. (1999) *Genoa and the Maghribi Traders: Historical and Comparative Institutional Analysis*, Cambridge University Press, Cambridge

Hearne, R. R. and Easter, K.W. (1997) 'The economic and financial gains from water markets in Chile', *Agricultural Economics*, vol 15, no 3, pp187–199

Holling, C. S. (1995) 'What barriers? What bridges?', in S. S. Light (ed) *Barriers and Bridges to the Renewal of Ecosystems and Institutions*, Columbia University Press, New York

Howe, C. W. (1998) 'Water markets in Colorado: Past performance and needed changes', in A. Dinar (ed) *Markets for Water: Potential and Performance,* Kluwer Academic Publishers, Boston

Keefer, P. and Shirley, M. M. (2000) 'Formal versus informal institutions in economic development', in C. Menard (ed) *Institutions, Contracts and Organizations: Perspectives from New Institutional Economics*, Edward Elgar, Cheltenham, UK

Kennan, G. (1973) *Memoirs 1950–1963*, Hutchinson, London

Khoshakhlagh, R., Brown, L. and DuMars, C.T. (1977) *Forecasting Future Market Values of Water Rights in New Mexico*, University of New Mexico Department of Economics, Albuquerque, NM

Levy, B. and Spiller, P. (1994) *Regulation, Institutions, and Commitment in Telecommunications*, Proceedings of the World Bank Annual Conference on Development Economics, World Bank, Washington DC

Loehman, E. T. and Kilgour, D. M. (1998) 'Introduction, social design for environmental and resource management', in D. M. Kilgour (ed) *Designing Institutions for Environmental and Resource Management*, Edward Elgar, Cheltenham, UK

Marshall, G. (2003) 'Towards a resource economics for adaptive managers', Paper presented at the 47th Annual Conference of the Australian Agricultural and Resource Economics Society, Fremantle, Western Australia, 12–14 February

Menard, C. (2000) 'Enforcement procedures and governance structures: What relationship?', in C. Menard (ed) *Institutions, Contracts and Organizations: Perspectives from New Institutional Economics*, Edward Elgar, Cheltenham, UK

National Competition Council (1998). 'Compendium of National Competition Policy Agreements: Second Edition', National Competition Council, June

Neale, W. C. (1994) 'Institutions', in G. M. Hodgson, W. J. Samuels, and M. R. Tool (eds) *The Elgar Companion to Institutional and Evolutionary Economics*, Edward Elgar, Aldershot, UK

North, D. C. (1990) *Institutions, Institutional Change and Economic Performance*, Cambridge University Press, Cambridge

North, D. C. (1995) 'Five propositions about institutional change', in I. Sened (ed) *Explaining Social Institutions*, University of Michigan Press, Michigan

North, D. C. (2000) 'Understanding institutions', in C. Menard (ed) *Institutions*,

Contracts and Organizations: Perspectives from New Institutional Economics, Edward Elgar, Cheltenham, UK

North, D. C. and Wallis, J. J. (1994) 'Integrating institutional change and technical change in economic history: A transaction cost approach', *Journal of Institutional and Theoretical Economics*, vol 150, no 4, pp609–624

Nunn, S. C. (1989) 'Transfers of New Mexico water: A survey of changes in place and purpose of use, 1975–1987', University of New Mexico, Department of Economics, Albuquerque, NM

Ostrom, E. (1993) 'Design principles in long-enduring irrigation institutions', *Water Resources Research*, vol 29, no 7, pp1907–1919

Ostrom, E., Gardner, R. and Walker, J. (1994) *Rules, Games, and Common-Pool Resources*, University of Michigan Press, Michigan

Pagan, P. (2008) 'Adaptive Management', in L. Crase (ed) *Water Policy in Australia: The Impact of Change and Uncertainty*, Resources for the Future, Washington DC, pp28–43

Ruys, P., van den Brink, R. and Semenov, R. (2000) 'Values and governance systems', in C. Menard (ed) *Institutions, Contracts and Organizations: Perspectives from New Institutional Economics,* Edward Elgar, Cheltenham, UK

Saleth, R. M. and Dinar, A. (2004) *The Institutional Economics of Water: A Cross-Country Analysis of Institutions and Performance*, Edward Elgar, Cheltenham, UK

Schotter, A. (1981) *The Economic Theory of Social Institutions*, Cambridge University Press, Cambridge

Shirley, M. M. (1995) *Bureaucrats in Business*, Oxford University Press, Oxford

Smith, D. I. (1998) *Water in Australia: Resources and Management*, Oxford University Press, Melbourne

Tinbergen, I. (1950) *On the Theory of Economic Policy*, Elsevier, Amsterdam

Wallis, J. J. and North, D. C. (1986) 'Measuring the transaction sector in the American economy, 1870–1970', in R. E. Gallman, *Long-Term Factors in American Economic Growth*, University of Chicago Press, Chicago

Williamson, O. E. (1985) *The Economic Institutions of Capitalism*, The Free Press, New York

World Bank (1998) 'Dividends and disappointments: Learning from the success and failure of foreign aid', World Bank, Discussion Draft, July

Young, H. P. (1998) *Individual Strategy and Social Structure: An Evolutionary Theory of Institutions*, Princeton University Press, Princeton

Young, M., Hatton MacDonald, D., Stinger, R. and Bjornlund, H. (2000) 'Interstate water trading: A two year review', CSIRO Land and Water, Australia

3

Dynamic Community Preferences: Lessons for Institutional Design and Measuring Transaction and Transformation Costs

Lin Crase

Introduction

The imperative for reforming the rules by which water is allocated between competing users is now widely acknowledged at all political levels in Australia. Even in Western Australia, where until only a few years ago the government had proclaimed that there was no 'major problem' with water over-allocation (WA Water and Rivers Commission, 2000, p16), institutional reform in the water sector is now considered essential. Increasingly, the reform agenda has been shaped and promoted at the national level, regardless of the constitutional constraints that beset federal intervention in this field. More specifically, the Australian Constitution clearly vests responsibility for water affairs in state jurisdictions such that any national approach to water policy relied heavily upon the assuasive powers of federal decision makers, at least in the first instances of reform. Ultimately, however, this has given rise to a relatively uniform policy approach to water management across different state jurisdictions and is typified by four broad themes.

First, the reform approach placed greater emphasis on the need to allocate additional water for environmental purposes. This can be traced to the progressive revelation of environmental harm caused by excessive extractions from both surface water and ground-water sources, particularly in the southern Murray-Darling Basin. Adding impetus to this approach has been the proclivity for the Australian electorate to favour increased environmental amenity, manifested in part by the emergence of the environmental lobby as a strong political force.

Second, the national water agenda has stressed the requirement to clarify the definition of individual water rights, particularly in the context of irrigation. In most jurisdictions this has resulted in the separation of land and water titles and the unbundling of rights into access and use regimes.

Accompanying the move towards stronger, less attenuated individual rights has been the devolution of the control of water infrastructure to end users. This is particularly the case in irrigation where the state has attempted to play a far less significant role than it has done historically. In some instances the result has been the divesting of all assets to irrigators while, in other cases, ownership has remained with the state while control and management now reside with irrigators or their representatives.

A final theme within the reform agenda has been the reliance on prices and markets to signal the preferred allocation of the resource. Usage charges are now determined by economic regulators and markets have been established to facilitate temporary and permanent water trade in most states. A stated policy ambition of reforms, embodied in statements like the National Water Initiative (NWI), is to expand water markets to a national scale wherever the hydrology makes it feasible.

A reflection on the processes that have seen the emergence of these four policy themes stands to provide valuable lessons about the process of water policy formulation and accompanying institutional reforms. In this chapter I attempt to trace the water reform agenda against other trends within the Australian community as a mechanism for exposing the apparatus of adjustment. This process is also aimed at providing insights into the operational dimensions of the various transaction costs frameworks developed by Challen (2000) and Marshall (2003) described in Chapter 2. This chapter also touches on important political economy and hierarchical decision-making issues not thoroughly explored in the earlier analysis.

The chapter itself is organized into four additional parts. The following section provides a brief overview of the major reforms in Australian irrigation since the 1980s and contextualizes these against long-standing social norms with respect to agriculture. The third section reintroduces an institutional perspective to policy change and endeavours to operationalize this framework specifically in the context of Australian irrigation. Some tentative lessons for institutional design are examined in the fourth section along with some cautionary notes on the transaction cost technique developed for conceptualizing change. Brief concluding remarks are then offered in the final section of the chapter.

An overview of Australian water reforms

Water reforms of the genre described earlier have occurred progressively in Australia since the 1980s. By and large, until that point water had been treated as an abundant resource which, if harnessed for productive pursuits, would act as a catalyst for generating rural and national prosperity. Randall (1981) describes this as the 'development' ethos. During this phase, only scant attention was paid to the true cost of extractive use or the costs that attended water infrastructure, which coincidentally remained largely in public hands because of the perceived wider benefits brought by water development, particularly irrigation.

Importantly, while this approach appears incompatible with present standards for organizing economic activity in Australia, the origins of policies of this kind can be traced back to deeply entrenched aspects of the Australian psyche. More specifically, it needs to be understood that non-indigenous Australian culture was (and arguably remains) heavily influenced by an affinity with agriculture that belies the urban existence of most of the current citizenry. These attitudes stood in stark contrast to the values held by the indigenous population which was largely displaced by European settlement. In this context Lloyd (1988, p20) observed that 'white settlers' ... exploitation of water was often injudicious and inequitable [and settlers] were patronizing, even contemptuous, about Aboriginal water management'. This exploitative approach to water and general disregard for indigenous values was heavily influenced by the background of early white settlers and the underlying ambition to recreate a familiar European environment within a radically different natural landscape.

Fuelled by the desire to secure a 'green land', water development became the norm throughout the 19th century and the first six decades of the 20th century. Within this timeframe Musgrave (2008) identifies two major phases of water management and law. First, the reform period of the late 19th and early 20th centuries was punctuated by the substitution of state control for the riparian doctrine, the use of licences to provide rights to use water, loans by the state governments to failed irrigation entities and the establishment of formidable water bureaucracies to influence the allocation of the resource. Collectively, these measures represented a response to the underlying concerns about drought-proofing a foreign and forbidding landscape and resulted in an expansion of agricultural output and accelerated settlement of the hinterland.

The second phase is described by Musgrave (2008, p30) as 'the march of irrigation' which expressed waning enthusiasm for state irrigation projects in the 1960s. However, throughout this second phase the use of public irrigation schemes as a vehicle for encouraging 'nation building' went virtually unquestioned. In this context Watson (2003, p220) observes that 'the popular enthusiasm for irrigation over a century or more was always inconsistent with a serious appraisal of physical or economic opportunities facing Australia'. Nevertheless, by the 1970s and 1980s the economic rationale of public irrigation was attracting serious criticism and this was accompanied by the abandonment of the notion of closer settlement. Wider fiscal constraints and broader shifts in public policy towards environmentalism were also evident at this time.

Against this background, the first series of national water reforms emerged from the Council of Australian Governments (CoAG) in 1994. The nationally agreed Water Reform Framework (followed by the Competition Principles Agreement in 1995) accelerated and unified various earlier initiatives at the state level – most of these had already begun to reshape the water sector, particularly irrigated agriculture. The main ingredients of the first CoAG reforms were:

- The reformation of pricing practices so that they are consumption-based and reflect the full economic cost of the resource.
- The separation of water service delivery from regulation functions and greater financial self-sufficiency. As part of this, irrigators were given increased control over the management of irrigation areas.
- Two-part tariffs were introduced for urban water users.
- Economic viability and ecological sustainability criteria were invoked to assess all future water investments.
- Jurisdictions were to recognize in legislation the environmental demands for water, and simultaneously break the nexus between land and water titles, thereby encouraging water trade.

In 2003 CoAG announced its intention to embark on an additional series of reforms, culminating in the National Water Initiative announced in 2004. Tasmania subsequently joined the agreement in 2005 followed by Western Australia. The National Water Initiative dealt with many of the areas raised a decade earlier but added three important ingredients. First, the development of institutional arrangements to deal with the catchment as a whole; second, the establishment of a robust, transparent regulatory water accounting framework; and third, a sharper focus on total urban water use in contrast to the narrow concentration on urban pricing under the 1994 framework.

Importantly, the National Water Initiative also requires that users' rights be specified as a perpetual share of the consumptive pool of the resource, once adequate allowance had been made for the requirements of the environment. This represents a significant departure from the 'development' approach which largely disregarded the needs of natural ecosystems. Accompanying the recognition of environmental needs was increased attention to the role of markets. In this context the National Water Initiative aimed to provide an 'expansion of permanent trade in water bringing about more profitable use of water and more cost-effective and flexible recovery of water to achieve environmental outcomes' (Department of Prime Minister and Cabinet, 2005, p1). This melding of economic and environmental outcomes characterized much of the current reform agenda up until the release of the National Plan for Water Security by the then Howard government. Throughout this period each state set about the process of implementing legislative changes that reflect the broad intentions of the National Water Initiative. Considerable attention was given to the property rights of different water users.

Arguably, there has been a non-trivial modification to the policy focus since the release of the National Plan for Water Security and the Rudd government's Water for the Future manifesto (see, e.g., Watson, 2007; Crase and O'Keefe, 2009). Nevertheless, several questions arise from the broader reforms evident in the Australian water sector between 1994 and 2007. First, what techniques are available to shed light on the radical transformation of water policy over this period, which appears diametrically opposed to the resource development ethos that had emerged over the preceding 100 years? Second, to what extent are the dual aims of increased economic efficiency or accountability and environmental enhancement reconcilable, and what institutional initiatives have been invoked to prima facie bolster compatibility? Third, what does the reform process suggest about the likely efficacy of future water policies or approaches employed elsewhere in the world?

In attempting to answer these questions within the scope of this chapter, the following discussion is underpinned by observations drawn from the New Institutional Economics literature, and revisits and embellishes some of the discussion from Chapter 2. The following section commences with a brief examination of the role of transaction and transformation costs in policy formulation.

The transaction costs of altering water policies

'One of the key premises in the institutional economics literature is that institutional change occurs only when the transaction costs of reform are less than the corresponding opportunity costs of doing nothing' (Saleth and Dinar, 2004, p13). As was noted in Chapter 2, transaction costs arising from policy change have been categorized by Challen (2000) into two main forms and collectively represent 'dynamic' transaction costs within his typology.

First, transition costs are conceptualized by Challen (2000) as those dynamic institutional costs that arise from constraints embedded in the history of present institutions. Here, the term 'institutions' refers to the set of rules that govern behaviour. Consider, for example, the historical implications of Section 100 of the Australian Constitution, which effectively assigns water management to the states and isolates the national government from important decisions about water use. This occurs regardless of the confluence of most of the nation's water resources. Thus, notwithstanding the benefits of a national approach to water policies and laws, institutional history has made it costly to develop a holistic approach to water management – the states have generally resisted attempts to cede the rights to water to a higher authority, regardless of whether this would yield a more efficient and less costly regime. Put simply, history does matter in these cases and can impose significant transition costs that might ultimately stymie the development of preferred institutional arrangements.

The second genre of dynamic transaction costs relates to the capacity to reverse institutional change. Challen (2000) described these as inter-temporal opportunity costs and they broadly represent the antithesis of transition costs.

In this instance, costs arise by selecting options that close off lower cost opportunities in the future. Thus, rather than arising from the existing history of institutions, these costs represent the 'future histories' of institutional choices. A fundamental tenet of inter-temporal opportunity costs is that it is always costly to reverse an earlier action that would have given stronger rights to individuals relative to group rights. By way of contrast, policy changes that cede strong rights to the few at the expense of the many usually attract limited costs; the few will always have the motivation to mobilize resources to support the assignment of rights in their favour, whereas the per capita motivation for the larger group is relatively weak (Horn, 1995).

Notwithstanding that there are always likely to be costs that attend change, the costs of doing nothing can also be substantial. In a neoclassical sense, the costs of doing nothing (static transaction costs in Challen's typology) can be considered analogous to the various forms of static 'inefficiencies' described in the conventional economics literature. For instance, there might be productive inefficiencies embodied in the rules that circumscribe the status quo, where the least-costly method of production is not employed because of institutional constraints. Alternatively, the output produced by a set of rules may not match with community preferences, giving rise to another genre of static costs. In the context of the latter, increased demand for environmental amenity that is not matched by government policies to protect or rehabilitate the ecosystems would fall into this group; i.e. this is one cost of 'doing nothing'.

The fact that institutions do not operate in a technological void has been recognized by Pagan (Chapter 2) where he draws on the work of Marshall (2003) to explain this relationship. In this case, the term 'transformation costs' was used to explain this technological link. As with institutionally derived transaction costs, transformation costs embody two dynamic elements: First, the cost of transition to a new technology (e.g. the technical cost of removing and replacing an old technology) and; second, the inter-temporal costs of a technological choice (e.g. technological lock-in).

Operationalizing transaction and transformation costs

To demonstrate how this typology can be employed and to illustrate why it might potentially require expansion I commence by sketching, by way of example, a modest technological development in water measurement devices and the related water allocation rules employed in several surface water irrigation districts in Australia.

Among the most common technologies for measuring and monitoring water use in surface water irrigation schemes in Australia is the Dethridge wheel. The wheel was first developed in 1910 and has been progressively refined from a technical perspective, partly in response to the need to limit unauthorized interference by farmers. Nevertheless, the fundamental hydraulic design principles have remained largely unchanged since the introduction of the device to irrigation districts almost a century ago (Australian Academy of Technological Sciences and Engineering, 2000).

In some instances, the Dethridge meter has been recorded as producing delivery errors of between plus and minus 20 per cent (Creighton et al, 2004). Clearly, in the context of the wider reforms aimed at promoting improved water efficiency, measurement errors of this magnitude have been viewed as unacceptable. In response, irrigation districts such as the Coleambally Irrigation Area have embarked on major infrastructure refurbishment projects have resulted in the deployment of alternative measurement technologies. Flume gates, which boast superior accuracy and measure the flow of water through a flume using differential pressure sensors (Creighton et al, 2004), are now widely employed.

Of particular interest is the relationship between the direct costs attendant on replacing the old technology and the extant institutional arrangements that circumscribe that technology. In this example, static transformation costs become manifest in the form of the inefficient metering of water use by the existing technology (i.e. the deficiencies of the Dethridge device). The accompanying static transaction costs encompass the rules that allow irrigation farmers to be under- and/or overcharged for their water consumption.

The technological transformation costs in this instance pertain to the expense of removing the Dethridge wheels and replacing them with flume gates. In addition, inter-temporal transformation costs might attend this change if flume gates limit the choice of alternative and superior technologies, should they emerge in the future. Institutional transition costs arise from the necessity to alter the rules as a result of modifications to water measurement. For instance, farmers who had previously been undercharged (oversupplied) for water though no fault of their own might require that some transitional arrangements be put in place. Inter-temporal transaction costs might plausibly arise if these 'new' rules then limit the use of 'better' rules in the future.

While the typology proffered by Pagan (Chapter 2) might adequately cover the range of costs that attend this modest technological and institutional adjustment, it does not specifically account for the hierarchical dimension of technological and transaction costs which substantially complicates the process. More specifically, the replacement of Dethridge wheels with flume gates and the development of new local rules in line with this technology represent a microcosmic response to technological and institutional changes occurring at several superordinate levels. In the framework developed in Chapter 2, these processes are subsumed into the aggregate behaviour of private and political entrepreneurs. Thus, while the distinction between technological and institutional costs can be gainfully employed to analyse these events, we run the risk of overlooking important influences that emanate from decisions emerging within an institutional hierarchy – and this is by far the most common architecture for establishing water allocation decisions.

If, for simplicity, we accept that the national authority represents the only superordinate level, static transaction costs arise when the current rules supported by the national government embody flaws. One source of transaction costs at this level occurs if the present rules do not adequately account for wider national community preferences. This form of cost might increase when the rules for water allocation are heavily biased in favour of 'development', even though community attitudes have changed to a 'conservationist' approach. Similarly, static transaction costs might occur if the community at large favours a less intrusive role for government and yet the rules imposed at the national level do not adequately reflect this preference.

At this ultimate level in the decision-making hierarchy, the 'technology of government' becomes an important variable. Put differently, there are 'technologies' that are required within decision-making bodies in order to bring about a modification to the rules. That is, the distinction between technologically related costs and transaction-related costs is not as clear as might be implied by Pagan's typology. Technologies in this instance might relate to a suboptimal capacity to draft meaningful and purposeful legislation or have agencies implement decisions.[1] Examples of static transformation costs at this level, and in the context of increased demand for environmental amenity, might occur because there is no extant environmental regulator, or important data on environmental criteria are missing, or the machinery for undertaking community consultation on environmental issues is nonexistent. Similarly, the absence of the 'technology' to allow for greater individualism (e.g. poorly defined property rights or the absence of a market) might conceivably be treated as a genre of static transformation cost at the ultimate level of this hierarchy.

The dynamic costs of change at the national level can similarly be considered against the dichotomy described by Pagan (Chapter 2). Institutional transition costs occur via the political process at the national level. This might include the costs associated with lobbying to achieve support for rules that better reflect society's aggregate preferences for environmental amenity or the costs of negotiating with irrigators who have previously enjoyed liberal access to water. Inter-temporal transaction costs will attend any amended rules that later prove difficult to adapt to the preferences of future generations. Technological transition costs emerge from the necessity to alter national statutes or national agencies (as the 'technology' of government) while inter-temporal transformation costs occur where the existence of such statutes or agencies places constraints over future and superior legislation or entities.

This analysis endeavours to highlight the relationships that exist within a hierarchical process of decision making. Conceivably, changes at the superordinate level of a decision-making hierarchy occur when the costs of the status quo at the national level (i.e. static transformation and transaction costs) can no longer be endured relative to the technological and institutional costs of change. Once these changes occur we might expect that changes cascade down the decision-making hierarchy, eventually reaching subordinate organizations that then embark on a process of adjustment – in turn invoking a microcosmic set of transformation and institutional comparisons. Put differently, the changes at the superordinate level stimulate a reassessment of the costs of doing nothing at lower tiers.

In the case of water management in Australia, these changes pass through several tiers within the decision-making hierarchy by virtue of the constitutional powers ascribed to water resources. This reinforces the necessity for 'technologies' to exist within each tier of the decision-making hierarchy to actually make a decision. These technologies are distinct from (although intimately related to) the rules that derive from those decisions. Importantly, this framework points to the necessity to consider the technological capacity at different tiers of governance and its relationship to performance. For example, the existence of capable leadership and informed governance committees, particularly for lower tier entities, might be significant in the context of communal irrigation organizations.

Three additional conceptual features of the hierarchical framework need to be addressed. First, there are probable additional transaction costs that occur between the levels of the decision-making hierarchy. As changes are implemented at a superordinate level there is a requirement to use resources at the subordinate level to interpret and respond to change. This implies some conceptual permeability at the boundaries of decision making but this is unlikely to be homogeneous for all changes proffered by the superordinate level.

Second, for convenience we have presented changes at the national level cascading down the decision-making hierarchy. In reality, this need not be the case. Change within institutions or technologies can also be prompted at subordinate levels. For instance, initiatives brought on within a state jurisdiction might promote adoption at an interstate or national level. However, it can be assured that if there is significant discord with the agenda at the superordinate levels of the hierarchy, these changes will probably be stymied.

Third, static and dynamic transaction costs should not be considered entirely independent. Consider, for example, the introduction of markets that allow for trading of water between users. Initially markets were introduced in response to the high static costs of retaining water in its historical uses in the face of increasing scarcity (say, as a result of the Murray-Darling Basin Cap on extractions). One of the consequences of water markets has been the revelation of the true reserve price held by some irrigators. Moreover, this has exposed considerable rents that have, in turn, added impetus to supplementary pricing reforms. Put simply, institutional changes to address static costs have revealed the need for additional institutional and technological adjustments.

Lessons for institutional change and a cautionary note on transaction costs

The hierarchical and transaction/transformation cost framework illustrated in the earlier section provides a useful lens through which to examine the process of adjustment on a variety of scales. Moreover, the framework is appealing inasmuch as it allows us to reconcile the manner in which community preferences can impact on both macro and micro institutional settings, in an ex post sense at least. However, two major deficiencies beset this approach. In essence, this framework provides us with a way of understanding the interactions between technology, institutions and decision making but falls short of providing direction for policy reform. Second, a related limitation resides in the absence of established empirical techniques by which to measure the range of costs, particularly inter-temporal transaction costs.

Pagan (Chapter 2) and Marshall (2003) have attempted to resolve this problem by applying a 'cost minimization' criterion – those institutions that give rise to lower costs are defined as preferable to those with higher costs. In addition, a set of heuristics were invoked to focus on those elements that advance institutional design. Pagan (Chapter 2) applies these heuristics specifically in the context of irrigation and offers five main features which are indicative of superior institutional performance. These institutions would comprise:

- clear objectives;
- interconnection with other formal and informal institutions;
- adaptiveness;
- appropriateness of scale; and
- compliance capacity.

Each of these institutional design elements is now briefly considered in the context of Australian irrigation. Notwithstanding that irrigated agriculture is far from homogeneous, generalized comments about the impact of water reform on the irrigation sector are proffered in the hope that they can prove instructive.

Clear objectives

We observed earlier in this chapter that irrigation in Australia was once considered synonymous with 'nation building' and was regarded as a manifestation of Australia's commitment to yeomanry. One of the most striking elements of irrigation reform has been its capacity to narrow the policy focus to the productive efficiency of irrigation and to more clearly define the role of irrigation entities. In this regard, the early CoAG reforms, that saw the devolution of the responsibility for irrigation to end users, have been critical. By and large this has made irrigation entities more responsive to the productive needs of irrigators while simultaneously providing greater decision-making power via water user committees, shareholder voting rights and the like. The clarification of water rights has also been pivotal in this context. In addition, those irrigators who are not part of larger schemes have benefited from improved definition of water rights, which provides a clearer productive focus for their activities.

These enhancements have not come entirely without cost, as the framework illustrated earlier would suggest. The irrigation lobby remains a powerful force in the Australian political milieu and has been reluctant to forgo its status as one of 'nation building'. Thus, regardless of institutional changes that have endeavoured to define the objectives of irrigation in a productive sense, attempts to invoke the earlier 'yeoman farmer' conceptualization of the sector (largely with the intention of preserving rents) remain commonplace.

Interconnection with other formal and informal institutions

Two main themes pervade the water debate in Australia. One concerns the productive efficiency of resource use and the other revolves around unease about the impact on the natural environment. Both of these themes resonate with the broad citizenry (Crase, 2009).

The use of markets to allocate all manner of resources and an emphasis on individual rights and decision making are far more prevalent in the 21st century than they were during the era when irrigation infrastructure received enthusiastic support from the public purse. A cursory review of workplace relations over the past two decades is illustrative of how Australians have come to expect that their formal and informal institutions enshrine individualism. Accordingly, the emphasis on cost recovery, user pay, individual rights and trade within the irrigation sector are all consistent with these wider social norms.

On the environmental front, the electorate has shown support for policy makers willing to improve environmental amenity, or at least halt further environmental degradation. Reconciling these preferences with the desire for institutional reforms to promote productive efficiency has necessitated innovative solutions. By and large this has required consultation with the irrigation community and the apportioning of a designated pool of the resource to achieve environmental objectives. The tradeoff for irrigators has been enhanced rights (albeit over a reduced quantum of water) and, in some instances, a commitment by government to defray the costs of structural adjustments. Unfortunately, these latter actions have provided additional scope for rent-seeking by some irrigation lobbyists and arguably weakened the productive efficiency objectives assigned to irrigation entities (see, e.g., Crase, 2009).

Adaptiveness

Much of Australia's water legislation includes reference to the necessity for environmentally sustainable development (ESD) and notes the precautionary principle in one form or another (see, for example, NSW Water Management Act). Prima facie we might expect that the strengthening of individual rights for irrigators makes it more difficult (i.e. costly) to change the behaviour of irrigators in line with revelations about ESD, particularly if the state chooses to rake additional water for environmental amenity. However, this need not be the case, and Pagan and Crase (2005) show that stronger rights for water users can bolster adaptive management by water resource agencies.

In addition, the National Water Initiative attempted to encapsulate institutional adaptiveness for irrigation by detailing the limits of, and adjustment mechanisms for, contingent claims against water. More specifically, the National Water Initiative proposed that changes to water rights that arise from government policy would be compensated by the state, while changes that attend new bona fide knowledge of deleterious effects would be shared between the individual and the state. In addition, the specification of irrigators' rights as a proportion of the available resource embeds some adaptiveness into the institutional arrangements in irrigation.

Notwithstanding these initiatives, Quiggin (2008) observes that numerous problems remain. Differentiating between government policy changes and those brought on by bona fide knowledge is likely to prove vexatious. In addition, in the immediate term an adequate mechanism for reducing water extraction rights to sustainable proportions of available resources has not been identified. In the case of surface water in the Murray-Darling Basin Commission, the original status of all allocations was honoured, regardless of use, and all right holders faced reduced extractions as part of the Murray-Darling Basin Cap (see Quiggin, 2004). In some districts state governments endeavoured to resolve this matter on the basis of 'history of use'. There are no easy answers to reaching consensus on an adaptive but sustainable institution for irrigation where there has been a record of over-allocation.

Appropriateness of scale

The hierarchical approach to decision making suggests that the scale or coverage of a set of rules can overlap. Notwithstanding the potential for change to emanate from lower tiers of the hierarchy, the rules established at a superordinate level impinge on the rules adopted at a lower level in the hierarchy. In the context of irrigation, the devolution of rights to individual irrigators and the expanded decision-making power of cooperative property institutions, such as irrigation companies or irrigator-managed state infrastructure, warrant mention.

Collectively, these reforms have shifted the locus of vital decisions about agricultural production down the hierarchy. The specification of water rights as a proportion of the extractive pool also ensures that production risks are primarily addressed at the individual irrigator or irrigation district level. This contrasts with earlier institutional arrangements which saw production decisions partially in the hands of state water bureaucracies by virtue of the manner in which they allocated water between competing users in a given season. The development of water markets has also acted as a vehicle for distributing production risks in a more efficient manner.

Notwithstanding the benefits of these reforms from a 'scale appropriateness' perspective, significant perverse outcomes can arise from the cascading influence of superordinate rules. For instance, the National Drought Policy provides financial assistance to farmers (in collaboration with the states) on the basis of the 'declaration' of districts assessed as being subject to 'exceptional circumstances' arising from low rainfall. One of the upshots of these arrangements is that farmers face incentives to undertake more risky practices, such as overstocking, or to fail to adequately prepare for the consequences of drought within their farming enterprises (Freebairn, 1983). Similarly, Quiggin and Chambers (2004) have shown that expectation of drought relief would induce farmers to adopt more risky production strategies. From an irrigation perspective, policies of this genre also reduce the potential returns to irrigation, which might be assumed to enjoy higher returns when competition from dryland agriculture declines. In sum, while significant progress has been made by shifting the scale of production-related decisions closer to the individual farmer, there is still scope for improvement.

Compliance capacity

In his original treatment of this component of institutional design Pagan (Chapter 2) argued that: 'Institutions that have high levels of internal enforcement support will have lower static and dynamic transaction costs where maintaining a contract for its full duration is mutually beneficial.' The manner in which irrigation infrastructure has been devolved to irrigators again proves instructive in this case. In many instances in Australian irrigation the enhancement of decision making for individual irrigators or cooperative irrigation schemes has been contingent upon the requirement to undertake activities that would (purportedly) lead to augmentation of the natural environment. For example, in the area presently controlled by Murray Irrigation Limited, irrigators were given ownership of the irrigation infrastructure in 1995. As part of these arrangements the New South Wales government acknowledged that there had been underinvestment in the infrastructure and undertook to assist in its refurbishment. Reciprocity was required from irrigators in the form of a commitment to land and water management plans that expire after 15 years. The plans require significant matching investments at the farm level to bolster irrigation efficiency, and to reduce the environmental harm caused by irrigation activities. These arrangements have proven reasonably successful in promoting on-farm investments in projects such as landforming and water recycling, although other targets have proven difficult to both quantify and meet (see, e.g., Toohey et al, 2005). The improvements in water measurement and distribution technologies discussed earlier are also illustrative of the drive towards compliance at the level of the irrigation district.

At a national level, similar reciprocity is evident in the National Water Initiative and earlier CoAG reforms. The strengthening of water rights for irrigators might arguably be regarded as the 'carrot' that encouraged irrigators to engage in the debate about reduced extractions and the establishment of environmental claims on the resource. The downside has been confusion among the public between irrigation efficiency and genuine environmental change. This might well be attributed to the citizenry's inability to distinguish between agricultural and natural landscapes and their categorization of all non-metropolitan areas of interest as 'the bush' (Crase, 2009).

A cautionary note

The transaction cost / transformation cost approach is particularly useful when contemplating institutional design and the allocation of water resources between competing demands. Moreover, Ostrom (1993) predicted over a decade ago that attention to institutional matters in water would outweigh the importance of engineering design for the foreseeable future. As I have attempted to illustrate in the context of Australian water reform, the institutional lens provides one way of conceptualizing the relationships between technologics, rules and the hierarchy of decision making in irrigation.

Unfortunately, this approach also carries severe limitations, not the least of which is its reliance on positivism and its bias towards ex post analysis. Collectively, these two limitations provide an opportunity for policy advisers to proffer mediocre solutions to demanding problems. Put simply, it has become possible for professionals to focus on the dynamic costs of change as an excuse for providing suboptimal policy choices that barely reduce static costs. Phrases such as 'it was as good as we could do on the day' become the norm in policy circles when the real question should be 'how can we do better?'

This is not to say that change in water institutions can occur without cost. Rather, it is important for professionals to be cognisant of the lessons offered by their disciplines and use these as the foundation for challenging the status quo.

Concluding remarks

Australian irrigation has undergone a radical transformation in the past two decades. Much of this has occurred on the institutional front inasmuch as the rules by which the irrigation sector operates are now vastly different to those that characterized irrigation for most of the 19th and 20th centuries. Following decades of state-sponsored development of water resources there was a determined push between 1994 and 2007 on the part of all Australian governments to address the productive deficiencies of irrigated agriculture and the environmental consequences of over-allocation of the resource.

I have illustrated in this chapter how changes of this magnitude can be considered as a suite of static and dynamic costs that occur on institutional (or rule-making) and technological fronts. Importantly, the relationships between national, interstate, state and district entities with an interest in water give rise to a hierarchy of decision making. This conceptual approach allows us to trace the relationships between costs borne at different levels of decision making and help account for the overt changes that ultimately manifest in irrigation districts or even irrigation farms.

Compared with the heuristics offered by Pagan, the changes witnessed in Australian irrigation during this period are consistent with institutional improvement. The objectives that circumscribe irrigation (and indeed the behaviour of individual irrigators) were more clearly specified and these changes were broadly consistent with wider trends within the Australian community. The capacity of irrigation institutions to adapt was challenged, although the clarification and strengthening of individual property rights seems likely to favour increased adjustment capacity. Decision making, in the context of production at least, was also devolved, arguably representing an improvement on the scale dimension of institutions. Finally, there is evidence that compliance capacity within levels of the decision-making hierarchy and between subordinate and superordinate entities in the hierarchy were enhanced.

Regardless of these admirable achievements there remains considerable scope for improvement and major challenges linger. In particular, the framework used here emphasizes the dynamic nature of community preferences. Moreover, rising incomes accompanied by the general malaise of agriculture relative to services and manufacturing sectors in Australia are important macro considerations. In addition, revelations brought by new information on a variety of fronts almost guarantees that the rules of today will be challenged by the social norms of tomorrow. In this context the transformation of water policy in Australia provides salutary lessons for others.

The hierarchical dimension of the framework also illustrates that modifications at one scale of the decision hierarchy, particular the superordinate levels, can produce a cascading response. Arguably, the more recent episodes of water policy in Australia and the U-turn evidenced by the renewed enthusiasm by the federal government to subsidize irrigation infrastructure without adequate scrutiny is illustrative of this point (see, e.g., Watson, 2007; Crase and O'Keefe, 2008). More specifically, the reversal of infrastructure funding witnessed in the Howard Plan for National Water Security and the subsequent emphasis on subsidized infrastructure in the Rudd government's Water for the Future have quickly transformed the way state and local irrigation entities respond on the institutional front.

Countries that presently rely heavily on agriculture and are encouraged to sponsor a 'developmentalist' approach to irrigation need to be cognisant that concerns about efficiency and environmental sustainability will probably emerge at some point – particularly as rising incomes stimulate preferences for greater environmental amenity. Developing current institutions that are amenable to improved productive efficiencies and that can simultaneously respond to environmental considerations seems to be a sensible approach. The Australian experience of trading off stronger irrigator rights for reduced extractions has yielded some successes, although the quantum of water required for genuine change on the environmental front remains highly contentious.

Finally, the hierarchical nature of decision making that circumscribes all water use cannot be ignored. Radical institutional change of the type witnessed in Australian irrigation requires sufficient coherence between each level of the decision-making hierarchy. This implies that cooperation between national, interstate, state and local entities is a prerequisite. Unfortunately, it also suggests that important changes will be delayed until the static costs of the status quo are so severe that they can no longer be ignored by any one of the levels of the hierarchy. In this context we need to be wary of those who would delay reform by resorting to arguments that focus solely on the difficulty of bringing about change.

Notes

1 The mechanics by which these agreed rules are transformed are assumed to be conceptually distinct from the institutional environment and constitute the 'technology of government'. They represent the means of transforming ideas or agreements reached in the politico-institutional domain into actions by government departments and their officers.

References

Australian Academy of Technological Sciences and Engineering (2000) *Technology in Australia 1788–1988*, Australian Science and Technology Heritage Centre, Melbourne

Challen, R. (2000) *Institutions, Transaction Costs and Environmental Policy: Institutional Reform for Water Resources*, Edward Elgar, Cheltenham, UK

Crase, L. (2009) 'Water policy in Australia: The impacts of change and uncertainty', in A. Dinar and J. Albiac (eds) *Policy and Strategic Behaviour in Water Resource Management*, Earthscan, London, pp91–108

Crase, L. and O'Keefe, S. (2009) 'The paradox of National Water Savings: Water use efficiency is not a solution', *Agenda,* forthcoming

Creighton, C., Meyer, W. and Khan, S. (2004) 'Farming and land stewardship. Case study – Australia's innovations in sustainable irrigation', Proceedings of the 4th International Crop Science Congress, Brisbane, Australia, 26 September–1 October, available online at www.cropscience.org.au/icsc2004/symposia/6/2/1838_creightonc.htm

Department of Prime Minister and Cabinet (2005) *About the National Water Initiative*, Department of Prime Minister and Cabinet, Canberra

Freebairn, J. (1983) 'Drought assistance policy', *Australian Journal of Agricultural Economics*, vol 27, no 3, pp185–199

Horn, M. (1995) *The Political Economy of Public Administration: Institutional Choice in the Public Sector*, Cambridge University Press, Cambridge

Lloyd, C. (1988) *Either Drought or Plenty: Water Development and Management in NSW*, Department of Water Resources NSW, Parramatta

Marshall, G. (2003) 'Towards a resource economics for adaptive managers', paper presented at the 47th Annual Conference of the Australian Agricultural and Resource Economics Society, Fremantle, WA, 12–14 February

Musgrave, W. (2008) 'Historical development of water resources in Australia: The case of irrigation policy in the Murray-Darling Basin', in L. Crase (ed) *Water Policy in Australia*, Resources for the Future, Washington, DC, pp28–43

Ostrom, E. (1993) 'Design principles in long-enduring irrigation institutions', *Water Resources Research*, vol 29, no 7, pp1907–1912

Pagan, P. and Crase, L. (2005) 'Property right effects on the adaptive management of Australian water resources', *Australasian Journal of Environmental Management,* vol 12, no 2, pp77–88

Quiggin, J. (2004) 'Discounting and policy options for sustainable management of the Murray-Darling River System', Working Paper 1/M04, University of Queensland: Risk and Sustainable Management Group, available online at www.uq.edu.au/economics/rsmg/WP/WP1M04.pdf

Quiggin, J. (2008) 'Uncertainty, Risk and Water Management: Water Policy', in L. Crase (ed) *Australia: The Impact of Change and Uncertainty*, Resources for the Future, Washington DC, pp61–73

Quiggin, J. and Chambers, R. (2004) 'Drought policy: A graphical analysis', *Australian Journal of Agricultural and Resource Economics*, vol 48, no 2, pp225–251

Randall, A. (1981) 'Property entitlements and pricing policies for a maturing water economy', *Australian Journal of Agricultural Economics*, vol 25, no 3, pp195–220

Saleth, R. M. and Dinar, A. (2004) *The Institutional Economics of Water: A Cross-Country Analysis of Institutions and Performance,* Edward Elgar and the World Bank, Cheltenham, UK

Toohey, D., Crase, L. and Paul, W. (2005) 'Review of Landholder Survey Data for Land and Water Management Plans', unpublished report prepared for Murray Irrigation Limited, Deniliquin

WA Water and Rivers Commission (2000) *Water Facts*, Water and Rivers Commission, Perth

Watson, A. (2003) 'Approaches to increasing river flows', *The Australian Economic Review,* vol 36, no 2, pp213–24

Watson, A. (2007) 'A National Plan for Water Security: Pluses and minuses', *Connections – Farm, Food and Resources Issues*, vol 7, no 1

4
Institutional Constraints and Organizational Dynamics: The Case of Water Trade between the Australian Capital Territory and New South Wales

Phil Pagan, Lin Crase, Vasant Gandhi

Introduction

In Chapter 3, Crase highlighted the complexity of institutional change when a hierarchical decision-making structure is in place. More specifically, it was argued that policy change is not only circumscribed by particular transaction and transformation costs of the forms described by Pagan (Chapter 2), Challen (2000) and Marshall (2003), but also that the occurrence of these costs at different levels within a decision hierarchy needs consideration. Moreover, there is a case for asserting that there are pervasive interdependencies between these costs. The upshot is that selecting and reaching an optimal (low-cost) set of rules for the allocation of water resources at a given point in time is no simple task. Bureaucracies, faced with the challenge of promoting change in a complex environment, may well settle for second-best solutions.

This chapter is used to expose the difficulty of institutional change, particularly in the context of water resources, and to highlight the role of organizational dynamics as part of this process. We do so by reflecting on the challenge of achieving the low-cost augmentation of urban water supplies in the Australian Capital Territory (ACT) by invoking water trade. Importantly, trade has long been sanctioned by superordinate authorities in this instance. While seemingly far removed from the allocation of water in Indian irrigation, the lessons revealed from this analysis provide a useful reference for further refinement of the generic institutional framework proffered here. In particular we conclude that the internal dynamics of organizations need to be considered when attempting to achieve wider institutional performance.

Water trade remains a contentious political issue in Australia, regardless of the acknowledged benefits to which economists continually refer. At least two sources of concern arise in discussions about water trade. First, disquiet is often expressed about inter-sectoral ramifications. These usually take the form of prophecies about the profligate growth of urban centres being achieved at the expense of regional and rural communities. This argument hinges on the perception that the distributional ill effects that attend trade outweigh potential economic gains. Poignantly, this is probably the most frequently cited issue, regardless of the grounds upon which it is based. Second, mention of unfettered trade between jurisdictions is usually sufficient to provoke rhetoric that draws upon long-standing rivalries between states. This chapter considers the benefits of water trade between agricultural interests in the Murrumbidgee Valley in New South Wales (NSW) and the predominantly urban users in the ACT. The chapter goes beyond the standard economic analysis by also pointing to the range of institutionally based constraints that circumscribe the operation of water markets.

The ACT provides an interesting study area for investigating issues of this type and holds appeal on several grounds. First, there has generally been a lack of pre-existing water trade, either within the ACT or interstate. Second, ACT's geographic location, which is entirely within the Murrumbidgee River catchment, means that the physical and economic potential for water trading is confined to a limited number of entities – namely, downstream residents in other states who currently hold access rights to water. Third, the existence of agricultural/urban water rivalries attends most trading issues – about 87 per cent of water consumption in the ACT is by urban users in Canberra and Queanbeyan (ABS, 2004) whereas 89 per cent of the diversions from the Murrumbidgee in NSW are accounted for by irrigation interests (Australian National Resource Atlas (ANRA), 2000). Poignantly, the former presently pay a marginal price of $A1250–$A3000 per ML while the latter pay a bulk price of about $A2–$A3 per ML, even after steep price rises in recent years.[1] Fourth, the magnitude of the extractions in the differing jurisdictions and the relatively modest call made by ACT residents on local water resources adds another salient dimension. More specifically, the ACT is estimated to consume about 63 gigalitres (GL) per year of the 494GL per year that emanates from within that state. In addition, the ACT presently makes no claim on the average 386GL that annually passes through its jurisdiction via the Murrumbidgee River to downstream users in NSW (ACT Electricity and Water (ACTEW), 2005).

Research into these issues in the ACT is also of interest because of the long-standing commitment by the ACT government to the principles embodied in the Murray-Darling Basin Cap. In simple terms, the ACT could not participate in water trade with NSW (or other jurisdictions) until a cap for ACT water extraction was agreed.[2] Thus, on the one hand the ACT stands to benefit from water trade in order to meet expanded demand from urban users, and yet on the other hand ratifying a cap on ACT extractions is itself attended by difficult institutional and political considerations. Nevertheless, these nuances and complexities did not dissuade the ACT Chief Minister joining other states (namely, NSW, South Australia (SA) and Queensland (Qld)) in offering in-principle support for the Howard government's National Plan for Water Security and the Rudd government's Water for the Future manifesto, which were themselves partially premised upon water trade.[3]

Most rudimentary neoclassical analysis of water trade would support interjurisdictional trade between NSW and the ACT as the least-cost alternative for shoring up water supplies. However, this approach substantially glosses over the role of institutional actors who hold responsibility for building the frameworks to enable trade to occur. Regrettably, failure to account for the perceptions and motivations of this group has resulted in overly simplistic predictions that focus primarily on the benefits of trade while downplaying the costs and complications associated with the establishment of trading regimes. In this chapter we do not argue that trade is itself a flawed policy response – rather, the aim is to highlight the range of institutional constraints that require urgent attention if the most is to be made from a policy that promotes exchange. In sum, any measurement of institutional performance needs to make some effort to account for the internal dynamics of organizations within the decision-making hierarchy.

The chapter itself comprises five additional parts. In the next section we review the important characteristics of water resource management in the ACT and the legislative obligations that circumscribe these issues. The following section is used to focus on the options for developing reliable water supplies to meet growing urban demands in the ACT. Special attention is given to the gains and limitations of the 'least-cost' options presently on offer to the Territory's water supply authority (ACTEW). This section also addresses the mechanisms for instigating interstate trade between NSW and the ACT. The fourth section is then used to present the results of an earlier empirical analysis of institutional stakeholders. Importantly, this analysis covers the range of policy makers and bureaucrats within organizations whose support is required to allow for the timely deployment of a policy based on water trade. This gives some indication of the costs and difficulty of transforming institutions in this context and partially explains the extant delays on this front. It also points to the need to include organizational effectiveness as a subset of measures aimed at enumerating institutional performance. The fifth section is used to draw out lessons for policy development and institutional analysis and briefly describes elements that could be valuably employed to embellish institutional analysis. The final section is used to offer some brief concluding remarks.

ACT water resources, the Cap and Trade

The ACT became a participant in the Murray-Darling Basin Initiative in 1998, when it signed a Memorandum of Understanding with the other initiative partners (Commonwealth, NSW, Victoria (Vic), SA and Qld) (MDBC, 1998). Joining the Murray-Darling Basin Initiative obliged the ACT to negotiate a cap on water extractions. In May 2006 the ACT became a full member of the Initiative, at which time it reaffirmed its original support for the Cap. The Cap had been formally implemented in NSW, Vic and SA by July 1997, while Qld imposed a moratorium on all new development in 2000. In essence, the Cap attempts to limit water extractions from the Murray-Darling Basin by constraining consumptive use to some pre-agreed level within each jurisdiction. In the case of NSW and Vic, the Cap limits diversions to those that would have occurred under 1993–94 levels of development, with the exception of two small allowances made for Pindari Dam and Lake Mokoan. Diversions in South Australia were set equivalent to the full development of existing high security entitlements, which is similar to about 90 per cent of the very high security entitlements in effect in 1993–94 (MDBC, 2004).

Notably, the Independent Audit Group (IAG, 2007), while reviewing the implementation of the Cap over 2005–06, concluded that 'the ACT should complete its consideration of the form and size of the Cap to apply to the ACT by early 2007 and finalize agreement on the actual Cap by October 2007'. By early 2008 these matters were yet to be settled, even though the Chief Minister of the ACT introduced the Murray-Darling Basin Agreement Bill to the ACT Parliament in August 2007. In introducing the bill the Chief Minister revealed the intention for the ACT Cap to 'reflect current levels of use as well as a requirement for the capacity for the future growth of the ACT' (ACT Parliament, 2007). In late May 2008, the ACT Cap was agreed and set at 40GL.

The Cap forms a key constraint on the extent to which the ACT can access its water resources. Water trading is important in this context because if growth in ACT water use moves beyond the limits of the Cap, entitlements to use this water will need to be purchased from outside the ACT. Establishing the Cap also theoretically enables water entitlement holders in the ACT to sell access rights to users in other states that are partners to the agreement.

It is important to recognize that trade in access rights (or even annual entitlements) is not simply constrained by the Cap on ACT extractions. There are three additional parameters that limit the development of water trade between the ACT and NSW: water pricing principles; water allocation principles;[4] and water storage capacity. First, bulk water pricing[5] is heavily influenced by the principles enshrined in the CoAG water reforms. In addition to being committed to the Murray-Darling Basin Initiative, the ACT also has obligations under the 1994 CoAG framework and, more recently, the National Water Initiative (NWI). Notwithstanding that both NSW and the ACT have made similar commitments to 'full cost recovery' as part of the NWI, the resulting pricing principles embody significant differences. More specifically, the ACT currently applies a Water Abstraction Charge (presently set at $A550 per ML) which purportedly captures resource rents that would otherwise accrue to the holders of water access rights.[6] No equivalent charge is imposed in NSW. Clearly, these differences will severely impact on the extent and direction of any trade in water access rights between jurisdictions – in essence, there is a strong incentive to discount the value of any ACT water access rights in an open market and a disincentive to trade water into the ACT if the abstraction charge is then imposed on those imported water rights.

Second, there are key differences in the water allocation principles that apply in NSW and the ACT. In NSW, holders of water access rights receive a number of unit shares in a specified pool of water. The responsible NSW department then publishes data indicating the long-term average volume of water that is likely to be available for extraction in each water source. But the amount of water (allocation) that the water access entitlement holder can use within a particular period is determined according to seasonal conditions (and according to the security of the entitlement they hold), with the only guarantee to access entitlement holders being that they will receive a constant share of the changing water resource pool (NSW Government, 2004).[7] By way of contrast, in the ACT water access entitlements are granted as a right to a volume of water within a particular period. Water allocations are based on average flows and do not expressly specify reliability, but the conservative management of ACT water resources means that water access entitlement holders are guaranteed to receive the full volumetric face value of their entitlement in all but extreme situations (National Competition Council, 2001). In extreme situations a hierarchy of uses (with some urban domestic uses being most highly protected) guides the reduction of water availability to individual access entitlement holders. In addition, informal voluntary agreements to restrict water use are also negotiated with water access entitlement holders in times of resource scarcity. In essence the 'water products' of the two jurisdictions differ in non-trivial ways. Moreover, recent evidence on the impact of 'tagging' as the preferred mechanism for facilitating trade between jurisdictions with different allocation principles points to the significance of this constraint.[8] For instance, Rooney (2007) claimed to have been unable to facilitate a single interstate trade since the introduction of 'tagging'. This is largely attributed to the administrative complexities that now attend the process.

Third, interstate trade between NSW and the ACT is inhibited by the limited water storage capacity in the ACT. This is perhaps the most formidable challenge to water trade between the two jurisdictions. While the ACT has significant excess consumptive rights relative to current consumptive needs, natural climatic variability (both within and between years) means that it is necessary to store this water to meet the time-dependent needs of urban and rural water users. The continual need for water restrictions since 2002 because of drought illustrates that ACT water storage capacity (rather than the ACT's average catchment resources) is the binding constraint on the ability to supply consumptive needs. While water trade could be used to gain additional water access rights, this counts for little without facilities to store and deliver the water when it is in greatest demand. This issue is discussed in greater detail in the context of the water supply options under consideration by the ACT government and its water utility (ACTEW).

Water supply options for the ACT

Constraints on the ACT's water storage capacity have been central to water planning in this jurisdiction for some time. In 2004–05 the ACT government considered four options to expand water storage capacity. These options included constructing a new dam at Mt Tennent; enlarging the existing Cotter Dam; buying water from the Snowy Mountains scheme in NSW for storage in Tantangara Dam, and then either letting it flow down the Murrumbidgee or piping it through a tunnel to Corin Dam; or undertaking a range of small-scale works and management changes to existing ACT water supply infrastructure. Ultimately, the government opted for the fourth option, including greater use of Cotter Dam, developing the capacity to transfer water from the Cotter system to Googong Dam, as well as other minor measures. Combined, these were to effectively increase ACT water supply capacity by around 12GL per year (ACTEW, 2005). By choosing this option the need for the ACT government to make decisions about water storage to meet longer term ACT urban water supply needs was also avoided.

By July 2007 the prolonged drought, accompanied by gloomy predictions of much lower runoff as a result of climate change, had prompted the release of another suite of water security recommendations by ACTEW. Reminiscent of the earlier investigations, four key proposals were presented to the ACT government. The first overarching recommendation pertained to sourcing carbon offsets to account for the additional energy usage associated with each of the water supply options. Second, ACTEW advocated the immediate commencement of the planning required to enlarge Cotter Dam from 4GL to 78GL. The capital cost of these works is expected to be about $A145 million. Third, additional pumping capacity to increase extractions from the Murrumbidgee River and to subsequently store water in Googong Reservoir was recommended at a cost of about $A70 million. Fourth, ACTEW recommended that water supplies which were independent of rainfall within the ACT catchments should also be developed. Two main alternatives were presented in this context. The first was euphemistically termed the Water Purification Scheme and amounts to blending reclaimed and treated sewage water with natural runoff into the Cotter Dam. This was expected to cost between $A181 million and $A274 million. The second alternative, which is particularly relevant in the context of water trade, is referred to as the Tantangara transfer (ACTEW, 2007; ACT Government, 2007).

In order to further scrutinize the options developed by ACTEW, the Chief Minister appointed a Water Security Taskforce to report back to the ACT government. As a result of the taskforce's deliberations, the government released five decisions pertaining to water supply and another three relating to demand management. On the demand front, the government has given approval to the extension of permanent water 'conservation' measures, primarily in the form of ongoing household water restrictions that limit outside water use. In addition, improved metering technology is to be trialled and ambitious targets for reduced per capita water consumption have been set. More specifically, there is now an expectation that per capita water consumption will fall by 12 per cent by 2013 and 25 per cent by 2023 (ACT Government, 2007).

The ACT government has also now approved the Cotter Dam enlargement (by 2011) and ratified progress on the Murrumbidgee-Googong transfer infrastructure. The proposal to develop a Water Purification Scheme, as an additional potable supply source, has been downgraded inasmuch as this is to be developed as a demonstration scheme focusing on non-potable water uses. Investigation of greenhouse gas offsets was also given less emphasis, with the government relying on ACTEW and ActewAGL to further investigate these issues on a voluntary basis. Importantly, the ACT government reached agreement that the Tantangara transfer option should be progressed (ACT Government, 2007).

As noted earlier, the Tantangara transfer provides access to water sources outside the ACT. The basic idea behind this option is that water would be transferred from the Snowy Mountains Scheme via Tantangara Reservoir to an ACT-controlled storage (either Googong or Corin Reservoirs). The merits of the Tantangara transfer had gained attention in earlier investigations by ACTEW and include the existing storage capacity of Tantangara, which stands at 239GL, well in excess of any existing or proposed storage in the ACT. This water supply option also offers increased flexibility in the management of existing ACT reservoirs and, with sufficient zeal on the part of the water bureaucracy, could realize enhanced supply within one year. The option is also very cost-effective with estimated capital costs of $A38 million and annual operating costs of $A3.4 million per year required to secure 20–25GL per year for urban use (ACTEW, 2007; ACT Government, 2007).

Three fundamental steps are required to operationalize the Tantangara transfer. First, water access rights need to be purchased from the owners of Snowy Mountain water, who typically are water users far downstream on either the Murray or Murrumbidgee Rivers. Most obvious in this context are irrigators in NSW, such as those in the Murrumbidgee Irrigation Area or Coleambally Irrigation Area, although rights could also be purchased from Victoria or South Australia. A precursor to these events was the necessity to reach agreement on the ACT Cap, which is now in hand. Second, the purchased water rights must result in water being physically stored in Tantangara Dam. Since this storage facility is effectively owned and managed by NSW there is an attendant requirement for the ACT to reach agreement with Snowy Hydro on operational issues. Put simply, these relate to compensating for the impacts of storing and releasing water for the benefit of ACT residents versus the current advantages that accrue to Snowy Hydro through generation of hydroelectricity. Third, the water from Tantangara (elevation 1230 metres) must be transferred to a point where it can be used to augment the ACT water supply. This third phase presently comprises two alternatives; one involving a 20km tunnel directly to the Corin Reservoir (elevation 1000 metres) and another allowing water to flow the long way down the Murrumbidgee River before pumping it via pipeline to the Googong Reservoir. The first of these alternatives offers medium- to long-term benefits, including the potential to generate hydropower en route, while the latter is the most attractive short-term approach. Regardless of the mechanism for augmentation, the Tantangara transfer has much in its favour when considered on the basis of capital and operating costs.

Empirical insights into the perceptions, motivations and interests of organizational stakeholders

Notwithstanding the apparent merits of arrangements such as the Tantangara transfer, there is clearly some reservation on the part of ACTEW about the feasibility of this approach. Poignantly, perceived constraints appear to be 'institutional' in nature, rather than technical or economic. For example, ACTEW observed recently that 'This proposal has always been very attractive in theory, but as ACTEW advised in the 2004/05 reports, *it involves a high level of legal and political assurance to provide the confidence to rely on such an option*' (ACTEW, 2007, pix; emphasis added). The government-sponsored fact sheets on this project also caution that this option requires 'a complex series of approvals and consent processes that include NSW, ACT, Vic and Commonwealth jurisdictions' (ACT Government, 2007, p1). At issue here is the concern that 'Tantangara water is currently controlled by NSW [and] this could mean ACT is denied water at a critical time when supplies are most limited' (ACTEW, 2005, pxiii). Of particular interest in the context of the arguments in this paper is the impact of institutional actors on the capacity to progress what prima facie appears to be a low-cost water supply option for the ACT (at least when viewed through the neoclassical lens), albeit accompanied by some obvious institutional challenges.

In order to shed some light on this issue we draw upon earlier survey work undertaken in 2005. The survey sought to uncover the objectives of regulators and agencies that might potentially participate in a market, or at least play some part in shaping the rules by which a water market could operate. A total of 30 organizations were approached and 22 respondents agreed to be interviewed. The data presented here emanate from in-depth, structured interviews with high-ranking officials from those organizations. Interviews were conducted in the first half of 2005 and the organizations that participated are listed in Table 4.1.

Table 4.1 *Organizations from which respondents to the institutional analysis were drawn*

NSW Department of Infrastructure Planning and Natural Resources
Murrumbidgee Catchment Management Authority
Environment ACT
Murray-Darling Basin Commission
Australian Government Department of the Environment and Heritage
ACT Department of Treasury
The Cabinet Office (NSW)
NSW Fisheries
State Water (NSW)
Murray Lower Darling Rivers Indigenous Nations
ACTEW Corporation
Murrumbidgee Irrigation Ltd
Coleambally Irrigation Cooperative Ltd
NSW Irrigators' Council
Nature Conservation Council of NSW
Conservation Council of the South East Region and Canberra
Australian Government Department of Transport and Regional Services
National Capital Authority
Department of Prime Minister and Cabinet
Murrumbidgee (Regulated) Water Management Committee
NSW Department of Environment and Conservation
Australian Government Department of Agriculture, Fisheries and Forestry

Clearly, interview participants were chosen for their institutional roles and in no way form a random sample of the population; the views elicited are not representative of the population of the Murrumbidgee Valley; and the analysis of the data cannot be used to indicate causality between different variables. The analysis of the data collected is essentially univariate, with the objective of identifying likely institutional constraints to progressing interstate water trade for the ACT.

The interview included a survey covering five main areas: (i) information about the participants; (ii) the perceived view of the organization towards water allocations; (iii) the role of the organization in developing, managing or participating in water markets; (iv) perceptions of the attitudes to water markets held by other stakeholders; and (v) perceptions of the likely views of irrigators about water trade. The discussion here focuses primarily on data drawn from the second, third and fifth sections of the survey.

Although there was a high prevalence of policy makers in the sample in Table 4.1, a range of other organizational goals and objectives other than policy making were represented. However, a notable exception was the very low representation of organizations with a role as a water market intermediary (one respondent with a current role and two with a future role).

Of particular interest was the series of questions within the survey which sought information about the relative importance of different organizational goals with respect to water allocation policy. Participants were asked to rank various policy goals that covered nine main topics.[9] The goals offered to respondents and identifiers for each are detailed in Table 4.2.

Table 4.2 *Alternative goals for water policy*

Goal identifier	*Policy goal*
1	Predictability in how water resources are used
2	Water use (technical) efficiency
3	Sustainable water resource use
4	Fairness in the sharing of water resources
5	Simple and transparent administration of water resources
6	That society's well-being from the use of water resources is maximized
7	To limit the pace of change from current water management policy positions until knowledge of consequences improves
8	To have water used in ways that are financially most valuable
9	To preserve policy adaptability

The cumulative ranking of the alternative goals by those surveyed is summarized in Table 4.3.

Table 4.3 *Frequency of ranking goals by institutional actors*

Goal identifier	*Frequency ranked most important*	*Frequency ranked second*	*Frequency ranked third*	*Frequency ranked <third*	*Total frequency*
1	1	2		6	9
2	2			2	4
3	12	6			18
4	2	1	5	2	10
5		2	3	8	13
6	8		1	1	10
7	1		1	3	5
8	1	1		2	4
9	1	1		3	5

Of the goals on offer, *sustainable water resource use* was ranked most highly, having been rated the most important policy goal by 12 respondents and the second most important for six others. However, when participants were questioned about their interpretations of 'sustainability', there was a range of responses. Interpretations included: 'maximizing long-term social welfare'; 'guaranteeing long-term ecological health'; 'ensuring sustainability of the capital investment in water delivery and production infrastructure'; 'maintaining access to water resources that preserves investment integrity'; and 'sustaining regional communities that rely on water resources'.

Responses to the policy goal of *simple and transparent rules* are of particular relevance in this case because of the direct link to transaction costs and the potential for bringing to fruition projects such as the Tantangara transfer. This policy goal was the second most commonly selected objective (13 times in total), but was rarely ranked as an objective of overall importance. No respondent ranked this item as their primary policy objective and only five organizations ranked it as the second or third most pressing objective.

Two of the policy goals specifically relate to long-term resource management outcomes (namely, *limit change while knowledge of consequences improves* and *to preserve policy adaptability*). Both of these options received low rankings by interview participants (five times for each), and the latter was the only objective regularly identified as being less relevant.

A key finding of the stakeholder analysis was that, without exception, interviewees claimed that there would be no material change to their organization's policy objectives in the foreseeable future. More detailed questioning revealed that most respondents acknowledged the necessity for changes at the margin, but expressed the view that the overarching objectives would not require adjustment over time.

Interviewees were also asked to judge the relative capacity of *market-based* and *planning-based* water allocation mechanisms to achieve the policy goals that had been ranked earlier. This was completed through the use of agreement scales. Low values (minimum of 1) indicate that respondents considered *market-based* allocation mechanisms to have relative advantages over the *planning-based* approaches for achieving a given policy objective. By way of contrast, high values (maximum of 5) indicate that respondents considered *planning-based* approaches to be superior in achieving that particular objective.

The ranking of objectives ranging from those with the strongest potential for *market-based* allocation through to *planning-based* systems are summarized in Table 4.4.

Analysis of variance indicates that the differences between the mean responses to pairs of objectives are significant ($p<0.05$) for 26 of the possible 36 combinations of objectives. That is, for each of these pairs there is a significant difference between the expected ability to achieve a given objective with either *market-based* or *planning-based* allocation mechanisms. Table 4.5 provides a summary of significant differences in mean responses.

Table 4.4 *Ranked mean usefulness of market-based approach for achieving policy goal*

Rank from market-based to planning-based approach	*Policy objective*
1	To have water used in ways that are financially most valuable
2	Water use (technical) efficiency
3	That society's well-being from the use of water resources is maximized
4	Sustainable water resource use
5	Simple and transparent administration of water resources
6	Predictability in how water resources are used
7	Fairness in the sharing of water resources
8	To preserve policy adaptability
9	To limit the pace of change from current water management policy positions until knowledge of consequences improves

Table 4.5 *Significant difference* in mean response to expected effectiveness of market-based approaches to achieving different water policy goals (lower score implies a higher rating of the market-based approach)*

Goal identifier	*1*	*2*	*3*	*4*	*5*	*6*	*7*	*8*	*9*
1		0.55			0.24	1.68	0.80		
2	0.55		1.85	1.69	1.05		2.73		1.77
3		1.85			0.30	0.54	1.38	1.10	
4		1.69			0.14	0.38	1.54	0.94	
5		1.05	0.30	0.14			2.18	0.30	1.22
6	0.24		0.54	0.38			2.42	0.06	1.46
7	1.68	2.73	1.38	1.54	2.18	2.42		1.98	0.46
8	0.80		1.10	0.94	0.30	0.06	1.98		2.02
9		1.77			1.22	1.46	0.46	2.02	

*p<0.05

The policy goal described as *limiting the pace of change from current water management policy positions until knowledge of consequences improves* was the only option to show a significantly different ($p<0.05$) mean response to all other policy ambitions. More specifically, this indicates that respondents considered markets to have a poor ability to contribute to this objective, relative to the contribution markets could make in accomplishing other water policy goals. Two other policy goals (*water use (technical) efficiency*, and *to have water used in ways that are financially most valuable*) were perceived by respondents as being well supported by market-based approaches. Importantly, neither of these objectives for which there was a clear perception about the usefulness of markets were ranked as being particularly important in the eyes of the respondents.

One final dimension of these data warrants closer scrutiny in the current context. This relates to the perceived motivation of irrigators to participate in water trade. The relevance of this aspect of the analysis hinges on the necessity for irrigators to sell water access rights, or at least water allocations, to make approaches like the Tantangara transfer feasible. Moreover, the policy makers' perceptions of the difficulty of inducing this behaviour among irrigators might arguably impact on their own enthusiasm for market-based reform.

In this part of the survey participants were asked to use a Likert scale[10] to indicate the proportion of irrigators who were expected to respond to a range of motivations to sell either annual allocation to irrigation water (referred to as a temporary sale) or water access rights (referred to as permanent sales). The eight statements derived from earlier interviews with irrigation interests and others with knowledge of water trade. The motivational statements appear in Table 4.6 along with identifiers for later reference.

Table 4.6 *Potential motivations for irrigators to sell water*

Identifier	*Irrigators' motivations*
1	Irrigators consider selling water temporarily that is surplus to cropping requirements.
2	Irrigators consider selling water temporarily to generate a higher net income than that from using the water on the irrigator's land.
3	Irrigators consider selling water permanently that is surplus to cropping requirements.
4	Irrigators consider selling water permanently to generate a higher net income than that from using the water on the irrigator's land.
5	Irrigators consider selling water permanently if making an adjustment to dryland farming.
6	Irrigators consider selling water permanently as a means of enabling on-farm retirement.
7	Irrigators consider selling water permanently and buying it back temporarily on an as-needs basis.
8	Irrigators would consider selling water (permanently or temporarily) even if this would significantly affect other water users (third parties).

The mean proportion of irrigators expected to comply with each of these motivational statements is summarized in Table 4.7.

To further scrutinize these data, analysis of variance was used to test whether perceived motivations differed significantly. The results indicate that there is no significant difference ($p<0.05$) between the perception that irrigators are driven to sell on the basis of 'generating higher net income' and the view that irrigators will sell water which is 'excess to requirements'. This is true for the sale of both temporary and permanent water entitlements. There is, however, a significant difference ($p<0.05$) in expectations about how irrigators view the selling of water temporarily in comparison to the permanent sale of water entitlements. Respondents consistently predicted a higher level of participation in temporary trade compared to permanent trade, regardless of the motivation for that trade (excess water or higher net income).

Table 4.7 *Perceived strength of motivation for potential water sellers*

Selling motivation	*Mean response (% agreement)*
1	63.9
2	58.6
3	28.6
4	29.7
5	42.4
6	47.5
7	20.1
8	37.3
Grand mean	41.0
Standard errors of differences of means (s.e.d.)	6.38
Least significant differences of means (l.s.d.) (5% level)	12.59

In summary, the bureaucrats who responded to the survey have a perception that irrigators view the temporary sale of water as being moderately acceptable (especially if it was surplus to requirements for that year), believed that farmers held a view that it was moderately unacceptable to sell permanently even if making a permanent exit from the irrigation industry (but without leaving the farm), but that it was totally unacceptable to farmers to sell water permanently if there was any chance that the irrigator may need it again in the future. For a policy maker looking for a market-based solution with low transition costs, these perceptions would not augur particularly well.

Importantly, respondents were also asked whether they expected irrigators' attitudes to water sales would change over time. The majority of respondents expected that more favourable attitudes to water trading would emerge in response to a range of factors including: cultural change; generational change; peer group influence; experience; settling of market values and the slowing of capital growth in water entitlement values over time. In practice, of course, irrigators have made substantial progress in adapting to the use of water markets, particularly in the context of the ongoing drought in many districts (see, e.g., RIRDC, 2007). However, respondents to the 2005 survey saw little need to adjust the organizational goals of agencies operating in this environment and arguably there is little evidence that the bureaucracy has changed its attitudes to trade in light of the actual trends in water trade.

Lessons for institutional analysis

So far we have considered the available options for increasing the reliability of urban water supply in the ACT. We have argued that market-based approaches, such as the Tantangara transfer, have offered much promise for some time but have failed to gain genuine policy traction. Ironically, this has occurred against a backdrop of policy rhetoric that supports interstate and inter-sectoral water trade. In an effort to shed light on the slow progress on this front we have considered original survey data that gives insights into the perceptions of organizational actors who have an influential role in developing the frameworks to support trade of this kind. Our analysis of these data reveals several useful findings.

First, some of the expectations held among organizational actors are inconsistent with common economic assumptions about resource reallocation once a water market is established. More specifically, the neoclassical approach to markets presumes that irrigators will dispassionately choose to sell on the basis of whether the water market price exceeds the marginal value product of water in irrigated agriculture; but this is resoundingly *not* the view of those surveyed. The failure of common economic assumptions to encompass more complex decision-making processes has been noted in a range of water-related studies (see, e.g., Tisdell et al, 2001). In a similar vein Young (1986) acknowledged over a decade ago that 'society may value water resources for non-commodity purposes'. Moreover, Young (1986) concluded that 'economists have some obligation to respect those values', and argued that there was a need to assess the impact of non-economic goals and devise exchange institutions with properties that permit the full range of social concerns to be reflected in transactions. All this is a formidable task, particularly in the eyes of policy makers who themselves may carry some doubt about the usefulness of the market.

While those interviewed on behalf of water-related agencies openly acknowledge the existence of a wide range of motivations underpinning water trading decisions, these same policy makers were not especially interested in focusing on these constraints in the development of water trading rules. In short, this would appear to lie squarely in the 'too hard basket' for most agencies. There is also support for the view that those charged with framing the rules for trade appear to be focused on developing conventions that tacitly meet criteria set by superordinate bodies, such as the National Water Commission or CoAG. The extent to which these efforts translate into efficacious policy outcomes that genuinely support water trade might be questionable.

Second, the results from the stakeholder analysis confirm the presence of a spectrum of values and objectives within the Murrumbidgee catchment's institutional environment. Notably, there is a strong organizational preference, as expressed by the stakeholders interviewed, to pursue an objective of sustainability in the management of water allocation. Despite variations within the definition of this goal, when coupled with two supporting observations this may at least partially explain the apparent policy inertia on ACT–interstate water trade.

The first of these observations is the extremely low level of expectations among key stakeholders of the necessity for any change in their own or each others' objectives in the future. This has important implications for potential intertemporal transaction costs, if policy arrangements do in fact require adjustment. Put simply, there is strong support for the view that it is likely to be difficult (and costly) to induce change if the institutional actors do not perceive it as being necessary or indeed their responsibility. In addition, there is a stark contrast between the perceptions that market participation will evolve over time and simultaneous perceptions that the goals and objectives of organizations that circumscribe these markets will remain static.

The second supporting remark pertains to the perceived role of market-based approaches to water allocation. In this regard, stakeholders do not have strong expectations that water markets can help in meeting the sustainability goal to which their organization aspires.

In concert these constraints result in significant policy inertia that makes it difficult to achieve trading solutions – not because they are unworthy, but because it is difficult to overcome the institutional constraints to achieve them, at least in the eyes of those who must undertake the policy work.

A way forward

This case clearly illustrates one of the main challenges of measuring institutional performance against a backdrop of change. In particular, it shows that transaction and transformation costs provide one set of lenses for considering the dynamics of water institutions and water policy but this approach is arguably incomplete. What is also required is a facility to consider the internal dynamics and operation of organizations and thereby incorporate actions of the players within those organizations. In this regard Gandhi et al (2006) indicate that the work on organizational effectiveness embedded in the management science literature can prove particularly instructive. Given that this is a well-developed area of analysis, we provide here only a synoptic overview of three core concepts which we adjudge as being complementary to the New Institutional Economics approaches outlined in preceding chapters. We draw particularly from the work of Nystrom and Starbuck (1981), Ackroyd (2002) and their consideration of good internal governance of organizations. The concepts of greatest interest in this context are political rationality, organizational rationality and technical rationality.

First, technical rationality focuses on efficient conversion of inputs into outputs. This centres on aspects such as the appropriateness of a given technology within an organization and the technical efficiency with which internal inputs are converted to outputs.

Second, when the organization involves a larger set of activities, division of labour invariably results. Thus, for larger organizations effectiveness will depend not only on the level of technical rationality but also on the ability to achieve the best coordination across various activities – this is the subject of organizational rationality.

Finally, in larger modern organizations that involve substantial human interaction, addressing issues of representation, fairness and justice become important. Thus, the organization needs to have in place mechanisms for addressing these demands – this is the subject of political rationality.

By adding these three constructs to the New Institutional Framework it then becomes feasible to consider the internal dynamics and operation of institutions within a given decision-making hierarchy. As we have seen with the case of water trade between the ACT and NSW, the internal actions and perceptions of important personnel within agencies are just as important as the structure of rules. For example, it is one thing to have a clear policy objective and rules that proclaim the encouragement of water trade. It is another thing altogether to have internal agents effectively deliver, which requires addressing the three rationalities within their organizations in order to achieve this objective. We anticipate that incorporating this additional lens will provide a richer analysis than that which would result from consideration of transaction and transformation costs alone.

Concluding remarks

The conclusions and lessons drawn from this analysis are generally consistent with other studies highlighting the impact of institutional barriers to change in the context of water resource management (see, e.g., Saleth and Dinar, 2004). Importantly, however, this case highlights the necessity to include internal organizational dynamics which may subvert efforts to move towards lower cost institutions within a wider decision-making hierarchy.

In the context of water resource allocation between the ACT and the neighbouring state of NSW there are clearly grounds for arguing that rules that facilitate trade would offer a low-cost solution to urban water scarcity in this jurisdiction. Moreover, these rules have been largely in place for almost a decade and are strongly supported by superordinate bodies such as CoAG. Quite clearly, however, there has been substantial resistance within organizations based in the ACT to embrace and promote the changes necessary to realize this low transaction/transformation cost solution.

Using this case as a backdrop, we contend that any attempt to measure overall institutional performance needs to adequately account for these nuances and this can be done by invoking relatively standard concepts drawn from the management science literature. This would then allow researchers to consider the internal capacity of organizations to manage technical, organizational and political elements, alongside the institutional elements developed in earlier chapters. The application of this approach to Indian irrigation forms the major component of later chapters of this book.

Notes

1 It needs to be conceded that these prices are illustrative only and are not strictly comparable. For instance, irrigators who form part of communal irrigation schemes would also pay a water delivery charge (circa $10 per ML) and the urban price relates to potable reticulated water. Potable water costs vary considerably by location, but as a general guide amount to around $550 per ML, including the cost of bulk water (Victorian Water Industry Association, 2003, p79). Thus, even after accounting for these nuances there are substantial differences in the prices paid

by urban water users in the ACT and irrigators in NSW.

2 After long delays and haggling, the ACT finally settled this matter in 2008.

3 The National Plan for Water Security provided support for water markets inasmuch as it foreshadowed spending $3.1 billion over ten years to purchase water entitlements in over-allocated systems. This approach has been followed by the Rudd government's approach to systems deemed to exceed sustainable extractions.

4 Notwithstanding legislative changes to define water allocations with more precision, the term 'water allocation' has retained differing meanings within the Australian vernacular. On the one hand the term is taken to mean the maximum annual volume of water available for extraction by a given user. In other contexts it is considered as the maximum volumetric access rights which can be drawn in perpetuity, subject to seasonal availability.

5 In this instance we refer to the regulated costs imposed on water right holders as distinct from the market price for water access rights.

6 Whether this is simply a mechanism for bolstering the state's coffers or a genuine resource tax remains a moot point (see, e.g., Dwyer, 2006).

7 NSW has taken a more aggressive approach to water allocations than other states, which results in generally lower reliability. Within a given season, however, allocations are conservatively structured, being progressively announced as inflows are received. Estimates of final allocations at any given point in time are based on the level of water held in storage and an allowance for the lowest 1 percentile of inflows. Arguably, this is a different form of conservatism but, as has recently been discovered, can be found wanting when new records are established for low inflows. The annual reliability of access entitlements in NSW also varies considerably between water sources (regulated, unregulated and ground water). Access entitlements from unregulated water sources are even less reliable than from regulated sources because of the absence of water storage infrastructure with which to spread availability between years.

8 Tagging amounts to ensuring that a water access right retains much the same supply reliability regardless of a change in ownership. For instance, a water access right that currently enjoys a reliability of seven years' full allocation in ten could be sold into a valley that is capable of delivering a higher reliability (say, nine years in ten) by virtue of additional upstream regulation. However, if the new owner were to invoke the access nine years in ten they would simultaneously undermine the reliability of existing users in that valley. In this context tagging is an attempt to prevent one of the potential externalities to trade. The involvement of a large number of agencies required to make judgements about reliability partly explains the high transaction costs associated with this approach and, thus, the paucity of trade since its introduction.

9 These options were developed from an earlier interview process. In addition to the nine choices available, respondents were given the opportunity to specify their own organizational policy goal. Few respondents exercised this choice and when doing so rated such goals as relatively minor considerations.

10 This comprised six points set at 20 per cent intervals and ranging from 0 per cent to 100 per cent.

References

ABS (2004) *Water Account, Australia,* Australian Bureau of Statistics, Canberra

Ackroyd, S. (2002) *Organization of Business: Applying Organizational Theory to Contemporary Change*, Oxford University Press, Oxford

ACT Government (2007) *Water Supply Security fact sheets*, accessed 21 December 2007 at www.thinkwater.act.gov.au/more_information/publications.shtml#water_security

ACT Parliament (2007) *Hansard of the Legislative Assembly of the ACT*, ACT Government, Canberra, Week 8, 2384

ACTEW (ACT Electricity and Water) (2005) *Future Water Options for the ACT in the 21st Century: The Tantangara Dam Option*, ACTEW, Canberra

ACTEW (2007) *Water Security for the ACT and Region: Recommendations to the ACT Government*, ACTEW, Canberra

ANRA (2000) *Water Resources: Allocation and Use in NSW*, accessed on 20 December 2007 at www.anra.gov.au/topics/water/allocation/nsw/index.html#sw_alloc

Challen, R. (2000) *Institutions, Transaction Costs and Environmental Policy: Institutional Reform for Water Resources*, Edward Elgar, Cheltenham, UK

Dwyer, T. (2006) 'Urban water policy: In need of economics', *Agenda*, vol 13, no 1, pp3–16

Gandhi V. P., Crase L. and Herath, G. (2006) 'Comparing Indian irrigation institutions: What determines institutional behaviour and performance? Preliminary Empirical Observations', paper presented at the Australian Agricultural and Resource Economics Society Conference, Sydney, 8–10 February

IAG (2007) *Review of Cap Implementation 2005/06 by the Independent Audit Group*, MDBC, accessed 20 December 2007 at www.mdbc.gov.au/__data/page/1658/IAG2005–6-full.pdf

Marshall, G. (2003) 'Towards a resource economics for adaptive managers', paper presented at the 47th Annual Conference of the Australian Agricultural and Resource Economics Society, Fremantle, WA, 12–14 February

MDBC (1998) *MoU on the ACT's Participation in the Murray-Darling Basin Initiative*, MDBC, Canberra

MDBC (2004) *The Cap*, accessed 20 December 2007 at www.mdbc.gov.au/__data/page/86/cap_brochure.pdf

NCC (2001) *Assessment of Government's Progress in Implementing the National Competition Policy and Related Reforms: ACT Water Reforms*, National Competition Council, Canberra

NSW Government (2004) *NSW Water Reforms, a Secure and Sustainable Future: Ministerial Statement*, NSW Government, Sydney

Nystrom, P. C. and Starbuck, W. H. (eds) (1981) *Handbook of Organizational Design*, Oxford University Press, Oxford

Rooney, T. (2007) 'Waterfind and Water Tagging', *Third National Water Pricing Conference*, IIR, Sydney

Rural Industries Research and Development Corporation (RIRDC) (2007) 'The economic and social impacts of water trading: Case studies in the Victorian Murray Valley', Rural Industries Research and Development Corporation, Canberra

Saleth, R. M. and Dinar, A. (2004) *The Institutional Economics of Water: A Cross-Country Analysis of Institutions and Performance*, Edward Elgar and the World Bank, Cheltenham, UK

Tisdell, J., Ward, J. and T Grudzinski (2001) *Irrigator and Community Attitudes to Water Allocation and Trading in the Murrumbidgee Catchment*, CRC for catchment hydrology, Technical report 01/2, Brisbane

Victorian Water Industry Association (2003) *Victorian Water Review 02–03*, VWIA, Melbourne

Young, R. (1986) 'Why are there so few transactions among water users?', *American Journal of Agricultural Economics*, vol 68, no 5, pp1143–1151

Part 2
Water Resource Development and Management in India

5
Institutions for Water Management in Developing Countries: Their Role, Nature and Analysis

Gamini Herath

Introduction

There has been a proliferation of irrigation investment and development programmes since independence in most countries in Asia (Aluvihare and Kikuchi, 1991). These irrigation programmes generally exhibit the following features: (a) heavy investment and management costs, (b) poor cost recovery, (c) a bias towards well-to-do farmers, (d) the head–tail problem, where those positioned in the headwaters receive preferential treatment over others, (e) low impact on poverty, (f) exacerbated income inequity in rural areas, (g) heavy subsidies, (h) poor water management, (i) dilapidated infrastructure and poor maintenance. Not surprisingly, irrigation investment programmes have been subjected to extensive study and by the mid 1980s economists had evolved an orthodoxy that challenged the usefulness and efficiency of such programmes. These views subsequently influenced policy attitudes of governments and international donor agencies.

Since the 1970s, economic theorists have sought to broaden their analysis of irrigation institutions and institutional change. The need for institutional change has arisen because decisions made at higher policy levels do not necessarily have the desired effects at the operational levels, where farmers actually make choices. This theme is given greater attention in the final section of this book, but here I focus primarily on pre-existing work on irrigation institutions.

The experience of several decades has revealed that institutions created by governments or bureaucratic hierarchies are not congruent with the rules and customs associated with informal indigenous institutional arrangements. This incongruence can induce suboptimal behavioural responses from irrigators, thereby increasing the social costs of managing scarce water resources. This 'institutional dissonance' occurs due to differences in the goals set by different elements of the decision-making hierarchy and conflicting views on the importance of institutions in efficient water resource management (Bromley, 1992). More specifically, institutional dissonance can occur due to divergent notions of the appropriateness of an institution in a given setting and inadequate appreciation of the role of local level rules, traditions and customs. Economists now strongly argue that operational level rules should be given due recognition as they are at the heart of any successful improvement of water resource use and management (see, e.g., Marshall, 2008).

A key factor influencing management of water resources is thought to be the lack of property rights and related institutional constraints. A better recognition of the role of local institutions is already becoming evident in most government policies with an apparent shift towards reallocating control of water resources management to communities (Baland and Platteau, 1998). For example, user groups for water management and irrigation now offer some degree of community property right, in some cases remarkably similar to those that broke down when top-down management was used to supplant indigenous rules.

The aims of this chapter are threefold. First, I attempt to identify the nature of institutions and their role in irrigation management with a particular emphasis on developing countries. In an effort to avoid duplicating the earlier discussion by Pagan (Chapter 2), I focus primarily on a subset of institutional concepts; particularly those that deal with collective action and social capital. Second, I use the chapter to examine the various perspectives in the analysis of institutions. Finally, I attempt to offer a synoptic review of irrigation performance from an institutional perspective.

The chapter itself offers an alternative, but nonetheless complementary, perspective to that developed in Part 1 of this book. It also provides the reader with a helpful segue to the more detailed analysis of institutional arrangements in India, since these are frequently grounded on behavioural analysis of collective action. The chapter is organized into four additional parts. In the following section I offer a brief overview of collective action as an institutional principle and consider the nature and role of institutions in that context. This section also briefly reviews institutional dynamics. Following this is an analysis of institutional performance and a critique of studies undertaken in this field. The final section comprises some brief concluding remarks.

The nature and role of institutions and institutional dynamics

As noted earlier, there is a voluminous literature on institutions, with several themes distinguishable. These include the rule of law as an institution as well as transactions costs and property rights approaches. There are many definitions of institutions that are discussed elsewhere in the book. Here I focus primarily on property rights and collective action.

Property rights are related to collective action and self-management. The absence of clearly defined and well-enforced property rights significantly increases the risks and costs associated with transactions. Coase (1960) argued that excessive government involvement might prove inefficient if property rights are already well established. Demsetz (1967) and Coase (1960) both contend that, in the absence of transactions costs, private property rights are likely to be the most efficient system for governing land use. Property rights have the capacity to lower transactions costs, and exclusive rights provide substantial incentives to encourage development and cultivation (North and Thomas, 1977). Property rights for water users encompass the right to access a certain amount and quality of water, collective protection against conversion of irrigated lands, use of irrigation infrastructure, and access to irrigation services, to name but a few. Notwithstanding the benefits of 'private rights' in some contexts, common property rights appear to reduce transactions costs when collective behavioural responses are required.

Collective action approaches and self-governance have been widely deployed to manage common property resources, such as irrigation water (Runge, 1986; Ostrom, 1990; Bromley, 1992). The rules, and the authority systems arising from them, encourage members to cooperate towards a group strategy. They also provide certainty about the expected actions of others (Runge, 1981; 1986). Collective action is affected by attributes such as group size, similarity of group characteristics, and goals (Olson, 1982). The more homogeneous a community, the more likely that the optimal structure is collective management, since people are more likely to share similar economic goals and view uncertainties as well as socially accepted norms of cooperation in a similar light. Ostrom (1990) identifies custom and social conventions as factors that facilitate collective action (Nabli and Nugent, 1989). According to Runge (1986) low incomes, critical dependence on a local resource and high uncertainty with respect to those resources can all be conducive to the adoption of collective forms of management.

Similarly, Runge (1986) argues that people will cooperate for their common good without the necessity for external (state) coercion if they can be assured that a critical mass of users obey a common property arrangement (Moorhead and Lane, 1993).

Historically, farmers in developing countries discovered favourable environmental niches via a process of trial and error and this then informed the accumulated production experience and helped perfect appropriate institutions for such environments. This is exemplified by the multitude of traditional water use and management institutions and indigenous institutions in Asia, Africa and Latin America. Indigenous management systems in west Africa, for example, often involve chiefs, religious leaders or councils of leaders as decision makers who worked for the benefit of the community by preserving valuable water resources and ensuring some level of universal access. However, important questions remain unanswered about the appropriateness of these indigenous arrangements in the context of the present problems with irrigation. For instance, to what extent can traditional forms of sanctions such as community exile or ritual penitence serve to maintain these institutions as community-held values are increasingly challenged by the government and the activities of the private sector?

Any new institutional form that fails to attract the support of the existing rights holders is unlikely to succeed. Privatization of common property resources by government decree may, in fact, worsen the relative position of those who subsist on common property resources. Widespread logging and mining where this has weakened or removed poor people's customary rights are arguably cases in point.

A society's institutions can also exist as cultural or social capital (Berkes and Folke, 1994). Social capital is especially closely linked to collective action in irrigation water management in developing countries. In this regard, social norms, cultural values, trust and reciprocity, and social sanctions might all be considered as social capital (Rudd, 2000; Woolcock, 1998). Social capital is productive, self-reinforcing and cumulative and can ultimately improve economic performance. Social capital enables participants to act effectively and to pursue shared objectives.

Social capital, such as cultural norms, reciprocity and trust among members of a given community are critical for success in development (World Bank, 2008). Social capital strengthens community-based collective action, and water resources often fall under collective management (Edwards and Steins, 1998; Quiggin, 1993). Failure to solve collective action problems can thus lead to the degradation of water resources and the systems designed for successful management of those resources. From an environmental perspective, there is also evidence that social capital can play an important role in sustainable water management.

The role of institutions and institutional dynamics

The introduction of market value concepts has not always been consistent with local management strategies. This was noted earlier by Pagan (Chapter 2) and North (1990) observed that markets work most effectively when the underlying values embodied in a market (such as competition and striving to win) are well-aligned with informal norms. Frequently the failure to recognize the people/nature interdependency in rural communities in developing countries has led to ineffective policies for water resource management. Against this background many researchers advocate a new vision for development based on shared concerns for place, devolution of power and revival of local institutions and civic norms and behaviours. In simple terms one would say that the aim of development planning is to remove 'institutional obstructions'. According to Ayers (1952), the strategic issue of present-day economic planning is institutional. The basic question is: at what point does our inherited institutional system inhibit economic progress? Put differently, where does the 'shoe pinch'?

(Ayers, 1952). There are historical precedents of note. In western Europe, for instance, the planning system itself was the obstacle to institutional innovation and adaptation.

Institutions do not remain static but are dynamic entities that evolve in response to emerging circumstances. Critically, institutional dynamics can also govern the rate at which environmental degradation occurs. According to Lopez (1977), the dynamics of institutional change relative to environmental dynamics is crucial in determining the rate of environmental degradation. Lopez (1977) argues that if environmental dynamics dominate institutional dynamics, then the environmental problems will simply be exacerbated. However, if institutional dynamics dominate environmental dynamics, then new institutions will emerge that protect the land and the soil while improving the economic status of farmers.

Many communities in developing countries use fragile soils and land to cultivate crops using irrigation (Kumar and Bhandari, 1992). Poorer societies require intensive production to meet rising demand for food, but intensification with irrigation leads to severe environmental damage. Instances of this cycle have been well documented for Nepal, Kenya and other countries (Metz, 1991). Under this scenario land degradation will continue and result in even lower productive capacity. These conditions are also found in many tropical countries where fragile soils predominate and population growth is rapid.

Greater intensification requires greater community cooperation to provide the labour for the construction of land-preserving measures. The lack of property rights to communal lands means that such cooperation may not be forthcoming. Monitoring is required but there may be no effective institutions able to provide the monitoring function. Traditional village institutions are often ill-equipped to deal with this situation. Such internally generated weaknesses further erode traditional institutions and ultimately accelerate resource degradation and perpetuate poverty (Lopez, 1977).

In contrast to this gloomy picture, the dry zone of Sri Lanka recorded good increases in paddy production helped by irrigation from large as well as small irrigation schemes in the 1980s. Similarly, there were spectacular successes in the Philippines and Indonesia and this resulted in self-sufficiency in food in both countries. However, the extent to which this success can be maintained and supported by institutional change remains contentious.

As noted in the introductory chapter, the image of the Punjab as India's 'bread basket' was severely tarnished by the end of the 1980s, due to soil erosion, waterlogging, pest infestations, depletion of local water sources and declining water tables (caused by excessive ground-water extraction). However, the overexploitation of ground water and environmental degradation are not limited to north or western India. China has substantial problems managing ground-water extraction. The increase in gravity irrigation has also resulted in salinization in the Indus river basin in south central Asia. In Mexico, a fourfold increase in grain production was accompanied by a 10 per cent diminution in usable cropland during the 1980s.

Private property rights are frequently considered the best means of minimizing land degradation and soil erosion, especially in fragile lands. However, private property rights may not emerge or might be slow to emerge (Lopez, 1977). One can envision a vicious circle where land degradation makes land less valuable and lowers incomes. Accompanied by rapid population growth, this will increase the demand for intensification of land use; so it becomes more likely that environmental dynamics will dominate institutional dynamics. Where the customary institutions are strong and cooperation exists, institutions are likely to develop faster to keep these perverse influences in check. Indigenous communities that develop customary land rights before population growth may well achieve a rapid transition to private property regimes, but this cannot be universally guaranteed.

If lands are fragile and institutions are weak, then irreversible damage to the land base can frequently occur. The result is a vicious cycle of environmental decay and degradation and increasing poverty. If initial institutions are strong, institutional dynamics will generally dominate environmental dynamics, leading to successful intensification of production and increased per capita income, even in relatively fragile areas. When the environmental base is solid, institutional dynamics continue to dominate environmental dynamics, leading to successful intensification of production (Lopez, 1977). Hence, in areas where land degradation continues unabated, it can be argued that environmental dynamics are manifestly dominating institutional dynamics.

In south Asia, intensive development of ground water is a major concern. Ground-water resources yield immediate benefits to individuals due to the relatively low investment required, the comparative ease of drilling wells and widespread availability of pumps and drainage devices. Important in this context is the overarching influence of relatively cheap energy ('free' in some cases). However, sustainable ground-water requires user participation in order to achieve effective longer term management and to allow for an integrated water resources framework to minimize environmental costs (Custodio, 2005).

While ignorance on the part of governments has sometimes resulted in the neglect of ground-water resources, a spectacular increase in the use of ground water for irrigation has taken place in the past decade in many developing countries. This development has occurred through the personal initiatives of millions of farmers in pursuit of the socio-economic benefits brought by ground water. However, the cost of exploitation of ground water borne by farmers is only a small fraction of the overall costs, and bringing extractions into check remains a formidable challenge in many countries.

Analysis of institutions

Economists have historically sought to successfully model economic behaviour through market analysis. However, even several decades after acceptance of the critical role of institutions in economic development, empirical analysis of institutions has lagged behind theory. The basic reasons for this lag reside in neoclassical economists' contention that institutional analysis lay outside the realm of the economist and institutions are themselves not easily amenable to neat analysis using the economist's familiar tools, such as mathematical equations and linear algebra (Manski, 2000). As a consequence, there is a dearth of empirical analysis of institutions that might provide information for irrigation policy. The available literature on institutions and irrigation deals with a multitude of issues, such as the role of institutions, factors affecting the effectiveness of institutions, quality of institutions and institutional dynamics. Below, I review some of these studies in an effort to highlight potential areas for improvement.

Cross-section studies of irrigation institutions

Many variables have been shown to be significant in determining the effectiveness of collective action. Some of these include resource characteristics, size of farm, income, family size, size of the group to whom the rules apply and the heterogeneity of members of the group (Olson, 1982). In addition, Ostrom (1990) highlights the importance of family ties and the characteristics of the beneficiaries in this context. Wealth distribution, income inequality, level of dependence of farmers on the water resource, rules of sharing water, social taboos, cultural and ethical factors, technology, indigenous knowledge and government policies have also proven influential in this context (Baland and Platteau,1996; Ostrom, 1990; Wade, 1988; White and Runge, 1994; Ostrom, 2000; Agarwal, 2001).

Several studies of irrigation institutions reported for Asia (Bardhan, 2000; Gandhi and Namboodiri, 2002; Samad, 2002; Gandhi and Marsh, 2003; Groottaert and Narayan, 2001; Chelliah, 2000) attempted to establish the micro-economic foundations of irrigation institutions. Most of these studies commonly used cross-sectional data to identify those factors that influence institutions. Generally, such studies are based on the premise that a better understanding of the factors which affect collective action in irrigation water management will assist the introduction of innovations in irrigation management (Rasmussen and Meinzen-Dick, 1995).

Bardhan (2000) examined cooperative action in canal and tank irrigation management in 48 irrigation communities in Tamil Nadu using cross-section data. All the canal systems were under some form of government management. Some associations were more than 20 years old, while others were less formal in nature and had shorter histories. Bardhan (2000) used three proxy variables for successful collective action, namely (a) absence of conflicts over water within the village during the last five years, (b) frequency of violations of water allocation rules, and (c) maintenance of distribution channels. Regrettably, these proxies do not reflect the institutions particularly well because they cannot accurately measure the impacts of institutions per se and there is a high degree of subjectivity. Put simply, such measures do not reliably capture the essential elements of institutions and collective action.

Meinzen-Dick et al (2000) examined the factors determining collective action in major canal irrigation in Karnataka and Rajasthan. They found closeness to the market, religious centres, size of the command, leadership and education to be important determinants of collective maintenance work. Gandhi and Marsh (2003) examined household income strategies and interactions within the local institutional environment in the State of Gujarat. Membership in dairy cooperatives, village service cooperatives, savings groups, village community associations and labour groups were all employed as proxies for institutions. The study found that membership of these village associations, particularly membership in savings/micro-credit groups and cooperative and community associations, significantly influenced income.

Other studies of institutional issues of irrigation tanks in Tamil Nadu are available within the literature. These include analyses relating to the modernization of tanks (Balasubramanian and Govindasamy, 1991), efficiency of crop production under tanks, and the interaction between private wells and tanks (Palanisami and Easter, 1991). In an extensive analysis Palanisami and Balasubramanian (1998) examined the impact of private wells on the performance of village tanks using cross-section data from 690 sites in Tamil Nadu. Notwithstanding the breadth of data, this study had serious measurement and specification problems because tank performance is also affected by the presence of wells, an important aspect that was not adequately accounted for in this instance. Other studies on collective action and property rights in irrigation tanks in Tamil Nadu have been reported by Palanasami and Balasubramanian (1998). These studies included the non-agricultural uses of tanks but additional work is required to explore the evolution of coping mechanisms by farmers under common property rights.

Balasubramanian and Selvaraj (2003) analysed the factors influencing tank degradation both at the macro and micro levels with the aim of addressing this issue from a collective action perspective. They found that more than 80 per cent of the poor people depend on tank water and spend a significant proportion of their income on the maintenance of the tank. Moreover, this group was shown to expend more than twice as much labour on this activity than their more affluent counterparts. The analysis showed that the presence of a common irrigator positively affected collective action. The study also found that an increase in the number of wells in the tank led to reduced collective action, migration and adoption of non-farm activities by the poor. Poignantly, private strategies appear to dominate over collective action in the cases reported by Balasubramanian and Selvaraj (2003) and a decline in local institutions governing tank maintenance was reported. This can result in changes in the socio-economic environment in which tanks are managed. The authors also argue that as the number of wells increases there is a reduction in collective action. They further contend that wells are partly a mechanism to privatize common pool tank water where only the well-to-do can benefit. These are important issues in the dynamics of tank irrigation but the study did not specifically focus on environmental dynamics, an issue that is equally important.

Aggarwal (2000) examined collective action for irrigation in India for group-owned wells. In particular, the extent to which norms, peer pressure and reciprocal obligations are effective in reducing transactions costs was considered in this analysis. One of the findings from this work was that the effectiveness of collective action can have a time dimension – collective action works well for daily water allocation but less so for regular maintenance activities and is even less effective for long-term expansion plans (Aggarwal, 2000).

Although complementarities among resource uses can promote cooperative management of such resources, competition among socially differentiated users can give rise to conflict. Bardhan and Dayton-Johnson (2002), Lam (1998) and Tang (1991) have all studied forms of heterogeneity with respect to irrigation water systems. These studies cover several countries. The inequality of income has generally been shown to exhibit a U-shaped relationship with successful collective action occurring in the presence of very low and very high levels of inequality (Bardhan, 2000; Balasubramanian and Selvaraj, 2003). These same studies show that the existence of traditional governance systems, including rules for allocating water, generally support collective action.

Game theory approaches to analysis of collective action

Institutional analysis commonly deals with situations characterized by uncertainty, and where opportunistic and strategic behaviour may be common. Such settings are amenable to analysis using game theory techniques. Many applications of game theory to water resource management have been reported in the literature (Runge, 1986; Sparling, 1993; Easter, 1993). Runge (1986) used game theory to illustrate how cooperation ensues if certain characteristics of the resource and resource users are present. This approach uses the familiar prisoners' dilemma game. This game suggests that defection is an inferior Nash equilibrium and there is a number (k>1) such that if k individuals cooperate and the rest defect, those who cooperate are still better off than if they had defected. Using this approach Runge (1986) compellingly illustrates that cooperation is optimal if a critical number of users cooperate, which has particular relevance to irrigation systems in many developing countries.

Runge (1986) suggested that the concept of assurance and reciprocity provides a better explanation for the observed variations in operation and maintenance activities in irrigation. Reciprocity implies that 'if everyone contributes to the Operation and Maintenance activities in irrigation you must do the same' (Easter, 1993). Various incentives and institutional arrangements can also be made to provide assurance. Thus, it can be argued that if farmers can be provided with assurance about other users' participation, it will elicit the desired behaviour from all members.

White and Runge (1994) also used game theory to examine collective action in a different setting and found that the physical distribution of farm land, the percentage of farmers adopting soil conservation measures, and sources of labour were all important determinants of the level of collective action.

Easter (1993) has examined water management systems in several countries in Asia employing an 'assurance' perspective. Four countries – namely,

Nepal, Sri Lanka, the Philippines and India – were analysed using this framework and showed that the level of assurance differed across countries. Easter (1993) comes to the following conclusions: (a) the assurance problem, if modified to include the concerns for fairness and commitment, will provide an improved explanation of farmers' behaviour regarding operations and maintenance activities in irrigation; (b) the best way to establish external assurance is to provide a dependable water supply, in addition to farmer participation, good communication, and penalties for poor water management. If farmers participate directly in system planning and maintenance it will also improve both external and internal assurance. This model is also conducive to offering explanations for the structure of some traditional irrigation management systems in various countries.

In this regard Martin and Verbeek (2006) refer to the *Muang Fai* system of water management in Thailand, which is a traditional water management system dating back over 1000 years and still persisting in many parts of Thailand. It is a collective action system where scarce water resources are managed in a cooperative manner and conflicts are usually minimized. The system is based upon cooperative sharing of the available resource pool. In a bad season, all entitlement holders get the same share. This has important behavioural implications. Where the individual, or group, obtains a share of the total resource, the dynamics of use is different to that occurring when the interests are expressed as a fixed volume of the resource. Under the sharing arrangement, self-interest results in maximizing the size of the pie: growing the collective resource, reducing waste, or winning in repeated rounds of bargaining among independent resource owners. Game theory suggests that bargaining is likely to lead to winners emerging mostly through collaboration rather than by cheating. In the *Muang Fai* system, mechanisms or rules of communication and negotiation have emerged among the members in order to maintain the cooperative behavioural dynamic (Martin and Verbeek, 2006).

Sparling (1993) also developed an analysis of the *Warabandi* system of water distribution in Pakistan using game theory. He noted that the *Warabandi* system has asymmetrical externalities and information. He used Schilling's tipping mechanism concept to support the case for generalized reciprocity/conflict. The results for the *Warabandi* system in 30 watercourses in Punjab support the concept of generalized reciprocity. If generalization of reciprocity is a common phenomenon, then the implications for social policy are non-rival and cooperation will flourish.

Regardless of the usefulness of the game theory approach, there are inherent difficulties in using it for all conceivable situations in irrigation. First, irrigation schemes are characterized by large numbers of people and this makes the simple analytic of game theory difficult to apply. Second, where numbers are large the transactions costs involved in negotiations will be high, and how this affects the incentives is not yet fully answered.

There are other problems that may bedevil any effort to adopt game theory for policy purposes. The difficulty of using game theory approaches in decision making in water management is accentuated by the lack of commitment by policy makers to utilize the techniques. Even in developed countries where game theory might expose useful policy lessons it is seldom considered. Most policy makers have not developed an interest and understanding for advanced decision-making approaches. Until that happens, game theory or innovations from game theory will go unrewarded, at least in the management and policy arenas in irrigation. Even if policy makers are interested in using game theory solutions, adoption is likely to be slow because of competing models. Criteria such as efficiency (maximizing output per unit of input), command and control methods, cost–benefit analysis and the like are generally more familiar and politically acceptable as analytical devices in most developing countries.

Ground-water markets and institutions

In an effort to cover the full array of institutional analyses available in the literature I now turn to the rich literature on the markets for ground water. Most of this literature analyses market institutions, even though many analysts would contend that ground water needs to be primarily considered from a broader institutional and environmental perspective. Dhawan's (1995) study of ground-water degradation systematically classifies degradation arising out of mining of water, and that arising from increasing salinity. He suggests that declining water tables are a matter of grave concern in India, but the problem is not as widespread in areas such as Haryana and Punjab, because of replenishment from Himalayan snow melt. Shah's (1993) study of ground-water markets identified a multitude of mechanisms through which water sales are undertaken, such as in-kind transactions and water contracts. Some of these are interlinked with land and/or other inputs and cash transactions, with per acre and per volume metrics also evident. Contracts in north India provide farmers with opportunities to buy water. Those not owning a water extraction mechanism are not necessarily disadvantaged by these arrangements.

The deep tube-well irrigation systems in Bangladesh have been studied in detail in the Comilla district. The village of Nabagram provides insights into institutional adaptations that can be useful for government and water users. Coward and Ahmed (1979) initially examined the patterns of local bureaucracy articulation, a process central to irrigation development in Bangladesh. They considered reasons for the adaptation and sustaining of cooperation. More specifically, they identified that timely operation of the irrigation pump was dependent on action by both village and bureaucracy, separately and in coordination. The village irrigation cooperative primarily established tubewells and pumps near the village cooperative. Channels were constructed and labour mobilized by the leaders. These adaptations were accomplished through three important locality-specific organizational changes; namely (a) the appointment of the *Panichalak* for the water distribution and pump operation; (b) the creation of differential water user charges; and (c) the use of private mechanics. Such studies highlight the importance and interlinking of seemingly minor local initiatives in the maintenance of successful cooperation on a wider scale.

According to Takase and Wickham (1976) the most difficult problems in irrigation institutions are the operation and maintenance capabilities and their integration with local engineering, agronomic, economic and social skills. Coward and Ahmed (1979) contend that the programme evidenced in Bangladesh evolved to overcome these constraints. The villagers in Nabaram were able to modify their own technological base while developing only limited dependency on a government agency. This was achieved to a large extent through the mobilization of locally provided and locally controlled resources (Coward and Ahmed, 1979).

Critique of earlier institutional analyses

Having provided an (albeit incomplete) overview of the types of institutional studies commonly undertaken in this field, I offer a brief critique of these works with the aim of informing future empirical analysis. This will also help contextualize the empirical analyses offered in the second section of this book.

Small-scale irrigation, farmer-managed irrigation and indigenous irrigation systems have evolved over time. This has usually involved repetition of a particular activity and a process of trial and error. Ultimately, farmers then form expectations about the scope and usefulness of coordinating their activities (Adams et al, 1994). During periods of rapid change the incidence of collective action is often observed to be quite low. This is because older norms may no longer be relevant while new norms are yet to emerge and gain acceptance (Aggarwal, 2000). The point is that research effort needs to be directed towards understanding how these groups form and evolve over time, how and to what extent they are able to control for the tendency to free-ride and for what kind of activities is it desirable to have such groups. Other important considerations attend how such groups change over time, or how they respond to local socio-economic challenges, development intervention and technological development. These interactions are complex and because they are occurring in a dynamic environment they are hard to trace and differentiate empirically. Yet such interactions are all too often ignored by researchers, despite their importance in establishing genuine relationships with institutions.

It is clear that in most of the studies described above the level of analytical rigour to deal with dynamics of this form has been found wanting. Accordingly, their capacity to shed light on how irrigation systems actually work in a period of change is limited. The proxies used do not always adequately reflect the actual interaction or the nature of that interaction. These problems are compounded when the statistical models are specified by seemingly random criteria or when variables are chosen solely on the basis of data accessibility. For example, establishing the total membership of an organization is surely an inadequate variable for capturing the dynamic of institutions. Similarly, Bardhan (2000) uses 'proximity to temples' as a proxy for institutions, but the role of a temple is complex and not purely production-oriented. A positive correlation does not provide robust evidence of the actual relationship. Arguably, such approaches fall short of being guided by deductive theory.

Much of the empirical research also fails to take account of the effects of contemporaneous changes in other economic factors, such as the technology that affects institutions or is related to it. The framework offered in earlier chapters in this book indicates the important link between technological costs and transaction costs and yet few other works have pursued this line of thinking. Thus, for many of these studies the estimated equations cannot capture the institutional role specifically but include the impact of other factors such as technology, climate, labour inputs and ownership. We cannot be sure that the relationship is linear but most of the regressions use linear multiple regression. Similar concerns attend the relationship between factors in these equations – do these factors operate additively, or do they interact in a more complex way? Empirical research therefore requires a counterfactual approach that isolates the effects by measuring the impacts of one group over another. Unless these factors are distinguished and isolated, the impact of a given institutional change cannot be precisely determined. Hence the failures or successes attributed to institutions may be as much a result of measurement error as this is tied to the hypothesized impacts of institutions.

These aggregate analyses also have a limited ability to predict with any detail the distributional consequences of institutional change. The accuracy of predictions should depend on the intrinsic features of institutions rather than the methodology used. Failure to capture the nuances and complexities found in the real world remains a problem with these approaches. On the one hand, market interaction is clearly defined in terms of preferences, expectations and constraints. On the other hand, the theoretical strands at play in institutions are less clearly defined.

The major weakness of most existing studies is that they fail to clearly unravel the complex web of causality among these factors. Problems of endogeneity and reverse causality plague most of this work. Reverse causality implies that institutions are the cause of improved incomes but institutions may, in fact, be the consequences of income. Put differently, are good institutions independent determinants of income or the consequences of higher incomes?

Because of these methodological weaknesses, it is difficult to delineate the exact magnitude of observed variations in incomes that are solely due to institutional changes. This lack of theoretical grounding undermines the accumulation of knowledge and the general applicability of the results – a task taken up later in this book. The complex relationships between poverty, private coping mechanisms and collective action have not been systematically studied by previous researchers (Balasubramanian and Selvaraj, 2003), although the analysis provided in later chapters of this book should, we hope, make some progress on this front.

Conceptual and practical problems attend empirical tests of hypothesized relationships, such as those purportedly existing between homogeneity and collective action, for example. Moreover, the effect of variables such as homogeneity depends on the type of collective action under consideration. The form of collective action in empirical research often cannot be correctly specified. Yet virtually all collective action situations have been portrayed as lying within three main categories – a prisoners' dilemma, tragedy of the commons, or public good provision problem. Common property regimes are seldom investigated or conceptualized as relics of earlier primitive institutions (McKean and Ostrom, 1995); and characterizing users as being trapped in continuous overuse of water resources needs to be reconsidered.

In most instances, the dynamic aspects of institutions are not examined. Hence it is not possible to use these approaches to separate the influence of transactions or information costs from those of cultural and other differences. A way forward would provide for insights on the dynamic elements of institutions. Such an approach would acknowledge and measure how dynamic effects are compounded by the fact that the relationship between modernization and environmental change may not be linear (Ehrhardt-Martinez, 1998). In sum, despite the important role of institutional dynamics, and because of analytical tractability and data availability problems, empirical analysis of institutions has hitherto focused on static effects and generally neglected critical dynamic issues.

The weak record of policy relevant to empirical research on institutions is a matter of concern for many theoretical economists and policy makers. To inform policy, we need credible empirical analysis of institutions. The challenge for economists is to unravel what institutions are prevalent in the world, the types of interactions they create and how they affect resource allocation in complex situations. There is a need to strengthen the standard of analysis and build knowledge that can enhance our understanding of the relevance of institutions to economic development. In particular, there is a compelling need for specific empirical research about the questions that bedevil irrigation management, since poor nations have invested so heavily in this activity.

Concluding remarks

In this chapter I have endeavoured to present collective action and cooperation as important institutional concepts. While differing somewhat from the transaction and transformation cost approaches discussed by Pagan and Crase in earlier chapters, this approach offers a useful complementary lens, particularly in the context of water resource management in developing nations. It also provides a useful insight into the operation of Indian irrigation, which is described in greater detail in subsequent chapters.

A brief review of a subset of studies dealing with collective action was also presented. However, despite the voluminous nature of this work, important policy questions remain unresolved. The extant research hints at some of the influential variables in this context and this may help us understand what makes for better institutions in irrigation and how these variables interact with other important factors such as poverty. Regrettably, reaching firm conclusions in this field has been hampered by either deficiencies on the methodological front or data constraints (or both). The upshot of the discussion is that there is considerable scope for more sophisticated methodologies in this area – a challenge taken up later in this book.

References

Adams, W. M., Potkanski, T., and Sutton, J. E. G. (1994) 'Indigenous farmer-managed irrigation', *Sonjo*, Tanzania, vol 160, pp17–32

Agarwal, A. (2001) 'Common property institutions and sustainable governance of resources', *World Development*, vol 29, pp1649–1672

Aggarwal, R. M. (2000) 'Possibilities and limitations to cooperation in small groups: the case of group-owned wells in Southern India', *World Development*, vol 28, pp1481–1497

Aluvihare, P. B. and Kikuchi, M. (1991) *Irrigation Investment Trends in Sri Lanka: New Construction and Beyond*, International Irrigation Management Institute, Colombo, Sri Lanka

Ayers, E. (1952) *The Industrial Economy*, Houghton Mifflin, Boston

Baland. J. and Platteau, J. P. (1996) *Halting Degradation of Natural Resources: Is there a Role for Rural Communities?* Clarendon Press, Oxford

Baland, J. M. and Platteau, J. P. (1998) 'Division of the commons: A partial assessment of the new institutional economics of land rights', *American Journal of Agricultural Economics*, vol 80, pp644–651

Balasubramanian, R. and Govindasamy, R. (1991) 'Ranking irrigation tanks for modernization', *Agricultural Water Management*, vol 20, pp155–162

Balasubramanian, R. and Selvaraj, K. (2003) *Poverty, Private Property and Common Pool Resource Management: The Case of Irrigation Tanks in South India*, South Asian Network for Development and Environmental Economics (SANDEE), Nepal

Bardhan, P. (2000) 'Irrigation and co-operation: An empirical analysis of 48 irrigation communities in South India', *Economic Development and Cultural Change*, vol 48, pp847–868

Bardhan, P. K. and Dayton-Johnson, J. (2002) 'Unequal irrigators: Heterogeneity and commons management in large-scale multivariate research', National Research Council, *The Drama of the Commons*, National Academy Press, Washington DC

Berkes, F and Folke, C. (1994) *Paradise Lost? The Ecological Economics of Biodiversity*, Earthscan, London

Bromley, D. W. (1992) 'The commons, common property and environmental policy', *Environment and Resource Economics*, vol 2, pp10–17

Chelliah, R. (2000) 'Institutional impediments to economic development in India', in S. Kahkonen and M. Olson (eds) *A New Institutional Approach to Economic Development*, Oxford University Press, Oxford

Coase, R. H. (1960) 'The problem of social cost', *Journal of Law and Economics*, vol 3, pp1–44

Coward, E. and Ahmed, B. (1979) 'Village, technology and bureaucracy: Patterns of irrigation organization in Comilla District, Bangladesh', *The Journal of Developing Areas*, vol 13, pp431–440

Custodio, E. (2005) 'Intensive use of groundwater and sustainability', *Ground Water*, vol 43, p291

Demsetz, H. (1967) 'Toward a theory of property rights', *American Economic Review*, vol 57, pp347–359

Dhawan, B. D. (1995) *Ground Water Depletion, Land Degradation and Irrigated Agriculture in India*, Commonwealth Publishers, India

Easter, K. W. (1993) 'Economic failure plagues developing countries' public irrigation: An assurance problem', *Water Resources Research*, vol 29, pp1913–1922

Edwards, V. M. and Steins, N. A. (1998) 'Developing an analytical framework for multiple use commons', *Journal of Theoretical Politics*, vol 10, pp347–383

Ehrhardt-Martinez, K. (1998) 'Social determinants of deforestation in developing countries: Cross national studies', *Social Forces*, vol 77, pp567–586

Gandhi, V. and Marsh, R. (2003) 'Development and poverty reduction: Do institutions matter? A study on the impact of local institutions in rural India', IIMA Working Paper, University of California, Berkeley

Gandhi, V. P. and Namboodiri, N. V. (2002) 'Investment and institutions for water management in India 's agriculture: Profile and behaviour', in D. Brennan (ed) *Water Policy Reform: Lessons from Asia and Australia,* ACIAR Proceedings No. 106, Canberra

Groottaert, C. and Narayan, D. (2001) 'Local institutions, poverty and household welfare in Bolivia', Policy Research Working Paper 2644, Policy Research Dissemination Center, World Bank, Washington DC

Kumar, M. and Bhandari, M. M. (1992) 'Impact of protection and free grazing on sand dune vegetation in the Rajastan desert, India', *Land Degradation and Rehabilitation*, vol 3, pp215–227

Lam, W. F. (1998) *Governing Irrigation Systems in Nepal: Institutions, Infrastructure and Collective Action*, ICS Press, Oakland, CA

Lopez, R. E. (1977) *Where Development Can or Cannot Go: The Role of Poverty–Environment Linkages*, Annual World Bank Conference on Development Economics, World Bank, Washington DC

Manski, C. F. (2000) 'Economic analysis of social interaction', National Bureau of Economic Research (NBER), Working Paper No. W7580, Northwestern University, Chicago, IL

Marshall, G. R. (2008) 'Nesting, subsidiarity and community-based environmental governance beyond the local level', *International Journal of the Commons,* vol 2, no 1, pp75–97

Martin, P. and Verbeek, M. (2006) *Sustainability Strategy*, The Federation Press, NSW

McKean, M. A. and Ostrom, E. (1995) 'Common property regimes in the forest: Just a relic from the past', *Unaasylvia*, vol 46, pp3–15

Meinzen-Dick, R., Raju, K. V. and Gulati, A. (2000) 'What affects organizations and collective action for managing resources? Evidence from canal irrigation systems in India', discussion paper, Environment and Production Technology Division, IFPRI, Washington DC

Metz, J. (1991) 'A reassessment of the causes and severity of Nepal's environmental crisis', *World Development*, vol 19, pp805–820

Moorhead, R. and Lane, C. (1993) *New Directions in African Range Management: Natural Resource Tenure and Policy*, International Institute for Environment and Development, London

Nabli, M. K. and Nugent, J. B. (1989) 'The new institutional economics and its applicability to development', *World Development*, vol 17, pp1333–1347

North, D. C. (1990) *Institutions, Institutional Change and Economic Performance*, Cambridge University Press, Cambridge, MA

North, D. C. and Thomas, R. P. (1977) 'The first economic revolution', *Economic History Review*, vol 30, pp229–241

Olson, M. (1982) *The Logic of Collective Action: Public Goods and the Theory of Groups*, Harvard University Press, Cambridge

Ostrom, E. (1990) *Governing the Commons: The Evolution of Collective Action*, Cambridge University Press, Cambridge

Ostrom, E. (2000) 'Collective action and the evolution of social norms', *Journal of Economic Perspectives*, vol 14, pp137–158

Palanisami, K. and Balasubramanian, K. (1998) 'Common property and private property: Tanks vs. private wells in Tamil Nadu', *Indian Journal of Agricultural Economics*, vol 53, pp600–613

Palanisami, K. and Easter, W. (1991) 'Hydro-economic interaction between tank storage and groundwater recharge', *Indian Journal of Agricultural Economics*, vol 46, pp174–179

Quiggin, J. (1993) 'Common property, equality and development', *World Development*, vol 21, pp1123–1138

Rasmussen, L. N. and Meinzen-Dick, R. S. (1995) 'Local organizations for natural resources management: Lessons from theoretical and empirical literature', EPTD Discussion Papers No. 11, International Food Policy Research Institute, Washington DC

Rudd, M. A. (2000) 'Live long and prosper: Collective action, social capital and social vision', *Ecological Economics*, vol 34, pp131–144

Runge, C. F. (1981) 'Common property externalities: Isolation, insurance and resource depletion in a traditional grazing context', *American Journal of Agricultural Economics*, vol 63, pp595–606

Runge, C. F. (1986) 'Common property and collective action in economic development', *World Development*, vol 14, pp623–635

Samad, M. (2002) 'Impact of irrigation management transfer on the performance of irrigation systems: A review of selected Asian experiences', in D. Brennan (ed), *Water Policy Reform: Lessons from Asia and Australia*, ACIAR Proceedings No. 106, Canberra

Shah, T. (1993) *Groundwater Markets and Irrigation Development: Political Economy and Practical Policy*, Oxford University Press, New Delhi

Sparling, E. W. (1993) 'Asymmetry of incentives and information: The problem of watercourse maintenance', in R. K. Sampath and A. Young (eds) *Social, Economic and Institutional Issues in Third World Development*, Westview Press, Boulder, CO

Takase, K. and Wickham, T. (1976) *Irrigation Management as a Pivot of Agricultural Development in Asia*, Asian Development Bank, Manila

Tang, S. Y. (1991) 'Institutional arrangements and the management of common-pool resources', *Public Administration Review*, vol 5, pp42–51

Wade, R. (1988) *Village Republics: Economic Conditions of Collective Action in South India*, Cambridge University Press, Cambridge

White, T. and Runge, C. F. (1994) 'Common property and collective action: Lessons from co-operative watershed management in Haiti', *Economic Development and Cultural Change*, vol 43, pp1–41

Woolcock, M. (1998) 'Social capital and economic development: Toward a theoretical synthesis and policy framework', *Theoretical Sociology*, vol 27, pp151–208

World Bank (2008) 'Overview of Social Capital', available at: http://web.worldbank.org/WBSITE/EXTERNAL/TOPICS/EXTSOCIALDEVELOPMENT/EXTTSOCIALCAPITAL/0,,contentMDK:20642703~menuPK:401023~pagePK:148956~piPK:216618~theSitePK:401015,00.html, accessed 20 December 2008

6
Water Institutions in India: An Institutional Design Perspective

Jayanath Ananda

Introduction

Water institutions[1] play a vital role in managing and sustaining water resources as well as encouraging economic development and poverty alleviation in India. Designing institutional mechanisms to allocate scarce water and river flows has long been an important legal, constitutional and social issue in India (Marothia, 2003). The water resource sector in India is confronted by several institutional challenges, which can be classified into three main areas: (a) poor performance and deterioration of public (canal and tank) irrigation systems, (b) high extraction levels of ground water and related economic and environmental problems, and (c) transition from a water management focus to an integrated management system that takes wider hydrological boundaries into account (Shah et al, 2004; Gulati et al, 2005). Most of these problems are manifestations of weak institutional design and therefore the task of reconfiguring water institutions remains a high priority in India.

The purpose of this chapter is to carry out a preliminary assessment and review of institutional responses to water management in India using a New Institutional Economics (NIE) framework. Earlier chapters presented institutions as 'the rules of the game in a society or, more formally, the humanly devised constraints that shape human interaction' (North, 1995, p5). Put differently, institutions epitomize formal rules, informal constraints (e.g. norms, conventions, codes) and the enforcement characteristics of both (Shah, 2005). Various authors have also emphasized the relationship between institutions and organizations (Nabli and Nugent, 1989; North, 1990). Saleth and Dinar (2004) distinguish between institutional environment and institutional arrangements.

The institutional environment encompasses a set of fundamental rules (social, political and legal) that a society adheres to, whereas institutional arrangements provide a governance structure within which members of a society cooperate or compete (Saleth and Dinar, 2004). In that sense, organizations are essentially manifestations of institutions. In this chapter, I present institutions from this broader 'institutional arrangement' perspective.

The chapter is organized as follows. The following section presents a review of various formal and informal institutional arrangements in water management that are currently in place in India. Various institutional responses such as federal and state legislation, water user associations (WUAs) and ground-water markets are briefly reviewed in this section. The next section presents a preliminary assessment of performance for selected Indian water institutions. This is done using the set of generic design characteristics developed by Pagan in Chapter 2. A discussion based on the institutional assessment is presented in the fourth section, while the final section provides some brief concluding remarks.

Institutional responses in irrigation and water management in India

Federal water institutions

A wide range of institutional responses has evolved over the years to use and manage ever-increasing demand for irrigation water in India. The State List (List II) of the Indian Constitution empowers the states to govern water resources. The regulation and development of interstate rivers is entrusted to the federal government through Entry 56 of List I. The core legislation emanating from this constitutional privilege includes the River Boards Act, 1956 and the Inter-State Water Disputes Act, 1956. The effectiveness of these Acts is clouded by a lack of clarity in terms of institutional objectives, fragmentation of basins by state boundaries, lack of cooperation among states, and intense political lobbying (Richards and Singh, 2001; Mohanty and Gupta, 2002).

The Ministry of Water Resources and its allied supporting agencies function as the apex body responsible for planning, policy formulation and coordinating water resources at the national level. The national policy regarding water resources in India is spelt out in the National Water Policy 2002, which emphasizes the need to reorient existing water-related institutions. The main thrust of the national policy has shifted towards a participatory, multi-sectoral approach leading to the establishment of river basin organizations (RBOs), which advocate a hydrological basis for water governance. Compared to surface water governance institutions, ground-water institutions at the federal and state levels are not yet fully established. Lack of integration of policy at central and state levels and lack of coordination within government ministries and line departments dealing with water remain core institutional deficiencies at the federal level (James, 2003). This is considered in the context of empirical work later in this volume.

State water institutions

Under state authority, Departments of Irrigation are responsible for development and maintenance of major, medium and minor irrigation schemes as well as ground-water development. Most state-level irrigation departments are plagued with corruption, mismanagement and inefficient bureaucratic procedures. They also suffer from chronic funding deficiencies and often subscribe to 'top-down' approaches to solve water management problems (Gulati et al, 2005).

In addition to state-level departments, *Panchayati Raj* institutions[2] (PRIs), which are the local self-governing bodies at the grassroots level, also control various water-related institutions. The main strength of the PRIs is their strong grassroots level contact and their capacity to offer many opportunities for effective agricultural development, including irrigation, under the distributed governance model (Gandhi, 1999). However, it appears that a number of ministries of the federal government have not taken substantive steps to integrate PRIs into their strategic planning (Planning Commission, 2001). Put differently, the state governments have not empowered and adequately internalized the subject of PRIs (Sehgal, 2004; Pillai, 2004). The political nature of PRIs, extant low skill level and the inability to deal with multiple tasks without becoming overburdened can also hinder their effectiveness. Ultimately, this can manifest in lower priority being given to agriculture than is optimal (Gandhi, 1999). Moreover, PRIs often lack the necessary power and authority as institutions for local governance (Shah et al, 2004). Although well interconnected with other informal institutions at the grassroots level, the PRIs lack compliance capacity and adaptiveness. Nevertheless, they may be well placed with appropriate social scale because of their decentralized structure.

Tank irrigation institutions

Tank irrigation is the primary source of traditional irrigation, which provided much needed livelihood security, through its multiple uses, to the poor living in economically fragile regions of India (Sakthivadivel et al, 2004). Tanks are inextricably linked to the social web of rural life and have been predominantly managed by local communities for centuries as 'common property' with a variety of local customs and norms. Tanks obtain water from a range of sources such as direct rain feed, river-fed or rainfed cascades, and they differ in their ownership and managerial regime (village community, village *panchayats*, registered WUAs, fishermen's cooperative, Revenue Department, Public Works Department, Minor Irrigation Department, etc.) (Sakthivadivel et al, 2004). The distribution of tanks is concentrated in the southern Indian states of Andhra Pradesh, Tamil Nadu and Karnataka.

Table 6.1 *Total area irrigated in India by type of irrigation (thousand hectares)*

Year	Sources of irrigation								Total net irrigated area
	Canals			Tanks	Wells			Other sources	
	Govt	Private	Total		Tube wells	Other wells	Total		
1998–99	17,093	212	17,305 (30%)	2792 (5%)	21,381	12,607	33,988 (59%)	3326 (6%)	57,411 (100%)
1999–00	16,842	194	17,036 (30%)	2535 (4%)	22,030	12,593	34,623 (61%)	2915 (5%)	57,109 (100%)
2005–06*	15,268	207	15,475 (26%)	2034 (3%)	23,224	12,148	35,372 (59%)	7314 (12%)	60,195 (100%)

Note: *provisional.
Source: Ministry of Agriculture (2007)

The area under tank irrigation has declined steadily and its share in the net irrigated area had declined from 18.5 per cent to 6.1 per cent between 1960–61 and 1996–97 (Narayanamoorthy, 2003). Since 1998–99, the net area irrigated by tanks has fallen steadily and in 2005–06 tank irrigation contributed only 3 per cent of the total net irrigated area (Table 6.1).The main reasons for this decline include the development of large-scale gravity irrigation systems, rapid spread of tube-well technology and the decline of traditional community management (Sakthivadievel et al, 2004). Perhaps not surprisingly, it has been pointed out that there is a strong negative relationship between tube-well density and tank performance in Tamil Nadu (Palanisami and Balasubramanium, 1998). This shift in common property governance to predominantly private property governance could be due to the high transaction costs associated with the use and maintenance of tank institutions. Rehabilitation of tank systems, while encouraging effective institutional change, is the major focus of current government policy to improve the productivity and performance of this form of irrigation.

Canal irrigation institutions

Canal irrigation provided the impetus for the green revolution and the rise of the agrarian economy in India. It is characterized by publicly funded and managed large-scale dams and canal infrastructure, predominantly constructed during the late 1960s to early 1980s. Although the investment in canal irrigation has enhanced the productive capacity of land in the past, severe management problems related to water use and allocation within the distribution network are exacerbated by poor maintenance and degraded infrastructure (Marothia, 2003). The area under irrigation has increased rapidly but resources needed for adequate operation and maintenance of this infrastructure are dwindling, mainly due to the poor cost recovery policies, which are threatening the physical and financial sustainability of systems. In response to these pressures, many irrigation economies, including India, implemented aggressive irrigation reforms aimed at securing farmer participation in irrigation management. In 2005–06, the extent of area irrigated using canal irrigation was 15,475 thousand hectares or 26 per cent of the total net irrigated area (Table 6.1). Canal irrigation schemes are classified on the basis of their command areas: major (>10,000ha), medium (2000–10,000ha) and minor (<2000ha) schemes (Gandhi, 2004a).

Water user associations (WUAs)

WUAs are the predominant canal irrigation institutions and have emerged with the advent of the participatory irrigation management (PIM) policy. Many states including Andhra Pradesh, Madhya Pradesh and Maharashtra have adopted legislation to promote PIM. The Andhra Pradesh Farmers Management of Irrigation Systems Act (enacted by the government in 1996 and granted approval in the legislative assembly in 1997) was the first legislation of this genre in India and is broadly representative of PIM arrangements. The key rationale of the Act was to negate the existing irrigation inefficiency and inequity, low-cropping intensities and yields by reorienting the irrigation department as a competent authority to provide technical support to WUAs (Vermillion, 1997). WUAs formed under the Act are responsible for the operation and maintenance of irrigation networks. Irrigation departments are responsible for making available a reliable water supply, rehabilitation of the distributary system, and the facilitation and determination of water charges paid by end users. Water charges are collected by the Revenue Department and WUAs in turn receive a portion of revenues to carry out designated tasks.

The basic structure of PIM in Andhra Pradesh, as stipulated by the Act, is presented in Figure 6.1. WUAs provide the basic platform for all water users. WUAs regulate and distribute water within a given command area. Landholders, title holders and tenants have voting rights and are members of the WUA. The other water users that do not have voting rights are referred to as coopted members. The Distributary Committee (DC) is comprised of a group of WUAs under a distributary channel. The DC is responsible for issues related to a given distributary. All the WUA presidents are members of the DC. They elect the managing committee and president of the DC. All the DC presidents will be members of the Project Committee (PC) which is in charge of the entire project command area. The Apex Committee is headed by the Minister for Major and Medium Projects and formulates broad policy guidelines to resolve conflicts (Reddy and Reddy, 2002).

WUAs can be classified according to their nature of origin: government-induced, farmer-initiated and NGO-facilitated. Under PIM initiatives, numerous government-induced WUAs were formed. In some instances, WUAs were promoted to jointly manage either main or branch canals of the irrigation systems (partial autonomy) with the irrigation agency. In such cases, a chosen group of farmers or a committee collaborates with the Irrigation

Department. In other instances, the whole system has been turned over to farmers (full autonomy).

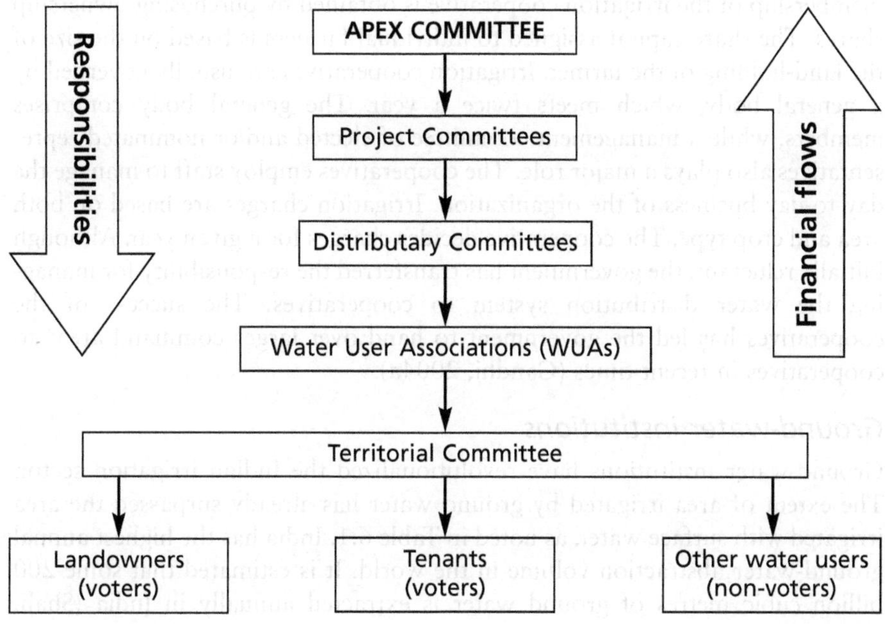

Figure 6.1 *Basic structure of the participatory irrigation management in Andhra Pradesh*

Source: Modified from Reddy and Reddy, 2002, p523

From an institutional design perspective, it is worth noting that farmer-developed and -managed irrigation institutions have been in existence for up to 2000 years in India. They have shown a high resilience to various adverse conditions and managed to survive. These institutions usually operate by adhering to basic principles relating to sustainable, fair and affordable services (non-cash basis) to beneficiaries. However, despite their historic record, community-managed systems cover less than 1 per cent of the total irrigated area in India and have failed to make any inroads into large-scale irrigation systems (Government of India, 1992, quoted in Reddy, 1998).

Irrigation cooperatives

Irrigation cooperatives have emerged as a response to inadequate and irregular water supply leading to numerous conflicts. State irrigation departments have often failed to deliver satisfactory irrigation management or O&M outcomes and this has been attributed to various factors. Frequent breakages of canal walls and unauthorized use of water by farmers have created chaos and inequity in canal systems, particularly in earthen canals,[3] often resulting in the tail-enders failing to receive any water at all (Gandhi, 2004a). The membership of the irrigation cooperative is obtained by purchasing ownership shares. The share capital assigned to individual farmers is based on the size of the land-holding of the farmer. Irrigation cooperatives are usually governed by a general body, which meets twice a year. The general body comprises members, while a management committee of elected and/or nominated representatives also plays a major role. The cooperatives employ staff to manage the day-to-day business of the organization. Irrigation charges are based on both area and crop type. The cooperative decides charges for a given year. Although initially reluctant, the government has transferred the responsibility for managing the water distribution system to cooperatives. The success of the cooperatives has led the government to hand over larger command areas to cooperatives in recent times (Gandhi, 2004a).

Ground-water institutions

Ground-water institutions have revolutionalized the Indian irrigation sector. The extent of area irrigated by ground water has already surpassed the area irrigated with surface water, as noted in Table 6.1. India has the highest annual ground-water abstraction volume in the world. It is estimated that some 200 billion cubic metres of ground water is extracted annually in India (Shah, 2002). Nearly 60 per cent of the total irrigated area (Table 6.1) is irrigated by ground-water and tube-well irrigation, which recorded an annual growth rate of 13.7 per cent from 1960 to 1999 (Department of Agriculture and Cooperation, 2004).

The emergence of ground-water markets is considered to be context-specific (Dubash, 2002). Tube-well technology and supply of electricity in the early 1970s intensified ground-water extraction and promoted some water trading. Higher water supply brought changes to cropping intensity and consequently, more formalized institutions emerged. Ground-water irrigation often requires a significant amount of private capital, which is not readily available for small farmers (Vakulabharanam, 2004). Moreover, lower castes facing resource constraints were commonly excluded from these arrangements. In sum, a ground-water revolution has redefined cropping patterns, labour practices, tenancy arrangements and caste relations in most parts of India (Dubash, 2002).

In areas where ground-water depletion is evident, such as in northern Gujarat, it is not uncommon for several farmers to band together to form cooperative tube-well organizations. Their primary aim is to secure irrigation water for members and sell the excess on the open market to maximize wealth. In some villages, group wells and tube-well cooperatives emerged because individual landholdings were small and the investment requirement was too high (Dubash, 2002). However, where there are large land-holdings, individual ownership is prominent. Further, access to credit required land as collateral and thus well ownership is often limited to well-off farmers. Institutional credit, subsidized inputs, power pricing policy, marketing facilities and technological interventions have thus played an important role in these events. In addition, as noted earlier, they have collectively contributed to the emergence of ground-water markets (Singh, 2002).

Problems related to ground-water governance include high extraction rates, fluctuating water tables, ground-water pollution and equity issues. Over-exploitation of ground water has also resulted in ground-water contamination triggering increased levels of fluoride, arsenic and iron (Planning Commission, 2007). Efforts are under way to arrest the exorbitant extraction levels of ground water and make the transition towards a more sustainable management of ground-water resources, but this is a formidable task. For example, moves in this direction have been challenged because ground water is in the hands of thousands of private farmers and government control over them is often negligible (Chaurasia, 2002). Another aspect is the availability of the electric subsidy, which has exacerbated extraction levels significantly. One element of the core legislation aiming to regulate ground-water management is the creation of a Groundwater Authority under the Environmental Protection Act, 1986. States are in the process of formulating their own ground-water legislation to control ground-water governance but adequate control of extraction seems a long way off. Many states are planning to transfer ground-water governance to *Panchayati* institutions at the village level (Chaurasia, 2002), although this is likely to prove costly and the potential for these changes to induce better governance arrangements seems questionable.

The nature of the water market

Mohanty and Gupta (2002) identified several unique characteristics of the informal water markets, including ground-water markets in India. First, an informal water market is localized and fragmented over short distances and periods. Unlike in Australia, there are no concrete legislation or regulatory mechanisms to ensure efficient water trade in India. Second, the market is driven by excess supply. In other words, the water market is dependent on rainfall and ground-water supply, where the sellers are often wealthy farmers owning deep wells. Third, it is a monopoly market where buyers have virtually no bargaining power and are tied to sellers due to their geographical location. Fourth, the transactions are sometimes influenced by agrarian relations between the buyers and sellers. For instance, in Bihar the buyer's social status rather than their ability to pay determines access to water (Wood, 1995, quoted in Mohanty and Gupta, 2002). Similarly, in Gujarat, there is evidence that many water transactions are inbuilt into existing landlord–tenant relations (Dubash, 2000).

Fifth, the payment mode is diverse: cash payments are made on the basis of time, volume or area irrigated and non-cash payments typically take the form of sharecropping.[4] There is a variety of pricing arrangements for ground-water transactions. Pricing arrangements vary from fixed payment per unit of land (*Uchhak*) to hourly payments and sharing of crop output. Prices are mostly dependent on crop and season (Dubash, 2002). Under hourly payments or time-based contracts, sellers provide water to buyers, who are then charged on an hourly basis. In villages where sharecropping is dominant ground-water trade is based on share payments. The negotiated share varies from two-fifths to one-quarter of crop output (Dubash, 2002). Sixth, there is evidence that excessive and competitive ground-water extraction has caused a decline in the water table as the current property regime symbolizes 'open access' and the scarcity value of ground water is not well captured by prices (Mohanty and Gupta, 2002).

While there is some evidence that small and medium landholders also operate wells (Singh, 2002), larger farmers dominate the supply of ground water in the trading market. The ability of large farms to engage in water trading is due to several factors. First, the large farms with wells are surrounded by small and marginal farms that do not have their own water sources. Second, large landholders reduce their own demand and increase supply by adopting less water-intensive crops and then selling the surplus water. Third, the availability of water is relatively higher with larger farmers since they have the financial means to extract water from deep sources (Singh, 2002). Well owners are encouraged to extract and sell the maximum volume of water because of the existing electricity pricing regime, which is set at a flat rate – sometimes close to zero (Singh, 2002).

Check dams

Check dams are constructed by building a barrier across the direction of water flow on shallow rivers for the purpose of water harvesting. The dam retains the excess water flow behind the structure during the monsoon season. The surface and subsurface water entrapped by the dam is primarily used for ground-water recharge. But there are other uses that attend check dams, such as limited surface irrigation and meeting livestock and domestic needs. One of the core benefits of check dams is their highly effective ground-water recharge. Check dams are popular among many resource-poor communities because compared to larger dams they require minimal technology, financial resources, skilled labour and maintenance (Development Alternatives, 1999). There are several government assistance schemes available for the construction of check dams and it is common for such structures to be viewed as communal property.

Check dams usually operate under common property institutional arrangements. Beneficiary farmers contribute to the construction and maintenance of check dams. The beneficiary farmers are required to pay a charge in accordance with the size of their land-holding. Village Committees (*Gram Samiti*) with wider community representation have been established to construct and manage check dams and they are responsible for raising money for construction, selecting suitable locations and securing government assistance and donations. In some cases, using water directly from check dams for irrigation purposes is strictly prohibited (Gandhi, 2004b).

A preliminary comparative assessment of selected water institutions

Undoubtedly, both the institutional environment and institutional arrangements in the water resource sector largely influence the welfare outcomes for the rural masses in India. However, there is no universal agreement on the appropriate institutional response and no criteria for successful institutional design. Various scholars have identified successful 'design principles' to manage common pool resources, including water. They include the seminal works by Olson (1965), Hardin (1968), Uphoff (1986), Wade (1987), Ostrom (1990, 1992 and 1993), Ostrom et al (1994) and Goodin (1996), which have been highly influential in debates on governance of water institutions. Hannah et al (1995) and Balland and Platteau (1996) also offer alternative sets of design principles (Hussain and Bhattacharya, 2004). These propositions have been primarily based on theories such as rational choice and collective action. Alternative propositions such as cultural theory and contextual theory have also been proposed to describe institutional arrangements and their performance. Cultural theory[5] (McCay and Acheson, 1987) involves the neo-institutional styles that define the behaviour and strategic choices of people, groups and organizations (Mollinga, 2001), while contextual theory (McCay, 2002) argues that the context in which the choice has to be made determines the rationality of the choice.

Quality of institutional design has a great impact on performance (Merrey, 1996).[6] Saleth and Dinar (2004) empirically evaluated the institution-performance interaction using multiple methods. Ostrom (1992) developed design principles of long-standing, self-organized irrigation systems. They include clearly defined boundaries, proportional equivalence between benefits and costs, collective choice arrangements, monitoring, graduated sanctions, conflict resolution mechanisms, external recognition of the rights to organize, and nested or federated organizations. These institutional design features essentially focus on which institutional conditions and design principles are most conducive to achieving and sustaining high performance in various irrigation systems.

This section offers a broad comparative assessment of selected water institutions using the generic institutional design criteria for good institutional outcomes developed by Pagan in Chapter 2. They include clear objectives, interconnection with other formal and informal institutions, adaptiveness, appropriateness of scale and compliance capacity. Since water institutions differ greatly in their physical attributes, geographical location, property rights structure, institutional attributes, sociopolitical and cultural contexts, it is not feasible to consider here all institutions and entities dealing with water management. The intention is to show that there are substantial variations among the 'good institutional design' criteria developed by Pagan. The assessment developed here is predominantly based on secondary literature. However, in some instances case studies conducted in several states of India and personal communication have been employed. The assessment provides a useful basis for any subsequent empirical analysis. A summary assessment of water institutions is presented in Table 6.2.

Table 6.2 *Design feature analysis of water institutions in India*

Institution	*Clarity of objective*	*Interconnectedness with other institutions*	*Adaptiveness*	*Appropriateness of scale*	*Compliance capacity*
Canal irrigation					
a Government-induced WUAs	Low, Moderate[1]	Moderate	Low[2]	–	Poor[3]
b Farmer-initiated WUA[4]	High	High	Very high	–	Moderate[5]
Tank irrigation					
a Traditional community-owned and managed[6]	High[7]	–	High[7]	–	High[8]
b Government-owned and managed[9]	Low	Low	Low[10]	–	–
c *Panchayati* Union managed[11]	Low	–	–	–	–
Ground-water irrigation					
a Privately owned and managed (single ownership)	High	Low	Moderate	Vary	High (self-enforced)
b Community-owned and managed (cooperatives and collective ownership)	High	High	Very high	High	High
c. Public tube-wells (government-owned and managed)[12]	–	–	–	–	–

Notes:

1 In the case of partial autonomy in IMT (DFID, 2001).
2 Mostly due to poor assessment of resource needs prior to turnover (DFID, 2001).
3 Priority water rights honoured by farmers, beneficiaries meet all O&M costs, violators of rules are promptly penalized (DFID, 2001).
4 Based on Centre for Civil Society (2003).
5 Lack of trust between WUA and Irrigation Department and poor procedures for collecting fees.
6 *Kudimaramathu* systems.
7 Sakthivadivel et al (2004).
8 See earlier section on compliance or Sakthivadivel et al (2004) for more details.
9 For example Public Works Department-controlled tanks.
10 The government-managed systems struggle in water distribution during scarcity periods due to inflexible rules enforced by corruptible agents (Bardhan, 2000). When rules are crafted by the government, there are more violations and less compliance.
11 Based on Palanisami and Balasubramanium (1998).
12 Public tube-well initiative, created to exploit the scale economies and improve the equity in access has more or less failed in all states (Mukherji and Kishore, 2003).

Assessment of canal institutions

Clarity of objectives

Various objectives are attributed to WUAs in general. They include securing an adequate and reliable water supply for irrigation, water distribution, conflict resolution, equitable access to irrigation water, undertaking O&M activities, and the like. The PIM Act empowers WUAs to prepare and implement rotational water distribution for each season (in line with operational plans approved by the Distributary Committee or Project Committee), to assist in collection of water charges, to maintain accounts and conduct general body meetings as required.

The degree of institutional clarity among government-induced WUAs varies and is assessed as being moderate to low. According to a study of 22 WUAs in Madhya Pradesh, there is evidence that membership of WUAs generally has good knowledge of the provisions of the PIM Act, how members should be elected and returned, water distribution and other collective choice rules (Marothia, 2002). Moreover, the study reported that there was total transparency in the functioning of WUAs and a well-specified work plan for the maintenance and repair of canal infrastructure (Marothia, 2002). Notwithstanding these findings, there are numerous on-ground examples where the objectives of WUAs are not well espoused.

Compliance capacity

Most government-sponsored WUAs suffer from erratic water distribution, theft and tail-ender problems (Kurian, 2001). Poor compliance can also arise from the elected nature of representation. Water theft and tampering with irrigation structures are quite common. Key criteria that can test members' compliance are the Irrigation Service fee payments. A World Bank evaluation of PIM projects revealed that cost recovery was unsatisfactory in 68 per cent of projects (World Bank, 1994, quoted in Kurian, 2001). This implies low compliance with Irrigation Service fee payments. Much can be attributed to the fact that most members are unaware how the collected money is being spent and there is often a sense of mistrust among the membership. For example, a canal irrigation study carried out in Madhya Pradesh reports that 91 per cent of the WUAs evaluated had low awareness of the financial status of their organization and performed poorly on financial management (Marothia, 2002). Another key criterion to test the degree of compliance is the level of water supply, since the adequacy of water supply is positively correlated with the degree of rule conformance (Marothia, 2002). The adequacy of water supply is arguably the most critical aspect of water governance. However, Marothia (2002) notes that only 5 per cent of WUAs had adequate water supply while 41 per cent and 55 per cent had moderate and scarce water supply respectively.[7] The same study reports that the voluntary labour contribution and efforts for water saving, social audit and fund generation were poor (Marothia, 2002).

Due to very low collection rates for water charges, there are instances where the government and the WUA together collect water charges from the farmers. Traditionally, the Revenue Department collected water charges using their administrative machinery. In this joint collection process, the Irrigation Department, the Revenue Department and WUA jointly inspect the area irrigated and the crops grown are noted. A corresponding cess [levy] is then tabulated and collected from the farmers. As an incentive to WUAs to participate in this cess collection process, a share of the water cess is then provided directly to the WUA (Nikku, 2002).

Interconnectedness with other institutions

Inadequate and erratic water supply has often been quoted as a reason for not establishing strong links within the PIM governance hierarchy. Marothia (2002) reports only moderate levels of performance for organizational linkages between WUAs and other related institutions. Some studies report that the leadership often resides with higher caste members (Nikku, 2002), indicating the tendency to follow deeply rooted social norms.

Adaptiveness

Given the universal application of the institutional design under the PIM Act, the adaptiveness and flexibility of WUAs is heavily constrained. For most WUAs, there is a well-specified work plan for O&M and each WUA has to submit their work plan for approval and release of funds. WUAs then receive compensation according to the irrigation revenue-sharing formula. In these situations, the flexibility of the organization and the ability to change plans quickly may be limited.

The performance of WUAs and farmer participation in irrigation management is mixed (Meinzen-Dick et al, 2000). In some areas they have worked but in others not. To sustain PIM requires substantial political and bureaucratic will and a preparedness to share power with farmers. Numerous observers have noted that PIM has not delivered to the extent originally envisaged (Marothia, 2003). Performance appears to depend in large part on whether the WUAs are strong enough to assume management.[8] There have been numerous instances where the additional direct and indirect costs, including intangible transactions costs, are not balanced by benefits and this can result in non-participation by farmers (Meinzen-Dick et al, 2000).

One of the most common problems with the farmer-managed irrigation schemes is the flawed water delivery systems where tail-enders do not receive water at all (World Bank, 1994, quoted in Kurian, 2001). With this in mind, the sustainability of the WUA heavily depends on their capacity to provide adequate water to all. Although spelt out as an objective of PIM, the lack of equity and reliable supply of irrigation water points to failure on the transparency front and the absence of an adjustment process. Although WUAs have succeeded in increasing the area irrigated predominantly with wet crops, such as rice, they have overwhelmingly failed to ensure an equitable water distribution between head-enders and tail-enders. Another criticism is the degree of equity prevalent when increased water availability arises in the system (International Irrigation Management Institute, 1997).

Assessment of tank institutions

Tank institutions can be classified into three distinct categories in terms of the property rights regime: community-owned and managed (*Kudimaramathu* systems), government-owned and managed, and *Panchayati* managed systems. Communities have managed tank systems as common property despite the presence of many adverse external conditions. Government-owned and managed tanks usually arise when the tank has undergone rehabilitation.

Clarity of objectives

Traditional tank institutions have well-defined, clear objectives and specific rules, including operation of sluice gates, allocation of water to various segments and rationing rules amid water scarcity (Sakthivadivel et al, 2004). Tanks have multiple functions including low-cost surface irrigation,[9] capturing rain water and reducing soil erosion, ground-water recharge, reducing the intensity of flash floods and droughts, and in some cases tank bed cultivation.[10] This multi-purpose nature of tanks is often associated with conflicting priorities for tank stakeholders,[11] which can trap them in a low-level performance equilibrium (Shah and Raju, 1999, quoted in Sakthivadivel et al, 2004).

Interconnectedness with other institutions

Traditional tank institutions generally have strong linkages to the sociocultural aspects of rural life (Sakthivadivel et al, 2004) and hence are well connected with other institutions. For example, in some traditional tank systems in Tamil Nadu, there are landholders from differing religious backgrounds such as Christian, Hindu and Muslim religions and the respective religious leaders appoint the irrigation functionaries. Moreover, the office bearers of the farmer associations are also elected from the representatives of these religions in rotation (Sakthivadivel et al, 2004).

Compliance

It appears that each tank system has it own institutional arrangements to acquire water and maintain feeder (supply) channels, which are critical for performance. A high compliance capacity is evident where it is mandatory for the users to participate in cleaning the feeder channels and those who are unable to participate are required to pay wages. In some tank systems in Tamil Nadu, there are exclusive field-level functionaries called *'kaval'* agents or *'neerkattis'* (common waterman) to facilitate water supply to the tank, organize and coordinate tank maintenance, mobilize resources for tank maintenance, lobbying with government departments for better maintenance of tank structures and so on (Palanisami and Balasubramanium, 1998; Sakthivadivel et al, 2004). Usually, these functionaries are paid for their duties from a common fund.

Compliance in deteriorating tanks is generally more problematic. In addition, the rapid expansion of lift irrigation has threatened the sustainability of some tank systems. With the availability of diesel pumps and cheap electricity, lift irrigators can pump water directly from the tank or canals. In some extreme cases where the well density has exceeded one well per hectare of tank command area, the tanks have become defunct (Palanisami and Balasubramanium, 1998). The lack of water in tanks has also encouraged people to encroach around the tank bed ('*petta*' farmers or tank-bed farmers) for cultivation (Palanisami and Balasubramanium, 1998). In certain cases, supply channels are encroached as well. The legality of tank-bed cultivation is a contentious issue and varies between states. In Madhya Pradesh, the state government has a policy of leasing tank beds to the poor, although people with political power control the access and allocation of tank beds (Satpathy et al, 2002). There are many conflicts between tank-bed farmers and command area farmers, particularly in the areas of desilting, timing of emptying the tank and rehabilitation of the canal system (Shah and Raju, 2001).

In some tank institutions participation in decision making is compulsory for members. For example, in the Pudukkottai district of Tamil Nadu, if anybody is absent from a meeting without prior notification, the absentee is fined 100 rupees (Sakthivadivel et al, 2004). In 'high performing' tank institutions sluice gate operation is usually entrusted to a non-member or to a person on a hereditary basis for a defined period of time (Sakthivadivel et al, 2004). In some instances, these positions are entrusted to people based on skill and managerial ability rather than caste-based criteria. Penalties for non-compliance include stern warning, imposition of fines, and cessation of water supply. In these situations, the social stigma that attends the punishment acts as a powerful incentive to comply.

Adaptiveness

The ability of members of a tank institution to make plans according to water availability so as to provide social safeguards against water scarcity is one measure of adaptiveness. Tank water allocation mechanisms frequently show great adaptability in the face of water scarcity. Sakthivadivel et al (2004) report on one such case. Water allocation during drought periods in this case is governed by the principle of equity and rotational irrigation. When the entire command area cannot be irrigated due to water scarcity, different systems of proportional water allocation are invoked by village leaders and this ensures that everybody receives a minimum irrigation to sustain livelihoods. When faced with water scarcity, farmers with up to one acre of land in the command area are permitted to cultivate their entire holding, farmers owning land between one and five acres in the command area are permitted to cultivate half their holding and farmers owning more than five acres are permitted to cultivate only one-third of their holding (Sakthivadivel et al, 2004). When the water level of the tank is very low, the tank association may decide not to supply water for that season at all.

There are a range of innovative mechanisms to raise funds for tank institutions. Many tank institutions raise funds from selling fishing rights and usufructs, and collecting fines and fees from the members (Sakthivadivel et al, 2004). If these funds are inadequate, some entities levy a tax based on landholding. This tax is also imposed on well owners as they can rely on the tank to recharge their wells. Some tank institutions use collective marketing arrangements and auctions for agricultural produce in order to raise funds for tanks (Sakthivadivel et al, 2004).

Assessment of private ground-water institutions

Private ground-water institutions are often classified as informal water markets. A considerable discrepancy exists in how they are perceived in a wider institutional context. There are two distinct groups of ground-water sellers: tube-well farmers and tube-well businessmen (Mukherji, 2004). Tube-well farmers are predominantly interested in self-irrigation, while the latter group is motivated by profit and is more interested in water trade. On the other hand, buyers are predominantly characterized as being small and marginal farmers (Mukherji, 2004).

A study carried out in North Gujarat, where a large number of ground-water irrigation organizations are functioning, shows that these organizations display the characteristics of strong and effective institutions for managing shared resources, in terms of rules and regulations, members' awareness, transparency in decision making, conflict resolution mechanisms, degree of equity in access, and efficiency in resource use (Kuman, 1995). Moreover, it can be seen that ground-water institutions are well interconnected with traditional institutions such as sharecropping. They also show a greater adaptability, although the capacity to restrain global extractions within sustainable limits remains problematic.

Institutional clarity

Ground-water rights are tied with land rights and are not clearly regulated. It is difficult to articulate a single objective for private ground-water operations because there may be objectives other than profit. For instance, price discrimination in ground water in favour of kith and kin and perceived social status attached to 'water lords' suggest that there are multiple objectives. However, there is also evidence that ownership of water pumps and other ground-water extracting machinery ('pump capital') has significantly shifted from large, upper-class farmers to medium- and small-scale backward caste and other schedule caste farmers (see Pant, 2003). Nevertheless, self-interest and profit motives dominate the operation of private tube-wells as they are virtually independent from any form of regulation. Landholders have the right to extract ground water freely for their own consumption as well as to sell it to other potential users. Tube-well partnerships usually have clear operational rules and mechanisms for changing rules when the need arises. The property regime of the ground water itself is complex as it is neither common property, because it lacks an identifiable group of individuals having equal user rights, nor genuine open access, because the ability to access ground water is limited by well ownership.

Interconnectedness with other institutions

Private tube-wells have very low interaction with other formal government agencies. The only agencies with whom a well owner is required to interact are either the electricity utility or a public bank. Nevertheless, there is some field evidence that suggests that participation in the ground-water market by various segments of the population (small farmers, medium farmers and large farmers) is high (Sharma and Sharma, 2004). A survey conducted in semi-arid Rajasthan revealed that almost 66 per cent of all farm households participate in water trade either fully or partially (Sharma and Sharma, 2004). Accordingly, some degree of connectedness with other institutions is required where trading takes place.

Adaptiveness

The evidence indicates that tube-well partnerships have a high resilience to adverse situations. For example, when the water table lowers, the members renegotiate a new plan of operation in terms of either constructing a new tube-well or buying a higher capacity water pump in order to sustain extractions (Gandhi, 2004a). The extent to which these arrangements are sustainable over the longer term is problematic.

Scale

The evolution of private tube-well partnerships suggests that most of the institutions have taken an adaptive management approach in determining the scale of operation. A case study conducted in Gujarat revealed that the membership increases as the partnership ventures into a greater capacity bore well, reflecting the greater need for pump capital (Gandhi, 2004a). This exemplifies Hardin and Sandler's argument that both the size of the group and the nature of the contract affect the outcome of collective action.

Discussion

Analyses of water institutions have generally followed two broad approaches. One group of researchers have placed a greater emphasis on internal institutional design principles and criteria as elements of governance, while the other focuses on identifying the external institutional conditions under which the water entity performs better. One weakness of the former approach is that it ignores the local political dynamics of institutional evolution and operation. Moreover, there is tremendous variability in water availability, climate, soil fertility, crop prices and other political and cultural practices. These factors invariably affect the success of a particular institution and separating out these effects from internal institutional criteria is not an easy task. A study from

Kerala revealed that the alternative institutional choices of farmers are determined or constrained by factors related to location, land–crop particulars and personal characteristics (Neetha, 2004).

Reorienting WUAs

PIM has been employed primarily with the aim of improving the performance of surface irrigation systems. As noted earlier, the outcomes have been mixed. The conditions inherent to large-scale irrigation projects (settler farmers with diverse origins and farming backgrounds and different tenurial conditions) make the formation of WUAs difficult. For example, in the Rajasthan Canal Project, secure tenure for farmers is non-existent. Changes to tenure patterns or relaxing the restrictions on tenure are needed to stimulate collective action leading to WUAs.

The *process* by which WUAs have been developed is not homogeneous across state jurisdictions. In some cases, the state has played the key role while in other instances the farmers themselves have been keen to develop this initiative. The preferred technique for developing WUAs is unexplored, at least from an empirical perspective, and this is given greater attention later in this book.

Irrigation agency reform

The devolution of power to the lower levels of government for the establishment of participatory village-level institutions with a clear charter and sound legal backing is essential for the effective functioning of WUAs. There is a huge challenge posed by the PIM to large, public irrigation organizations such as state irrigation departments. At risk here are the power and authority of the entity and the job security of public servants. The relationship between public irrigation officials and water users has become increasingly uneasy. However, there may well be a role for these public entities with a reformed mandate of responsibility (see Johnson et al, 2002 for a brief review of organizational options in irrigation agency reform).

The tank systems assessment provided here offers some interesting insights. It appears that traditional tank institutions rate highly on most design criteria, yet all available evidence suggests that traditional tanks are on the decline. This shows that although traditional tank systems appear to have useful elements, at least in the medium term, they do not guarantee the long-term sustainability of the institution. Breakdown of traditional social institutions and lack of formal institutions are seen as catalysts for degradation of the traditional irrigation infrastructure (Singh, 1994). Disintegration of traditional institutions due to the changing economy and globalization has also hampered the performance of tank systems. An important point to note here is that traditional institutions functioned under a totally different sociopolitical set-up, often dominated by feudal or semi-feudal production relations (Reddy, 1998). There is also evidence that elements of social and economic heterogeneity and mutual trust heavily influence the emergence and sustenance of institutions (Kahkonen, 1999). Hence the importance of external and/or contextual factors to the performance of water institutions cannot be overlooked.

Against this backdrop, the emergence of ground-water institutions has revolutionalized the Indian irrigation sector, at least in terms of the area irrigated. Despite the virtual absence of regulation and consequential environmental problems, ground-water institutions have embedded well into the existing institutions and have been able to improve the welfare of millions of farmers in India. However, recent research indicates that the current rate of ground-water use is not sustainable and seems likely to prove harmful in the long term, resulting in irreversible damage to aquifers. Accordingly, in a holistic sense, current ground-water institutions require greater investigation before being proclaimed as successful.

Concluding remarks

Indian water institutions portray a complex mosaic of socio-economic, cultural and political realities in concert with numerous environmental challenges. This chapter presented a provisional assessment of Indian water institutions using the generic institutional design criteria developed earlier in this volume. Comparative studies and testing hypotheses about institutional performance using quantitative data are important steps required to establish a better understanding in this field. The analysis indicates that there is a variety of formal and informal institutions operating collectively as well as in isolation. The large irrigation schemes face continued physical deterioration, silting up of dams, lack of O&M, poor cost recovery and disintegration of institutions. Additional water to meet new urban, industrial and environmental demands must be found. The RBOs may be a step in the right direction but it is obvious that there is not a simple recipe for a 'winning water institution'. Most institutions have at least several desirable design qualities. How these qualities influence performance requires additional research, although it is likely to be difficult to generalize across all types of water institutions and across all geographical regions. The task of designing winning institutions poses even greater challenges because institutional performance depends not only on embedded design criteria but also on the ability to adapt and respond to changing socio-economic, political and cultural challenges.

Notes

1 As noted in earlier chapters, there are various interpretations of the notion of institutions. Here, water institutions are divided into three distinct components: water law, water policy and water administration (Saleth and Dinar, 2004).
2 PRIs have been conferred constitutional status through the 73rd Constitutional Amendment Act of 1992.
3 This is common in earthen irrigation canal systems.
4 In sharecropping, a proportionate share of output is given to the supplier of the input (water in this case).
5 Cultural theory emphasizes the role of culture in common property resources by

signifying the presence (or absence) of rules about uses of commons (McCay and Acheson, 1987).

6 There is a strong positive correlation between the institutional design and performance with four broad categories of performance indicators identified in the literature: technical impact, productivity impact, financial impact and environmental impact (Meinzen-Dick et al, 1994).

7 It should be noted that, of the WUAs surveyed in this study, water availability varied considerably (55% – water scarce, 40% – moderate and 5% – adequate) due to a number of factors including size of the command area, total number of farmers covered, etc.

8 This theme is taken up in other parts of this volume.

9 Most tanks have only unlined earthen canals (*'kuchcha'*).

10 Tank-bed cultivation is locally known as *petta* cultivation.

11 Tank stakeholders include command area farmers, tank-bed farmers, fishermen and village communities.

References

Balland, J. N. and Platteau, J. P. (1996) *Halting Degradation of Natural Resources: Is there a Role for Rural Communities?* FAO and Clarendon Press, Oxford

Bardhan, P. (2000) 'Irrigation and cooperation: An empirical analysis of 48 irrigation communities in South India', *Economic Development and Cultural Change*, vol 48, no 4, pp845–865

Centre for Civil Society (2003) 'Managing water resources: Communities and markets', CCS Briefing paper, March, New Delhi

Chaurasia, P. R. (2002) *Organizational Change for Participatory Irrigation Management: India (2),* Report of the APO Seminar on Organizational Change for Participatory Irrigation Management, 23–27 October 2000, the Philippines, Asian Productivity Organization, Japan

Department for International Development (DFID) (2001) *Sustainable Irrigation Turnover: Report on System Infrastructure,* KAR Project R7389, London

Department of Agriculture and Cooperation (2004) *Land Use Statistics at a Glance*, 1988–89 and 1999–2000, Ministry of Agriculture, Government of India, available at www.agricoop.nic.in, accessed 12 November 2004

Development Alternatives (1999) *Check-Dams and Irrigation, DA Sustainable Livelihoods,* available at www.dainet.org/livelihoods/checkdams2.htm, accessed 16 November 2004

Dubash, N. K. (2000) 'Ecologically and socially embedded exchange: Gujarat model of water markets', *Economic and Political Weekly,* vol 35, no 16, pp639–656

Dubash, N. K. (2002) *Tubewell Capitalism: Groundwater Development and Agrarian Change in Gujarat,* Oxford University Press, New Delhi

Gandhi, V. P. (1999) 'Institutional framework for agricultural development', *Indian Journal of Agricultural Development,* vol 54, no 1, pp48–52

Gandhi, V. P. (2004a) 'Kiyodar farmers bore-well partnership: An unregistered partnership tube-well irrigation system', unpublished paper, ACIAR project, La Trobe University, Melbourne

Gandhi, V. P. (2004b) 'Ibrahimpatan water users association on a minor irrigation project in the Ranga Reddy District, Andhra Pradesh', unpublished paper, ACIAR project, La Trobe University, Melbourne

Gandhi, V. P. (2004c) 'Check dams at Khopala Village: A rare achievement', unpublished paper, ACIAR project, La Trobe University, Melbourne

Goodin, R. E. (1996) *The Theory of Institutional Design*, Cambridge University Press, Cambridge

Gulati, A., Meinzen-Dick, R. and Raju, K. V. (2005) *Institutional Reforms in Indian Irrigation*, IFPRI and Sage Publications, New Delhi

Hannah, S., Folke, C. and Maler, K. G. (1995) 'Property rights and environmental resources', in S. Hannah and M. Munasinghe (eds) *Property Rights and the Environment: Social and Ecological Issues,* Beijer International Institute of Ecological Economics and the World Bank, Washington DC, pp15–29

Hardin, G. (1968) 'The tragedy of the commons', *Science*, vol 162, December

Hussain, Z. and Bhattacharya, R. N. (2004) 'Common pool resources and contextual factors: Evolution of a fishermen's cooperative in Calcutta', *Ecological Economics,* vol 50, pp201–217

International Irrigation Management Institute (IIMI) (1997) *Impacts of Irrigation Management Transfer: A Review of the Evidence*, Research Report No. 11, Colombo, Sri Lanka

James, A. J. (2003) 'Institutional challenges for water resources management: India and South Africa', WHIRL Project Working Paper 7, Department for International Development (DFID), London, accessed 5 November 2004 from www.nri.org/whirl

Johnson, I., Sam, H., Svendsen, M. and Gonzalez, F. (2002) 'Options for institutional reform in the irrigation sector', discussion paper prepared for the International Seminar on Participatory Irrigation Management, 21–27 April, Beijing, China

Kahkonen, S. (1999) 'Does social capital matter in water and sanitation delivery?' Social Capital Initiative Working Paper No. 9, The World Bank, Washington DC

Kuman, M. D. (1995) 'Institutions for efficient and equitable use of groundwater: Irrigation management institutions and water markets in Gujarat, Western India', *Asia-Pacific Journal of Rural Development,* vol 10, no 1, pp52–65

Kurian, M. (2001) 'Farmer-managed irrigation and governance of irrigation service delivery – Analysis of experience and best practice', Working Paper 351, Institute of Social Studies, The Hague

Marothia, D. K. (2002) 'Institutional arrangements for participatory irrigation management: Initial feedback from central India', in D. Brennan (ed) *Water Policy Reform: Lessons from Asia and Australia, Proceedings from an International Workshop held in Bangkok, Thailand, 8–9 June 2001,* ACIAR Proceedings No. 106, Australian Centre for International Agricultural Research, Canberra, pp75–105

Marothia, D. K. (2003) 'Enhancing sustainable management of water resources in agriculture sector: The role of institutions', *Indian Journal of Agricultural Economics*, vol 58, no 3, pp406–427

McCay, B. J. (2002) 'Emergence of institutions for the commons: Contexts, situations and events', National Research Council, *The Drama of the Commons,* Washington DC, National Academy Press, pp361–402

McCay, B. J. and Acheson, J. M. (1987) 'Human ecology of the commons', in B. J. McCay and J. M. Acheson (eds) *The Question of the Commons*, University of Arizona Press, Tucson

Meinzen-Dick, R., Mendoza, M., Sadoulet, L., Abiad-Shields, G. and Subramaniun, A. (1994) 'Sustainable water user associations: Lessons from a literature review', paper presented at World Bank Water Resources Seminar, Landsdowne, Virginia, 13–15 December

Meinzen-Dick, R., Raju, K. V. and Gulati, Ashok (2000) 'What affects organization and collective action for managing resources? Evidence from canal irrigation systems in India', paper presented at 8th Biennial Meeting of the International Association for the Study of Common Property, Bloomington, Indiana, 31 May–4 June

Merrey, D. J. (1996) *Institutional Design Principles for Accountability in Large Irrigation Systems,* Research Report No. 8, International Irrigation Management Institute, Colombo, Sri Lanka

Ministry of Agriculture (2007) *Agriculture Statistics at a Glance, 2007*, Ministry of Agriculture, India

Mohanty, N. and Gupta, S. (2002). 'Breaking the gridlock in water reforms through water markets: International experience and implementation issues for India', Julian L. Simon Centre for Policy Research Working Paper Series, Liberty Institute, New Delhi

Mollinga, P. (2001) 'Water and politics: Levels, rational choice and south Indian canal irrigation', *Futures,* Oct–Nov, pp733–748

Mukherji, A. (2004) *Groundwater Markets in the Ganga-Meghna-Brahmaputra (GMB) Basin: A Review of Literature*, International Water Management Institute-Tata Water Policy Program, Gujarat

Mukherji, A. and Kishore, A. (2003) 'Public tubewell transfer in Gujarat: Marketing approach to IMT', Water Policy Research Highlight No. 2, IWMI-TATA Water Policy Program, accessed 5 June 2004 at www.iwmi.org/iwmi-tata

Nabli, M. K. and Nugent, J. B. (1989) 'The New Institutional Economics and its applicability to development', *World Development,* vol 17, no 9, September, pp1333–1347

Narayanamoorthy, A. (2003) Book review: *Tank Irrigation in the 21st Century: What Next?* by K. Palanisami and K. W. Easter, Discovery Publishing House, New Delhi

Neetha, N. (2004) *Alternative Irrigation Institutions in Canal Command: The Case of the Chalakkudy River Diversion Scheme in Kerala*, Water Policy Research No. 16, International Water Management Institute-Tata Water Policy Program, Gujarat

Nikku, B. R. (2002) 'Water user associations in irrigation management: Case of Andhra Pradesh, South India – Opportunities and challenges for collective action', paper presented at the 9th Biennial Conference of the International Association for the Study of Common Property, Victoria Falls, Zimbabwe, 12–17 June

North, D. (1990) *Institutions, Institutional Change and Economic Performance*, Cambridge University Press, Cambridge

North, D. (1995) 'The New Institutional Economics and third world development', in J. Harriss, J. Hunter and C. M. Lewis (eds) *The New Institutional Economics and Third World Development*, Routledge, London

Olson, M. (1965) *The Logic of Collective Action,* Harvard University Press, Cambridge, MA

Ostrom, E. (1990) *Governing the Commons,* Cambridge University Press, Cambridge

Ostrom, E. (1992) *Crafting Institutions for Self-Governing Irrigation Systems,* ICS Press, San Franscisco

Ostrom, E. (1993) 'Design principles in long-enduring irrigation institutions', *Water Resources Research*, vol 29, no 7, pp1907–1912

Ostrom, E., Gardiner, R. and Walker, J. (1994) *Rules, Games and Common-Pool Resources*, University of Michigan Press, Michigan

Palanisami, K. and Balasubramanium, R. (1998) 'Common property and private property: Tanks vs. private wells in Tamil Nadu', *Indian Journal of Agricultural Economics,* vol 53, no 4, pp600–613

Pant, N. (2003) *Key Trends in Groundwater Irrigation in the Eastern and Western Regions of Uttar Pradesh*, IWMI-TATA Water Policy Program, Anand, Gujarat

Pillai, S. (2004) 'Strengthening Panchayati Raj Institutions', *The Financial Express,* 11 September 2004, accessed 27 September 2004 at www.financialexpress.com

Planning Commission (2001) *Report of the Task Force on Panchayat Raj Institutions*

(PRIs), The Planning Commission, New Delhi

Planning Commission (2007) *Report of the Expert Group on Ground Water Management and Ownership,* The Planning Commission, New Delhi

Reddy, V. R. (1998) 'Institutional imperatives and coproduction strategies for large irrigation systems in India', *Indian Journal of Agricultural Economics,* vol 53, no 3, pp440–445

Reddy, V. R. and Reddy, P. P. (2002) 'Water institutions: Is formalisation the answer? (A study of water user associations in Andra Pradesh)', *Indian Journal of Agricultural Economics,* vol 57, no 3, pp519–534

Richards, A. and Singh, N. (2001) *Inter State Water Disputes in India: Institutions and Policies*, Department of Environmental Studies and Department of Economics, University of California, Santa Cruz

Sakthivadivel, R., Gomathinayagam, P. and Shah, T. (2004) 'Rejuvenating irrigation tanks through local institutions', *Economic and Political Weekly*, 31 July, pp3521–3526

Saleth, R. M. and Dinar, A. (2004) *The Institutional Economics of Water: A Cross-Country Analysis of Institutions and Performance*, Edward Elgar, Cheltenham, UK

Satpathy, M., Malik, A., Ganguly, U. and Arya, V. (2002) *Who Should Manage the Tanks? Findings from a Study of Tanks in Tikamgarh, Madhya Pradesh*, International Water Management Institute-Tata Water Policy Program, Gujarat

Sehgal, R. (2004) 'The challenge is to make *Panchayati Raj* institutions vehicles for both governance and delivery', *Info Change Analysis News and Features*, July, Centre for Communication and Development Studies (CCDS), accessed 27 September 2004 at www.infochangeindia.org

Shah, M. (2002) 'Water policy blues', *The Hindu*, 7 June 2002

Shah, T. (2005) 'The New Institutional Economics of India's water policy', paper presented at the international workshop on 'African Water Laws: Plural Legislative Frameworks for Rural Water Management in Africa', 26–28 January, Johannesberg, South Africa

Shah, T. and Raju, K. V. (2001) 'Rethinking rehabilitation: Socio-ecology of tanks and water harvesting in Rajasthan, north-west India', CAPRi Working Paper No. 18, International Food Policy Research Institute, Washington DC

Shah, T., Giordano, M. and Wang, J. (2004) 'Irrigation institutions in a dynamic economy: What is China doing differently from India?', *Economic and Political Weekly,* 31 July, pp3452–3461

Sharma, P. and Sharma, R. C. (2004) 'Groundwater markets across climatic zones: A comparative study of arid and semi-arid zones of Rajasthan', *Indian Journal of Agricultural Economics,* vol 59, no 1, pp138–150

Singh, D. (2002) 'Groundwater markets in fragile environments: Key issues in sustainability', *Indian Journal of Agricultural Economics,* vol 57, no 2, pp180–196

Singh, K. (1994) *Managing Common Pool Resources: Principles and Case Studies,* Oxford University Press, New Delhi

Uphoff, N. (1986) *Local Institutional Development,* Kumarian Press, West Hartford, CT

Vakulabharanam, V. (2004) 'Agricultural growth and irrigation in Telenganal: A review of evidence', *Economic and Political Weekly*, 27 March, pp1421–1426

Vermillion, D. L. (1997) *Impacts of Irrigation Management Transfer: A Review of Evidence*, IIMI, Research Report No. 11, Colombo, Sri Lanka

Wade, R. (1987) 'The management of common property resources: Collective action as an alternative privatisation or state regulation', *Cambridge Journal of Economics,* vol 15, pp95–106

7
Legal Dimensions of Water Resource Management in India: A Review of Legal Instruments Controlling Extractions to Sustainable Limits

Videh Upadhyay

Introduction: Regulatory frameworks and rights for better water management

The role of drafting and enforcing water legislation, regulatory frameworks and water rights is increasingly seen to be central in meeting the challenge of water mismanagement the world over. There are reports by the United Nations identifying both the need 'to strengthen the enabling role of the government to enact and enforce water legislation' and 'to strengthen local water management and service capacities' as being among the paramount strategies that are critical in promoting and facilitating sustainable water development and management (UN Secretary General, 2001). Perceptive observers in India also advocate a clutch of instruments in law and rights for better water management, including: (a) a water law and regulatory framework for coordinated action for sustainable water resources management; (b) treating water as an economic good by pricing water resource as well as services, especially outside lifeline uses, to reflect its scarcity value so that it is efficiently used and allocated to high value uses; (c) creation of water rights, preferably tradable, by instituting a system of water withdrawal permits; and (d) participatory water resource management with involvement of women so that 'water becomes everybody's business' (Shah and Van Koppen, 2006).[1]

There has also been ever-increasing enthusiasm – and more so through the last few years – on the need to replace 'government oriented centralized supply-driven rural water programs' with 'people oriented, decentralized and demand driven water programs'. Together with this there are strong voices articulating the need for 'Integrated Water Resources Management' across the country. Indeed, policy documents and discourse in official reports speaking of the need and significance of integrated resource management are increasing by the day (Ministry of Water Resources, 2003). While it is true that the government policies have to date emphasized integrated resource management, it is notable that there has been little reflection of these pronouncements in the law and in this sense one may add that there is a law and policy disconnect on integrated water resource management (Upadhyay, 2007). In realizing policy mandates for an integrated approach, legal regimes also need to press for structural changes.[2] The present chapter aims to show the legal and regulatory dimensions of some of these policy questions while also offering preliminary insights into related pressing issues. The intent of the chapter is to review the range of legal instruments that seek to control water extractions such that they remain within sustainable limits. Special attention is given to those instruments available at the state level with particular emphasis on the extant water law in Andhra Pradesh and Maharashtra. In addition, I briefly address some of the issues relating to water law in Gujarat.

Water and the Constitution of India: States' jurisdiction, mandate for local bodies and water rights

States' legislative competence on water and obligation to devolve

Under the Constitution of India, water is a state subject.[3] This means that the state legislatures are competent to legislate on 'Water, that is to say, water supplies, irrigation, and canals, drainage and embankments, water storage and water power'.[4] The states of the Indian Union thus have exclusive power to regulate ground water. It has been rightly pointed out that 'looking to the diversity of the problems and corresponding solutions across different states, the constitutional framework appears sound as it enables legal solutions on a region specific basis' (Ishwara Bhat, 2004).

While the legislative competence to enact laws rest with states, the 73rd Amendment of the Constitution has also cast a constitutional imperative on all state governments to come up with appropriate laws detailing meaningful democratic devolution of functions, functionaries and funds to the rural and urban local bodies, i.e. the *Panchayats* and the municipalities. Specifically, it empowers states to endow *Panchayats* with such powers and authority to enable them to function as institutions of self-government and goes on to list 'Water Management', 'Minor Irrigation' and 'Watershed Development' as subjects under the jurisdiction of *Panchayats*.[5] It is useful to keep in mind this constitutional mandate while reading the discussion that follows on legal instruments on water management.

Human right to water and limits to right over 'subsoil water'

A most significant aspect while discussing water under the Indian Constitution is that the 'right to pollution-free water' and the 'right of access to water' have been read by the Supreme Court and the High Courts as an integral part of the right to life under Article 21 of the Constitution of India.[6] The commission that reviewed the Constitution of India recently also recommended that a new article in the Constitution be inserted thus: 'Every person shall have the right: (a) to safe drinking water.' The recommendation may be seen as saying in plain terms what the higher courts have been upholding in similar words in the last few years. In this sense it can be seen as only recognizing a pre-existing right, not creating a new one! (National Commission to Review the Working of the Constitution, 2002)[7]

A more relevant pronouncement for the immediate purposes of this chapter is that of the High Court of Karnataka, which has specifically interpreted 'the right to have subsoil water for irrigation and business purposes' in the context of the right to life under the Constitution of India. The relevant part of the interpretation is worth quoting in full:

> *In a developing country like India, no citizen can claim absolute right over the natural resources ignoring the claims of other citizens. It is true that life without water cannot be conceived. But, it is equally true that water resources being limited, its use has to be regulated and restricted in the larger interests of the society and for the welfare of the human beings. We are, therefore, of the opinion that the right under Article 21, which is available to all the citizens, can be held at the most to have water for drinking purposes, as, admittedly, without it, the life cannot be enjoyed at all. However, the right to have water for irrigation purposes cannot be stretched to the extent of bringing it within the ambit of Article 21 of the Constitution of India. The right to have subsoil water for irrigation and business purposes may at the most amount to a right conferred under Article 300A of the Constitution or a statutory right bestowed upon the citizens under any statute incorporated in accordance with the provisions of law. We are of the opinion that even without a right to draw subsoil water for irrigation and business purposes, a person can enjoy his life to the extent it has been intended to be protected by Article 21 of the Constitution of India.*[8]

The above observations of the Court on the limits to drawing subsoil water for irrigation and business purposes serve as a useful backdrop for discussing in some detail the existing national legal context on ground-water regulation and management in India today.

National legal context on ground-water regulation and management

From private ownership to state as trustee of ground water

Under the Indian legal system ground water is considered an easement connected to the land.[9] Thus, traditionally, the owner of land has an unrestricted right to use the ground water beneath it. The Indian Easements Act, 1882 points to 'the right of every owner of land to collect and dispose within his own limits of all water under the land which does not pass in a defined channel and all water on its surface which does not pass in a defined channel' (Indian Easements Act, 1882). The use of the words 'collect and dispose' seems to suggest that there is an unrestricted right to extract ground water from under one's land. This then leads to a general understanding from the existing legal regime that, while surface water is a state property, ground water belongs to the land owner.

The above legal position, however, is not absolute and it is not feasible to take a simplistic view that ground water by law is the property of the owner of the land above. All over the world various instruments for regulation of ground-water prospecting, extraction and use are evolving with the backing of the law. There is a growing perception that ground water is public property and that only user rights accrue to the owners of overlying lands. Thus, governmental assertions of control can accrue from statutory vesting in the state of superior user rights or in the state as 'public trust' in the resources on behalf of the people. Furthermore, it can also accrue from the pronouncements of the court of law, as with 'public trust doctrine', developed and adopted by the Courts (Burchi, unpublished).

In this context the High Court of Andhra Pradesh in an important recent verdict held that 'Deep Underground Water' is the property of the state under the doctrine of Public Trust.[10] The holder of land has only a user right towards the drawing of water in tube-wells. Thus, neither his action nor his activity can in any way harm his neighbours and any 'such act would not violate Article 21 of the Constitution'. In another well-known 'Coca-Cola Case' involving centrally the question of the power of the *Panchayats* to control and regulate ground water in their territorial jurisdictions, the High Court of Kerala also held in clear terms that 'the underground water belongs to the public'. The state and its instrumentalities should act as trustees of this great wealth. The state has a duty to protect ground water against excessive exploitation and the inaction of the state in this regard is tantamount to infringement of the right to life of the people guaranteed under Article 21 of the Constitution of India.[11]

The nature of state obligation stemming from the legal position, as laid out above by the High Courts, is that 'Deep Underground Water is the property of the state under the doctrine of Public Trust' and that the 'State should act as trustee of the great wealth of underground water'. These matters deserve closer scrutiny. The Supreme Court of India, while adopting the public trust doctrine as part of Indian jurisprudence, has held that: 'The state is the trustee of all natural resources which are by nature meant for public use and enjoyment ... The state as a trustee is under the legal duty to protect the natural resources.'[12] In the year 2006 separate cases made clear that the above represents 'an articulation of the doctrine from the angle of the affirmative duties of the State with regard to public trust'. This approach is important for all those searching for greater state responsibility and enforcement of sustainable water use and is succinctly articulated by Sax (1970) thus:

> *Formulated from a negatory angle, the doctrine does not exactly prohibit the alienation of the property held as a public trust. However, when the state holds a resource that is freely available for the use of the public, it provides for a high degree of judicial scrutiny upon any action of the Government, no matter how consistent with the existing legislations, that attempts to restrict such free use. To properly scrutinize such actions of the Government, the Courts must make a distinction between the government's general obligation to act for the public benefit, and the special, more demanding obligation which it may have as a trustee of certain public resources.* (Sax, 1970)

The legal position as it is evolving should make clear that the government of the day both has an obligation and is empowered to regulate ground water in the public interest. It can thus legislate to restrict the duration of the groundwater exploitation permits, limit the amount of ground water used and lay down spacing norms between wells and water sources, among others. Even in areas where the rule of private ownership of ground water by the landowner would apply, it is empowered to declare areas as 'Groundwater Conservation Areas' or 'Water Scarcity Areas' or 'Over-Exploited Watersheds', whereupon the state can set stringent requirements and norms. In fact this is the way some states in India have adopted specific ground-water laws. However, before we examine closely the nature of regulation by some of those states, a brief overview of the proposed Central Ground Water Bill and the nature and role of the Central Ground Water Authority is in order.

The proposed model bill of the Union government on ground water

With a view to regulating ground-water resources, the government of India first formulated a draft model bill in 1970. This was subsequently revised in 1992, 1996 and 2005. Some of the salient features of this bill, as it stood before the 2005 amendment, were identified by a Commission of the Union Ministry of Water Resources itself as follows:

- The state governments were to acquire powers to restrict the construction of ground-water abstraction structures (including wells, bore wells, tube-wells, etc.) by individuals or communities for all uses except that of drinking water in any area declared as a notified area based on a report from the Ground Water Authority of State.

- For discharging the various functions to be acquired by the government under the legislation, a Ground Water Authority was to be constituted by each state.
- Applications for sinking wells for purposes other than domestic use were to be considered by the Ground Water Authority keeping in view the purpose for which water was to be used, the existence of other competitive users, the availability of ground water, and any other relevant factors.
- Persons or organizations desirous of taking up the business of sinking wells/tube-wells were required to register with the Ground Water Authority. The authority was also to be vested with the power to cancel any permits, registrations or licences issued by them.
- The Authority was to be provided with complete legal support to enforce the various provisions of the legislation. The civil courts were to be barred from granting injunctions on any decision taken by the Authority (Ministry of Water Resources, 1999).

One important chapter was added to the model bill through an amendment in 2005. The amendment introduced the chapter on 'Rainwater Harvesting for Ground Water Recharge' and had the following specific provision, among others:

> *To improve the groundwater situation, the Authority may identify the recharge worthy areas in the State and issue necessary guidelines for adoption of rain water harvesting for groundwater recharge in these areas. In rural areas, watershed management to facilitate groundwater recharge may be encouraged through community participation. The Authority may give appropriate directions to the concerned departments of the State/UT Government to include Rain Water Harvesting in all developmental schemes falling under notified areas. In urban areas, falling in notified areas, the Authority may issue directives for constructing appropriate rain water harvesting structures in all residential, commercial and other premises having an area of 100m² or more in a manner prescribed within the stipulated period, failing which the Authority may get such rain water harvesting structure constructed and recover the cost incurred along with a penalty as may be prescribed.*

In addition to having a hand in the model bill, the central level of the Ministry of Environment and Forest, Government of India, constituted the Central Ground Water Authority (CGWA) as an 'Authority' under the Environment Protection Act, 1986. The intention was that the CGWA was to regulate overexploitation of underground water in the country. The circumstances leading to the birth of this Authority are detailed in Box 7.1.

Box 7.1 *Coming of the Central Ground Water Authority through intervention of the Supreme Court*

The Supreme Court of India has held that prima facie the Constitution (Article 253) and provision of the Environment Protection Act, 1986 (EPA) empowers the centre to regulate ground-water exploitation. These observations were made by the Apex Court on an application before it whereby the Court also directed the Union Ministry of Environment and Forests to constitute the Central Ground Water Board as an Authority under Section 3 (3) of the EPA. (See *M. C. Mehta* vs *Union of India*, 1997 (11) SCC 312.)

In pursuance of the above order of the Supreme Court the Ministry of Environment and Forest, Government of India, constituted the Central Ground Water Authority (CGWA) as an 'Authority' under the EPA to regulate overexploitation of underground water in the country. Specifically, CGWA was required to regulate indiscriminate boring and withdrawal of ground water and to issue necessary regulatory directions in this regard. The authority exercises its power of issuing directions under the EPA. (Section 5 read with Section 3(2) of EPA.) In addition, it can also resort to the penal provisions contained in the said Act (Sections 15 to 21). The Authority functions under the administrative control of the Union Ministry of Water Resources and has jurisdiction over the whole of India. The CGWA has since drafted 'Environment Protection Rules for Development and Protection of Ground Water' which were also circulated to all states for their comments before its notification. (As per the National Commission for Integration Water Resources Development Plan; Government of India 1999.)

The evidence presented in Box 7.1 shows that the CGWA has been established to regulate overexploitation of underground water in the country. While later sections show that it is the state laws that are at the 'business end' of regulating ground-water extractions and use, the CGWA continues to issue guidelines on the matter and a typical example of such guidelines recently issued by CGWA is presented in Box 7.2.

Box 7.2 *Revised policy guidelines by Central Ground Water Authority issued in August 2008 'For construction of tube wells/bore wells for drinking and domestic purposes'*

I For notified areas:

- i Only one tube well is allowed for construction in the premises to meet the drinking and domestic purposes. No tube well/bore well will be constructed, if any working tube well already exists. In case the existing well has become non-functional and is to be replaced, it should be converted to a recharge well, if possible, or properly sealed and no water to be pumped from it.
- ii The person(s) intending to construct a new tube well will intimate the authorized officer/advisory committee 10 days in advance along with the name and address of the drilling agency that will undertake construction of the tube well.
- iii The maximum diameter of the tube well should be restricted to 100mm and the capacity of the pump should not exceed 1h.p.
- iv Concurrent with the construction of the tube well, the owner of the tube well shall undertake installation of the rainwater harvesting system in the premises.
- v The water from the tube well/bore well will be used exclusively for drinking and domestic purposes only.
- vi All details of the drilling such as formations encountered, the depth and diameter of the constructed tube well, type of pipes used in tube well, yield of bore well/tube well and ground-water quality etc., shall be kept for the record.
- vii Any violation to the above conditions will attract legal action under section 15 of the Environment Protection Act, 1986.

II For non-notified areas:

Since there is no regulation in force in non-notified areas, there is no restriction for construction of tube wells for drinking and domestic purposes. (Central Ground Water Authority, 2008)

Participatory ground-water regulation and the new national policy climate

As it is almost four decades since the first draft of the 'model bill', it is evident that the states have shown virtually no inclination to adopt the draft model bill and the draft rules (see Box 7.2 above).[13] Among the major reasons behind the proposed Central Ground Water Bill not taking shape in law, and most states not adopting the bill, has been the concern that a 'licensing type control' under the law could lead to widespread corruption on one hand and alienation of the people on the other (Dubash, 2002).[14]

The bill, as it stands today, is also seen as being against the dominant thinking of water management inasmuch as this presently emphasizes decentralized and participatory decision making. Perhaps the strongest reflection of this thinking from within the official circles came from a Working Group on Legal, Institutional and Financing Aspects constituted by the Union Ministry of Water Resources. It suggested that the best option is to introduce the participatory process in ground-water management, whereby the role of the state could be that of facilitator and the role of the user organization/*Panchayat* an implementing regulatory agency. In this context the Working Group specifically suggested that in 'dark' and 'overexploited areas':

- *Gram Sabha* as a whole may decide on ground-water management; where villages are large, the *Sabha* could be formed for smaller areas. ('*Gram Sabha*' is a term in Hindi and refers to 'Village Assembly'. Village Assembly comprises all the adults in village who have a right to vote.)
- The use of ground water for irrigation and sale of ground water should be approved by the village community.
- The central and state ground-water officials may be required to extend full cooperation, rendering technical service and advice to the village communities (Ministry of Water Resources, 1999).

In the context of a possible greater role of the *Gram Sabha* and the village community in ground-water management, it is also noteworthy that the bulk of the 'Rural Water Supply Programme' in India (more than 85 per cent) is ground-water-based. When it comes to rural water supply a nationwide scheme, namely *Swajaldhara*, has already been launched in this decade. The scheme seeks to put in place a people-oriented, decentralized and demand-driven water management regime across the country. In doing so it aims to utilize the *Panchayat Raj* Institutions (PRIs) while empowering them in the process.[15] Close on the heels of *Swajaldhara*, another national-level scheme for watershed development was also launched called the '*Haryali*' where, again, *Panchayats* were the agents of implementation. In the context of watershed development it is arguably logical that, since the watershed development leads to greater recharge of ground water, the additional water resource should belong to the watershed community. On the basis of this logic, a recent technical group of the Union Ministry of Water Resources recommended that the watershed community must be involved in regulating ground water (Ministry of Water Resources: Subgroup on Micro Watershed Development, 1999). However, this also needs to be considered against other recommendations by another subgroup of the same Union Ministry. In this case it was argued that the *Gram Sabha* had a role in ground-water management. As noted earlier, in 'dark' and 'overexploited areas' the *Gram Sabha* as a whole may decide on ground-water management and the use of ground water for irrigation and sale should be approved by the village community. When seen together these reports from the Ministry of Water Resources themselves underline the imperative to develop clearer and satisfactory functional relationships between the watershed community, the *Gram Sabha* and the *Gram Panchayat.* In addition, much of the rhetoric emanating from the new schemes, the recommendations of the various Working Groups of the Ministry of Water Resources of the government of India and, indeed, the larger water policy climate illustrates the national commitment to bolster the critical role of users/village groups in ground-water use and recharge. How much of this 'commitment' is actually reflected in the various state water laws is another issue, and one which is specifically considered in the next section of this chapter.

State legal context on ground-water regulation and management

Only a few states in India have enacted specific ground-water legislation. These laws apply in restricted areas, have limited purposes and generally suffer from a low level of implementation. A review of the extant state water laws in India from several states shows that most tend to include: (a) restriction of the depth of wells/bore wells/tube-wells, and (b) declaration of ground-water conservation and protection zones, especially around sources of drinking water. The implementation of those provisions, including all actions to be taken under these Acts, generally rests with the District Collector with no specific role therein for village/community-level institutions.

Some detailed examples of these laws may be noted here. Gujarat amended its Irrigation Act in 1976, requiring landowners to apply for a licence to extract ground water from below a depth of 45m. The Regional Canal Officer (RCO) was vested with the sole power of granting or denying a licence. The amendment applied to only a few districts and even where it was applied it was not possible for the RCO to supervise all districts.[16] The state of Madhya Pradesh also came up with a specific law, namely the Madhya Pradesh Peya Jal Prirakshan Adhiniyam, 1986 that provided for regulation of digging of tube-wells in order to maintain the water supply to the public for domestic purposes. The Collector has the power and authority under this Act to grant or refuse permission for the digging of tube-wells. Contravention of the provisions of this Act could lead to imprisonment for up to two years.[17]

The Karnataka Ground Water (Regulation for protection of sources of drinking water) Act, 1999 was enacted with regulatory measures that included the following: (i) sinking a well for the purpose of extracting or drawing water within a distance of 500m from a public drinking water source without obtaining permission of the appropriate authority i.e. the Deputy Commissioner is prohibited; (ii) the appropriate authority, in times of water scarcity may declare an area to be a water scarcity area for such period as may be specified in the order, but not exceeding one year at a time; (iii) upon declaration of any area as a water scarcity area, the appropriate authority may order for restricting or prohibiting extraction for any purpose where such well is within 500m of the public drinking water source; (iv) the appropriate authority on the advice of the technical officer may declare a watershed as overexploited; (v) the appropriate authority shall have powers to prohibit sinking of wells in over-exploited watersheds; (vi) if the appropriate authority is satisfied that any existing well in the area of an overexploited watershed is already affecting any public drinking water source it may prohibit the extraction of water from such well during the period from February to July every year.

The Kerala Ground Water (Control and Regulation) Act, 2002 also creates a State Ground Water Authority in the state of Kerala which is 'empowered to notify areas for the control and regulation of groundwater development in the State'. Any person desiring to dig a well or to convert the existing well into a pumping well, for his own or social purposes in the notified area, shall submit an application before the Authority for the granting of a permit. The applicant shall not proceed with any activity connected with such digging unless a permit has been granted by the Authority. The Act further lays down a procedure for registration of existing wells of the notified area and adds that no person shall, without the permission of the Authority, dig a well for any purpose within 30m of any drinking water source from where water is pumped for public purposes.

Box 7.3 *Factors taken into account by state authorities before granting/refusing permit for water extraction under state laws*

Most of the state laws have similar provisions saying that in granting or refusing a permit the appropriate state authority shall have regard to:

(a) the purpose or purposes for which water is to be used;
(b) the existence of other competitive users;
(c) the availability of water;
(d) quality of ground water to be drawn with reference to proposed usage;
(e) spacing of ground-water structures keeping in view the purpose for which water is to be used;
(f) minimum distance of 200m in case of shallow well and 300m in case of tube-well from the existing source of water supply scheme or irrigation scheme, as the case may be;
(g) long-term ground-water level behaviour; and
(h) any other factor relevant thereto.

Source: Himachal Pradesh Ground Water (Regulation and Control of Development and Management) Act, 2005; West Bengal Ground Water Resources (Management, Control and Regulation) Act, 2005; Kerala Ground Water (Control and Regulation) Act, 2002

The West Bengal Ground Water Resources (Management, Control and Regulation) Act, 2005 was enacted 'to manage, control and regulate indiscriminate extraction of groundwater in West Bengal' and create an authority at the state level known as the West Bengal State Level Ground Water Resources Development Authority. To enable the State Level Authority 'to perform its functions and exercise its powers efficiently' the government also established the District Level Ground Water Resources Development Authority at the district level in the state. Under the Act no user shall sink any well for extracting or using ground water without obtaining a permit issued by the State Level Authority or the District Level Authority. The District Level Authority shall have power to issue a permit for sinking a well for extraction or use of ground water at a rate not exceeding 50m^3 per hour from each well under intimation to the State Level Authority. For offences a fine up to 10,000 rupees is provided for under the Act.

The Himachal Pradesh Ground Water (Regulation and Control of Development and Management) Act, 2005 establishes the Himachal Pradesh Ground Water Authority at the state level. If the Authority feels that it is necessary or expedient in the public interest to control and/or regulate the extraction of ground water in any form in any area, it shall advise the state government to declare any such area to be a notified area and the state government, after examining the advice of the Authority, may declare such an area as a notified area under the Act. Any user of ground water desiring to sink a well within a notified area, for any purpose, shall apply to the Authority for grant of a permit, and shall not proceed with any activity connected with such sinking unless a permit has been granted by the Authority. If any user of ground water sinks, constructs or uses a well in contravention of the provisions of the Act imprisonment for a term which may extend to six months is also provided for.

There are useful additional provisions under this Act, including that every user of ground water in a notified area shall pay to the state government a royalty for extraction of ground water at such rates and in such manner as may be prescribed. However, a user of ground water who irrigates less than one hectare of land, whether owned or leased or both, shall be exempted from payment of royalties. Further, the Authority may, in order to improve the ground-water situation, identify the areas of ground-water recharge and issue guidelines for adoption of rain-water harvesting for ground-water recharge in such areas. On this aspect the Authority may issue directions to the concerned departments of the state government to include rain-water harvesting in all developmental schemes within notified areas.

Against the broad legal setting across different states in India, it is useful to closely examine the experience of some of these states in more detail and this is done in the next section.

Controlling extractions to sustainable limits: Mapping the experience of devising legal instruments in Maharashtra and Andhra Pradesh

Against the backdrop of the brief discussion on the various legal instruments aimed at controlling water extractions to sustainable limits it is useful to map the legislative experience on the subject at the state level more closely. This is done in just a couple of states where there have been recent attempts to introduce new legal mechanisms for sustainable water management. The states of Maharashtra and Andhra Pradesh are specifically reviewed. The discussion begins first with experience in Maharashtra.

Searching for effective ground-water management: Experience in Maharashtra

In addition to the states mentioned in the section above, Maharashtra has also separately enacted a law for ground-water regulation and management – The Maharashtra Groundwater (Regulation of Drinking Water Purposes) Act, 1993 (hereinafter GWA). The Act seeks to regulate the exploitation of ground water for the protection of ground-water resources. The GWA seeks to prevent sinking of any well within 500m of a public drinking water source, regulates extraction of water from any well within 1km of the public drinking water source in a declared water scarcity area and prevents sinking of a well in a declared and 'overexploited' watershed. The declaration of an overexploited watershed or a water scarcity area is to be done by the 'appropriate authority' which is the Collector/Deputy Collector of the District. Contravention of the provisions of the Act could entail payment of compensation as well as imprisonment for up to six months.

It is also useful to assess the state of implementation of the GWA and findings of one of the committees constituted by the government of Maharashtra to investigate this matter. The government of Maharashtra appointed a high-powered committee under Shri D. M. Sukhthankar for an in-depth study of the situation in respect of operation, management and maintenance of the water supply schemes in the state. According to the Committee only 10 per cent of water withdrawal in scarcity areas is 'declared' – a declaration that is required to be made as per Section 4 of the GWA, 1993. The committee also recorded that during 1996–2000, action to restrict water withdrawal in scarcity areas, as per Section 5, was taken in only 15 cases. Similarly, under Section 7, which places restrictions on sinking wells in overexploited watersheds, action was taken in only 16 cases. Action under the GWA was thus very limited, to say the least (Government of Maharashtra, 2001).

The nature of minimal implementation of GWA prompted the state to rethink ground-water management and regulation in the state. The Suktankar committee itself recommended in 2001 the creation of 'local watershed management units' (LWMU) to collect information on water usage in the watershed, implement the ground-water regulations and resolve water usage disputes. The LWMU, according to the committee, should ideally comprise local stakeholders and users and this body should be statutorily created. In the context of the GWA, the State Government Resolution dated 14 February 2002 tried to address the problem of management of ground water in greater detail while admitting that, even though the Collectors of the Districts were empowered to protect the drinking water sources through the provisions of the GWA, 'it has not helped much'. The alternative resolution required the Village Water Supply Committee – as a committee of the *Gram Panchayat* – to compile all the relevant information on the water resources and further insisted that the *Gram Sabha* prepare a draft plan for the use of available water in the village. The *Gram Sabha* was also given the power and the discretion to invite the District/Taluk Level Officers of the Zila Parishad and Ground Water Survey and Development Agency (GSDA) if their guidance was necessary. Further, the agency for the implementation of the action plan and the programme was to be decided by the *Gram Sabha*. This initiative was a clear departure from the typical 'command and control' model that was envisaged by the GWA and rules in the state. It basically attempted to address concerns about overexploitation by merely empowering the district officials through a law to prevent ground-water pollution and depletion. Arguably, these measures seem destined to not help, on the one hand, and to alienate many rural people on the other.

In order to achieve state-wide applicability of the government resolution, the Water Supply and Sanitation Department, Government of Maharashtra, also formulated comprehensive legislation for ground water around this time. The legislation sought to include provisions for *Gram Sabha* to manage ground water at the local level and for the establishment of District Ground Water Authorities (DGA) under the chairmanship of the District Collector.[18] However, the draft in that form did not take shape as law.

However, soon there was to be another law that is likely to regulate ground water in significant ways in the future. This is the Maharashtra Water Resources Regulatory Authority Act, 2005 (MWRRA). The provisions of the Act seek to strengthen the control of the state over all water resources. Section 11 of this Act defines roles, responsibilities and powers of the Authority which is to be set up under the Act. It empowers the Authority, inter alia, to make a state water-use plan, assign priority for use of water, determine water allocations to various users, prevent people not allotted water allocations from using it, regulate owners of lift irrigation equipment (after five years from the date of coming into force); it also requires all drilling contractors to register, and requires prior permission before drilling new tube-wells. The provisions of the Act are enforceable either in watersheds declared as overexploited (this declaration is of a permanent nature) or if a specific locale (generally defined as a micro watershed) is notified as scarcity-affected in a particular year.[19] These provisions provide the basis to substantially regulate ground water though the precedence of the Groundwater Regulation (Drinking Water) Act and is accepted explicitly the MWRRA Act. More specifically, these documents contend that 'the Authority shall abide by the relevant provisions of the Maharashtra Groundwater Regulation (Drinking Water Purposes) Act, 1993' (Section 12 (8), Maharashtra Water Resources Regulatory Authority Act, 2005).

Some of the earlier thinking on empowering the *Gram Panchayat* and the *Gram Sabha* in the state by vesting in them powers for regulation of ground water has been restored. Rules made under the MWRAA require that the *Gram Panchayat* (GP) must be cognisant of violations and make a written complaint to the Block Development Officer (BDO) should a violation be observed. However, there are observers who have seen problems, both with the mechanism envisaged under the Act and the capacity of the *Gram Panchayat* to deliver the goods. The effect of the provision under the rules is that, even when the Scarcity Department or the geologist makes an assessment that a violation of the Act occurs, nothing can be done unless the *Panchayat* makes a complaint (Phansalkar and Kher, 2006).[20]

Legislative experience of ground-water management in Andhra Pradesh

The state of Andhra Pradesh had a law similar to the Maharashtra Groundwater (Regulation of Drinking Water Purposes) Act, 1993. This was the Andhra Pradesh Ground Water (Regulation for Drinking Water Purposes) Act, 1996. In terms of the legislative mechanism that it created, this Act fell into the same pattern as the Maharashtra 1993 Act. However, unlike the Maharashtra Act, which is very much an existing law, the Andhra Pradesh Act, 1996 has been repealed and replaced by the Andhra Pradesh Water, Land and Trees Act, enacted in 2002.

The Andhra Pradesh Water, Land and Trees Act, 2002 has a large and ambitious mandate. The preamble of the Act points out that it aims to 'promote water conservation, and tree cover and regulate the exploitation and use of ground and surface water for protection and conservation of water sources, land and environment'. Under the Act the state government has constituted an authority called the Andhra Pradesh State Water, Land and Trees Authority. The Act also notes that the government, may also, in consultation with the state Authority, constitute by notification authorities at district and *mandal* (i.e. block) levels.[21] The functions of the Andhra Pradesh State Water, Land and Trees Authority include the following: promotion of water conservation and enhancement of tree cover in the state; regulation of exploitation of ground and surface water in the state; making regulations for the functioning of the authorities at district and *mandal* level constituted under the Act; advising the government on the legislative and administrative measures to be taken from time to time for the conservation of natural resources; advising on economic measures to be taken by the government as incentives or disincentives relating to taxes, levies, fees or other charges to promote conservation of natural resources; and advising on strengthening public participation in conservation of natural resources from time to time in such a way that equity in access to water in different basins, sub-basins and regions in the state is maintained (Section 6, Andrah Pradesh Water, Land and Trees Act, 2002).

After declaring that all ground-water resources in the state shall be regulated by the Authority, the Act lays down that 'the owners of all the wells including those which are not fitted with power-driven pumps and water bodies in the state, shall register their wells/water bodies with the Authority' (Section 8, Andrah Pradesh Water, Land and Trees Act, 2002). Under the Act there is also a prohibition on water pumping by individuals, groups or private organizations in any particular area, 'if such water pumping in such area is likely to cause damage to the level of groundwater or cause deterioration or damage to natural resources or environment' (Section 9, Andrah Pradesh Water, Land and Trees Act, 2002). Further, the Act provides that to preserve the supply of the requisite quantity of water for drinking purposes from the public drinking water source, no person shall sink any well in the vicinity of a public drinking water source within a distance of 250m. Other provisions in the area of ground-water management include registration of all the bore wells with concerned revenue authorities at the *mandal* level; prior permission for digging of new bore wells from revenue authorities, and registration of all the rigs with the government.

The government of Andrah Pradesh amended the 2002 Act in 2004 and rules were brought out for effective implementation of the Act.[22] The most important features of the recent amendment are the introduction of a single-window approach for speedy clearance of the applications for new bore wells and insuring all new bore wells to assist the farmers wherever bore wells fail.[23] It should also be noted that the state government has designated the Commissioner, Rural Development as the Administrator for the purpose of the Act. However, there have been concerns about the administration of various provisions within the Act. It has been pointed out that 'much as the government and the well-meaning citizens may wish implementation of the recently amended Andhra Pradesh Water, Land and Trees Act (WLATA), aimed at regulating and spacing bore wells to check overexploitation of ground water, it seems to have hit roadblocks, with grossly inadequate [number of] hydrogeologists and geophysicists, ill-equipped machinery, lack of database and uncooperative rig owners' (Venkateshwarlu, 2004).

A notable point is that there has been no attempt made under the Andhra Pradesh Water, Land and Trees Act, 2002 to vest powers with the *Gram Panchayat* or the *Gram Sabha*, as envisaged in Maharashtra.[24]

Towards better irrigation management: Legally empowered water user associations in states

The focus of this chapter to date has been on the nature and experience of various legal instruments regulating ground-water extraction and use. However, in addition to new and evolving laws in the area of ground-water management, there is another area which has seen a flurry of recent laws which have direct implications for better surface water management, especially around canal networks in the country. These laws relate to the creation of water user associations (WUAs) under the policy of 'participatory irrigation management' across different states in India.[25] While some details on this issue were provided by Ananda (Chapter 6), a brief review of the legal regime under which the WUAs are mandated is added here for completeness.

Over the last two decades there have been significant attempts to involve farmers – the beneficiaries of the irrigation canals – in operation and management of the irrigation systems in India, as in other parts of the developing world. Farmers' direct involvement in irrigation system management through farmer associations or UWAs is now almost universally seen as a lasting response to systemic inadequacies in irrigation. It is now believed that where the state failed in the past, farmers will not, and that operation and management of irrigation systems by farmers themselves can lead to substantial improvements. The result has been that state after state in India, as in other parts of the world, came up with policies and then laws supporting 'participatory irrigation management (PIM)'.[26] In a number of states, including the states of Andhra Pradesh, Orrisa, Madhya Pradesh, Rajasthan, Kerala, Karnataka, Tamil Nadu, Maharashtra and Chhattisgarh the law enabling farmers' participation in irrigation management has come via the enactment of specific 'farmers' participation in management of irrigation systems' Acts.[27] Typically, all these laws empower the 'project authority' to delineate every command area under each of the irrigation systems 'on a hydraulic basis which may be administratively viable' and declare it as a water users' area. Every water users' area is to be divided into territorial constituencies. The laws then provide for establishing a democratically elected WUA for every water users' area. Every WUA is to consist of members who comprise all water users who are landowners in such water users' areas.[28]

One striking aspect of India's PIM programmes is that relatively little attention appears to have been given to the specification of water rights. This has meant that the governments' rights to water are largely unchallenged, while its obligations to deliver water to WUAs are rarely legally binding (Mosse, 2003).[29] A closer look at the various state laws creating WUAs reveals that legislation rarely considers or specifies the rights of the WUAs or of the individual water user. However, there are two sets of rules developed under two different laws which make explicit mention of the rights and responsibilities of the WUAs. These two rules are: the Andhra Pradesh Farmers' Management of Irrigation Systems Rules, 2003 and the recently notified Chhattisgarh Sinchai Prabandhan Me Krishkon Ki Bhagidari Niyam, 2006. These rules explicitly discuss both the rights and responsibilities of the WUAs as well as the rights and responsibilities of each of the water users within these associations. This (perhaps mistakenly) gives the impression that under these rules there is an equal emphasis on both the individual and the group rights.[30]

There is a specific set of rights under these two state rules, mentioned above, that directly impact on sustainable use and extraction of both surface water and ground water. Under the Andhra Pradesh Farmers' Management of Irrigation Systems Rules, 2003 and the Chhattisgarh Sinchai Prabandhan Me Krishkon Ki Bhagidari Niyam, 2006 within the territorial limits of the specific WUA, the WUA has the right to:

(a) participate in planning and designing of micro-irrigation systems;
(b) suggest improvements/modifications in the layout of field channels/field drains to supply water to all the farmers in the command;

(c) plan and promote use of the ground water;
(d) carry out other agro-based activities for economic upliftment of its members;
(e) utilize the canal bunds – as long as such use is not obstructive, or destructive to hydraulic structures – by planting timber, fuel or fruit trees or grass for augmenting the income of the farmers organization; among others.

On closer scrutiny, however, many of these rights amount to little more than a say in management and planning functions and are not rights in the strict legal sense of the term. Given the state of the laws and the state of the irrigation systems in large parts of the country today, it is a moot point as to how much WUAs are actually empowered through the vesting of a range of functions and responsibilities under the laws. For the sake of better water and irrigation management the balance between rights, responsibilities and decision-making expertise requires closer attention in the future.

Concluding remarks

The exclusive private ownership right of the landowner over ground water has given way to increasing attempts to assert public control over ground water in recent times across India. The proposed Central Ground Water Bill and the enactment of specific ground-water laws establish that the basic feature of these legal regimes is to create a permit system and declare special zones where the use of ground water is subject to strict controls. The mechanisms envisaged predominantly use the 'command and control' approach, whereby regulation is sought using licences and permits.

However, as the Maharashtra experience shows, things are beginning to change. User participation is seen as being particularly important for ground-water management, not only in principle but also in terms of strategy. User participation has also been the basis on which several states have come up with specifically created legal regimes that have transferred some responsibilities for irrigation management from government agencies to the WUAs and these have been discussed above. However, the argument for enhanced participation as the only way out of the present problems in water management should also have critical caveats, especially given the situation prevailing today. As a comprehensive study in the context of ground-water management and markets in Gujarat points out: 'Farmers, small and large, invoke the state as the means out of the impending water crisis. However, they do not envisage the state as regulator or facilitator of collective action to limit ground-water use. Instead, they consider it the state's role to enhance supply by providing alternative, surface sources of water. That farmers in this region now look to the state to take over is a sobering sign that North Gujarat farmers do not consider sustainability of ground water to be their concern but that of the state' (Dubash, 2002).

At another level the reasons for the failure of the Central Ground Water Bill have been identified by the working group of the Union Ministry of Water

Resources. This bill advocated a 'licensing type control' that is susceptible to corruption and likely to lead to the alienation of rural people. On the other hand, the main constraints with the half-hearted state laws on ground-water management include: (a) lack of 'clear, meaningful and objectively measurable' definitions of water scarcity; (b) political difficulties facing district authorities charged with its implementation due to strong and influential farmers' lobbies who resist such regulation; (c) lack of awareness among the general public; and (d) lack of capacity and mandate with the State Department's technical body for ground-water survey and development for the requisite policing functions.[31]

The nature of problems in the implementation of the ground-water laws in India points to the need to closely identify and assess the locally water-scarce areas, the need to somehow generate compliance with 'uncomfortable' regulations and for this to look beyond technical state-level 'expert' bodies. Finally, there is also a pressing need to generate awareness among the local populace.[32] Regulation to restrict ground-water usage is invariably unpopular, especially with people owning the land above, but it needs internalization by one and all. Without such restrictions 'the beneficiaries of today may be the losers of tomorrow'.[33]

Notes

1 In addition, in the Indian context from time to time there has been a range of suggestions for resolution of the problem of access to fresh water, including the introduction of a rational water pricing policy, cutting the subsidy on power to curb ground-water over-extraction, lessening government participation in water management and regulating ground-water withdrawals, a massive awareness campaign on the judicious use of water and encouraging widespread rain-water harvesting, among others.

2 To take just one example, it may be easy to say as a policy that 'Water resource development and management shall be planned for a hydrological unit', but it is an open question as to how this approach can be implemented when the existing legal regime is based only on administrative boundaries and does not recognize ecological/hydrological boundaries for water management.

3 The allocation of legislative competence between the Centre and the states is enshrined in Articles 246–254 read with Schedule VII to the Constitution of India.

4 Entry 17 of list II under the Schedule VII of the Constitution of India. This is, however, subject to the power of the Union Parliament to regulate on interstate rivers and river valleys. This is due to the entry in the Union list under Schedule VII of the Constitution of India, which reads thus: 'Regulation and development of interstate rivers and river valleys to the extent to which such regulation and development under the control of the Union is declared by Parliament by Law to be expedient in the public interest.' See Entry 56 of list I under Schedule VII of the Constitution of India.

5 See Schedule XI to the Constitution of India.

6 This has been possible by a liberal and activist interpretation of the fundamental right to life, both by the Supreme Court and the High Court of the country in a series of cases before them.

7 In the context of the right to water the present author had felt that this right is not forcing things on the ground, not forcing the state to reorient its priorities, and not helping the state to set its minimum irreducible goal.

8 See *Venkatagiriyappa* vs *Karnataka Electricity Board, Bangalore and Others*, 1999.

9 Section 4 of the Indian Easement Act, 1882 defines an easement as 'A right which the owner or occupier of certain land possesses, as such, for the beneficial enjoyment of that land, to do and continue to do something, or to prevent and continue to prevent something being done, in or upon, or in respect of certain other land not his own.'

10 *M. P. Rambabu* vs *District Forest Officer*, 2002).

11 *Perumatty Grama Panchayat* vs *State of Kerala*, 2004. The Kerala High Court added: 'The Apex Court has repeatedly held that the right to clean air and unpolluted water forms part of the right to life under Article 21 of the Constitution ... the *Panchayat* and the state are bound to protect ground water from excessive exploitation'.

12 See *M. C. Mehta* vs *Kamal Nath* and *M. I. Builders* vs *Radhey Shyam Sahu*, (1999).

13 The relative absence of legislative action on ground water in fact was the major spur for 'Judicial Activism' through pronouncements of the Supreme Court and the High Courts in this area.

14 Dubash (2002) adds 'The Model Bill is a highly unimaginative document. It rests on mechanisms to control ground-water use through heavy-handed regulation from above, insulates regulatory officials from public scrutiny and provides no scope for information or management feedback from ground-water users.'

15 Notably, the institutional mechanism envisaged by the scheme has a village-level water supply committee as its cornerstone, which would be generating the demand for specific water supply schemes while being responsible for its implementation. The scheme required that the Centre funds the various rural water supply schemes suggested by the *Panchayats* by 90 per cent, the remaining 10 per cent being footed by the *Panchayats* proposing the scheme.

16 The same problem exists with the proposed Draft Ground Water (Regulation) Bill in Rajasthan, which provides for licensing of new bore wells and gives authority to the District Collector to grant or deny permits in this regard. It is argued here too that as the Collector himself would not be able to go into the merits of each case, the *Patwaris* and the *Kanungos* have an incentive to start selling the licences at a premium.

17 Notably, the Act defined and excluded 'domestic purpose' from the licence requirement.

18 The draft law also provided for the intervention of the DGA, either on its own or on the request of *Gram Sabha*.

19 This declaration follows a certain cycle of actions: assessing the ground-water situation after noting the rainfall till 30 September and then preparing a list of the areas (villages) likely to be scarcity affected. The notification has to be made by January. Often this itself is delayed or manipulated (Phansalkar and Kher, 2006).

20 Phansalkar and Kher (2006) add: 'So we have this bizarre situation of the ZP functionary trying to persuade the GP people to make a complaint about a serious problem under its nose! Clearly, since emergency about drinking water scarcity and its serious consequences on law and order have to be avoided, when the GP does not make a complaint and when action can not be taken under the Act, the department in any case has to move to make alternate arrangements.'

21 Section 3, Andhra Pradesh Water, Land and Trees Act, 2002. The Andhra Pradesh State Water, Land and Trees Authority was constituted, see GOMs No. 240, PR & RD Dept, dated 25 June 2002. For effectively implementing the Act, provision was made in GOMs No. 244, PR & RD Dept, dated 26 June 2002 for the constitution of subsidiary Authorities at District and *Mandal* levels.

22 This was done through GOMs No. 339, PR & RD Dept, dated 6 November 2004.

23 The single-window approach under the Act works as follows: the farmers desiring to drill a bore well apply to the Village Secretary/MRO. The *Mandal* Authority (*Tahsildar*) assesses the feasibility of electricity from the APTRANSCO and feasibility of water from the Ground Water Department. When both are feasible, the MRO accords permission for the drilling of a new agricultural bore/tube-well.

24 See Policy Brief on DFID-NRSP Project R8192 'Enabling Rural Poor for Better Livelihood through Improved Natural Resource Management in SAT India', being implemented by CRIDA and BAIF in Mahaboobnagar and Anantapur in Andhra Pradesh and Tumkur district in Karnataka (Central Research Institute for Dry Land Agriculture, 2004). The study added:

> *It was clear from the experience of working with farmers in this project that they do respond to messages of ground-water alert and are willing to adopt more (ground-water) resource-friendly crop options. What is needed is to effect these attitudinal changes on a long-term perspective so that it has a lasting impact on sustainable resource use. Facilitating the communities by providing technical backstopping and networking with developmental agencies, NGOs, village Panchayat and state line departments is very crucial for scaling-up this kind of approach.*

25 Participatory irrigation management refers to the programmes that seek to increase farmers' direct involvement in irrigation canal system management, either as a complement or as a substitute for the state role.

26 Even the Approach to the Eleventh Five-Year Plan (2007–12) attests to this point of view. The Approach to the Eleventh Five-Year Plan argues:

> *Participatory Irrigation Management (PIM) by democratically organized water user associations empowered to set and collect water charges, and retain a substantial part of the collection, would help to maintain field channels, expand irrigated area, distribute water equitably and provide the tail enders their just share of water. Experience in Andhra Pradesh and Gujarat has shown the effectiveness of such PIM. The 11th Plan must expand reliance on PIM on a large scale.* (Government of India Planning Commission, 2006)

27 The specific laws include the Andhra Pradesh Farmers' Management of Irrigation Systems Act, 1997; Madhya Pradesh Sinchai Prabandhan Me Krishkon Ki Bhagidari Adhiniyam, 1999; the Tamil Nadu Farmers' Management of Irrigation System Act, 2000; Kerala Irrigation and Water Conservation Act, 2003; Orrisa Pani Panchayat Act, 2002; Karnataka Irrigation Amendment Act, 2003; Maharashtra Management of Irrigation System by Farmers Act, 2005; and the

Chhattisgarh Sinchai Prabandhan Me Krishkon Ki Bhagidari Adhinyam, 2006.

28 Though there are useful variations from these positions in some states and most notably by the Chhattisgarh Sinchai Prabandhan Me Krishkon Ki Bhagidari Adhinyam, 2006. Typically under the above-mentioned state laws these WUAs are required to
   (a) prepare and implement a warabandi schedule for each irrigation season;
   (b) prepare a plan for the maintenance, extension, improvement, renovation and modernization of irrigation systems;
   (c) regulate the use of water among the various outlets under its area of operation;
   (d) maintain a register of landowners as published by the revenue department;
   (e) monitor flow of water for irrigation;
   (f) resolve the disputes if any, between its members and water users in its area of operation.

29 Mosse (2003) adds: 'The result (of this position on rights) has been that the government may have lost little control over irrigation resources, and arguably, in establishing registered WUAs has retained its rights and also acquired a new mechanism to extend its influence in rural society.'

30 It is important to note that all the laws have sought to vest powers in farmer associations and thus the rights regime needs to evolve conditions under which a group and not an individual can become a right holder so that an entity like a legally constituted water user association can exercise such a right to its advantage.

31 These are the reasons, among others, identified by the Sukhthankar Committee Report, Government of Maharashtra, 2001.

32 'It must be noted that nowhere in India does the obvious need for stopping rapacious exploitation of groundwater enjoy popular recognition and support' (Phansalkar and Kher, 2006). The authors also note that 'people have realized that the state will always take some necessary action to obviate emergencies on drinking water supply. This may involve water supply through tankers for ensuring that people do not die of thirst. Thus they see a real possibility of addressing their problem of drinking water without taking the unpleasant step of complaining against violation of the Act by some farmer.'

33 See Karnataka High Court in *Venkatagiriyappa* vs *Karnataka Electricity Board, Bangalore and Others*, 1999.

References

Burchi, S., 'National Regulations for Groundwater: Options, Issues and Best Practices', unpublished script available from the author

Central Research Institute for Dry Land Agriculture (2004) 'Enabling Rural Poor for Better Livelihood through Improved Natural Resource Management in SAT India', *Policy Brief*, CRIDA and Karnataka, Hyderabad, India

Dubash, N. K. (2002) *Tubewell Capitalism – Groundwater Development and Agrarian Change in Gujarat*, Oxford University Press, New Delhi

Government of Maharashtra (2001) *The Findings of the Sukhtanker Committee Report*, Government of Maharashtra, India

Ishwara Bhat, P. (2004) 'A comparative study of ground water law and policy in South Asia', *Indian Juridical Review*, vol 1

Ministry of Water Resources (1999) *Report of the National Commission for*

Integrated Water Resources Development Plan, Government of India

Ministry of Water Resources (1999) *Report of the Sub-Group on Micro Watershed Development*, Government of India

Ministry of Water Resources (2003) *Vision for Integrated Water Resources Development and Management*, Government of India, New Delhi

Mosse, D. (2003) *The Rule of Water: Statecraft, Ecology, and Collective Action in South India*, Oxford University Press, New Delhi

National Commission to Review the Working of the Constitution (2002) *Report*, 2002, available at http://lawmin.nic.in/ncrwc/finalreport.htm, accessed 20 December 2008

Phansalkar, S. and Kher, V. (2006) 'A decade of the Maharashtra groundwater legislation: Analysis of the implementation process', *Law, Environment and Development Journal*, vol 2, no 1, pp67–83

Sax, J. (1970) 'The public trust doctrine in natural resource law: Effective judicial intervention', *Michigan Law Review*, vol 68, no 3

Shah, T. and Van Koppen, B. (2006) 'Is India ripe for integrated water resources management? Fitting water policy to national development context', *Economic and Political Weekly*, 5 August

UN Secretary General (2001) *Water: A Key Resource for Sustainable Development*, Report of the Secretary-General, UN Division for Sustainable Development, Economic and Social Council, UN, New York

Upadhyay, V. (2007) 'The water challenge and the poor: How can India's water regime respond to those living on the edge?', *Sustainability Tomorrow*, vol 2

Venkateshwarlu, K. (2004) 'State lacks muscle to regulate sinking of bore wells', *The Hindu*, 8 September

8
Water Resource Development and Institutions in India: Overview and Profile

Vasant Gandhi and N. V. Namboodiri

There is a water crisis today. But the crisis is not about having too little water to satisfy our needs. It is a crisis of managing water badly – such that billions of people and the environment suffer.

World Water Vision

Introduction

The management of water resources in India is facing a crisis, and this is becoming increasingly evident as development accelerates. Scarcities are becoming frequent and deteriorating water quality also common. Maintaining the area under irrigation is also proving increasingly difficult with a negative trend being evident in some recent years. As noted in the introductory chapter, water resource management is crucial to India given the growing demand for food, the imperative to raise rural incomes, and the dependence of 60–70 per cent of the population on agriculture.

Many of the problems that have beset surface water irrigation, as outlined by Herath (Chapter 5), are particularly evident in India. Surface water management dilemmas include huge investment requirements, project implementation delays, poor maintenance, dysfunctional institutions, and environmental degradation. There is also a crisis emerging in the management of ground water as a result of excessive exploitation and inadequate recharge.

As Pagan (Chapter 2) and others noted in earlier chapters, the major problems are often not technical or strictly financial in nature. Rather, they owe their origins to institutional difficulties – whether they be associated with the design, implementation or management of appropriate institutions in the political economy.

Against this background we use this chapter to set the scene for the empirical work that follows. More specifically, this chapter aims to describe the context of water resource development, particularly in the states of interest. The chapter itself is arranged into four additional parts. We commence by providing a macro overview of the status of water resources in India and position this in the extant data on global resource endowment and use. For convenience, this is done by providing a suite of summary data accessed from reliable sources. In the third section we detail the development of water resources in India before briefly summarizing the institutional layout in the three states of interest – Andhra Pradesh, Gujarat and Maharashtra. A précis of the contemporary issues is also provided and this offers a rationale for the empirical analysis that follows in Part 3 of this book. The chapter ends by offering some brief concluding observations.

The macro water situation in the world and in India

World Water Vision

According to World Water Vision (2000), the blue or renewable water resource available in the world is 40,000km^3, and the green or soil water resource available is 60,000km^3. These data imply that there is a substantial quantity of fresh water available in the world, which goes much beyond current or projected use levels.

World Water Vision indicates that agriculture is the largest user of water, and also predicts that in the future, from 1995 to 2025, the annual withdrawal for agriculture will increase by 6 per cent to reach 2650km^3. By way of contrast, annual withdrawal for industry is expected to increase by 7 per cent to reach 800km^3 in the same timeframe (see Table 8.1 below). Importantly, these projections are based on achieving significant improvement in the efficient use of water in both agriculture and industry. Municipalities across the globe are expected to increase annual water use by 43 per cent to reach 500km^3 by the year 2025. Nevertheless, of the total withdrawal of 4200km^3 in the year 2025, agriculture is expected to remain the largest user at 2650km^3 (63 per cent), indicating that efficiency of water use in agriculture will remain crucial to global water resource management. Against this global backdrop the use of water for irrigation in India assumes considerable significance.

The Indian water landscape

Why is irrigation so important in India? Because the distribution of rainfall across India is highly uneven. Only 8 per cent of the land area receives very

Table 8.1 *Renewable water use according to World Water Vision*

User	*Cubic km 1995*	*Cubic km 2025*	*% increase 1995–2025*	*Notes*
Agriculture				
Withdrawal	2500	2650	6	Food production increases 40%, but much higher water productivity limits increase in harvested irrigated area to 20% and increase in net irrigated area to 5–10%
Consumption	1750	1900	9	
Industry				
Withdrawal	750	800	7	Major increase in developing countries is partly offset by major reduction in developed countries.
Consumption	80	100	25	
Municipalities				
Withdrawal	350	500	43	Major increase and universal access in developing countries, stabilization and decrease in developed countries
Consumption	50	100	100	
Reservoirs (evaporation)	200	220	10	
Total				
Withdrawal	3800	4200	10	
Consumption	2100	2300	10	
Ground-water overconsumption	200	0		Increased recharge of aquifers makes ground-water use sustainable

Note: Totals are rounded.
Source: World Water Vision, 2000

high/assured rainfall, and another 20 per cent receives high rainfall. The remainder of the land area (i.e. 72 per cent) is in the low, dry or medium rainfall range (see Table 8.2).

Even during the year the rainfall is highly concentrated in just a few months. As shown in Table 8.3, about 73.7 per cent of rainfall is received in the southwest monsoon period which spans June to September. Thus, agriculture in other areas and indeed agriculture generally at other times of the year depends substantially on artificial methods of providing water. Statistics indicate that nearly 70 per cent of the foodgrain production in India, which has to feed over 1 billion people, comes from irrigated areas (Kumar et al, 1995).

The profile in Figure 8.1 shows that of the annual precipitation of 400 million hectare metres (Mha-m), 115Mha-m enters surface flows and 215Mha-m enters the soil. Only 25Mha-m is finally used through surface irrigation, which constitutes a mere 6 per cent of the total water available through annual precipitation and inflows from outside the country. The figure also indicates that of the 215Mha-m infiltrating into the soil, only 13Mha-m is utilized for ground-water irrigation and other uses. This again constitutes a mere 6 per cent of the annual precipitation infiltrating into the soil, indicating substantial potential for expanded harvesting and use.

Table 8.2 *Distribution of annual rainfall according to area*

Rainfall classification	*Amount of rainfall (mm)*	*% of total geographical area*
Low/dry	Less than 750	30.0
Medium	750–1150	42.0
High	1150–2000	20.0
Very high/assured	Above 2000	8.0
Total		100.0

Source: Fertilizer Association of India (2007) – based on reports of India, Meteorological Department, Pune

Table 8.3 *Distribution of annual rainfall according to seasons in India*

Rainfall	*Duration*	*Approx. share of annual rainfall*
Pre-monsoon	March–May	10.4
Southwest monsoon	June–September	73.7
Post-monsoon	October–December	13.3
Winter or northeast monsoon	January–February	2.6
Total	Annual	100.0

Source: Fertilizer Association of India (2007) – based on reports of India, Meteorological Department, Pune

Official estimates and projections given in Tables 8.4–8.6 below show that India's estimated utilizable surface water resource' is 690km^3 and the utilizable ground-water resource is 432km^3. The total water requirement in the year 2000 was about 605 billion m^3, and this is expected to rise to 1093 billion m^3 by 2025. Irrigated agriculture was by far the largest water user in the year 2000 and is expected to continue be so for the foreseeable future. The percentage use in agriculture is actually predicted to rise slightly from 82 per cent to 83 per cent by 2025. Given the fixed water stock and the growing population, per capita water availability is continuously falling. It stood at 5177m^3 per capita in 1951, fell to 1869 m^3 in 2001, and is forecast to decline to 1140m^3 by 2050. Clearly, there is growing pressure on the available water resources and the need for better water resource management is palpable.

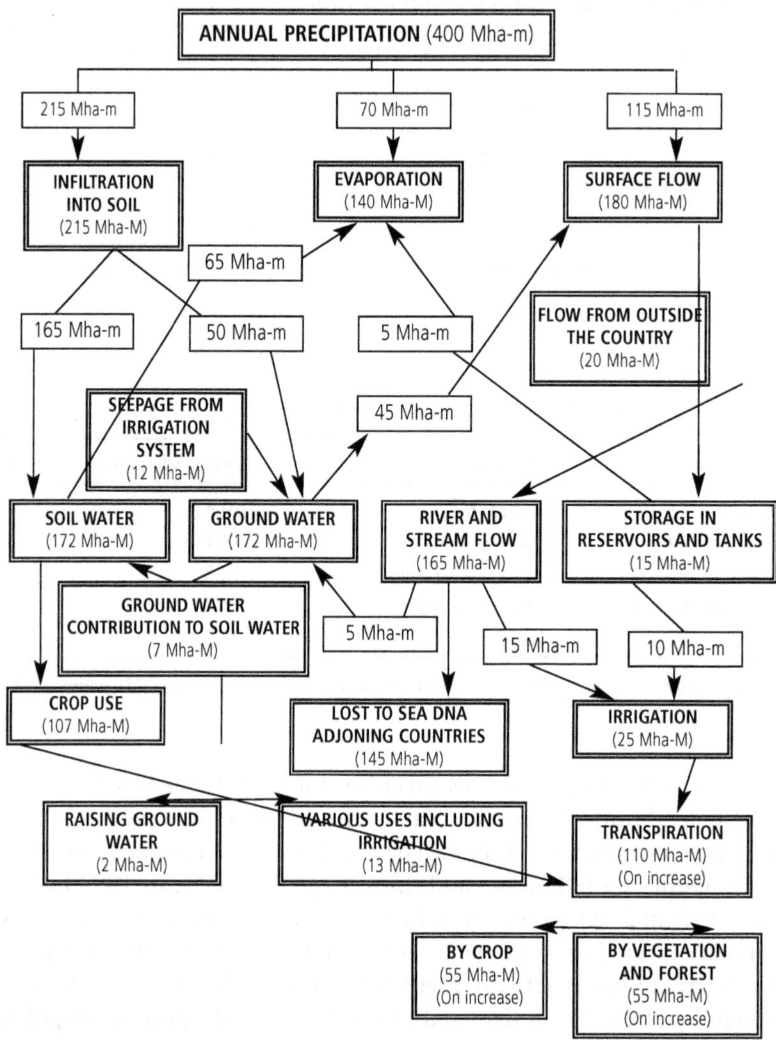

Figure 8.1 *Water Wealth and Irrigation in India*

Source: Majumdar, 2000

Table 8.4 *Estimated total utilizable water resource in India*

Resource	*Volume*
Surface water resource	690km^3
Ground-water resource	432km^3

Source: India, Ministry of Water Resources (2007)

Table 8.5 *Water requirement in India (billion m³)*

Use	2000	2010	2025
Domestic	30	56	73
Irrigation	501	688	910
Industry	20	12*	23
Energy	20	5*	15*
Other	34	52	72
TOTAL	605	813	1093

Note: * partial estimates.
Source: India, Ministry of Water Resources (2007)

Table 8.6 *Annual per capita availability of water in India*

Year	m³
1951	5177
2001	1869
2025	1341
2050	1140

Source: India, Ministry of Water Resources (2007)

Water resource development in India

Historically, before investments in irrigation by the state became an accepted practice in India, many emperors and local chiefs devised ways of storing water in ponds and tanks (Singh, 1991). Some excavated inundation canals and 'anicuts' to draw water from rivers. Even though most of these efforts were initiated by emperors and influential people, the responsibility for maintenance of the irrigation works and the distribution of water often remained with farmers. Since agriculture was critical for human survival, communities developed norms and social systems for managing irrigation, cognisant of the consequences of failing to manage the resource appropriately. The beneficiaries assumed responsibility for repairs and also undertook supervision of the system, sometimes with the help of paid staff. There was also often a desire to seek an equitable distribution of water. Some old works that still survive are typically looked after by the water users themselves with minimal support from the government (Singh, 1991). These works bear testimony to the potential of farmer initiative and the strength of sustained human efforts in water management in some contexts in India. Similar enduring indigenous initiatives set in different contexts were described by Herath (Chapter 5).

During British rule in India the government began intervening by harnessing water for irrigation (Singh, 1991). Some large barrages and reservoirs were built to store water in order to sustain agriculture in years of lean rainfall. At the time of independence in 1947, India had 22.5 million ha under irrigation, of which 9.7 million ha constituted major and medium schemes developed by government. There was considerable acceleration in government intervention in irrigation affairs after independence and by 1985 a total potential of 68.0 million ha had been created, 30.6 million ha from major and medium projects and 37.4 million ha from minor irrigation projects.

Table 8.7 gives the statistics on major and medium irrigation projects undertaken and projects completed since independence. It indicates that by the eighth plan (5-year plan 1992–97) a total of 1637 projects had been taken on, and 1239 projects were completed. The number of medium irrigation projects is the largest among these. In total, 1075 medium projects were taken up with 911 of these being completed. These statistics point to the substantial number of large and medium irrigation project institutions that are in existence in the country and reveal the legacy of the public endeavours in this field.

Table 8.7 *Government investment: Major and medium irrigation projects*

Periods	*Projects taken up*			*Projects completed*		
	Major	*Medium*	*Modernization*	*Major*	*Medium*	*Modernization*
Pre-plan period	74	143	–	74	143	–
Plan period (1951–92)	278	894	146	120	668	51
Eighth plan (1992–97)	14	38	50	38*	100*	45*
Total	366	1075	196	232	911	96

Note: * provisional.
Source: India, Ministry of Water Resources (1997)

Figure 8.2 below indicates that there has been considerable growth in the government expenditure on irrigation development in India in nominal terms (India, Ministry of Agriculture, 1996; 2002; 2006). Of the different kinds of expenditure, major and medium irrigation projects have absorbed most resources. The expenditure on minor irrigation projects has been relatively modest, as has the funding of command area development and flood control projects.

When these data are adjusted to reflect constant prices a different story is revealed, as exposed in Figure 8.3. Here, the real expenditure on irrigation shows very little growth over most of the period apart from a steep increase in the late 1970s. The expenditure in real terms remained more or less constant from 1980 to 1997. More recently, following strong concerns expressed about inadequate government investment in irrigation development, there has been an increase.

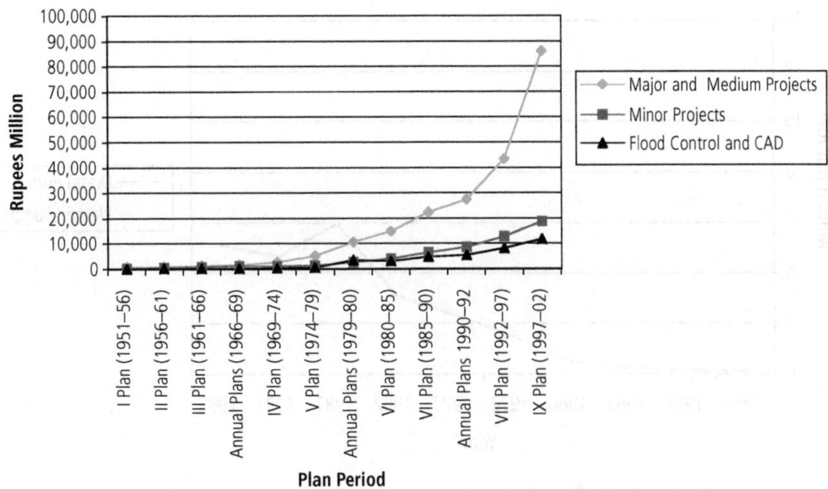

Figure 8.2 *Average annual financial expenditure by central and state government*

With respect to private investment in irrigation, an important indicator is the investment in irrigation pumpsets. Figure 8.4 indicates that there has been considerable growth in the number of pumpsets purchased and used by farmers. The electric pumpsets in particular show rapid growth since the mid 1980s, whereas diesel pumps have declined in importance after initial early growth.

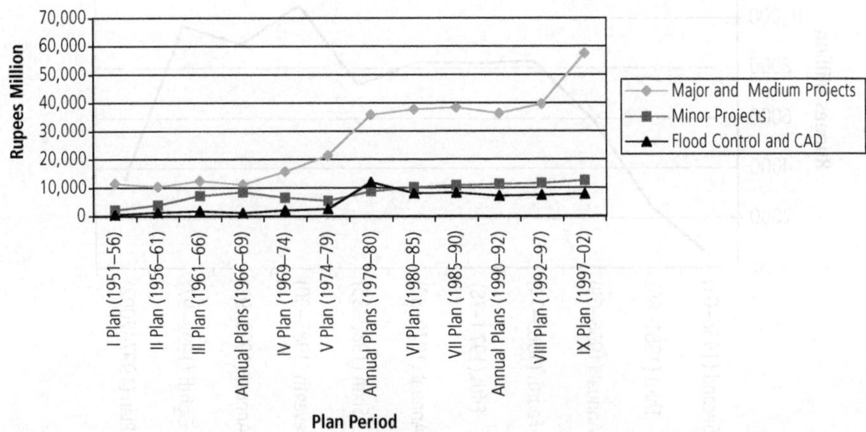

Figure 8.3 *Average annual financial expenditure by central and state government (at 1993–94 prices)*

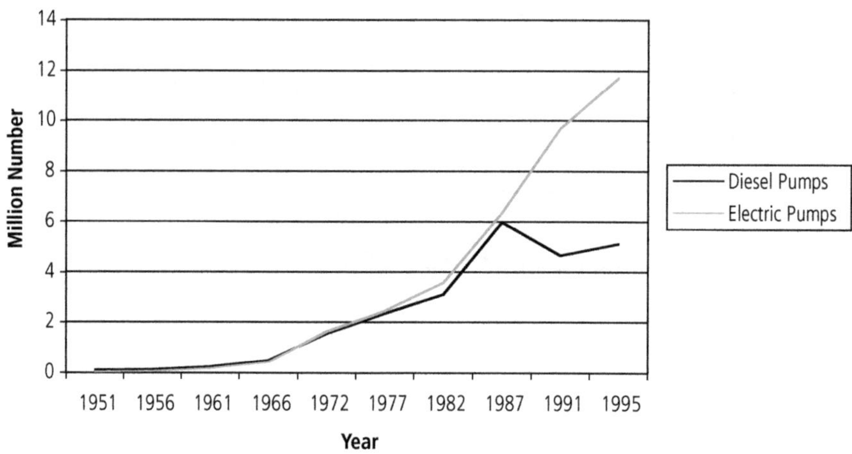

Figure 8.4 *Number of irrigation pumpsets in millions*

In order to shed some light on the broad pattern of private investment in irrigation, the available data on institutional finance pertaining to private irrigation investment was examined and converted to constant prices. Figure 8.5 indicates that this investment has stagnated from the early 1970s to the mid 1990s, and since then is showing a decline. Thus, the real private investment in irrigation also appears to be on a downward trend in recent times.

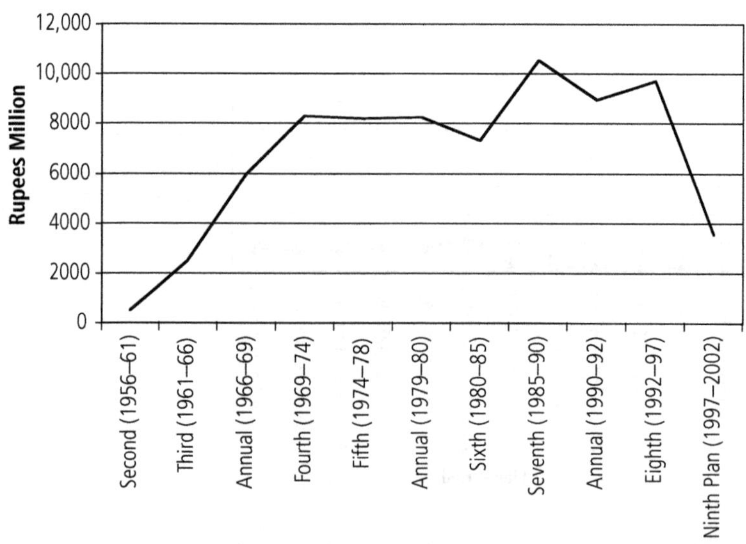

Figure 8.5 *Private investments in irrigation (based on institutional finance): Rupees million at 1993–94 prices*

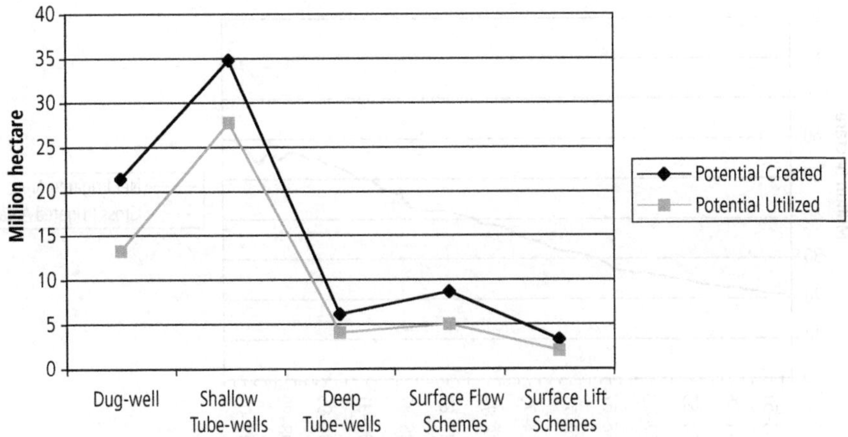

Figure 8.6 *Irrigation potential created, utilized and the actual irrigated area*

Figure 8.6 shows that in terms of the overall irrigation potential created, there has been considerable growth. But there is an emerging gap between the potential created and the potential utilized. Moreover, a similar gap is evident between the potential utilized and the actual gross irrigated area and this shows some evidence of actually widening. There is a widely felt concern in policy circles that this trend is substantially due to poor institutional development and performance in irrigation (see Vaidyanathan, 1999; Meinzen-Dick and Mendoza, 1996).

Figure 8.7 indicates that there has been considerable growth in the actual irrigated area in India, both in net and gross terms (gross = for successive irrigated crops on the same land in a year, the area is counted again). However, the data also reveal a marked slowdown in the early 2000s. Again, one possible explanation for these events is the extant difficulties in sustaining growth, some of which are tied to institutional issues.

Table 8.8 provides an analysis of the overall growth in planted (sown) area and irrigated area. It indicates that the net sown area shows some growth until 1970–71, but since then has remained largely static. Moreover, the annual growth rate is showing a slight negative trend since 1990–91 (–0.10 per cent) as land is diverted to other uses. The gross sown area follows a similar pattern, but shows some modest growth (0.15), mostly because of increased cropping intensity. By 2005–06 the gross sown area reached 190 million ha and the cropping intensity was 135.7 per cent. In comparison, the irrigated area is showing more rapid growth, with the net irrigated area growing at 1.92 per cent per year and the gross irrigated area growing at 2.36 per cent per year since 1950. Nevertheless, since the 1990s the growth rate of both net and gross irrigated areas is showing a considerable slowdown. By 2005–06, the proportion of arable land irrigated had risen to 43.3 per cent and 43.5 per cent for net and gross measures respectively.

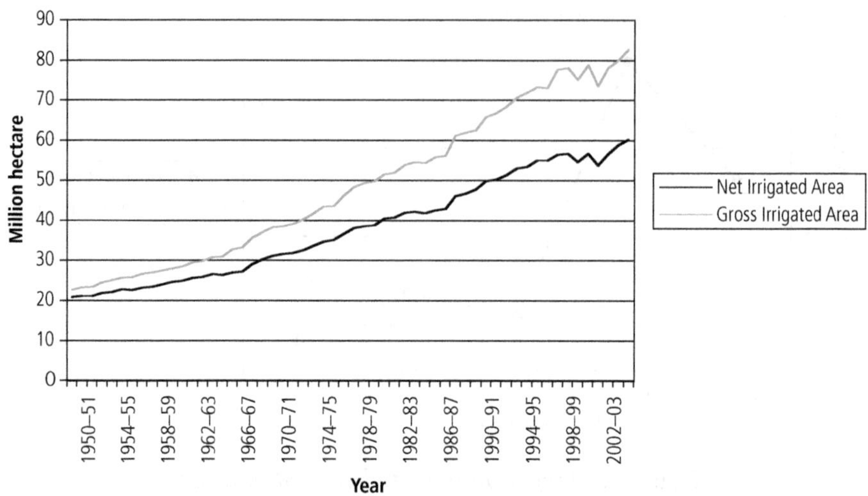

Figure 8.7 *Net and gross irrigated area (million ha)*

Table 8.8 *Trends in overall crop area and irrigated area (million ha)*

Year	*Net sown* area	*Gross sown area*	*Cropping intensity* (%)	*Net irrigated area*	*Gross irrigated area*	*Irrigation Intensity* (%)	*Percentage area irrigated* Net	*Gross*
1950–51	118.8	131.9	111.1	20.9	22.6	108.2	17.6	17.1
1960–61	133.2	152.8	114.7	24.7	28.0	113.5	18.5	18.3
1970–71	140.3	165.8	118.2	31.1	38.2	122.8	22.2	23.0
1980–81	140.0	173.1	123.6	38.7	49.8	128.6	27.7	28.8
1990–91	142.2	185.9	130.7	47.8	62.5	130.7	33.6	33.6
1998–99	142.6	193.0	135.4	56.5	77.6	137.4	39.6	40.2
1999–00	141.1	190.3	134.9	56.8	78.0	137.4	40.2	41.0
2000–01	141.1	187.9	133.2	54.7	75.1	137.4	38.8	40.0
2001–02	141.4	189.7	134.2	56.7	78.7	138.8	40.1	41.5
2002–03	132.7	175.7	132.4	53.8	73.5	136.6	40.5	41.8
2003–04	140.9	190.4	135.1	56.6	77.9	137.6	40.2	40.9
2004–05	141.4	190.9	135.0	58.8	80.0	136.1	41.6	41.9
2005–06	140.0	190.0	135.7	60.2	82.6	137.2	43.3	43.5
Annual growth rate								
1950–2006	0.30	0.66	0.36	1.92	2.36	0.43	1.64	1.70
1990–2006	–0.10	0.15	0.25	1.54	1.86	0.32	1.69	1.72

Source: India, Ministry of Agriculture, 1996; 2002; 2006

Table 8.9 contains data on the irrigated area by water sources. There has been a substantial change in the composition by source in recent years. The total canal irrigated area grew at a slow pace of 0.78 per cent between 1971–72 and

2005–06. However, between 1991–92 and 2005–06, this growth rate was negative at –0.86 per cent. Similarly, tank irrigation is also showing a negative trend of –2.64 per cent in the last decade. These trends are illustrative of the problems that beset surface water irrigation in this country, particularly those of an institutional nature. By way of contrast, ground-water-based tube-well irrigation shows rapid growth at 6.87 per cent in the last 35 years, but this has reduced substantially to 3.49 per cent since 1991–92. Irrigation by other wells shows less rapid growth, with total ground-water-based irrigation growing at 4.54 per cent but then slowing to 2.57 per cent more recently. As a result of these trends, the share of canals in irrigation has reduced to 25.71 per cent and the share of wells has increased to 58.76 per cent by 2005–06. Unequivocally, ground water is becoming the dominant source of irrigation, creating its own set of institutional challenges.

Table 8.9 *Sources of irrigation (area in '000 ha)*

	Govt canal	*Private canal*	*Total canal*	*Tanks*	*Tube-wells*	*Other wells*	*Total wells*	*Other sources*	*Total net area irrigated*
1970–71	11,972	866	12,838	4112	4461	7426	11,887	2266	31,103
1980–81	14,450	842	15,292	3182	9531	8164	17,695	2551	38,720
1990–91	16,973	480	17,453	2944	14,257	10,437	24,694	2932	48,023
1995–96	16,561	559	17,120	3118	17,910	11,787	29,697	3467	53,402
2000–01	15,111	199	15,710	2518	22,324	11,451	33,775	2831	54,833
2005–06	15,268	207	15,475	2034	23,224	12,148	35,372	7314	60,196
Percentage	25.36	0.34	25.71	3.38	38.58	20.18	58.76	12.15	100
1971–2006	1.01	–5.96	0.78	–2.93	6.87	2.05	4.54	4.88	2.75
1991–2006	–0.76	–6.01	–0.86	–2.64	3.49	1.08	2.57	6.53	1.61

Source: India, Ministry of Agriculture, 1996, 2002, 2006

Figure 8.8 graphically illustrates the changing composition of irrigation by source and shows that since 1995–96 tube-wells have become the largest single source of irrigation. This is followed by canals and then other wells. Tank irrigation shows a decline throughout this period. It is also worth noting that the growth in tube-well irrigation has shown signs of tapering off in recent years.

What is the pattern of irrigation by crops? The total irrigated area by crop is given in Figure 8.9. It shows that the largest share of irrigated area is under rice, followed by wheat. The data also reveal that the irrigated area under wheat was relatively small in 1965–66, but has risen sharply since and has become almost equal to that of rice. Among the other crops, oilseeds hold the largest single share, followed by sugar cane. The figure supports the view that irrigation has become crucial for foodgrain production, particularly rice and wheat.

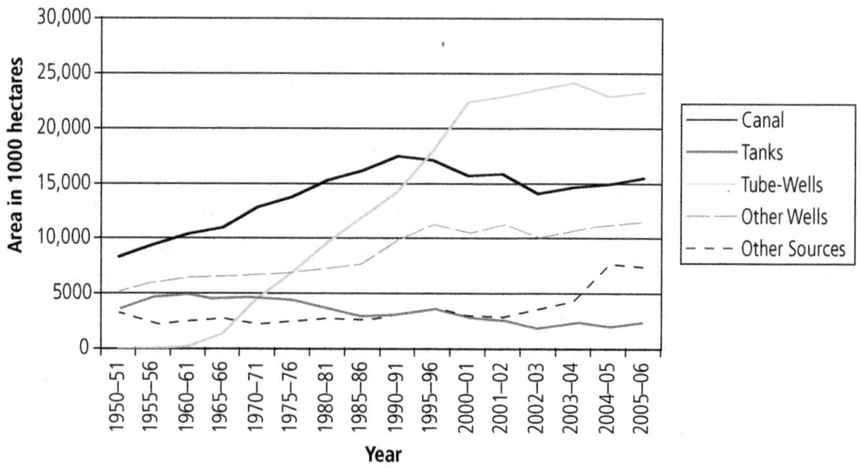

Figure 8.8 *Net area irrigated by type of irrigation*

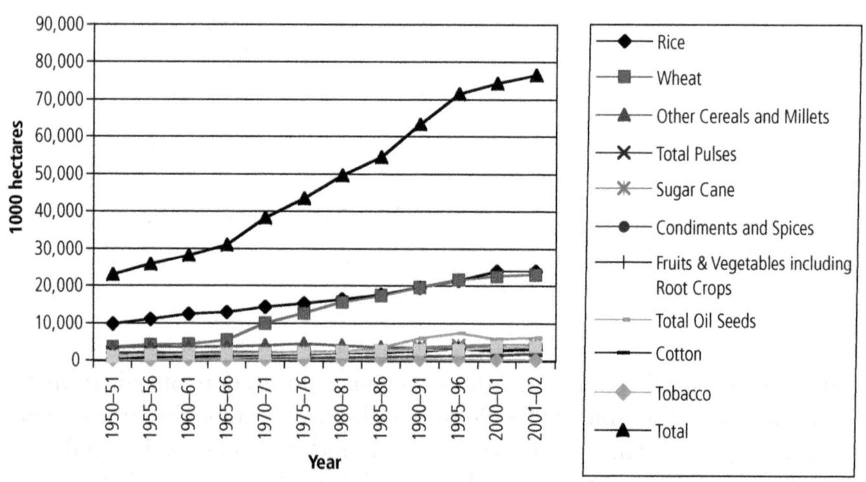

Figure 8.9 *Irrigated area under major crops*

Table 8.10 gives the percentage each crop area subject to irrigation and the percentage share of each crop in the total irrigated area. It indicates that even though rice holds the largest share in the total irrigated area, only 54.8 per cent of the rice area is actually irrigated. On the other hand, 89.8 per cent of the wheat area and 96.5 per cent of the sugar-cane area is subjected to irrigation.

Only 31.5 per cent of the oilseeds area and 33.0 per cent of the cotton area are irrigated. Importantly, nearly 65 per cent of the foodgrain area is irrigated and hence irrigation development has substantial implications for the level as well as the growth of foodgrain production in India.

Table 8.10 *Percentage of area under major crops irrigated and their share in total irrigated area*

	% of area under crop irrigated		*% share of each crop in total irrigated area*	
	1991–92	2004–05	1991–92	2004–05
Rice	47.3	54.8	30.7	27.8
Jowar	6.5	9.0	1.2	1.0
Bajra	6.5	8.2	1.0	0.9
Maize	22.5	20.5	2.0	1.8
Wheat	83.7	89.8	29.8	28.7
Total cereals + millets	43.4	53.6	66.0	63.1
Gram	24.2	31.6	2.1	2.6
Total pulses	10.7	14.5	3.7	4.0
Foodgrains	37.4	44.6	69.7	64.8
Sugar cane	88.0	96.5	5.5	4.3
Condiments and spices	49.7	62.9	1.8	2.2
Fruit and vegetables	38.7	73.8	4.1	6.5
Groundnut	19.1	17.8	2.5	1.4
Oilseed	25.5	31.5	10.4	10.5
Cotton	33.3	33.0	3.9	3.5
Tobacco	39.0	46.9	0.3	0.2
All crops	36.0	43.5	100	100

Source: India, Ministry of Agriculture, 1996; 2002; 2006

We now briefly turn to the specifics of the states considered in the empirical research that follows – that is Andhra Pradesh, Maharashtra and Gujarat. Figure 8.10 indicates that Andhra Pradesh has the largest irrigated area of the three, followed by Maharashtra and then Gujarat. The irrigated areas of Gujarat and Maharashtra are very similar in magnitude and the irrigated area in Andhra Pradesh demonstrates large fluctuations. All three states show only modest growth in irrigated area, and some declines are evident in recent years. Again, some of these recent trends are attributable to the difficult institutional challenges that have thwarted irrigation in recent years.

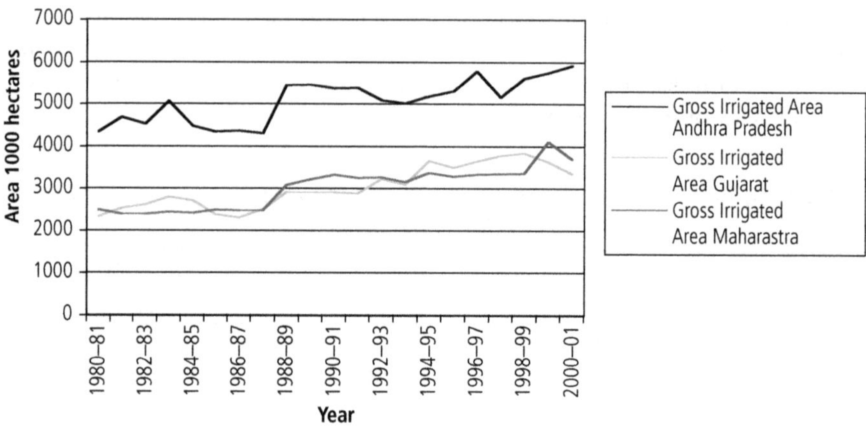

Figure 8.10 *Gross irrigated area in Andhra Pradesh, Gujarat and Maharashtra*

Institutions for water resource development

Water resource development in India, as indicated above, was often initiated by kings and nobles in the early days, and later development was continued on a larger scale by the government under British rule. After independence, there was considerable acceleration in the government effort and investment in irrigation, which is clearly evident in these data. However, by the 1970s, serious concerns about unsatisfactory management, delivery and utilization of water at the farm level emerged. A large number of commissions and committees were set up to examine the issues (Singh, 1991).

As a result of these concerns, Command Area Development Authorities (CADAs) were established from 1973 onwards in various parts of the country, as explained by Ananda (Chapter 6). The primary responsibilities of CADAs included management, delivery and water utilization. This signalled the beginning of an integrated approach to irrigation development that went far beyond construction. This approach worked in some areas and failed miserably in others, but it nevertheless resulted in the formation of yet another government bureaucracy. The farmers in many parts of the country did not take kindly to the principles of CAD and it was usually seen as a government programme imposed from the top rather than one generated by farmers themselves (Singh 1991).

Following this experience, the government increasingly sought to give the responsibility for irrigation management to the farmers. A large number of local institutions of different kinds were formed for water resource management. Table 8.11 below gives data on the number of institutions created and the membership in the states studied. Experience also shows that this arrangement often did not work effectively. A large number of these entities had institutional problems and performed poorly or became defunct. However, in the process, the need and potential for better institutional arrangements were recognized at different levels (Uphoff, 1996). It was also realized that proper institutional design and policies would be necessary for such a new decision-making structure to succeed.

Table 8.11 *Registered irrigation cooperatives in selected states as of 1996*

	Number	Membership	Average membership	Share in all India
Andhra Pradesh	370	26,076	70	5.9
Gujarat	882	29,281	33	14.0
Maharashtra	3081	268,906	87	48.8
All India	6310	399,557	63	100
Number of WUAs formed (2003)				
Andhra Pradesh				
Major	1664			
Medium	413			
Minor	7845			
Total	9922			

Source: Gandhi and Namboodiri, 2002; India, Ministry of Water Resources, 2007

Institutional considerations and emerging trends

In an earlier chapter in this volume (see Upadhyay, Chapter 7) a detailed description of the legal status of water in several Indian states was provided. It was noted that under the laws and legal system in India, water is a state subject and therefore the setting of water laws and policies comes under state jurisdiction. The only exception is in the case of interstate rivers, where the central government is involved. As described earlier by authors commenting on the Australian situation, the larger financial resources available with the Indian central government provide substantial leverage over the water policy and investment strategies of the states. This has given rise to national consistency in some areas.

The general legal principle in India is that surface water belongs to the state but the ground water notionally 'belongs' to the owner of land above it. Under government schemes, there are three types of irrigation systems: canal, tank (small reservoirs) and lift systems. The schemes are also classified into major, medium and minor (Brewer et al, 1999). The major schemes have a command area greater than 10,000ha, the medium schemes between 2000 and 10,000ha and minor schemes below 2000ha.

Water resources are governed by central and state irrigation/water resource departments of governments. The central and state agriculture departments are also heavily involved in particular dimensions of water resource management, such as watershed development. With respect to surface irrigation, different institutional systems for the distribution of water are followed in the different states (Mitra, 1997; Brewer et al, 1999). These include *Warabandi*, *Shejpali*, land class and assured irrigation systems that were briefly described in Chapter 1. Most of these arrangements have legal sanction in state jurisdictions, although implementation is often difficult. The local institutions for water resource management come under the state framework of cooperative laws, or fall under special laws and Acts passed for that purpose.

As we noted at the start of this chapter, managing surface water is posing serious challenges (Reddy, 1998). A major problem is the lack of new investment in surface water irrigation, as evidenced by the data presented earlier. In addition, the maintenance of irrigation works is frequently poor, resulting in water use inefficiency and wastage. This problem is compounded by situations where agronomic practices do not reflect the real scarcity of water and there is also inequity in distribution (Dhanasekaran, 1998). Some of these problems result in serious environmental harm and, in the case of large projects, there is often substantial opposition from environmentalists. Rehabilitation of displaced people is also a serious implementation problem for larger projects in particular (Wood, 2007).

In the case of ground water, the overriding concern is overdraft of water (Foster et al, 2000). This arises because of the high demand as well as the low energy/electricity cost (Shah, 1993). Moreover, there is virtually no control on the use of ground water in most areas, despite the elaborate legislative initiatives detailed by Upadhyay (Chapter 7). The upshot is that ground-water recharge is inadequate, water tables are falling and the quantity and quality of water is on the decline. These problems are resulting in a rising cost of water, both capital and operational.

Much is happening in response to these issues, but progress is slow and varied. In some instances there has been a move towards bringing about new government investment in surface water irrigation and participatory irrigation management (PIM) is being seriously promoted by many governments as a panacea to address maintenance and management problems (Gandhi and Namboodiri, 2002). Some governments are also raising water use charges and creating river basin organizations for integrated water resource management. Some large projects, such as the Interlinking of Rivers project, are being pursued to link areas in surplus to areas in deficit, but these are mostly at the planning stage.

In the case of ground water, licensing is being seriously considered as a vehicle for controlling the number of wells, although this is proving problematic, as noted by Upadhyay (Chapter 7). In other instances, farmers are organizing themselves to exploit and regulate water together (Kumar, 2000). Property rights for water are being considered and the joint construction of check dams to improve the recharge of ground water is testament to the benefits of collective action in particular locales. Local institutions are also beginning to charge for water on the basis of the crop/use and less so on the basis of area. There is also a move to raise energy cost and introduce metering, which would undoubtedly modify some behaviour.

Many governments and donor agencies are undertaking watershed development activities for better conservation and use of land and water. In addition, numerous rain-water harvesting methods are being implemented. A number of NGOs and self-help groups are getting involved in water resource management and there are substantial efforts being made to promote more efficient use of water through micro-irrigation, in both sprinkler and drip forms (India, Ministry of Water Resources, 2007).

Recent policy experience demonstrates that getting prices right alone is not enough. Determining the right price hardly solves the problem of water scarcity and water sharing. The problem lies in the associated implementation and management that must accompany the 'right price' and cost/price recovery rates are often very poor (Gandhi, 1998). Pricing alone generally does not solve the problems, since institutional arrangements for operation and investment are weak (Gandhi and Namboodiri, 2002). Farmers are willing to pay two to three times the price as long as adequate water is provided and water is available at the right time (Reddy, 1998).

A large number of analysts and commentators have argued that water resource management in India is heading for a crisis unless policies and institutions are radically transformed (see, for instance, Saleth, 1996; Svendsen and Rosegrant, 1994; Gulati, 2002). This would require better design of water resource institutions, including a water rights regime that can effectively limit and regulate use (Meinzen-Dick and Mendoza, 1996). However, worldwide experience indicates that managing water is difficult because of the basic nature of the water resource, and market failures and government failure are common in this field (Saleth and Dinar, 1999).

In general, water resource management is very challenging because by nature, water is 'fugitive, lumpy and rife with externalities' (Livingston, 1993). Managing water also usually involves large transaction costs and serious information deficiencies. There is a need to design institutions to deal with the peculiarities of water, and to create the right incentives, controls and efficiencies. Many disappointing investments in water resources have resulted from institutional failure. There is a need to understand how rules combine with particular physical, economic and cultural environments to produce appropriate institutions (Ostrom, 1992). Some of the major institutional questions that emerge in the Indian context are:

1 How can the institutions be designed so that the water use reflects the real *scarcity* of the resource and leads to its efficient use?
2 How can the institutions be designed so as to achieve an *equitable* distribution in water use?
3 How can institutions be designed to be financially viable so that required rates of *investment* in irrigation are achieved and financial support generated?
4 How can institutions be designed so that the development and utilization take place with fewest ill effects on the soil and the *environment*?

These questions are taken up in subsequent chapters, with particular references to the empirical data collected as part of this study.

Concluding observations

There is a crisis in water resource management in India. The crisis is largely not about physical or technical issues but about poor institutional development. Water resource management is critical for India due to rainfall limitations, growing demand, and the large dependence on agriculture for livelihoods. Substantial effort and investment have been made by the government but this is still inadequate. Moreover, the utilization of this investment is often poor and there is much scope for improvement. Growth in the irrigated area has been faltering in recent years and water resource management requires urgent attention; otherwise it will severely constrain development. However, water institutions and water resource management are complex topics and there are no easy solutions.

Notes

1 Conversions:
1Mha-m = 1 million hectare metres
1ha-m = 10,000m^3
1Mha-m = 10 billion m^3
1km^3 = 1,000,000,000m^3 = 1 billion m^3
1Mha-m = 10km^3

References

Brewer, J., Kolavalli, S., Kalro, A. H., Naik, G., Ramnarayan, S., Raju, K. V. and Sakthivadivel, R. (1999) *Irrigation Management Transfer in India: Policies, Processes and Performance*, Oxford & IBH, New Delhi

Dhanasekaran, K. B. (1998) 'Role of management in the distribution of irrigation water in Periyar Vaigai project', *Indian Journal of Agricultural Economics*, vol 53, no 3, pp510–511

Fertilizer Association of India (2007) *Fertilizer Statistics,* Fertilizer Association of India, New Delhi

Foster, S., Chilton, J., Cardy, F., Schiffler, M. and Moench, M. (2000) 'Groundwater in rural development: Facing the challenges of supply and resource sustainability', World Bank Technical Paper No. 463, World Bank, Washington DC

Gandhi, V. P. (1998) 'Rapporteur's report on institutional framework for agricultural development', *Indian Journal of Agricultural Economics*, vol 53, no 3, pp552–564

Gandhi, V. P. and Namboodiri, N. V. (2002) 'Investment and institutions for water management in India's agriculture: Profile and behaviour', in D. Brennan (ed) *Water Policy Reform: Lessons from Asia and Australia*, ACIAR, Canberra

Gulati, A. and Narayanan, S. (2002) 'Subsidies and reforms in Indian irrigation', in D. Brennan (ed) *Water Policy Reform: Lessons from Asia and Australia*, ACIAR, Canberra

India, Ministry of Agriculture (1996) *Agricultural Statistics at a Glance*, Ministry of Agriculture, New Delhi

India, Ministry of Agriculture (2002) *Agricultural Statistics at a Glance*, Ministry of Agriculture, New Delhi

India, Ministry of Agriculture (2006) *Agricultural Statistics at a Glance*, Ministry of Agriculture, New Delhi

India, Ministry of Water Resources (1997). *Annual Report 1996–97*

India, Ministry of Water Resources (2007). *Annual Report 2006–07*

Kumar, D. (2000) 'Institutional framework for managing groundwater: A case study of community organizations in Gujarat, India', *Water Policy* 2, Elsevier, London, pp423–432

Kumar, P., Rosegrant M. and Hazell P. (1995) 'Cereals Prospects in India to 2020: Implications for policy', *2020 Vision Brief 23*, IFPRI, June

Livingston, M. L. (1993) 'Designing water institutions: Market failures and institutional response', Policy Research Working Paper 1227, World Bank, Washington DC

Majumdar, D. K. (2000) *Irrigation Water Management: Principles and Practice*, Prentice-Hall of India, New Delhi

Meinzen-Dick, R. and Mendoza, M. (1996) 'Alternative water allocation mechanisms: Indian and international experiences', *Economic & Political Weekly*, 30 March

Mitra, A. K. (1997) 'Irrigation management and pricing of water', Occasional Paper No. 4, NABARD, Mumbai

Ostrom, E. (1992) *Crafting Institutions for Self-Governing Irrigation Systems*, ICS Press, San Francisco

Reddy, R. V. (1998) 'Institutional imperatives and coproduction strategies for large irrigation systems in India', *Indian Journal of Agricultural Economics*, July–September

Saleth, M. R. (1996) *Water Institutions in India: Economics, Law and Policy*, Commonwealth Publishers, New Delhi

Saleth, M. R. and Dinar, A. (1999) 'Water challenge and institutional response: A cross-country perspective', Policy Research Working Paper 2045, World Bank, Washington DC

Shah, T. (1993) *Groundwater Markets and Irrigation Development: Political Economy and Practical Policy*, Oxford University Press, Bombay

Singh, K. K. (ed) (1991) *Farmers in the Management of Irrigation Systems*, Sterling Publishers, New Delhi

Svendsen, M. and Rosegrant, M. (1994) 'Irrigation development in Southeast Asia beyond 2000: Will the future be like the past?', *Water International*, March

Uphoff, N. (1986) *Improving International Irrigation Management with Farmers' Participation*, West View, London

Vaidyanathan, A. (1999) *Water Resource Management: Institutions and Irrigation Development in India*, Oxford University Press, New Delhi

World Water Vision (2000) *Making Water Everybody's Business* (eds W. J. Cosgrove and F. R. Rijsberman) World Water Council

Wood, J. R. (2007) *The Politics of Water Resource Development in India: The Narmada Dams Controversy*, Sage, New Delhi

Part 3
Water Institutions and their Performance in Three States in India

9 Institutional Analysis of the Performance of Water Institutions in Three Major States of India

Vasant Gandhi, Lin Crase and Ashutosh Roy

Introduction

The development of the necessary institutions to structure the interactions and arrangements required for good management of water resources has received insufficient attention in the scholarly literature. In particular, it has been observed that there is relatively little empirical work in this field and some of the earlier empirical analyses were hampered by theoretical or practical flaws (for a synopsis of the empirical flaws see, for example, Herath, Chapter 5). Accordingly, there is a substantial lack of information or understanding regarding the design and operation of institutional arrangements to complement technological change (Brewer et al, 1999; Saleth, 1996; Gandhi, 1998; Vaidyanathan, 1999; Gandhi and Namboodiri, 2002). It follows that the performance of irrigation and the agriculture sector generally may be suffering and the welfare of those who rely on agriculture is diminished as a result.

The previous two sections of this text were used to set the scene for some novel empirical work that aims to partially fill the empirical void around institutional performance in irrigation generally, and in India in particular. First, the authors of Part 1 developed the conceptual basis for the work that follows. This initial section drew heavily upon the experiences of policy and institutional reform in Australia and collectively established generic lessons or principles for application in other settings. Second, the authors of Part 2

(Chapters 5 to 8) provided insights into the Indian irrigation landscape. This was accomplished by sketching the role of collective action in developing countries, reviewing existing organizational arrangements for water management in India, outlining the legal status of the resource, and reviewing recent trends in irrigation production and development.

This chapter builds on these foundations and provides the introduction to the third section of the book; a section given to the empirical analysis of irrigation performance. The chapter is based on a study of water institutions and their components. As noted in the introductory chapter, the study was conducted collaboratively by researchers from India and Australia and was supported by the Australian Centre for International Agricultural Research (ACIAR). Importantly, the data were drawn from a variety of local water resource institutional initiatives and experiments in the three major states of Andhra Pradesh, Maharashtra and Gujarat. In each instance the motivation for forming these institutions was the necessity to overcome institutional problems faced in water resource management. All the states sampled confront significant water scarcity and farmers in these regions are heavily dependent on seasonal rainfall. Moreover, the predicament of farmers has generally worsened with the acceleration of economic development.

The aim of this chapter is to provide an overview of the data that forms the basis of important empirical analysis. We do not attempt to disaggregate the performance of irrigation institutions at this point, but deal with the data as a whole and describe overall salient trends. The chapter is arranged into seven additional parts. In section two we briefly review the conceptual background and provide an overview of sampling procedures. The third section is used to provide a summary of the characteristics of the farm households in the sample and the agro-institutional status of respondents. We then turn to the key governance and institutional elements embodied in the study in section four. This analysis is initially undertaken by considering the overall distribution of responses to questions relating to key governance and institutional features. The fifth section briefly considers the performance of differing institutional arrangements against the national priorities for water management, before moving to a more detailed investigation of performance in section six. This is accomplished by reporting the results of a bivariate statistical analysis dealing with general considerations, matters relating to governance and concepts directly pertaining to New Institutional Economics (NIE). In section seven we present the results of a multivariate analysis centring on the drivers of institutional performance before offering some brief concluding remarks in section eight.

Synoptic overview of conceptual background and sampling

Key concepts

Without dwelling on the literature covered earlier, it is worth repeating that the principal premise of NIE is that the real total cost of an economic activity includes not only transformation costs but also transaction costs. However, transaction costs are often ignored, despite usually being very large and having the potential to substantially reduce efficiency and effectiveness. In this context, the measure of a 'good institution' is its ability to reduce the costs of an activity.

We saw earlier that there is an expanding literature that attempts to deal with this issue and Pagan (Chapter 2) argues that much of this work can be reduced to five key elements of good institutional design. These are:

1 Clear objectives
Good institutions have clear objectives and show clarity of purpose. Clear objectives and clarity among stakeholders result in greater congruence, less conflict, and lower transaction costs.
2 Good interaction
An important feature of good institutions is good internal interaction among constituents. This helps in reducing transaction costs and obtaining cooperative solutions. Good institutions show good interaction with other institutions so that external transaction costs are also minimized.
3 Adaptiveness
Institutions typically face variation and change in the internal and external environment. In light of this, successful institutions demonstrate good adaptiveness. Through this process the organization can survive and grow while also keeping transaction costs low.
4 Appropriateness of scale
Good institutions are appropriate in scale with respect to their size and scope. If the institution is too large, transaction costs are too high. On the other hand, if the institution is too small, it has very little control over its relevant affairs.
5 Compliance ability
Good institutions demonstrate the required compliance ability. If the rules and processes of the institutions are not followed by a large section of the participants – i.e. compliance is poor – the institution in all likelihood ceases to be effective and meaningful, and transaction costs are high.

We have hypothesized that the existence of these institutional characteristics can be mapped against the performance of particular entities and thus provide useful insights into the relative impact (or combination of impacts) that attend particular institutional features.

However, as noted in Chapter 4, there are also internal mechanics of organization that can play a major part in subverting institutional/organizational effectiveness. In this regard the observations of Nystrom and Starbuck (1981), Groth (1999) and Ackroyd (2002) within the literature on the management theory of organizational design provide a useful embellishment to the NIE criteria. More specifically, good governance in organizations/institutions requires that they address three important rationalities. These are: (i) technical rationality, (ii) organizational rationality and (iii) political rationality.

This theory is summarized in Table 9.1, putting it in the context of the developmental phases of an organization.

Table 9.1 *Good governance and rationalities to address in organizations*

Form of rationality	*Purpose sought*	*Developmental phase*
Technical	Efficiency	Early growth of structurally simple organizations
Organizational	Coordination	Moderate maturity of structurally complex organizations
Political	Regime maintenance and justice	Full maturity of structurally complex organizations

Collectively, this study focused on eight key conceptual elements – five drawn from NIE and three drawn from the management science literature.

Sampling

The study used data collected in the states of Gujarat, Maharashtra and Andhra Pradesh in India. These states all face water scarcity and have attempted to address the situation through various measures, including different institutional innovations. The study sampled a variety of local institutions involved in water resource management. In the state of Gujarat, these included tube-well-based cooperatives, tube-well-based partnerships and check dam groups. The tube-well cooperatives and partnerships have sought to address two main problems. First, there is a problem pertaining to the high investment requirements and operational costs of deep tube-wells which arise as ground water progressively recedes. Second, there are problems relating to the distribution of the scarce available water among farmers participating in ground-water extraction. By way of contrast, the check dam groups have sought to achieve village-wide rain-water harvesting and recharge of wells through the creation of series of check dams.

In Maharashtra there has been a long history underpinning the evolution of farmer irrigation cooperatives to manage the distribution of canal water, and for lifting waters from rivers. These initiatives are the subject of analysis in that state and sampling was developed around this theme. In Andhra Pradesh there has been a massive government initiative to form water user associations (WUAs) across the state to bring a participative approach to the management of canal and village tank (small reservoir) water distribution and maintenance. Accordingly, this government-led initiative has shaped the sampling undertaken in that state.

Based on the information available from the government and academic institutions in each jurisdiction, a set of diverse local water institutions were selected that covered the all the aforementioned institutional initiatives. The institutions were then studied using detailed institutional questionnaires as well as household questionnaires. In the state of Gujarat, which has the largest diversity of water institutions, 19 such entities were covered. In this instance 250 beneficiary farm households were sampled. The sampling is shown in Figure 9.1 and the distribution across types of institutions is given in Table 9.2. In the state of Maharashtra five canal institutions including river-lift cooperatives were covered and 100 beneficiaries sampled. In the state of Andhra Pradesh five WUAs across major, medium and minor irrigation projects were studied. Again a sample of 100 beneficiary households was drawn from this state. The results reported here are thus based on data from 29 differing water institutions in total and were developed using 450 beneficiary households.

The household survey included a variety of questions detailing the respondent profile, land-holding, village setting, institutional association and activities, and institutional performance. There was also a series of questions related to institutional structure and function based on the conceptual frameworks of NIE and governance, as discussed above. The survey pertained to the 2004–05 cropping year.

Table 9.2 *Sampling plan: Number of sample households*

Type of local water institution	*Gujarat*	*Maharashtra*	*Andhra Pradesh*	*Total*
Canal cooperative	50	100	0	150
Water user association	0	0	100	100
Tube-well cooperative	40	0	0	40
Tube-well partnership	60	0	0	60
Check dam group	100	0	0	100
Total 2	50	100	100	450

Profile of farmer households and agro-institutional features

Farm households

The land-holding and educational profiles of the sample households are shown in Tables 9.3 and 9.4. The mean land-holding was found to be 2.63 hectares per farm household showing the very small farm sizes common in India. There was some leasing-in and leasing-out of land which modified this slightly and resulted in an average operational holding size of 2.68 hectares. The irrigated area being operated averaged 2.33 hectares per household for the years in question. The irrigated area stood at 87 per cent of the total land-holding and was much higher than the national average of 42 per cent, clearly reflecting the sampling focus on irrigated farms. Table 9.4 also highlights the relatively poor education level of the households with nearly 70 per cent of those surveyed having less than tenth grade education.

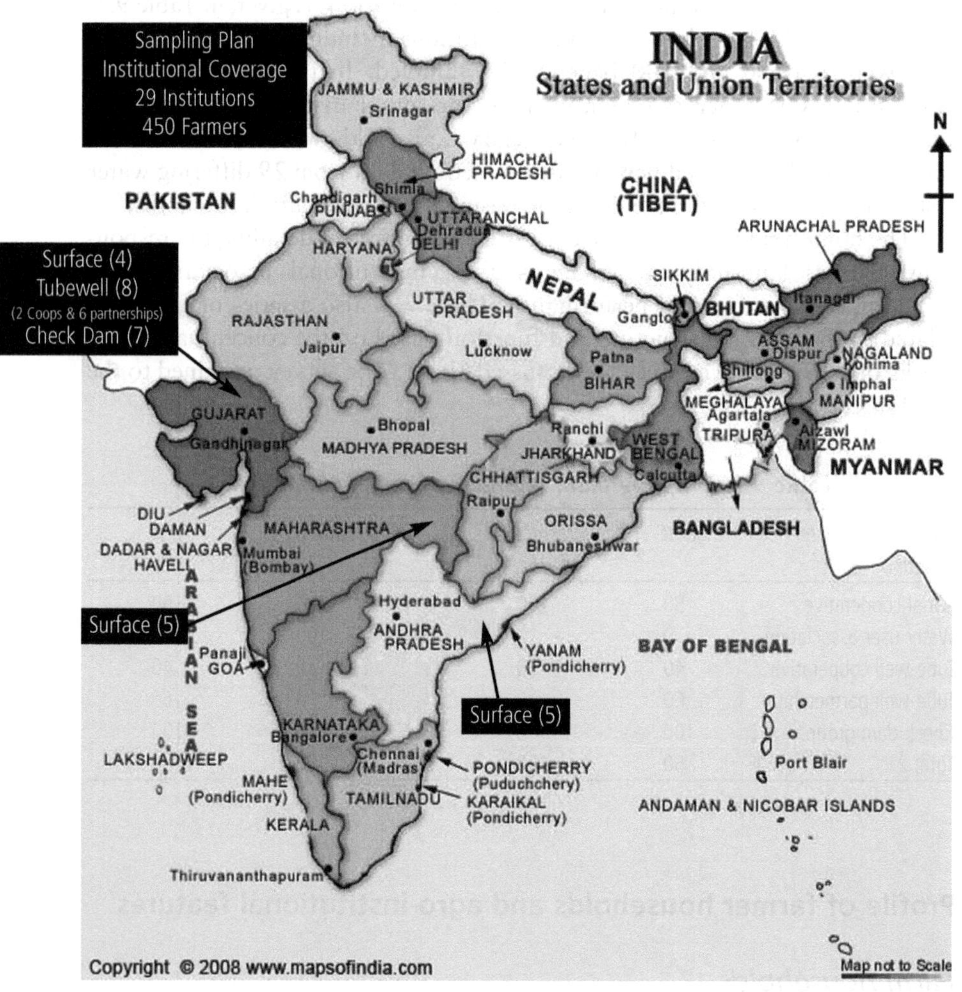

Figure 9.1 *Sampling plan*

Relationship with the water institutions

Findings on the relationship with the water institutions, participation level in the institutions, and the reliance of the household on the institution are shown in Table 9.5. About 93 per cent of respondents were ordinary members of the institutions, whereas 6 per cent held positions of responsibility in the institu-

Table 9.3 *Land-holding profile (ha)*

Land-holding	*Number of households*	*Minimum*	*Maximum*	*Mean*	*Std Dev*
Owned	450	0.00	40.00	2.63	2.97
Leased in	35	0.10	10.00	1.68	1.93
Leased out	6	2.00	3.20	2.62	0.43
Total	450	0.10	40.00	2.68	2.93
Irrigated operated area	450	0.10	40.00	2.33	2.67

Table 9.4 *Education*

Education	%
Illiterate	16.9
Grade 1–4	16.7
Grade 5–9	36.0
Grade 10–12	22.7
Below graduate	1.8
Graduate	4.7
Above graduate	1.3
Total	100.0

tion. Thus, the data primarily reflects the views of the ordinary members rather than officials per se. The data show that about 72 per cent of the respondents were active or very active in their participation in the activities or decision making of the institutions, while the remainder indicated that they primarily took on a passive role. A very large percentage of the respondents (i.e. 83 per cent) indicated that their reliance on the institution is either substantial or very substantial. These findings support the view that respondents were seriously dependent on and generally involved with the functioning of the entity under scrutiny.

Nature and status of the water resource

Other data were assembled that reveal the source of irrigation water and the nature of the water resource (Table 9.6). These data indicate that ground water, including open wells and tube-wells, were the water source for more than 50 per cent of the households surveyed, while another 39 per cent indicated that canal water was their primary source of irrigation. The remainder of the sample was made up of farmers lifting water from tanks and rivers. About 43 per cent of the households in the sample were in the middle reach, 25 per cent at the head reach and 31 per cent could be found at the tail end in the local watershed/water distribution network. Accordingly, these data potentially account for distributional nuances that can arise within irrigation and

Table 9.5 *Position in the institution, participation in activities and reliance on the institution*

Position in the institution			
Membership type	%	Membership type	%
Non-member	0.4	Member	92.7
Managing committee member	4.4	Chairman	1.3
Vice-chairman	0.2	Secretary	0.4
Staff	0.2	Director	0.2
Total	100.0		
Participation in activities/decision making			
Participation	%	Participation	%
Very active	6.9	Active	64.7
Passive	28.4	None	0.0
Total	100.0		
Reliance on the institution			
Reliance	%		
Very substantial	24.7	Substantial	58.7
Some	4.7	Very little	5.8
None	6.2	Total	100.0

which have not always been specifically considered (see, for example, Herath, Chapter 5).

Table 9.6 also indicates that scarcity is a common feature, with 41 per cent indicating scarcity or acute scarcity, and another 27 per cent indicating occasional scarcity. Not surprisingly, water availability is a significant problem for many of the households in the sample. In about 35 per cent of cases, water availability has declined over the years, whereas there has been no discernable change in water availability for others. About 25 per cent of the households indicated that there had been deterioration in water quality.

Social and economic cohesion in the village community is often considered an important determinant of the success of institutional activities. Accordingly, additional data was collected on this attribute. The responses obtained show that the social and economic cohesion was regarded as good to excellent by almost all respondents with only 1 per cent indicating some conflict. Presumably, such an environment is conducive to the operation of good institutions.

Membership and participation in water institutions

Table 9.7 provides an overview of the nature of membership and participation in water institutions. In most instances the mechanisms for gaining member-

Table 9.6 *Sources of irrigation, location in watershed, general water situation, change in water availability and water quality*

Source of irrigation			
Sources	%	Sources	%
River	4.4	Open well	26.9
Tube-well	24.7	Canal	39.3
Tank	0.7	Rainfed	3.6
Lift from tank	0.4	Total	100
Location in watershed area			
Location	%	Location	%
Head end	25.4	Middle	43.1
Tail end	31.4	Total 1	00.0
General water situation on the farm			
Situation	%	Situation	%
Excess water	2.7	No scarcity	29.3
Occasional scarcity	26.7	Scarcity	35.3
Acute scarcity	6.0	Total	100.0
Change in the availability of water over the years			
Change	%	Change	%
Increase	0.7	No change	64.4
Decline	30.7	Sharp decline	4.2
Total	100.0		
Change in water quality over the years			
Current situation	%	Current situation	%
Improvement	0.0	No change	75.6
Deterioration	23.1	Sharp deterioration	1.3
Total	100		
Social/economic cohesion in the village community			
Social/economic cohesion	%	Social/economic cohesion	%
Excellent cohesion	6.2	Good cohesion	92.7
Some conflict	1.1	Several conflicts	0.0
Total	100.0		

ship were clear to respondents, regardless of the institutional form. Similarly, members generally participated in the organization, not because of social or economic pressures per se, but because of the perceived benefits that the organization provided. The respondents also indicated that even though all members do not have the opportunity to join the management group, in most cases mechanisms were in place for the management to listen to the opinions of members.

Table 9.7 *Membership and participation in water institution/organization*

	Strongly agree (Yes)	*Agree*	*Partially agree/ disagree*	*Disagree*	*Strongly disagree (No)*
	5	*4*	*3*	*2*	*1*
The way to become a member of the institution/organization is clearly documented and widely known	38.9	52.4	2.0	1.1	5.6
Members participate in the activities of this organization because of social or economic pressure	2.2	2.4	2.2	21.3	71.8
Members participate in the activities of this organization because it benefits them directly	14.9	64.7	4.4	3.1	12.9
All members have the opportunity to join management teams/committees	4.9	23.1	13.3	11.8	46.7
There are mechanisms in place for management to listen to the opinions of members	2.7	44.9	5.6	18.9	28.0

Key governance and institutional considerations

Governance

As discussed above in the conceptual framework, a major determinant of the success of institutions is expected to be their ability to deliver good governance along the lines of three rationalities: technical, organizational and political. In local institutions such as these, the technical rationality seems likely to be delivered primarily by the staff, while the organizational rationality relates mainly to the activities of the managing committee. Political rationality hinges on the chairman and the relationship to the general body. The key question is whether these forms of rationality are being adequately addressed in the water institutions. The results in Table 9.8 below indicate that the general body is very active in 21 per cent of the cases, active in 40 per cent and passive in 28 per cent. The chairman, managing committee, and secretary are considered active or very active in most cases. But clearly there appears to be considerable variation in the extent to which each entity is addressing these rationalities and this may well be reflected in the overall performance of institutions.

As far as the government is concerned, the data show that government officials and local government bodies (*Panchayats*) were considered inactive or having no role in more than 60 per cent of the cases. The village headman (*Sarpanch*) also usually had little to do with the functioning of the water institutions. Again, critical questions arise around data such as these. For instance, do those involved in governance have the necessary expertise to actually do a good job? After all it is one thing to be 'active'; it is another thing altogether to be effective. According to Table 9.8, 45 per cent of the respondents perceived that management had the expertise to do a good job and nearly 78 per cent considered that management was putting this into practice and delivering. However, satisfaction with staff expertise and performance was of a lower order. These variations may again be reflected in institutional performance, an issue dealt with later in this and other chapters.

Table 9.8 *Governance – Role of the following in the running of the institution (percentages)*

Role of	*Very active*	*Active*	*Passive*	*None*
General body	21.1	40.7	27.8	10.4
Chairman	37.3	29.1	7.1	26.4
Managing committee	32.7	32.7	8.0	26.7
Members	13.6	49.6	26.7	10.2
Non-members	4.2	11.6	10.9	73.3
Secretary	29.3	32.0	5.3	33.3
Other staff	13.3	22.9	6.7	34.9
Government officials	8.4	16.0	13.3	62.2
Panchayat	3.1	22.0	10.7	64.2
Sarpanch	1.6	24.2	6.4	67.8

Table 9.9 *Governance expertise and quality*

	Strongly agree (Yes)	*Agree*	*Partially agree/ disagree*	*Disagree*	*Strongly disagree (No)*
	5	*4*	*3*	*2*	*1*
Management has the expertise to do a good job	13.1	32.7	12.2	4.4	37.6
The management does a good job	8.4	70.2	4.0	3.1	14.2
Staff have the necessary expertise to do a good job	1.8	52.9	2.0	2.0	19.1
In general, the staff do a good job	1.6	54.2	1.1	1.8	18.9

The government is a mega-force in irrigation affairs and often plays a major role in the creation and functioning of water institutions. Table 9.10 provides findings on the role of the government. While about 23 per cent agree that the institution had been created directly as a result of government activity, more than 50 per cent of the sample was made up of institutions where government action was trivial or insignificant. In addition, more than half the household respondents indicated that there was no necessity to report to government at all. In these cases the rules were not considered to be determined by government and the supervision and working of the organization lay outside the purview of the state. Nevertheless, a sizable proportion of the sample report that the government played a significant role in these activities. This undoubtedly arose because of the coverage of ground-water and surface water institutions within the sample itself.

Table 9.10 *Role of the government*

	Strongly agree (Yes)	*Agree*	*Partially agree/ disagree*	*Disagree*	*Strongly disagree (No)*
	5	*4*	*3*	*2*	*1*
The institution/organization has been created by the government	22.2	0.7	25.6	19.8	31.8
The institution/organization reports to the government	7.6	10.4	19.1	14.2	48.4
The rules of the organization are mainly determined by the government and not the members	12.9	7.3	4.9	33.6	41.3
The government supervises the working of the organization	3.8	6.7	4.4	35.6	49.6

Features related to New Institutional Economics

This section provides an overview of the data as it relates to the features based on the NIE framework discussed in the conceptual background above and detailed in the introductory chapters. In that context we focus primarily on the delineation of clear objectives, good interaction, adaptiveness, appropriateness of scale, and compliance ability. Table 9.11 provides findings on the issue of clarity of purpose and objectives. Whereas a majority of the respondents indicated that the institution had a clear set of objectives, a large number reported that the objectives were not well communicated and shared across the institution. Moreover, in many cases the institution was perceived as not deliberately pursuing the achievement of objectives on a regular basis. With respect to deviations from the objectives, the opinions expressed within the sample were highly divided with only partial agreement from most members.

Table 9.11 *Clarity of purpose/objectives*

	Strongly agree (Yes)	*Agree*	*Partially agree/ disagree*	*Disagree*	*Strongly disagree (No)*
	5	*4*	*3*	*2*	*1*
This organization has a clear set of objectives/purpose	26.9	62.2	1.3	0.7	8.7
The objectives of this organization are clear to the members of the organization	18.9	62.7	3.8	1.6	13.1
The objectives are well communicated and shared across the institution	5.1	21.8	4.4	15.3	53.1
The institution pursues and regularly makes plans towards achievement of these objectives	9.6	18.0	16.7	12.7	43.1
Deviations from these objectives are not frequent	8.9	25.6	47.1	3.1	14.4

Table 9.12 gives the results on items relating to good interaction. A majority of the respondents indicated that there was good interaction between the members, between the management and the members, and between the staff and the members. However, with respect to good leadership to facilitate interaction and regular meetings, the overall opinion was highly divided. A large number of respondents indicated that good interaction between the institution and the government did not exist, and that the institution did little to help settle disputes.

Table 9.13 provides an overview of the responses to questions relating to adaptiveness. A majority of the respondents indicated that the rules and systems of the organization were not especially rigid, and that there were clear mechanisms and processes for adapting the rules and systems of the organization. Nevertheless, this opinion was far from universal with considerable variation within the data. Respondents also indicated that the management generally had the authority to adapt the rules and systems, but again this was not unanimous across the sample. Most respondents thought that there were no mechanisms for regular review of the rules and systems within the organization.

Another important feature is the appropriateness of the scale and size of the entity under consideration. Overall the data summarized in Table 9.14 indicate that the institutions are considered neither too large nor too small in most cases and were generally perceived as being of appropriate scale. The systems of the institutions are also considered to scale. However, respondents frequently indicate that higher level issues were not appropriately addressed by higher level institutions – a response consistent with the earlier observations of Upadhyay (Chapter 7).

Table 9.12 *Good interaction*

	Strongly agree (Yes)	*Agree*	*Partially agree/ disagree*	*Disagree*	*Strongly disagree (No)*
	5	*4*	*3*	*2*	*1*
There is good interaction between the members of the institution	28.0	64.0	1.3	4.9	1.8
There is good interaction between the management and the members	27.1	63.6	1.6	2.7	5.1
There is good interaction between the staff and the members	35.8	43.3	3.1	2.0	13.8
There is good leadership to facilitate, improve and guide the interaction	16.7	40.4	28.9	1.6	12.2
There are regular meetings	11.8	46.2	2.7	12.7	26.2
There is good interaction between the institution and the government	2.0	5.1	44.2	5.6	42.4
This organization helps members to settle disputes	4.2	15.8	22.0	10.2	47.6

Table 9.13 *Adaptiveness*

	Strongly agree (Yes)	*Agree*	*Partially agree/ disagree*	*Disagree*	*Strongly disagree (No)*
	5	*4*	*3*	*2*	*1*
The rules and systems of the organization are very rigid	3.56	15.33	10.67	26.44	44.00
There are clear mechanisms for changing the rules of this organization if the need arises	11.6	64.4	3.1	5.3	15.6
There are processes for adapting the rules and systems according to the needs and setting	2.22	47.56	13.33	12.44	24.44
There is a regular review of the rules and systems of the institution	3.56	10.89	23.78	12.00	49.56
The management has the authority to adapt the rules and systems	24.44	31.56	2.22	4.00	37.78

Table 9.14 *Scale/size*

	Strongly agree (Yes)	*Agree*	*Partially agree/ disagree*	*Disagree*	*Strongly disagree (No)*
	5	*4*	*3*	*2*	*1*
The scale of the institution is too large	0.67	4.00	4.22	35.33	55.78
The scale of the institution is too small	0.67	1.33	7.33	27.56	63.11
The scale of the institution is appropriate for efficient management	26.00	56.67	8.22	2.22	6.89
The systems of the institution are appropriate for the scale of operation	12.67	68.67	8.22	2.44	8.00
The higher level issues are appropriately addressed by higher level institutions	7.11	15.78	27.78	8.44	38.22

Table 9.15 *Compliance*

	Strongly agree (Yes)	*Agree*	*Partially agree/ disagree*	*Disagree*	*Strongly disagree (No)*
	5	*4*	*3*	*2*	*1*
Members are aware of and willingly follow the rules set down by this organization	18.0	61.8	4.9	2.4	12.7
The management has enough powers to bring compliance with institutional objectives and rules	21.11	59.33	2.89	1.33	15.33
The institution uses its powers to bring compliance	14.89	43.78	22.89	1.78	16.67
The compliance with the rules is sufficient	22.00	28.89	5.11	3.56	40.44
There is external monitoring and enforcement for compliance	0.00	2.67	2.44	28.00	66.67
The institution is able to ensure fairness and justice	6.22	50.22	24.00	1.33	18.00

The ability of the institution to bring compliance among members is the final dimension of interest and the items used to gauge this attribute are summarized in Table 9.15. In most cases respondents were aware of and willing to follow the rules and management had sufficient powers to effect compliance. Again, there was variation within the data, with many disagreeing. On the issue of whether the organization used its powers and whether compliance was sufficient, opinions were also widely divided. Most respondents indicated that there was no external monitoring or enforcement for compliance, but about 56 per cent of the respondents indicate that the institution was able to ensure fairness and justice.

Institutional actions to address national priorities for water management

To address the national crisis in water resource management, water institutions in India need to focus their activities on the key challenges of scarcity, equity, environmental degradation and financial viability. This section presents an overview of the items used to capture information on these challenges. Table 9.16 examines the actions taken by the institutions to deal with the scarcity of water. The results indicate that in most cases, opinions are highly divided, again reflecting considerable variation in the data, presumably tied to different institutional forms and settings. In a large number of cases institutions seem able to assess water availability in a season and have a process for allocating the resource to farmers. However, pricing of water according to its scarcity and crop use was not commonly practised. Penalties for misuse and maintenance activities to prevent losses were also reported as frequently inadequate.

Table 9.17 provides results on the issue of equity. While appropriate mechanisms were in place in most cases to deal with distribution between small and large farmers, this was considered somewhat less so between the head, middle and tail-end farmers. Monitoring and enforcement of equitable allocations was also perceived as being inadequate in many cases.

Environmental considerations were also gauged as part of the survey and an overview of the responses for all participants is provided in Table 9.18. As a general rule the activities of the organization seldom led to water-logging or flooding; perhaps not surprisingly given the water scarcity in these states. However, in many cases (30 per cent) it was acknowledged that the activity of the institution was leading to depletion of ground water. Very few respondents felt that there were mechanisms to consider or become aware of environmental issues. Very few respondents reported the existence of organized activities to reduce environmental harm/depletion.

On the issue of financial viability, less than half of the respondents indicated that their institutions were financially viable and less than 30 per cent agreed that their institution was likely to be able to raise a recurring payment from the beneficiaries (Table 9.19). Most of the respondents indicated that the support from the government, donors and financial institutions was either unavailable or inadequate. Most indicated that banking and financial institutions would be unwilling to invest in the activities undertaken by the organization.

Given the superordinate nature of government, additional information was collected on the broad perceptions of household farmers dealing with the relationship between government and the lower-order institutions. The data in Table 9.20 illustrate the diverse opinions proffered by respondents in this context. About 55 per cent of respondents believed that members had benefited because of government policy intervention while about 44 per cent believed that the activities and services of the institutions had improved because of policy.

Table 9.16 *Scarcity*

Particulars	*Strongly agree (Yes)*	*Agree*	*Partially agree/ disagree*	*Disagree*	*Strongly disagree (No)*
	5	*4*	*3*	*2*	*1*
The institution assesses the quantity of water available in a season/year	29.3	4.0	16.9	6.7	22.7
The institution has processes for determining the allocation of this water to the farmers	25.8	25.6	14.4	8.2	24.0
The institution prices the water according to its scarcity value.	4.7	14.7	20.2	20.9	38.9
The institution prices the water according to the crop	18.9	20.2	7.1	9.1	44.7
The staff of the institution allocate and monitor the use	29.3	24.2	7.3	3.8	33.3
The penalties for misuse/abuse are enforced	12.0	21.3	11.1	11.1	44.2
The institution does good maintenance to prevent water loss	18.7	9.1	23.6	9.1	39.1

Table 9.17 *Equity*

Particulars	*Strongly agree (Yes)*	*Agree*	*Partially agree/ disagree*	*Disagree*	*Strongly disagree (No)*
	5	*4*	*3*	*2*	*1*
The institution has processes for equitable distribution of water among farmers	23.8	37.1	6.0	8.4	24.7
There is proper distribution of water between small and large farmers	27.3	34.2	10.4	3.6	24.4
There is proper distribution of water between head, middle, and tail-end farmers	27.1	26.7	9.8	5.3	31.1
Equitable allocation of water is monitored and enforced	4.9	23.8	28.7	7.3	34.9

Table 9.18 *Environment*

Particulars	*Strongly agree (Yes)*	*Agree*	*Partially agree/ disagree*	*Disagree*	*Strongly disagree (No)*
	5	*4*	*3*	*2*	*1*
The activity of the institution is causing flooding/water-logging in some areas	5.6	6.0	6.4	40.2	41.8
The activity of the institution is rapidly depleting ground water in the village	8.4	20.2	7.3	21.6	42.4
The institution is aware of and monitors such environmental harm/depletion	15.1	12.7	47.1	4.9	20.2
The institution undertakes activities to reduce such environmental harm/depletion	1.3	3.6	47.6	20.7	26.9

Table 9.19 *Financial viability*

Particulars	*Strongly agree (Yes)*	*Agree*	*Partially agree/ disagree*	*Disagree*	*Strongly disagree (No)*
	5	*4*	*3*	*2*	*1*
The institution is financially viable	21.6	25.3	41.6	8.0	3.6
The institution is able to raise recurring payments from the beneficiaries	12.2	16.9	35.3	19.6	16.0
The institutions has penalties to encourage regular payment	9.3	19.1	13.1	20.4	38.0
The institution is able to raise sufficient funding support from the government	10.4	16.0	8.7	18.4	46.0
The institution is able to raise funding from donors and public	14.2	9.8	8.7	18.2	49.1
Banking and financial institutions would be willing to invest in the institution	0.4	1.1	10.7	30.7	57.1

Table 9.20 *Impact of policy*

Particulars	*Strongly agree (Yes)*	*Agree*	*Partially agree/ disagree*	*Disagree*	*Strongly disagree (No)*
	5	*4*	*3*	*2*	*1*
Membership of this organization has improved because of government policy	21.8	12.0	11.6	39.1	15.6
The financial performance of this organization is threatened by government policy	5.6	4.0	19.6	34.4	36.4
The activities and services of the organization have improved because of policy	18.7	25.6	35.3	8.4	10.7
Members have benefited because of policy	19.3	36.0	33.8	3.3	7.3

Institutional performance

Enumerating performance

Having provided a broad overview of the range of responses within these data, we now turn to the question of institutional performance. This is done against the backdrop of the earlier theoretical chapters where it was hypothesized that good institutional design and sound governance were the keys to unlocking superior performance in irrigation. The performance of institutions can be judged in various ways, such as their impact on the issues of scarcity, equity, environment and financial viability. However, objective evaluation of variables such as these is very difficult, particularly in the context of a developing country where consistent and historically reliable data cannot easily be drawn upon. Table 9.21 provides a summary of the responses of the sampled households to questions pertaining to some dimensions of institutional performance. In essence, these data attempt to draw upon the historical indigenous knowledge of households as it relates to perceptions of changed performance over time. A large number of respondents indicated that there has been a positive impact on the efficiency indicators – such as timely and good quality of water, changes to high value crops and better maintenance – all attributable to the institutional initiatives in question. Positive impacts were also indicated in the areas of equity, social cohesion and empowerment. However, little impact was shown in the context of adding choice to the sequencing and timing of irrigation.

A broader way of examining the performance of institutions would be to establish the impact on the village community as a whole, and its different constituent parts. A summary of the responses to questions dealing with this approach is shown in Table 9.22. In general, these data indicate that, in the view of large numbers of respondents, the impact has been either positive or substantially positive. This result holds not only for the village as a whole but also for various groups within the community; low-income groups such as small/marginal farmers and labour/wage earners, for example.

An alternative approach to considering performance revolves around negative outcomes and their prevalence. The data in Table 9.23 give a summary of the outcome from this approach and review the response of households to questions focusing on performance deficiencies. The data in the table indicate that among the major problems are non-availability of water at source, the high cost of electricity, and the high cost of maintenance. Other concerns, such as lack of member cooperation and non-payment of water charges, do not appear to be significant for most respondents.

Table 9.21 *What has been the impact of the institution on the following? (percentages)*

Particulars	*Strongly agree (Yes)*	*Agree*	*Partially agree/ disagree*	*Disagree*	*Strongly disagree (No)*
	5	*4*	*3*	*2*	*1*
A Efficiency					
Timely water availability	24.9	36.4	37.3	0.2	1.1
Adequate water availability	22.9	36.7	18.7	11.8	10.0
Change in cropping pattern in favour of high value crops	31.6	25.3	42.4	0.0	0.2
Better maintenance of irrigation structure	19.8	28.0	43.1	6.4	2.7
B Equity					
Equitable distribution of water	27.1	32.9	39.3	0.4	0.2
Empowerment of farmers to manage irrigation systems	32.7	37.6	20.4	6.7	2.7
C Social cohesion and empowerment					
Beginning of a sense of ownership by farmers	45.8	24.4	29.1	0.4	0.2
Resolution of disputes and dealing with offences	20.7	45.1	33.8	0.0	0.2
D Other					
Price/cost of water	21.6	30.7	46.9	0.2	0.7
Diversification of cropping pattern	29.8	22.9	46.7	0.2	0.4
Choice in deciding irrigation timings	3.1	19.8	76.7	0.0	0.4

Finally, one alternative for tackling the dilemma of performance measurement is to delve into the household members' overall perceptions of success and impact of a given institution. Notwithstanding the caveats that would apply to this approach, it should be remembered that institutional analysis is primarily based on humanly devised constraints and therefore the humanly perceived impact of institutions is entirely consistent with the NIE philosophy. Table 9.24 contains information about the overall assessment of water institutions as offered by respondents. The data indicate that about 17 per cent consider that their institution had been very successful and another 26 per cent rated performance as successful. About 12 per cent consider the performance of their institution as poor. With respect to the financial health of the institution, about 7 per cent indicated this to be very strong or strong and about 76 per cent indicated it to be satisfactory. Again, the variation in these data is substantial, suggesting scope for greater empirical scrutiny.

Table 9.22 *Has the institution contributed directly or indirectly to the development of the following? (percentages)*

Type	*Impact of the institution*				
	Substantially positive	*Positive*	*No impact*	*Negative*	*Substantially negative*
	5	*4*	*3*	*2*	*1*
Village as a whole	48.2	31.8	19.3	0.0	0.7
Women	40.7	36.9	22.4	0.0	0.0
Poor	18.0	28.7	53.3	0.0	0.0
Large/medium farmers	26.2	51.6	22.2	0.0	0.0
Small/marginal farmers	27.3	48.9	22.9	0.9	0.0
Labour/wage earners	23.3	53.6	22.7	0.0	0.2
Head-reach farmers	23.3	42.9	11.6	0.0	0.0
Tail-reach farmers	16.2	38.7	12.4	6.0	4.4
Environment and natural resources	18.4	7.3	72.9	0.9	0.0

Table 9.23 *Indicate if the institution and its members suffer due to the following problems (percentages)*

Particulars	*Rating*			
	Very major	*Major*	*Light/occasional*	*None/no*
	4	*3*	*2*	*1*
Inadequate maintenance	4.9	14.2	27.6	53.3
High cost of maintenance	0.7	53.1	8.2	38.0
Lack of members cooperation	1.6	4.2	8.2	86.0
Non-availability of water at the source	26.7	9.3	19.3	44.0
Poor quality of water	21.3	3.6	0.9	69.8
High cost of electricity	32.9	18.4	1.6	44.9
Water table receding fast	22.7	3.8	1.3	71.8
Non-payment of water charges	0.0	5.3	7.6	86.9

Table 9.24 *Overall assessment of the success and financial health of the institution by the respondents*

Success of the institution			*Financial health of the institution*		
Success	*Rating*	*%*	*Financial health*	*Rating*	*%*
Very successful	4	16.7	Very strong	4	3.3
Successful	3	26.0	Strong	3	3.8
Satisfactory	2	44.9	Satisfactory	2	75.8
Poor	1	12.4	Poor	1	17.1
Total		100.0	Total		100.0

Results of bivariate statistical analysis

The analysis here applied bivariate statistical techniques to examine the statistical significance of a large number of associations across the generalized study results presented above. This has been done through the analysis of variance (ANOVA) framework. The findings are presented in terms of the mean values of each group and the statistical significance of the difference across the means. Where the institutional performance is involved, this is gauged on the basis of the opinion of the respondents on the overall success of the institution (ranging from 4 to 1 as described above).

General findings

The association between cohesion and institutional performance is presented in tabular form in Table 9.25. The results confirm that there is a positive and statistically significant relationship between the performance of the institution and cohesion. Excellent cohesion is associated with superior performance.

Table 9.25 *Relationship between cohesion and institutional performance*

Cohesion	*Excellent cohesion*	*Good cohesion*	*Some conflict*	*Several conflicts*	*Severe conflict*	*F-Statistic*	*Statistical significance*
Performance-mean	3.29	2.42	1.80	–	–	13.85	***

Note: *Significant at 10%; ** Significant at 5%; *** Significant at 1%.

The analysis of the participation level of the members in their institutions (Table 9.26) indicates that the differences are statistically significant across institution type, with tube-well partnerships showing the highest level of participation, followed by check dam groups. This is consistent with the grass-roots foundations and close association witnessed in these institutions. Among the states, Gujarat shows the highest level of participation, followed by Andhra Pradesh (Table 9.27).

Table 9.26 *Relationship between institution type and participation*

Institution type	*Check dams group*	*Tube-well cooperative*	*Tube-well partnership*	*Canal cooperative*	*Water user association*	*F-statistic*	*Statistical significance*
Participation-mean	1.99	1.65	2.10	1.62	1.69	14.45	***

Note: *Significant at 10%; ** Significant at 5%; *** Significant at 1%.

Table 9.27 *Relationship between the states and participation*

State	*Andhra Pradesh*	*Gujarat*	*Maharashtra*	*F-statistic*	*Statistical significance*
Participation-mean	1.69	1.96	1.44	38.88	***

Note: *Significant at 10%; ** Significant at 5%; *** Significant at 1%.

As shown in Table 9.28, the reliance of members on the institutions differs significantly by state, with Gujarat showing the highest reliance followed by Maharashtra and then Andhra Pradesh. This is consistent with the water scarcity situation across these states. The reliance also varies by institution type, but there is not much difference across institutions except for the substantially lower reliance shown for WUAs (Andhra Pradesh), see Table 9.29.

Table 9.28 *Relationship between state and reliance on institution*

State	*Andhra Pradesh*	*Gujarat*	*Maharashtra*	*F-statistic*	*Statistical significance*
Reliance-mean	2.99	4.26	3.91	69.39	***

Note: *Significant at 10%; ** Significant at 5%; *** Significant at 1%.

Table 9.29 *Relationship between institution type and reliance on institution*

Institution type	*Check dams group*	*Tube-well cooperative*	*Tube-well partnership*	*Canal cooperative*	*Water user association*	*F-statistic*	*Statistical significance*
Reliance-mean	4.19	4.30	4.33	4.03	2.99	33.28	***

Note: *Significant at 10%; ** Significant at 5%; *** Significant at 1%.

Tables 9.30–9.35 present the results on institutional performance in relation to various features, such as the extant water situation and location. The institutional performance does not vary greatly between ground and surface water institutions. This indicates that there may be successes and failures in both settings. Even though institutions under excess water scenarios show greater success, this is followed by institutions confronting scarcity, indicating that the need for the institution also plays an important role. However, acute scarcity is related to poor institutional performance. An increase in water availability is predictably related to institutional success, although causation remains in dispute (see Herath, Chapter 5). The institutional success rating does not vary significantly with the position of the respondent in the watershed: head, middle or tail. Check dam groups show the highest performance rating, followed by canal cooperatives and then tube-well cooperatives. The institutional performance is indicated as being the highest in Gujarat, followed by Maharashtra.

Table 9.30 *Relationship between source of water and institutional performance*

Source	*Ground*	*Surface*	*F-statistic*	*Statistical significance*
Performance-mean	2.21	2.54	10.56	*

Note: *Significant at 10%; ** Significant at 5%; *** Significant at 1%.

Table 9.31 *Relationship between water situation and institutional performance*

Water situation	*Excess water*	*No scarcity*	*Occasional scarcity*	*Scarcity*	*Acute scarcity*	*F-statistic*	*Statistical significance*
Performance-mean	3.50	2.28	2.63	2.64	1.26	23.09	***

Note: *Significant at 10%; ** Significant at 5%; *** Significant at 1%.

Table 9.32 *Relationship between change in water availability and institutional performance*

Water availability	*Increase*	*No change*	*Decline*	*Sharp decline*	*F-statistic*	*Statistical significance*
Performance-mean	4.00	2.66	2.20	1.26	26.05	***

Note: *Significant at 10%; ** Significant at 5%; *** Significant at 1%.

Table 9.33 *Relationship between location in watershed and reported institutional performance*

Location	*Head*	*Middle*	*Tail*	*F-statistic*	*Statistical significance*
Performance-mean	2.25	2.23	1.99	4.22	–

Table 9.34 *Relationship between institution type and institutional performance*

Institution type	*Check dams group*	*Tube-well cooperative*	*Tube-well partnership*	*Canal cooperative*	*Water user association*	*F-statistic*	*Statistical significance*
Performance-mean	3.56	2.25	2.18	2.59	1.46	177.07	***

Note: *Significant at 10%; ** Significant at 5%; *** Significant at 1%.

Table 9.35 *Relationship between states and institutional performance*

State	*Andhra Pradesh*	*Gujarat*	*Maharashtra*	*F-statistic*	*Statistical significance*
Performance-mean	1.46	2.85	2.52	131.77	***

Note: *Significant at 10%; ** Significant at 5%; *** Significant at 1%.

Variables relating to governance

The results of the analysis of the association between the dimensions of good governance and institutional success are shown in Tables 9.36–9.38. The results support the view that the activity level of the general body is a very important determinant.[1] Good governance provided by an active chairman, management committees and secretaries are all strongly associated with success. Moreover, active government officials are also strongly so associated. The results indicate that where management and the secretary have the expertise to do their jobs, the performance is significantly better. Thus, training could play a significant role if this provided improved decision-making capacity, a theme taken up in later chapters. If the organization has been created by the government and the rules are determined by the government, then there is a significant reduction in the chances of success. Thus, direct government involvement does not seem to lead to a successful institution in its own right.

Table 9.36 *Governance: Relationship between activity level and institutional performance*

	None	*Passive*	*Active*	*Very active*	*F-Statistic*	*Statistical significance*
		Performance-mean				
General body[1]	1.26	3.14	2.26	2.58	84.10	***
Chairman	1.86	1.47	2.78	2.85	64.89	***
Managing committee	1.88	1.50	2.78	2.87	64.45	***
Secretary	1.80	1.75	3.05	2.73	85.64	***
Government officials	2.19	2.08	3.36	3.47	76.47	***

Note: *Significant at 10%; ** Significant at 5%; *** Significant at 1%.

1 These results are somewhat skewed because check-dam general bodies become passive after structure creation.

Table 9.37 *Governance: Relationship between expertise and institutional performance*

	Strongly disagree	*Disagree*	*Partially agree/ disagree*	*Agree*	*Strongly agree*	*F-statistic*	*Statistical significance*
			Performance-mean				
Management has the expertise to do a good job	2.03	1.65	1.84	2.95	3.41	77.28	***
The staff have the necessary expertise to do a good job	1.47	1.22	2.67	2.40	2.88	47.20	***

Note: *Significant at 10%; ** Significant at 5%; *** Significant at 1%.

Table 9.38 *Governance: Relationship between role of government and institutional performance*

	Strongly disagree	*Disagree*	*Partially agree/ disagree*	*Agree*	*Strongly agree*	*F-statistic*	*Statistical significance*
			Performance-mean				
The organization has been created by the government	2.36	2.52	3.46	1.67	1.47	153.50	***
The rules of the organization are mainly determined by the government and not the members	2.70	2.79	2.32	1.61	1.45	46.77	***

Note: *Significant at 10%; ** Significant at 5%; *** Significant at 1%.

Variables relating to New Institutional Economics

Next, the relevance of the fundamentals drawn from NIE is examined against the success of water institutions. The association between success and clear objectives as well as success and good interaction are examined in Tables 9.39 and 9.40 respectively. Results indicate that when clear objectives are in existence, and when these are obvious to all members, there is a strong association with institutional success. The regular pursuit of plans to achieve objectives shows a mixed performance but this is largely because of the inclusion of the check dam groups in the samples, where planning is largely a one-off activity. Good interaction between the members, and between the management and members is positively associated with success. Good interaction with the government appears to be of even greater importance, with very high levels of success shown where this attribute is strong. With respect to assistance in settling disputes, the results are mixed, perhaps because of the questionable effectiveness of the institution in this regard.

Table 9.39 *New Institutional Economics: Relationship between clear objectives and institutional performance*

	Strongly disagree	*Disagree*	*Partially agree/ disagree*	*Agree*	*Strongly agree*	*F-statistic*	*Statistical significance*
			Performance-mean				
This organization has a clear set of objectives/purpose	1.23	1.33	1.50	2.44	2.99	42.29	***
The objectives of this organization are clear to all members of the organization	1.36	2.00	1.65	2.56	3.14	57.10	***
The institution pursues and regularly makes plans towards achievement of these objectives	2.39	3.14	1.87	2.67	2.60	20.42	***

Note: *Significant at 10%; ** Significant at 5%; *** Significant at 1%.

Tables 9.41–9.43 examine the association between institutional performance and the characteristics of adaptability, scale and compliance. The results indicate that where the rules of the organization are very rigid, the chances of success are significantly reduced. Clear mechanisms for changing the rules and the authority to change rules would appear to lead to greater success. Appropriate scale and systems of the institutions are also strongly related to higher success rates. The results indicate that the appropriate handling of higher level issues by higher level institutions is of the greatest importance in the context of scale. The more frequently higher-order decision makers deal appropriately with higher-order problems the more likely there is to be success within the lower-order entities, such as WUAs. In addition, where members are willing to follow the rules of the organization, the chances of success are substantially increased. The use of powers by the institutions to bring compliance shows mixed results, but, where compliance with the rules is sufficient, the success rates are generally higher.

Table 9.40 *New Institutional Economics: Relationship between good interaction and institutional performance*

	Strongly disagree	*Disagree*	*Partially agree/ disagree*	*Agree*	*Strongly agree*	*F-statistic*	*Statistical significance*
			Performance-mean				
There is good interaction between the members of the institution	1.00	1.59	1.67	2.39	2.93	24.01	***
There is good interaction between the management and the members	1.35	1.58	1.86	2.37	3.02	30.83	***
There is good interaction between the institution and the government	1.88	2.04	3.03	2.74	3.22	67.16	***
There is good leadership to facilitate, improve and guide the interaction	1.35	1.57	2.34	2.75	2.95	45.71	***
This organization helps members to settle disputes.	2.34	3.41	2.53	2.13	2.53	18.53	***

Note: *Significant at 10%; ** Significant at 5%; *** Significant at 1%.

Results of multivariate analysis: Factor analysis and TOBIT analysis

The above analysis examined the relationships through a bivariate approach with one explanatory factor considered at a time. A number of factors emerge with significant association, particularly for institutional performance, and these confirm the relevance of the conceptual background of NIE, as well as management theories of good governance. In this section we expand the analysis to enable us to contemplate more complex issues, such as the collective effect of these variables on institutional performance. To accomplish this task we use a multivariate approach with regression (TOBIT) analysis. In simple terms, this approach enables us to load several explanatory factors together in a statistical model to predict the marginal impact of each variable.

Table 9.41 *New Institutional Economics: Relationship between adaptability and institutional performance*

	Strongly disagree	*Disagree*	*Partially agree/ disagree*	*Agree*	*Strongly agree*	*F-statistic*	*Statistical significance*
			Performance-mean				
The rules and systems of the organization are very rigid	2.40	3.04	1.92	2.03	2.56	24.74	***
There are clear mechanisms for changing the rules of this organization if the need arises	1.41	1.75	1.93	2.66	3.31	67.59	***
The management has the authority to adapt the rules and systems	1.88	1.61	1.80	2.85	3.09	67.15	***
There is a regular review of the rules and systems of the institution	2.41	2.67	2.45	2.55	2.44	1.00	–

Note: *Significant at 10%; ** Significant at 5%; *** Significant at 1%.

Table 9.42 *New Institutional Economics: Relationship between scale and institutional performance*

	Strongly disagree	*Disagree*	*Partially agree/ disagree*	*Agree*	*Strongly agree*	*F-statistic*	*Statistical significance*
			Performance-mean				
The scale of the institution is appropriate for efficient management	1.19	1.50	1.65	2.52	3.03	54.37	***
The systems of the institution are appropriate for the scale of operation	1.25	1.55	1.57	2.64	3.05	53.73	***
The higher level issues are appropriately addressed by higher level institutions	1.93	2.11	2.56	3.52	3.41	88.40	***

Note: *Significant at 10%; ** Significant at 5%; *** Significant at 1%.

Table 9.43 *New Institutional Economics: Relationship between compliance and institutional performance*

	Strongly disagree	*Disagree*	*Partially agree/ disagree*	*Agree*	*Strongly agree*	*F-statistic*	*Statistical significance*
			Performance-mean				
Members are aware of and willingly follow the rules set down by this organization	1.37	1.55	1.68	2.57	3.25	70.15	***
The institution uses its powers to bring compliance	1.39	2.25	2.47	2.73	2.96	50.69	***
Compliance with the rules is sufficient	1.86	1.88	3.22	2.79	3.09	65.44	***

Note: *Significant at 10%; ** Significant at 5%; *** Significant at 1%.

Factor analysis

One of the major problems with multivariate analysis is the potential for multicollinearity between explanatory variables. For example, in production functions, irrigation and fertilizers, even though they are separate determinants of crop production, usually move together in the data – the more irrigation, the higher the fertilizer use. Therefore, the multivariate procedure finds it difficult to separate the specific effects of irrigation and fertilizer on production. In the case of water institutions, an active management committee may well be associated with management showing greater expertise, or the presence of a good secretary and adequate compliance. Thus, the multivariate analysis may find it difficult to distinguish these impacts on performance.

In light of this problem, factor analysis was undertaken to reduce the potential for multicollinearity within the data. In addition, this phase allowed us to identify important factors as explanatory variables in their own right. The resulting factor loading matrix resulted in the identification of seven key factors with variable loadings as follows:

- Factor 1: Managing committee (active), secretary (active), management has expertise, management has authority to adapt rules, compliance is sufficient;
- Factor 2: Organization created by government (negative), rules of organization determined by government (negative), objectives are clear, clear mechanism for changing rules, scale is appropriate, organization uses its powers;
- Factor 3: Good interaction between members of the institution, good interaction between management and members;

- Factor 4: General body active, institution regularly plans and pursues objectives;
- Factor 5: Higher-level issues are appropriately addressed by higher-level institutions;
- Factor 6: Good leadership to facilitate interaction;
- Factor 7: Management has expertise.

Apart from identifying these factors, analysis also showed that many determinants of institutional performance are empirically associated within the data – i.e. they fall on the same factor. Nevertheless, the analysis also successfully revealed many independent items and a number of different independent factors that determine institutional performance.

TOBIT analysis

Since the performance indicators are range-bound with values, say from 1 to 4 and 1 to 5, the classical regression assumptions would be violated and an alternative procedure such as a limited dependent variable procedure is required for correct multivariate estimation. The TOBIT model is suitable for the nature of the data and was selected for the econometric estimation.

The TOBIT model is used to study the behaviour of institutional performance with the aim of identifying important determinants. Various measures of institutional performance were used as the dependent variable, including the overall rating of institutional performance, and other measures addressing the performance objectives of water delivery, scarcity (efficiency), equity, environmental degradation, financial strength and development.

The model used 19 explanatory variables, including dummies for groundwater and check dam institutions. The explanatory variables were selected after taking into account the broader theoretical literature, the framework developed earlier in this text, and the results of several rounds of factor and correlation analysis to identify independent factors. In general, it was considered desirable to include representatives of as many variables as possible covering the different kinds of determinants. This was done to increase the explanatory power of the model and yet this comes at the risk of increased multicollinearity. Given the nature of the data, it was not possible to eliminate multicollinearity entirely, and the results should be interpreted appropriately within those limitations.[2]

The results of the TOBIT model estimation with the dependent variable specified in three different forms are presented in Table 9.44. In this instance the dependent variable is specified as institutional performance or success (i.e. the respondents' overall rating), increase in irrigated area, and the frequency of pricing according to scarcity. Several factors that were hypothesized in the conceptual background emerge as significant determinants of performance. The performance was found to be positively related to the general body, managing committee activity and management expertise, indicating the importance of addressing the internal mechanics of organizations, particularly technical and organizational rationality.[3]

The results indicate that if the institution regularly pursues plans to achieve stated objectives, then success is significantly improved. If the organization has been created by the government and the rules are determined by the government, the chances of success are predicted to be significantly reduced. Where the institution uses its powers to bring compliance, the chances of success are significantly better. These results indicate the importance of the NIE framework in explaining institutional performance.

As noted earlier, another model was estimated using the impact on increasing irrigated area as a dependent variable. The results indicate that the managing committee being active, good leadership and sufficient compliance with the rules emerged as being significantly and positively related to increases in the irrigated area. The creation of the organization solely by government was predicted to be negatively related to the area under irrigation.

Finally, a third equation was estimated using a variable that captured the extent to which water prices were set in accordance with scarcity. The rationale for this approach lies in the importance of this variable as an indicator of the water institutions' capacity to treat water as an economically valuable and scarce resource. The results indicate that good interaction between the members, clear mechanisms for changing rules, having higher-level issues being dealt with by higher-level institutions, and compliance with rules were all conducive to establishing pricing regimes along economic lines.

In order to further explore other salient relationships, additional models were developed that sought to uncover the role played by institutional factors in determining equity and maintenance of irrigation infrastructure. Table 9.45 presents the TOBIT model estimation results where the dependent variables were specified as better maintenance of irrigation structures, the frequency of having rules for equitable distribution of water, and the respondents' rating of the extent to which equity was achieved within the structure of the organization. In the context of better maintenance, which is an important indicator of attempts to address scarcity, it was found that there was a positive association with general body activity, having clear objectives, the regular making of plans to achieve objectives, and having higher-level issues being appropriately addressed by higher-level institutions.

To examine the issue of equity, two different models were used. The first contains a dependent variable that focuses on the existence of rules for ensuring an equitable distribution of water. This model revealed that there was a positive association with the objectives of the organization being clear, good interaction between members, and the institution using its powers to bring compliance. By way of contrast, the model exposed a negative relationship between this dimension of equity and the creation of the institution by the government.

The second model dealing with equity considerations specified the dependent variable as the extent to which equity was achieved within the structure of the organization. The results indicated that there was a positive relationship

Table 9.44: *Tobit regression results for overall institutional performance rating, increase in irrigated area, and pricing of water according to scarcity*

Explanatory variable	*Dependent variables*		
	Institutional performance or success	*Increase in irrigated area*	*Pricing of water according to scarcity*
	Parameter estimates and significance		
Intercept	1.420091***	4.076893*	1.410308
General body active	0.250914***	−0.069159	−0.066155
Managing committee active	0.187092**	0.265481***	0.099475
Secretary active	−0.287871***	−0.04304	−0.015379
The organization has been created by the government	−0.149422***	−0.25024***	−0.139544
The rules of the organization are mainly determined by the government and not the members	−0.08607	−0.057786	−0.118937
Management has the expertise to do a good job	0.234816***	0.084181	0.101575
The objectives of this organization are clear to all members of the organization	0.100343	−0.20820***	−0.255083
The institution pursues and regularly makes plans towards achievement of these objectives	0.268053***	−0.080258	−0.237644**
There is good interaction between the members of the institution	−0.063359	−0.003387	0.475615***
There is good leadership to facilitate, improve and guide the interaction	−0.169503***	0.239415***	0.211716
There are clear mechanisms for changing the rules of this organization if the need arises	−0.001211	−0.007377	0.29315**
The management has the authority to adapt the rules and systems	−0.090217	0.099452	−0.097824
The scale of the institution is appropriate for efficient management	−0.170791***	−0.145137**	−0.333062***
The higher-level issues are appropriately addressed by higher-level institutions	0.068449	0.076801	0.432666***
The institution uses its powers to bring compliance	0.163848***	0.03968	−0.254228**
The compliance with the rules is sufficient.	0.002516	0.111427*	0.417881***
Check-dam dummy	2.08165***	0.445611	−9.007202
Ground-water dummy	0.260732	0.215121	−0.416754
N = 450			

Note: *Significant at 10%; ** Significant at 5%; *** Significant at 1%.

Table 9.45 *TOBIT regression results for better maintenance of irrigation structures, rules for equitable distribution of water, and equity achieved within the structure*

Explanatory variable	*Dependent variables*		
	Institutional performance or success	*Increase in irrigated area*	*Pricing of water according to scarcity*
	Parameter estimates and significance		
Intercept	2.184783	0.865103	2.691568***
General body active	0.161418*	−0.053271	0.128444
Managing committee active	−0.070948	0.035073	0.172179**
Secretary active	−0.042258	0.144124	0.008209
The organization has been created by the government	0.035662	−0.280849***	−0.244929***
The rules of the organization are mainly determined by the government and not the members	−0.008707	0.05329	0.165364***
Management has the expertise to do a good job	0.260157***	−0.086964	−0.014157
The objectives of this organization are clear to all members of the organization	0.148892**	0.246791**	−0.153588**
The institution pursues and regularly makes plans towards achievement of these objectives	0.308167***	0.075920	0.014838
There is good interaction between the members of the institution	−0.005304	0.578960***	0.013341
There is good leadership to facilitate, improve and guide the interaction	−0.232613	−0.108166	0.056266
There are clear mechanisms for changing the rules of this organization if the need arises	−0.014414	−0.075976	0.089766
The management has the authority to adapt the rules and systems	0.040387	0.189608*	−0.002157
The scale of the institution is appropriate for efficient management	−0.057051	−0.104382	−0.026575
Higher-level issues are appropriately addressed by higher-level institutions	0.274928***	−0.039760	0.046489
The institution uses its powers to bring compliance.	−0.395888***	0.252684**	0.010793
The compliance with the rules is sufficient	0.024219	−0.008054	0.199314***
Check-dam dummy	0.401172	−10.952037	1.090317**
Ground-water dummy	3.273710***	0.822417	1.048941***
N=450			

Note: *Significant at 10%; ** Significant at 5%; *** Significant at 1%.

Table 9.46 *TOBIT regression results for activities to reduce environmental harm, the institution being financially viable, the impact on the whole village, and the impact on labour and wage earners*

Explanatory variable	*Dependent variables*			
	Activities to reduce environmental harm	*Institution is financially viable*	*Impact on whole village*	*Imapct on labour and wage earners*
	Parameter estimates and significance			
Intercept	1.013432	1.983687***	2.438957***	2.724603***
General body	−0.227194*	−0.080576	0.113985	0.111588*
Managing committee	−0.013498	0.065312	0.085222	−0.088264
Secretary	−0.103777	−0.126746	−0.003935	0.152946*
The organization has been created by the government	−0.162456**	−0.30127***	−0.186443**	−0.033801
The rules of the organization are mainly determined by the government and not the members	0.037021	0.055063	0.110334	−0.041491
Management has the expertise to do a good job	0.256080***	0.170645***	−0.002147	0.127217***
The objectives of this organization are clear to all members of the organization	0.073119	0.002937	−0.064158	−0.143711***
The institution pursues and regularly makes plans towards achievement of these objectives	0.007371	0.290509***	0.080999	−0.060217
There is good interaction between the members of the institution	0.302305***	0.387007***	0.075067	0.032975
There is good leadership to facilitate, improve and guide the interaction	−0.072640	−0.166068**	0.089606	0.020929
There are clear mechanisms for changing the rules of this organization if the need arises	0.163347	−0.019349	0.211390**	−0.058104
The management has the authority to adapt the rules and systems	−0.012764	0.141572*	−0.016034	0.150765***
The scale of the institution is appropriate for efficient management	−0.235257***	−0.334343	0.029707	0.010978
Higher-level issues are appropriately addressed by higher-level institutions	0.471946***	0.473933***	0.029610	0.074944
The institution uses its powers to bring compliance	−0.371419***	−0.060407	−0.222861**	0.088943*
The compliance with the rules is sufficient	0.253350***	0.037992	0.265635***	0.029809
Check-dam dummy	1.100617*	−0.021508	3.104188***	0.120237
Ground-water dummy	1.098932**	1.120363***	0.942875*	1.460313***
N=450				

Note: *Significant at 10%; ** Significant at 5%; *** Significant at 1%.

between this variable, activity by the managing committee, and compliance with the rules. Arguably, these results are consistent with the hypothesized importance of organizational rationality and compliance. As with the previous model, a negative association with equity was apparent when the organization was created by the government. However, when the government had influence over determining the initial rules there was a significant and positive impact on equity, indicating at least some role for government in achieving better equity outcomes.

We now turn to four additional dimensions of institutional performance using the multivariate approach. Table 9.46 presents the results where the dependent variables were specified in four other ways:

1 undertaking activities to reduce environmental harm;
2 the institution being financially viable;
3 the impact of the institution on the well-being of the whole village, and;
4 the impact on labour and wage earners (as distinct from land owners).

In the case of model 1, expanded environmental activities were found to be positively associated with clear mechanisms for changing rules, good interaction between members of the institution, higher-level issues appropriately addressed by higher-level institutions, and compliance with the rules. Environmental activities were found to be negatively associated with the creation of the institution by government.

Model 2 (based on the financial viability of the institution) again highlights the pivotal role of the internal mechanics and the institutional principles described earlier. Here there was a positive association with management expertise, regular planning to achieve objectives, good interaction between members, management having authority to adapt rules, and higher-level issues being dealt with by higher-level institutions. In a familiar tone, there was a negative association when the institution was created by government.

In a broader sense, the success of the institution may be considered against its impact on the village as a whole (Model 3). In this case there were positive associations with clear mechanisms for changing the rules, and compliance with the rules. The organization was less likely to have a positive impact on the village as a whole when created solely by government.

From the development perspective, considering the benefits to the poor, who are mainly found among labourers and wage earners, is very important and this matter is examined in Model 4. There was a positive impact on labour when the general body was active, the secretary was active, and management possessed the requisite expertise. In addition, where management had the authority to adapt rules and the institution used its powers to bring compliance, it was more likely that labour would be better off.

In sum, there is a strong case for arguing that good governance, embodied in serious attempts to address the technical, organizational and political rationalities, plays a key role in irrigation performance. In addition, many of the rudiments of good institutional design are significantly related to preferred performance outcomes.

Concluding observations

This study sought to examine the nature and performance of local institutions in water resource management in India, using the NIE framework, and theories of good governance emerging from management sciences. A large number of lessons and findings emerge. A number of factors indicated by the NIE materialize as relevant and very important in determining the performance of water institutions. This includes having clear objectives, good interaction, adaptability, appropriate scale, and sound compliance measures. Accordingly, there is strong support for addressing these factors when designing better water institutions and improving the performance of existing water resource management in India – just building better infrastructure is insufficient.

Issues of good governance, including the need to address technical rationality, organizational rationality and political rationality also emerge as very important determinants of institutional performance. The importance of the secretary and the staff being well-trained, active and having the right expertise indicates the importance of addressing technical rationality. Moreover, the management committee being active and having the necessary skills was also found to be very important. This supports the view that it is critically important to address coordination and organizational rationality; however, these are unlikely to be sufficient in their own right. The importance of the general body along with the elected chairman being active indicates that without adequately addressing political rationality, the water institutions cannot be successful. The need for good leadership, often projected as the key essential element, does not emerge in this case as being especially critical. Put differently, while leadership may be important, the results indicate that it is far more important to have the correct institutional design with the required structure, active processes and effective systems to create successful institutions.

In this light, the NIE fundamentals are very important, particularly in indicating ways of reducing transaction costs and promoting cooperative solutions. Having clear objectives which are stated, shared and actualized by the institutions is a critical success driver. Promoting good interaction between the members, and between the management, government and the members, thereby reducing transaction costs, was also found to be very important. However, direct involvement of the government in creating institutions and determining their rules is negatively associated with success and hampers the achievement of many specific aims, such as addressing scarcity, equity, environmental and financial viability. Adaptability of rules and having in place processes to facilitate that adaptation are also clearly important ingredients. Appropriate scale also comes through as being relevant, especially the capability of higher-level issues being adequately addressed by higher-level institutions. Compliance with the rules – both voluntary and through institutional effort – was also found to be a significant determinant of institutional success.

The results show that the failure of water resource institutions witnessed in many parts of India is not insurmountable. Institutional deficiencies can be overcome through the implementation of coherent responses based on the features of institutional design emerging from NIE and management theories of good governance. Ideally, this approach will address the particular deficiencies evident in a specific irrigation setting, as there is clearly much variation in the relative importance of the different components of the NIE framework and the attributes of good governance. This challenge is taken up in the following three chapters where ground-water, surface water and rain-water-harvesting irrigation are treated separately.

Notes

1 The result is somewhat bimodal because of the inclusion of check dam groups in the sample, where general bodies are mostly passive after the construction phase. However, if these are excluded, the results clearly bring out a positive unimodal association of performance with general body activity.

2 Some signs may be incorrect and some significances low because of this. That said, multicollinearity can seldom be dismissed from any analysis – it is more a question of 'degree' rather than exclusion.

3 Managing committee and secretary activity fall in the same factor within the data. Accordingly, we suspect that the coefficient sign for secretary may be turning negative due to multicollinearity.

References

Ackroyd, S. (2002) *Organization of Business: Applying Organizational Theory to Contemporary Change*, Oxford University Press, Oxford

Brewer, J., Kolavalli, S., Kalro, A. H., Naik, G., Ramnarayan, S., Raju, K. V. and Sakthivadivel, R. (1999) *Irrigation Management Transfer in India: Policies, Processes and Performance*, Oxford & IBH, New Delhi

Gandhi, V. P. (1998) 'Rapporteur's report on institutional framework for agricultural development', *Indian Journal of Agricultural Economics*

Gandhi, V. P. and Namboodiri, N. V. (2002) 'Water resource management in India: Institutions and development', in D. Brennan (ed) *Water Policy Reform: Lessons from Asia and Australia*, Australian Centre for International Agricultural Research (ACIAR), Canberra

Groth, L. (1999) *Future Organizational Design: The Scope for IT-Based Enterprise*, John Wiley & Sons, Chichester

Nystrom, P. C. and Starbuck, W. H. (eds) (1981) *Handbook of Organizational Design*, Oxford University Press, Oxford

Saleth, M. R. (1996) *Water Institutions in India: Economics, Law and Policy*, Commonwealth Publishers, New Delhi

Vaidyanathan, A. (1999) *Water Resource Management: Institutions and Irrigation Development in India*, Oxford University Press, New Delhi

10
Institutional Analysis of the Performance of Surface Water Institutions in India

N. V. Namboodiri and Vasant Gandhi

Introduction

As we noted earlier, water scarcity, especially in agriculture, is a major concern in India. The rising demand for water due to population growth, economic development, food production needs and industrial growth is making scarcity even more acute. Accordingly, improving the efficiency of water use in agriculture has become far more important.[1] Irrigation systems, particularly those related to canal irrigation, are besieged by a number of problems such as poor maintenance, degraded infrastructure, difficulties in the allocation of water, water-logging and salinity. Perhaps not surprisingly then, it has been persuasively argued that the economic gains from many surface irrigation projects are not commensurate with the large public investments and subsidies given to them (Vaidyanathan, 1994; Marothia, 1997). Frequently, government or state management and control of canal irrigation have shown a poor record. Better institutional arrangements are required and farmers' groups and cooperatives can play a crucial role in this regard, potentially overcoming some of these problems and improving the economic yield from irrigation (Joshi, 1997; Gandhi and Namboodiri, 2002).

There has been a substantial focus on the development of surface water irrigation in India, but the emphasis has been mainly on the physical and technical dimensions of the task and, as noted elsewhere in this book, the attention given to institutional design has lagged behind that given to engineering design. This chapter builds on the broader analysis presented in the previous chapter and focuses specifically on the functioning of surface water institutions. In this context, the study examines a variety of institutional initiatives and experiments that have been trialled in an effort to develop surface water irrigation and overcome the problems of surface water management. As noted earlier, the study covered three major states of India, that is Andhra Pradesh, Maharashtra and Gujarat. These states have substantial water scarcity and depend heavily on rainfall for crop production. Consistent with the analysis used in the previous chapter, we draw directly from the New Institutional Economics (NIE) framework and the management theories of good governance that were systematically integrated in the first section of this book.

The remainder of this chapter is divided into four main parts. In the following section we establish the context of surface water irrigation in India by providing a brief historical perspective, outlining the scope and development of surface water resources, reflecting on the development of local institutions and summarizing key issues and concerns. The second section provides an overview of the data pertaining to surface water entities and decision-making domains within those organizations. In section three we revisit the constructs drawn from NIE and the theory of good governance and test their empirical relationships with performance. This section follows a similar approach to that outlined in the previous chapter with a series of bivariate tests and multivariate modelling used to evaluate the data. The final section of the chapter comprises a brief summary and some concluding remarks.

Background to surface water irrigation in India

Context and history

In Chapter 8 Gandhi and Namboodiri provided a general overview of water resources and irrigation in India. This section focuses specifically on the nature of surface water resources to establish the context for the empirical analysis offered later.

With a geographical area of 329 million ha India has a large surface water resource and is crisscrossed by numerous small and large rivers, some of them among the mightiest rivers of the world. The rainfall has a highly skewed seasonal and geographical distribution with frequent departures from normality. For example, precipitation averages over 2500mm per year along the west coast, mountain ranges and over Assam, but falls short of 150mm per year in many parts of the peninsular. The surface water resources in the country include rivers, canals, reservoirs, tanks, ponds and a few small water bodies. Surface water irrigation dates back centuries in India, although advances in the construction of inundation canals, where water is blocked by constructing bunds across streams, became more commonplace during the 19th century.

Under British rule, irrigation development began in earnest with innovations, improvements and extensions of the existing works. Subsequently, major river diversion works such as the Ganga, Krishna and Godavari Delta canal systems were taken up. The recurrence of drought and famine during the second half of the 19th century further spurred the development of irrigation.

The gross area irrigated in British India under public works was about 7.5 million ha of which 4.5 million came from surface water. The overall net irrigated area in India at the time of independence was 19.4 million ha, the bulk of it through surface irrigation. At the time of the partition of India and Pakistan, surface water intervention works shared between jurisdictions were mostly designed around flood prevention.

During the government planning periods after Independence, rapid harnessing of water resources was given top priority. As a result, the construction of a large number of projects comprising dams, barrages and canal networks was undertaken as part of successive five-year plans. As it stands, the potential of surface irrigation under major, medium and minor projects is estimated to be 75 million ha but the present utilization is still less than half this (India Planning Commission, 2001).

Surface irrigation in India is dominated by canal systems that are often very large. Irrigation systems in India are classified into three categories based on the size of the command area. Those with a command area of more than 10,000ha are classified as major, those with a command area between 2000 and 10,000ha are classified as medium, and those with less than 2000ha in the command area are classified as minor. In most states the major and medium systems are managed by state government agencies and the small systems are usually managed by local government bodies, such as village *Panchayats*. The basic logic of this bifurcation is that building and operating large systems requires technical knowledge calling for the involvement of the state.

The water distribution systems differ from area to area and some were detailed in the introductory chapter. Generally these include:

(i) *Warabandi* system: government agency managed canal systems mainly found in northwestern India whose users are entitled to a fraction of the total water flow available, proportionate to land area.
(ii) *Shejpali* system: also managed by government agencies, this system is responsible for delivering water in a specific quantity under a given schedule to bring the crop to maturity. These are generally found in western India.
(iii) Land class system: a government agency-controlled system generally found in the southern parts of the country, in which water rights are land-based and classified as single cropped, double cropped, etc.
(iv) *Satta* system: mainly found in the northeastern states with assured irrigation; government agencies are supposed to supply water to bring the crop to maturity.
(v) *Phad* system: small-scale irrigation systems managed by communities, often found in Maharastra; there is usually no involvement of the government or other public bodies. However, in most cases, government

agencies *are* substantially involved in the operation of surface water irrigation systems.

Development and scope of surface water irrigation

On the eve of independence in 1947, canals accounted for almost 70 per cent of the total net irrigated area in the country. Major expansion in canal irrigation took place between the 1950s and the 1980s with the country aggressively following a policy favouring the construction of large dams. The area irrigated through canal systems almost doubled during this period. At the same time, the share of tank systems was declining, not only due to the decline in the command area under tanks, but also due to the rapid expansion in canal irrigation. By the early 2000s tanks constituted less than 13 per cent of irrigation by area (see Table 10.1). The area irrigated through canals was about 8.5 million ha on the eve of independence and by 1980–81 this had expanded to more than 15 million ha. However, the growth in canal irrigation has slowed since then. It is worth noting that the role of private agencies in the development of canal irrigation has been very small.

The irrigation potential developed under surface irrigation through major, medium and minor projects during the successive planning periods is given in Table 10.2. The actual utilization of the potential created under the major and medium projects until the mid 1970s was over 90 per cent but this declined to around 85 per cent by the 1990s, where it has remained since. The gap between irrigation potential developed and irrigation potential utilized has been growing due to delays experienced between the infrastructure development and the transfer of water from dams to fields. Under minor irrigation schemes, the entire potential created was utilized until 1980, but since then the unutilized potential has also been increasing.

Surface water irrigation now accounts for about 40 per cent of the total irrigated area in the country (Table 10.3 and Figures 10.1 and 10.2). The states where the share of surface irrigation is less than one-third are Gujarat, Punjab, Uttar Pradesh, Rajasthan, Bihar and Madhya Pradesh. Tank irrigation has a significant share in states such as Tamil Nadu, Andhra Pradesh and Jharkhand. Thus, there are wide variations in the prominence of surface irrigation systems across states.

Development of local institutions in surface water

Participation in irrigation management was formalized in India in 1974 when Command Area Development Authorities (CADA) were mandated. The main objective of these authorities was to improve the downstream utilization of the created irrigation potential by garnering farmers' cooperation. Additional efforts to mobilize farmers in canal areas were also made in the 1980s under the National Water Resource Management Project. However, user participation under the CADA programme was often ineffective and components of the programme were arguably ad hoc. In 1995, the Union Ministry of Water Resources set up a high-level committee to investigate legal, economic and

Table 10.1 *Growth in surface water irrigation in India (area in '000ha)*

	Canal			*Tanks*	*Total*
	Public	*Private*	*Total*		*surface*
1950–51	7158	1137	8295	3613	11,908
1955–56	8025	1360	9385	4423	13,808
1960–61	9170	1200	10,370	4561	14,931
1965–66	9859	1099	10,958	4258	15,216
1970–71	11,972	866	12,838	4112	16,950
1975–76	12,933	858	13,791	3972	17,763
1980–81	14,450	842	15,292	3182	18,474
1985–86	15,715	465	16,180	2765	18,945
1990–91	16,973	480	17,453	2944	20,397
1995–96	16,561	559	17,120	3118	20,238
2000–01	15,511	199	15,710	2518	18,228
2001–02	15,670	206	15,876	2336	18,212
2002–03	13,868	201	14,069	1802	15,871
2003–04	14,464	196	14,660	1908	16,568
2004–05	14,707	195	14,902	1727	16,629
2005–06	15,286	190	15,476	2034	17,510
Percentage distribution					
1950–51	60.1	9.5	69.7	30.3	100
1955–56	58.1	9.8	68.0	32.0	100
1960–61	61.4	8.0	69.5	30.5	100
1965–66	64.8	7.2	72.0	28.0	100
1970–71	70.6	5.1	75.7	24.3	100
1975–76	72.8	4.8	77.6	22.4	100
1980–81	78.2	4.6	82.8	17.2	100
1985–86	83.0	2.5	85.4	14.6	100
1990–91	83.2	2.4	85.6	14.4	100
1995–96	81.8	2.8	84.6	15.4	100
2000–01	85.1	1.1	86.2	13.8	100
2001–02	86.0	1.1	87.2	12.8	100
2002–03	87.4	1.3	88.6	11.4	100
2003–04	87.3	1.2	88.5	11.5	100
2004–05	88.4	1.2	89.6	10.4	100
2005–06	87.3	1.1	88.4	11.6	100

Source: India, Ministry of Agriculture (1996; 2002; 2006)

technical questions relating to the transfer of public irrigation projects to end users. The report favoured a gradual, selective and stage-wise process of transfer to user management.

Table 10.2 *Irrigation potential created and utilized under surface irrigation (cumulative: million ha)*

Plan period	*Major and medium irrigation*		*Minor irrigation*		*Potential utilized under major and medium (%)*	*Potential utilized under minor %)*	*(Minor irrigation share in surface water utilization (%)*
	Potential	*Utilization*	*Potential*	*Utilization*			
Pre-Plan (up to 1951)	9.7	9.7	6.4	6.4	100.0	100.0	39.8
First Plan (1951–56)	12.2	11.0	6.4	6.4	90.0	100.0	36.9
Second Plan (1956–61)	14.3	13.1	6.5	6.5	91.1	100.0	33.1
Third Plan (1961–66)	16.6	15.2	6.5	6.5	91.6	100.0	29.9
Annual Plan (1966–69)	18.1	16.8	6.5	6.5	92.5	100.0	28.0
Fourth Plan (1969–74)	20.7	18.4	7.0	7.0	88.8	100.0	27.6
Fifth Plan (1974–78)	27.7	21.2	7.5	7.5	76.3	100.0	26.2
Annual Plan (1978–80)	26.6	22.6	8.0	8.0	85.1	100.0	26.1
Sixth Plan (1980–85)	27.7	23.6	9.7	9.0	85.1	92.9	27.7
Seventh Plan (1985–90)	29.9	25.5	10.9	10.0	85.1	91.5	28.1
Annual Plan (1990–92)	30.7	26.3	11.5	10.3	85.6	89.8	28.1
Eighth Plan (1992–97)	33.0	28.4	12.5	11.1	86.3	88.5	28.0
Ninth Plan (1997–02)	37.1	31.0	13.6	11.4	83.7	84.1	26.9
Tenth Plan (2002–07)	42.4	34.4	14.3	12.0	81.3	83.9	25.9

Source: India Planning Commission (2001)

Figure 10.1 *Sources of irrigation (net area irrigated)*

Table 10.3 *State-wise surface irrigation sources in India: 2001–02 (1000ha)*

State	Total surface sources	Share of surface irrigation in total net irrigated area	Percentage share of various surface sources		
			Canal	Tanks	Other sources
Andhra Pradesh	2310	54.5	67.6	24.6	7.8
Assam	168	98.8	88.1	0.0	11.9
Bihar	1210	35.0	79.8	9.3	11.0
Chhattisgarh	974	84.5	85.7	5.6	8.6
Goa	4	17.4	100.0	0.0	0.0
Gujarat	404	13.5	94.6	3.2	2.2
Haryana	1436	48.9	99.0	0.1	1.0
Himachal Pradesh	89	87.3	4.5	0.0	95.5
Jammu and Kashmir	308	99.4	92.2	1.0	6.8
Jharkhand	89	54.3	19.1	30.3	50.6
Karnataka	1510	58.9	59.8	16.1	24.1
Kerala	261	69.2	38.3	19.2	42.5
Madhya Pradesh	1696	35.8	51.9	5.5	42.6
Maharashtra	1053	35.4	100.0	0.0	0.0
Manipur	65	100.0	0.0	0.0	100.0
Meghalaya	59	100.0	100.0	0.0	0.0
Mizoram	16	100.0	100.0	0.0	0.0
Nagaland	64	100.0	0.0	0.0	100.0
Orissa	1163	60.0	75.7	24.3	0.0
Punjab	964	23.9	99.8	0.0	0.2
Rajasthan	1604	29.6	90.5	6.5	2.9
Tamil Nadu	1352	48.3	59.2	39.7	1.0
Tripura	32	88.9	68.8	15.6	15.6
Uttaranchal	145	41.8	71.0	0.0	29.0
Uttar Pradesh	3020	24.4	91.0	2.2	6.8
West Bengal	966	40.7	27.2	18.1	54.7
Delhi	4	11.8	50.0	0.0	50.0
All India	21040	37.7	75.5	11.1	13.4

Source: India Planning Commission (2001)

The proposed organizational structures for the irrigation user groups varied across states but were broadly as follows: (1) three-tier system: water user associations (WUAs) at the user level, WUAs at the 55ha level and the system-level Joint Managing Committee (example: Kerala, Orissa and Tamil Nadu); (2) two-tier system: village WUAs and WUAs for distributaries with a command over 10,000ha (like Bihar); (3) minor level WUAs, 400–750ha units (example: Andhra Pradesh and Madhya Pradesh); (4) cooperative WUA for

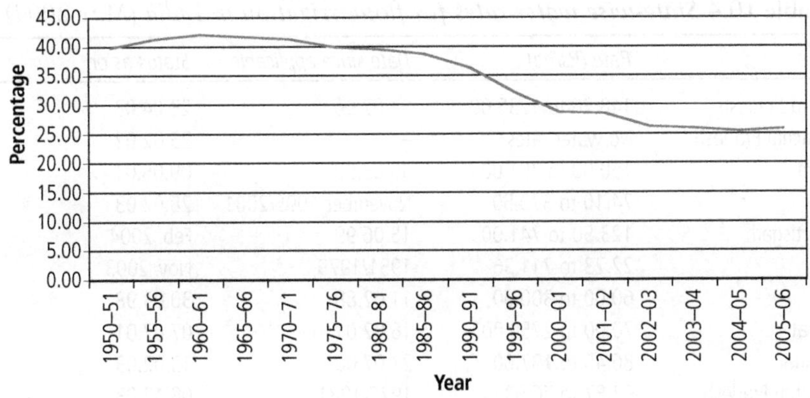

Figure 10.2 *Share of canal in net irrigated area*

500ha blocks, minor level in Gujarat and Maharashtra; (5) outlet level WUAs (example: Haryana).

In northern India, by and large, a rotational system is followed by farmers. Here water is delivered to the farmers according to a pattern of rotation at watercourse level and is established in advance. In western India the intermittent flow system is followed and water delivery is scheduled according to the area served and the types of crops grown. In southern and eastern India, where a rice-based cropping system is prevalent, water is released into the command area at a fixed rate from the beginning of the crop season till the maturity of the crop, subject to water availability in the reservoir of course. Thus, variation in the structure of WUAs is further complicated by regional differences in the mechanisms employed for sharing water.

Against this backdrop it is not surprising that water rates also vary substantially across states (see Table 10.4). In some instances in the northeastern states, public agencies levy no charge on water at all while the rate can be as low as Rs 2.77 per ha in states such as Tamil Nadu. On the other hand, the rate can be as high as Rs 2750 per ha, say in Gujarat. In some states, such as Tamil Nadu, water rates have not been revised since 1962.

Despite these clear differences in organizational structure, distribution system and water rates, several common themes emerge across the states. First, the transfer of irrigation management responsibilities to WUAs is organized on a hydrological basis. Second, the government has retained ownership of large irrigation systems and taken responsibility for their maintenance. Third, the major responsibilities that have either been transferred or were intended to be transferred relate to water distribution, maintenance of distributaries and collection of government irrigation fees. Finally, the resources available for the functioning of WUAs comprise a share of the collected irrigation fee, labour contributed by members and, in some cases, crop area fees. The states also assist WUAs by maintaining an operation and maintenance (O&M) fund.

Table 10.4 *State-wise water rates for flow irrigation in India (May 2004)*

	Rate (Rs/ha)	*Date since applicable*	*Status as on*
Andhra Pradesh	148.20 to 1235.00	01.07.96	23.04.03
Arunachal Pradesh	No water rates	–	25.02.02
Assam	150.00 to 751.00	30.03.00	09.05.01
Bihar	74.10 to 370.50	November 1995/2001	28.02.03
Chhattisgarh	123.50 to 741.00	15.06.99	Feb. 2004
Delhi	22.23 to 711.36	1951/1979	Nov. 2003
Goa	60.00 to 300.00	11.02.88	30.03.98
Gujarat	70.00 to 2750.00*	16.02.01	07.07.01
Haryana	86.45 to 197.60	27.07.00	13.02.03
Himachal Pradesh	63.87 to 76.03	1977/1981	08.12.03
Jammu and Kashmir	19.76 to 49.40	01.04.00	28.07.01
Jharkhand	74.10 to 370.50	26.11.01	25.11.03
Karnataka	37.05 to 988.45	13.07.00	26.08.02
Kerala	37.00 to 99.00	18.09.74	06.04.02
Madhya Pradesh	123.50 to 741.00	15.06.99	15.06.01
Maharashtra	180.00 to 4763.00*	01.09.01	28.02.02
Manipur	22.50 to 75.00	1977/78	26.03.02
Meghalaya	No water rates	–	27.06.01
Mizoram	No water rates	–	04.08.03
Nagaland	No water rates	–	31.05.01
Orissa	28.00 to 930.00	05.04.02	24.05.02
Punjab	Abolished	14.02.97	22.08.02
Rajasthan	29.64 to 607.62	24.05.99	21.06.01
Sikkim	No water rates	–	02.03.02
Tamil Nadu	2.77 to 61.73	01.07.62	04.03.02
Tripura	312.50	Yet to start	06.08.01
Uttaranchal	49.00 to 143.00	18.09.95	08.12.03
Uttar Pradesh	30.00 to 474.00	18.09.95	April 2002
West Bengal	37.05 to 123.50	06.04.77	16.05.03
Andaman and Nicobar Islands	No water rates	–	06.02.04
Chandigarh	No water rates	–	12.06.01
Dadra and Nagar Haveli	110.00 to 830.00	29.01.96	13.07.01
Daman and Diu	200.00	1980	03.01.02
Pondicherry	12.50 to 37.50	31.03.79	02.08.79

Note: * Subject to increase – Rs. 155 to 255 per annum.

Major issues in surface water irrigation management

The ability of the government to operate and maintain various surface irrigation systems in an efficient manner is currently a major concern. Various factors are responsible for this state of affairs. The poor physical condition of the irrigation systems, absence of appropriate staff, lack of incentives relating to efficiency of the irrigation systems, missing links between the users and the water distribution agencies, and inadequate financial resources are all commonly cited (see Herath, Chapter 5). The major constraints facing the surface irrigation systems can be broadly classified into physical, institutional, financial and social challenges. The problems begin at the physical level, often with the construction phase. This is characterized by high cost and time overruns as well as faulty design and subsequent ongoing rehabilitation costs. In addition, most of the surface irrigation systems lack proper maintenance and in many parts are functioning far below their designed capacities. The upshot is inequity in the distribution of water between the head and tail reaches (see for example, Vaidyanathan, 1999). Poor maintenance also results in the physical deterioration of the hydraulic system, which leads to large conveyance losses and untimely water deliveries. Cumulatively, these shortcomings resulted in poor water distribution at user level.

At institutional level, it is important to note that all surface water in the country is legally under the control of the state governments and the government agencies manage the system by delivering water to outlets, each serving a number of farmers.[2] The major institutional constraints faced by various state governments fall into several groups. First, there are limited specialized staff to operate the system. Second, there is a lack of coordination among the various public agencies, and the state departments involved in planning, monitoring and water distribution do not always communicate adequately. A subset of this problem is the relatively limited involvement of farmers. Third, financial constraints arise, primarily due to low water charges and poor cost recovery, resulting in revenue deficits in the irrigation account. Clearly, scarcity of finance has a direct bearing on the poor maintenance of the irrigation system. More specifically, it has been widely acknowledged that the revenue realized from the sale of water does not even meet the operation and maintenance expenditure in the major and medium irrigation schemes (Gulati et al, 1995).

If the goals in managing irrigation water are efficiency, equity and sustainability, then past experience shows that the centralized agencies in charge of planning and operating surface irrigation systems have largely failed to achieve these basic objectives. Even though users are often willing to pay irrigation fees, poor services provided by the centralized agencies persist, thereby undermining any incentive for payment. Such weaknesses provide the backdrop to the participatory approach in irrigation management, which hinges on involving users at appropriate levels in the irrigation systems. In the National Water Policy document of 2002, institutional mechanisms were proposed that would see the planning, development and management of the water resources organized on the basis of a hydrological unit and invoke participatory approaches. The aim was to integrate quality, quantity and environmental aspects of the resource. It was further suggested by this framework that water allocations in an irrigation system should be made with due regard to equity and social justice. Ideally, the disparities in the availability of water between head-reach and tail-end farms and between large and small farms should be obviated by adopting a rotational water distribution system and supplying water on a volumetric basis, subject to certain ceilings and rational pricing. Similarly, management of water resources should be based on a participatory approach, involving not only governmental agencies but also the users and other stakeholders. This ambitious approach should lead to effective and decisive planning, design, development and management of water resources schemes. Formation of WUAs with genuine authority and responsibility should be encouraged as part of this approach, in order to facilitate the maintenance of irrigation systems in a time-bound manner. Needless to add, all this is easier said than done!

Study overview and decision-making domains

Study overview

The broad study objectives and the relationship between the theoretical rationale and the data collection processes were described in detail in the previous chapter. To reiterate, the sample for this empirical work covers local institutions involved in canal and tank irrigation areas of Andhra Pradesh, Maharashtra and Gujarat. Andhra Pradesh has recently implemented a major programme where a large number of WUAs was formed. Maharashtra has a large number of irrigation cooperatives, and many of these have a long-established history. By way of contrast, Gujarat is well known for its cooperative movement, especially in dairying and a number of irrigation cooperatives have also been formed using the cooperative industry experience as a foundation. The data reported here cover a sample of 14 surface water institutions: five in Andhra Pradesh, five in Maharashtra and four in Gujarat. The survey pertained to the 2004–05 cropping year. In total a sample of 250 beneficiary farmer households were sampled: 100 from Andhra Pradesh, 100 from Maharashtra and 50 from Gujarat (see Table 10.5).

Table 10.5 *Sample profile*

Type of local water institution	*Gujarat*	*Maharashtra*	*Andhra Pradesh*	*Total*
Canal cooperative	50	100	0	150
Water user association	0	0	100	100
Total	50	100	100	250

Tables 10.6 and 10.7 provide a summary of the basic features of the sample. The average farm size within the sample was 2.17ha and after leasing-in and leasing-out activities the operational farm size stood at 2.21ha – again showing the very small farm sizes involved. Clearly, most of the land is irrigated. While one-quarter of the respondents had no formal education, 40 per cent had some schooling and 26 per cent had attended high school. About 90 per cent of the respondents were ordinary members of water institutions, with the

remainder holding positions of responsibility within these institutions. Only 58 per cent of the respondents claimed to be active participants with the organization. The distribution of the sample respondents, based on their location in the canal system, showed that 25.4 per cent were located at the head end, 43 per cent were located in the middle and the remainder were positioned at the tail end. Over half (55 per cent) reported scarcity of water although socio-economic cohesion in the village was generally reported to be good (Table 10.7).

Table 10.6 *Land-holding pattern in ha*

Landholding	*N*	*Min*	*Max*	*Mean*	*Std deviation*
Owned	250	0	40	2.17	3.31
Leased in	24	0.1	4.8	1.32	1.15
Leased out	2	2	3.2	2.60	0.85
Total	250	0.1	40	2.21	3.17
Irrigated operated area	233	0.1	40	2.08	3.15

Table 10.7 *Basic features of the sample respondents, water availability and social cohesion in the village*

1 Education (%)		***4 Location in watershed area***	
Illiterate	24.0	Head end	25.4
1–4 years of schooling	10.0	Middle	43.1
5–9 years of schooling	30.8	Tail end	31.4
10–12 years of schooling	26.0		
Below graduation	2.4	***5 General water situation on the farm***	
Graduation	5.6	Excess water	4.8
Above graduation	1.2	No scarcity	40.4
		Occasional scarcity	25.6
2 Position in the water institution (%)		Scarcity	20.0
Membership type		Acute scarcity	9.2
Member	89.6	***6 Change in water quality over the years (%)***	
Managing committee member	6.8	Improvement	0.0
Chairman	2.0	No change	84.0
Vice-chairman	0.4	Deterioration	14.0
Secretary	0.8	Sharp deterioration	2.0
3 Participation in activities/decision making of institution		***7 Social/economic cohesion in the village community (%)***	
Participation	%	Excellent cohesion	1.2
Very active	7.2	Good cohesion	96.8
Active	50.4	Some conflict	2.0
Passive	42.4		

Decision-making domains

The question of decision-making responsibility is important in this context and a summary of responses to these questions is provided in Table 10.8. These data show that the government appears to dominate decisions with respect to the pricing of water and the release of water for irrigation. On the other hand, local institutions play a significant role in the areas of planning for capital investment, actual release of water for irrigation to farms, collection of dues, and monitoring the use of water. The responses suggest that there was some uncertainty about who actually undertook investment in the irrigation structure. Cropping decisions resided with farmers.

Table 10.8 *Who makes the decisions on the following activities? (percentages)*

Decision/activity	*Govt*	*Institution*	*Individual farmers*	*Joint*	*Others*	*Nobody/ don't know*
Planning for capital investment in irrigation structures	33.2	66.4	0.0	0.4	0.0	0.0
Actual capital investment in irrigation structures	32.4	23.2	0.4	20.8	0.0	23.2
Actual release of water	76.4	8.4	0.0	0.0	0.0	15.2
Distribution of water among farmers	23.2	63.2	0.0	0.0	0.0	13.6
Pricing of water received	84.0	0.0	0.0	0.0	0.0	16.0
Pricing of water distributed to farmers	24.0	60.0	0.0	0.0	0.0	16.0
Collection of dues from farmers	24.0	60.0	0.0	0.0	0.0	16.0
Implementation of maintenance/repair	18.4	51.6	0.0	0.0	0.0	30.0
Monitoring use of water	8.4	61.2	1.2	0.0	0.0	29.2
Stopping misuse/waste	8.4	60.8	1.2	0.0	0.0	29.6
Crops to be grown	1.6	0.0	98.4	0.0	0.0	0.0

Governance

As discussed above in the conceptual framework, and in other chapters, a major determinant of the success of institutions is expected to be their ability to deliver on three rationalities: technical, organizational and political. Following the same line of argument employed in the previous chapter, we contend that in institutions of this form technical rationality will be linked primarily to the staff, while organizational rationality is tied to the attributes of the management committee. Political rationality relates primarily to the activities of the chairman and the general body.

The results in Table 10.9 indicate that the general body is reported to be active to very active by 71 per cent of the respondents, but passive by 10 per cent and having no role by 19 per cent, suggesting an institutional weakness in a significant number of cases. The most active entity is reported to be the chairman, followed by the managing committee and the secretary. Non-members are generally not active, and government officials – *Panchayat* (local government) and *sarpanch* (headman) – are widely reported as playing no role or being passive.

Do those involved in governance have the necessary expertise and do they do a good job? The data in Table 10.10 suggest that 49 per cent of the respondents believed that management had the expertise to do a good job and 62 per cent appeared to be of the view that management did do a good job. The opinions reported on staff expertise were higher than those reported for management (58 per cent), although performance was adjudged slightly lower (at 60 per cent). There is some prima facie evidence in these data that there exists a considerable gap between expertise and performance on several fronts. There is also substantial variation which may be ultimately be reflected in institutional performance.

Table 10.9 *Governance: Role of the following in the running of the institution (percentages)*

Role of	*Very active*	*Active*	*Passive*	*None*
1 General body	38.0	33.2	10.0	18.8
2 Chairman	47.6	24.4	12.4	15.6
3 Managing committee	37.2	33.2	14.0	15.6
4 Members	21.6	46.0	14.0	18.4
5 Non-members	7.6	20.8	19.6	52.0
6 Secretary	33.2	29.2	9.6	28.0
7 Other staff	24.0	33.2	12.0	30.8
8 Government officials	0.0	4.0	24.0	72.0
9 *Panchayat*	0.0	5.2	19.2	75.6
10 *Sarpanch*	0.0	6.4	11.6	82.0

As noted in the preceding chapter, the government has been a major force in irrigation and often played a role in the creation and functioning of water institutions, particularly those based on surface water use. Table 10.11 provides findings on the role of the government. A large number of respondents (40 per cent) agreed that the institution had been created by government but this was also rejected by over 50 per cent of respondents. Regardless of the perceived origins of the organization, most disagreed or partly disagreed that the institution reported to government. About one-third of the sample agreed that the rules were determined by the government, but most (81 per cent) disagreed that the government supervised the actual workings of the organization.

Table 10.10 *Governance expertise and quality*

	Strongly agree (Yes)	*Agree*	*Partially agree/ disagree*	*Disagree*	*Strongly disagree (No)*
	5	*4*	*3*	*2*	*1*
Management has the expertise to do a good job	8.4	40.4	22.0	7.2	22.0
The management does a good job	6.0	56.0	6.8	5.6	25.6
Staff have the necessary expertise to do a good job	3.2	55.2	3.6	3.6	34.4
In general, the staff do a good job	2.8	57.8	2.0	3.2	34.1

Table 10.11 *Role of the government (percentages)*

	Strongly agree (Yes)	*Agree*	*Partially agree/ disagree*	*Disagree*	*Strongly disagree (No)*
	5	4	3	2	1
The institution/organization has been created by the government	40.0	1.2	6.0	35.6	17.2
The institution/organization reports to the government	13.7	18.9	34.5	13.3	19.7
The rules of the organization are mainly determined by the government and not the members	23.2	13.2	8.8	45.2	9.6
The government supervises the working of the organization	6.8	12.0	8.0	48.8	24.4

Institutional performance and empirical analysis

Features related to New Institutional Economics

In line with the theoretical underpinnings of the work, we commence the empirical analysis by considering a number of the aspects drawn from NIE.

Clarity of objectives and purpose

Findings on the issue of clarity of purpose and objectives are given in Table 10.14. As with the sample of all water institutions, a majority of the respondents indicated that these institutions had a clear set of objectives. However, a large number reported that the objectives were not especially clear to members, or well communicated and shared. About 50 per cent of the sample indicated that the institution appeared to plan for and pursue the achievement of objectives but about 30 per cent only partly agreed with this view. A similar proportion reported that there were frequent deviations from the stated objectives.

Table 10.12 *Clarity of objectives/purpose*

	Strongly agree	*Agree*	*Partially agree/ disagree*	*Disagree*	*Strongly disagree*
	5	*4*	*3*	*2*	*1*
This organization has a clear set of objectives/purpose	48.8	39.2	2.4	0.8	8.8
The objectives of this organization are clear to the members of the organization	12.4	54.8	6.8	2.4	23.6
The objectives are well communicated and shared across the institution	9.2	39.4	8.0	14.1	29.3
The institution pursues and regularly makes plans towards achievement of these objectives	17.2	32.4	30.0	4.4	16.0
Deviations from these objectives are not frequent	16.3	44.3	7.7	5.3	26.4

Good interaction

Over 80 per cent of the respondents reported that there was good interaction between the members, and between the management and the members. Many respondents indicated that this was not the case for interaction between the staff and the organization's members. More than half of those sampled (60 per cent) indicated that there was good leadership capable of facilitating interaction and ensuring that there were regular meetings. Respondents were somewhat divided on the level of interaction between the organization and government, with 40 per cent indicating this was adequate and 37 per cent indicating that it was less than adequate. About 40 per cent of the sample partly agreed that the institution was equipped to help settle disputes although 23 per cent disagreed with this view.

Adaptiveness and compliance with rules

As per the theoretical framework, adaptiveness should be an important characteristic of sound institutions. Results given in Table 10.14 indicate that the respondents were divided on the question of whether surface water institutions had rigid rules and systems – about 34 per cent agree and 46 per cent disagree. Nevertheless, a majority of the sample agreed that there were clear mechanisms in place for changing the rules noting that, when required, rules can be modified according to the needs of the prevailing conditions. By way of contrast, respondents were less clear on the question of regular review of rules. Overall, respondents strongly agree that management had sufficient power to bring compliance and possessed the ability to ensure fairness and justice to its members.

Table 10.13 *Good interaction*

	Strongly agree	*Agree*	*Partially agree/ disagree*	*Disagree*	*Strongly disagree*
	5	*4*	*3*	*2*	*1*
There is good interaction between the members of the institution	26.0	59.6	2.4	8.8	3.2
There is good interaction between the management and the members	21.6	61.6	2.8	4.8	9.2
There is good interaction between the staff and the members	39.8	24.9	5.8	3.7	25.7
There is good leadership to facilitate, improve and guide the interaction	14.1	48.2	12.9	2.8	22.1
There are regular meetings.	21.4	44.0	4.8	6.9	23.0
There is good interaction between the institution and the government	3.6	9.3	40.5	9.7	36.8
This organization helps members to settle disputes	7.6	28.4	39.6	1.2	23.2

Appropriateness of scale/size

More than two-thirds of those sampled indicated that the size of their institution was neither too small nor too large against a number of criteria. On the question of relationships within the institutional hierarchy for surface water, respondents generally expressed some reservation about the capacity of higher-order decision-making bodies to appropriately interact with lower-order organizations, such as WUAs.

Table 10.14 *Adaptiveness and compliance (percentages)*

	Strongly agree	*Agree*	*Partially agree/ disagree*	*Disagree*	*Strongly disagree*
1 Adaptiveness					
There are clear mechanisms for changing the rules of this organization if the need arises	7.2	50.0	5.6	9.2	28.0
The rules and systems of the organization are very rigid	6.4	27.6	19.2	20.8	26.0
There are processes for adapting the rules and systems according to the needs and setting	4.0	45.6	24.0	5.2	21.2
There is a regular review of the rules and systems of the institution	6.4	19.6	42.8	8.8	22.4
The management has the authority to adapt the rules and systems	22.0	38.8	4.0	7.2	28.0
2 Compliance					
Members are aware of and willingly follow the rules set down by this organization	9.2	54.6	8.8	4.4	22.9
The management has enough powers to bring compliance with institutional objectives and rules	15.2	49.6	5.2	2.4	27.6
The institution uses its powers to bring compliance.	11.6	14.0	41.2	3.2	30.0
Compliance with the rules is sufficient	15.6	36.0	9.2	6.4	32.8
There is external monitoring and enforcement of compliance	0.0	4.8	4.4	39.8	51.0
The institution is able to ensure fairness and justice	11.2	50.6	3.6	2.0	32.5

Table 10.15 *Scale/size (percentages)*

	Strongly agree (Yes)	*Agree*	*Partially agree/ disagree*	*Disagree*	*Strongly disagree (No)*
1 Scale/size					
The scale of the institution is too large – e.g. for proper control	1.2	7.2	7.6	42.8	41.2
The scale of the institution is too small – e.g. for viability	1.2	2.4	13.2	30.4	52.8
The scale of the institution is appropriate for efficient management	17.6	51.2	14.8	4.0	12.4
The systems of the institution are appropriate for the scale of operation	6.8	59.6	14.8	4.4	14.4
Higher-level issues are appropriately addressed by higher-level institutions	0.0	1.3	52.5	16.0	30.3

Performance of the institutions

About two-thirds of the respondents indicated that the impact of the institution was positive on efficiency parameters such as adequate and timely delivery of water, better maintenance of the irrigation structure, and changes in the cropping pattern towards high value crops. The remaining one-third indicated little impact. A generally positive trend was discernable in the context of the equitable distribution of water, with over 70 per cent of farmers noting improvement on this front. Responses were mixed on the empowerment of farmers in managing the irrigation system (Table 10.16).

The opinions were also divided on a number of other questions such as the ability of the institution to establish a sense of ownership among the members, or the capacity for resolving disputes and bringing active participation among all classes of farmer. A large majority of those sampled would appear to believe that the activities of the institution did no harm to the environment through flooding, water-logging and depletion of ground water. However, these results need to be treated with some caution as many respondents seemed unsure about the extent to which the organization actually monitored or was aware of environmental considerations. There was also some evidence that the farmers themselves had only limited understanding of environmental indicators. A majority of the sample indicated that the introduction of the surface water institution had reduced the cost of water and had played an active part in encouraging crop diversification. There was no clear trend in these data about farmers' opinions on flexibility in irrigation timings and the quantity of water supplied.

Table 10.16 *What has been the impact of the institution on the following? (percentages)*

Particulars	Highly positive	Positive	No impact	Negative	Highly negative
	1	2	3	4	5
A Efficiency related					
Timely water availability	27.2	42.8	29.2	0.4	0.4
Adequate water availability	18.8	48.4	32.0	0.4	0.4
Change in cropping pattern in favour of high value crops	35.1	27.8	36.7	0.0	0.4
Better maintenance of irrigation structure	11.6	34.8	37.2	11.6	4.8
B Equity related					
Equitable distribution of water	23.6	44.4	30.8	0.8	0.4
Empowerment of farmers to manage irrigation systems	15.2	31.2	36.8	12.0	4.8
C Social cohesion and empowerment					
Beginning of a sense of ownership by farmers	32.4	14.0	52.4	0.8	0.4
Resolution of disputes and dealing with offences	12.4	28.1	59.0	0.0	0.4
Active involvement of all classes	26.8	39.6	32.8	0.4	0.4
D Environment					
The activity of the institution is causing flooding/water-logging in some areas.	10.0	10.8	11.6	35.6	32.0
The activity of the institution is rapidly depleting ground water in the village.	0.8	10.8	13.2	17.6	57.6
The institution is aware of and monitors such environmental harm/ depletion.	2.4	7.6	44.8	8.8	36.4
E Others					
Price/cost of water	14.4	39.6	44.4	0.4	1.2
Diversification of cropping pattern	42.0	14.8	42.4	0.0	0.8
Choice in deciding irrigation timings	5.6	32.4	61.2	0.0	0.8
Choice in deciding quantum of water	4.8	38.8	55.2	0.4	0.8

There was a large variation in the responses to questions on financial performance and financial viability of the institutions, although most respondents indicated that the organizations were generally viable and had the capacity to raise funds by levying beneficiaries. By way of contrast, many respondents indicated that surface water organizations were unable to raise sufficient funds from the government or from donors. Moreover, banks and financial institutions were perceived as being reluctant to invest in these institutions (Table 10.17).

Table 10.17 *Financial aspects (percentages)*

	Strongly agree (Yes)	*Agree*	*Partially agree/ disagree*	*Disagree*	*Strongly disagree (No)*
Finance					
The institution is financially viable	20.4	29.6	29.2	14.4	6.4
The institution is able to raise recurring payments from the beneficiaries	21.2	28.0	26.8	12.4	11.6
The institution has penalties to encourage regular payment	16.8	34.4	23.2	5.2	20.4
The institution is able to raise sufficient funding support from the government	0.8	6.9	15.7	14.1	62.5
The institution is able to raise funding from donors and public	0.4	2.8	15.6	16.4	64.8
Banking and financial institutions would be willing to invest in the institution	0.8	2.0	19.2	22.4	55.6

In the context of the overall rating of performance, 49 per cent of respondents indicated that the performance of the surface water organization was satisfactory, and 28 per cent of the respondents rated their institution as being successful or very successful overall. On financial health, only 13 per cent indicated that this was perceived as being strong or very strong (Table 10.18).

Table 10.18 *Success and overall health of the institution*

1 Assessment of the success of the institution		*2 Assessment of the financial health of the institution*	
Success	%	Financial health	%
Very successful	7.6	Very strong	6.0
Successful	20.8	Strong	6.8
Satisfactory	49.2	Satisfactory	57.2
Poor	22.4	Poor	30.0
Total	100	Total	100

Results of bivariate statistical analysis

We now turn briefly to bivariate analysis to examine the relationship between various conceptual elements of the research. It should be remembered that the chief aim is to distinguish those elements of NIE and governance that are most relevant to delivering improved performance in the management of different water resources. Following the approach developed in Chapter 9, analysis of variance is employed here to examine potentially meaningful relationships (Table 10.19).

The relationship between institution type and performance was considered initially, where institutional performance was measured on the basis of overall performance, being rated on a five-point scale. Applying this approach, the performance of canal cooperatives was found to be significantly better – perhaps because many of these organizations are older and well established. However, the mean values for 'participation' and 'reliance' were slightly higher for WUAs.

An interesting trend emerges when we consider the relationship between institutional performance, participation and reliance against the various state jurisdictions from which these data were drawn. Results indicate that these differences are statistically significant by jurisdiction, with Gujarat having higher values on all three parameters (Table 10.20). Results also suggest that the farmers' satisfaction with the performance of the surface water organizations was greatest in Gujarat.

The relationship between institutional performance and change in water availability indicated, as might be expected, that where water availability had improved, the institutional performance was rated more highly (Table 10.21). The relationship between location in the watershed and institutional performance showed the lowest values from tail-end users, indicating that they are generally less satisfied with performance, although the differences were not large (Table 10.22). Finally, the ANOVA results clearly support the view that, where cohesion in the village community is better, the overall performance of the surface water entity is also superior (Table 10.23).

Table 10.19 *Analysis of relationship between institution type and institutional performance, participation and reliance on institution*

1 Institutional performance				
Institution type	*Canal cooperative*	*Water user association*	*F-statistic*	*Statistical significance*
Performance-mean	2.59	1.46	183.00	***
2 Participation				
Participation-mean	1.62	1.69	14.45	***
3 Reliance on institution				
Reliance-mean	2.26	2.73	30.99	***

Note: * Significant at 10%; ** Significant at 5%; *** Significant at 1%.

Table 10.20 *Analysis of relationship between location of state and institutional performance, participation and reliance on institution*

1 Institutional performance					
State	*Andhra Pradesh*	*Gujarat*	*Maharashtra*	*F-statistic*	*Statistical significance*
Performance-mean	1.46	2.72	2.52	93.94	***
2 Participation					
Participation-mean	1.69	1.98	1.44	14.90	***
3 Reliance on institution					
Reliance-mean	2.99	4.26	3.91	25.60	***

Note: * Significant at 10%; ** Significant at 5%; *** Significant at 1%.

Table 10.21 *Analysis of relationship between change in water availability and institutional performance*

Water availability	*Increase*	*No change*	*Decline*	*Sharp decline*	*F-statistic*	*Statistical significance*
Performance-mean	4.00	2.17	2.21	1.18	14.31	***

Note: * Significant at 10%; ** Significant at 5%; *** Significant at 1%.

Table 10.22 *Analysis of relationship between location in watershed and institutional performance*

Location	*Head*	*Middle*	*Tail*	*F-statistic*	*Statistical significance*
Performance-mean	2.34	2.20	1.93	4.58	***

Note: * Significant at 10%; ** Significant at 5%; *** Significant at 1%.

Table 10.23 *Analysis of relationship between cohesion and institutional performance*

Cohesion	*Excellent cohesion*	*Good cohesion*	*Some conflict*	*Several conflicts*	*Severe conflict*	*F-statistic*	*Statistical significance*
Performance-mean	3.33	2.13	1.80	–	–	3.45	**

Note: * Significant at 10%; ** Significant at 5%; *** Significant at 1%.

Other relationships are examined through multivariate analysis.

Results of multivariate analysis

The analysis above sought to consider relationships through a bivariate approach with one explanatory factor scrutinized at a time. Next, a multivariate approach with regression analysis was employed since this allows us to load several explanatory factors into a single explanatory model. As noted in the previous chapter, a major problem with multivariate analysis of almost any realistic data is the potential for multicollinearity between the explanatory variables. Further, since the performance indicators employed in this instance are range-bound, with values such as from 1 to 4 and from 1 to 5, the classical regression assumptions would be violated and an alternative procedure is required for estimation. The TOBIT model is suitable for the nature of the data and was selected.

The TOBIT model is used to study the behaviour of institutional performance and identify the important determinants of performance. Various measures of institutional performance were used as the dependent variable, including the overall rating of institutional performance, and those measures addressing the performance objectives of water delivery, scarcity (efficiency), equity, environmental stewardship, financial strength and development. The preferred models ultimately used 17 explanatory variables. The explanatory variables were selected after taking into account the theoretical framework, and the results of several rounds of factor and correlation analysis to identify independent factors. Given the nature of these data, it is not possible to completely eliminate multicollinearity, and the results should be interpreted accordingly.[3]

The output from this approach is given in Tables 10.24 and 10.25. The results for the model developed to test overall institutional performance/success indicate several positive and significant influences: namely, an active general body and management committee; expertise of the management; regular plans for achievement of objectives; and when institutions use their powers to bring compliance. By way of contrast, where the institution had been created by government there was generally a negative influence on performance

If we consider the analysis of institutional achievement in the context of pricing water according to scarcity a different set of relationships emerges. First, a positive and strong influence arises from factors such as the expertise of the staff, good interaction between the members, good leadership to facilitate interaction, higher-level entities appropriately dealing with higher-order issues, and the compliance capacity of the organization. Again, the origins of the organization proved influential, with government-created entities less likely to perform well on this front.

Considering institutional performance in the context of 'better maintenance' reveals similar trends. Positive and significant variables in this instance include the necessity for clarity of objectives to the members, regular planning for achieving objectives, expertise of the management, expertise of the staff, and having higher-level issues appropriately addressed by higher-level institutions.

Table 10.24 *TOBIT analysis: Estimates*

Parameter	*Institutional performance/ success*	*Pricing of water according to scarcity*	*Better maintenance*
Intercept	1.77472*	0.753157	2.176775*
General body active	0.261092*	−0.08403	0.024465
Managing committee active	0.189365	0.077713	−0.00578
Secretary active	−0.31116*	−0.0953	0.003593
Management has the expertise	0.301601*	0.021971	0.285715*
The staff have the expertise	−0.13462	0.55088*	0.194682
Created by the government	−0.19101***	−0.03713	0.05312
Rules are determined by the government.	−0.14724	−0.08238	−0.02518
The objectives are clear to the members	−0.01001	−0.25125***	0.155352
The institution regularly plans for achievement of objectives	0.190192*	−0.25556*	0.308469*
There is good interaction between the members	−0.00607	0.473419***	0.031263
There is good leadership to facilitate interaction	−0.20385	0.218295	−0.22659*
There are clear mechanisms for changing the rules.	0.044407	0.198579	−0.07434
The management has authority to adapt the rules and systems	0.038278	−0.14275	0.011893
The scale of the institution is appropriate.	−0.08641	−0.31047**	−0.16003***
Higher-level issues are addressed by higher-level institutions	0.093095	0.377494*	0.337882*
The institution uses its powers to bring compliance	0.153954***	−0.28778**	−0.51255*
The compliance with the rules is sufficient	−0.06876	0.346305	0.047772
N=250			

Note: * Significant at 10%; ** Significant at 5%; *** Significant at 1%.

Next, we considered the impact of the institution on achieving equity within the structure of the organization. The results support the view that there are four major factors pertinent to improving equity in surface water organizations: expertise of the staff in the institution; sufficient compliance with the rules; an active management committee; and ensuring that the scope for rules is set out by the government in the first instance. All factors appear positively related to enhancements in equity. This is an important finding inasmuch as it suggests that government has a critical role in setting the parameters for rule formulation but needs to be careful not to overstep the mark. More specifically, the earlier models showed a clear negative trend when the institution was actively 'created' by government, suggesting there is a fine line between

Table 10.25 *TOBIT analysis: Estimates*

Parameter	*Equity achieved within the structure*	*Activities to reduce environmental harm*	*Financial viability*	*Impact on village as a whole*
Intercept	2.461632*	1.911319	2.91786*	2.234168*
General body active	0.108346	−0.36703**	0.011654	0.111909
Managing committee active	0.197954***	0.032563	0.071794	0.10287
Secretary active	−0.03842	−0.36167**	−0.31949	−0.07385
Management has the expertise	0.060879	0.119149	0.137628	−0.2016**
The staff have the expertise	0.193267***	0.539792*	−0.05172	0.219142**
Created by the government	−0.17083***	−0.39831*	−0.39659*	−0.1169
Rules are determined by the government	0.139641	0.107862	−0.01226	0.086593
The objectives are clear to the members	−0.13129	−0.00884	0.002602	0.001933
The institution regularly plans for achievement of objectives	−0.05892	0.021774	0.303588*	0.158544**
There is good interaction between the members	0.027286	0.442488*	0.391112*	0.069363
There is good leadership to facilitate interaction	0.013617	0.07921	−0.21889**	0.031776
There are clear mechanisms for changing the rules	0.104428	0.215486	0.058827	0.079625
The management has authority to adapt the rules and systems	−0.05176	−0.19191	0.090519	0.052082
The scale of the institution is appropriate	0.022869	−0.52054*	−0.42326*	−0.00404
Higher-level issues are addressed by higher-level institutions	−0.0351	0.675725*	0.536235*	0.041824
The institution uses its powers to bring compliance.	−0.04969	−0.6289*	0.015236	−0.19901*
The compliance with the rules is sufficient	0.177849*	0.314833	0.061147	0.26946*
N=250				

Note: * Significant at 10%; ** Significant at 5%; *** Significant at 1%.

enhancing equity by greater involvement of government and enhancing efficiency by allowing individuals to craft institutional objectives.

In the context of environmental impacts, those institutions that had more expert staff, undertook regular planning for achievement of objectives, had better capacity to bring compliance and were circumscribed by higher-level issues being appropriately managed by superordinate bodies were more likely to perform well on this front.

The TOBIT analysis of financial viability revealed significant and positive influences along similar lines to most of the other models. Regular plans for achievement of objectives, good interaction between the members, and appropriate superordinate decision making were all more conducive to financial viability. Finally, the results from the model of factors influencing the well-being of the village as whole showed that, where staff had good expertise and where regular planning occurred that focused on the achievement of goals, then village well-being was likely to be higher.

Summary and conclusions

Scarcity of water is a major concern in India especially in the context of agriculture. Accordingly, there is much policy interest focused on improving the efficiency of water use in this sector. There has been substantial interest in the development of surface water irrigation in India, but the emphasis has been mainly on the physical and technical aspects. Developing the necessary institutions to efficiently manage surface water resources has received relatively little attention, despite that fact that surface irrigation accounts for about 40 per cent of the total irrigated area in the country. The major local institutions involved with surface water now include canal cooperatives and WUAs which largely owe their genesis to government enthusiasm for devolving some control over water resources to user groups. This trend can be traced to the administrative and financial limits of government agencies in managing natural resources at the local level.

Using the concepts of NIE and management concepts of governance, the research has tried to analyse the performance of these local level WUAs and irrigation cooperatives in three major states – Andhra Pradesh, Maharashtra and Gujarat. Field-level data were collected to examine a range of issues, such as participation of members in the activities and decision making of the organization. Socio-economic cohesion in village communities was also considered as this can be traced to organizational operations and the mechanisms for establishing rules or decisions and how these relate to other agencies/bodies. The data also give insights into the perceived adaptiveness of surface water organizations, their compliance capacity, and whether their scale and scope were perceived as appropriate. Finally, the data also shed light on different dimensions of institutional performance, such as the ability to address water scarcity, equity, environmental issues and financial viability.

The information on decision making showed that governments dominated decisions on pricing and the actual release of water for irrigation. On the other hand, lower-order institutions play a major role in the distribution of water at the farm level. These organizations were also intimately involved in the collection of dues from farmer members and monitoring the use of water. Respondents to the survey were divided on whether the rules embodied in these surface water institutions were excessively rigid and whether there was scope for adequately reviewing the rules to meet new needs.[4] The respondents strongly agreed that the rules of the institution were clear and that members were well aware of them. In addition, the sample showed a widely held view that the management of the entity had sufficient power to bring compliance in line with institutional objectives. Management also had the ability to ensure fairness and justice to members. Most of the farmers sampled indicated that the activities of the institutions did little, if any, harm to the environment, although there remains some doubt about the overall awareness of environmental metrics from an institutional and member point of view.

The bivariate statistical results showed that the performance of canal co-operatives was somewhat better than that of WUAs. The relationship between institutional performance and change in water availability indicated, as may be expected, that where the water availability had improved, the institutional performance was rated higher. The relationship between location in the watershed and institutional performance revealed that tail-end users consistently rated institutional performance lower than their upstream neighbours, although the differences were not large. The results show that where cohesion in the village community was better, the performance of the surface water organization was also better. Other relationships were examined through multivariate analysis.

In the multivariate analysis undertaken to assess overall institutional performance/success, several factors stood out with significant and positive influences. These were: an active general membership body; an active managing committee; expertise of the management; regular plans for assessing the achievement of objectives; and using the authority vested in the institution to bring compliance. Importantly, where the institution was directly created by the government there was a negative impact on performance. The pricing of water according to its scarcity values was significantly and positively related to the expertise of the staff, having good interaction between the members, the presence of good leadership to facilitate interaction, and sufficient compliance with the rules. On better maintenance, variables such as clarity of objectives to the members, regular planning for achieving objectives, having sound expertise of the management and good expertise of the staff all operated positively and significantly. In addition, where higher-order issues were adequately addressed by superordinate bodies, then maintenance was likely to be positively impacted.

Other multivariate models were developed around environmental outcomes, financial viability and the well-being of the village as a whole. In the case of the former, significant positive influences emanated from the expertise of the staff as well as good interaction between members. In the case of the financial viability, having the ability to make regular plans for achievements of objectives, having good interaction between the members, and capable superordinate governance structures proved significant. Good expertise of staff and regular planning for achievements of goals had a significant and positive association with improvements in the overall well-being within the village.

Modelling the relationship between surface water institutions and equity within the structure of the organization showed that a range of similar variables were important (e.g. expertise of the staff in the institution, sufficient compliance with the rules, active management committee), but there was one notable exception. More specifically, equity was enhanced when the rules of the entity had been strongly influenced by government guidelines or decree. We cautiously predict that this will be an ongoing challenge for policy makers since heavy-handed government would appear to significantly hamper progress on the efficiency front for surface water institutions.

Notes

1 It is worth noting that increasing the efficiency of water use in agriculture may not be a panacea for the water problems of India or elsewhere. For an excellent review see Perry (2007).
2 For a more detailed description of the legal context see Upadhyay, Chapter 7.
3 Some signs may be incorrect and some significances low because of this.
4 This is perhaps not that surprising. The New Institutional Economics framework embodies somewhat of a contradiction in that it favours clear objectives and yet also advocates adaptiveness. In the minds of some, these two features might appear irreconcilable.

References

Gandhi, V. P. and Namboodiri, N. V. (2002) 'Water resource management in India: Institutions and development', in D. Brennan (ed) *Water Policy Reform: Lessons from Asia and Australia*, Australian Centre for International Agricultural Research (ACIAR), Canberra

Gulati, A., Svendsen, M. and Chaudhury, R. (1995) 'Operation and maintenance costs of canals and their recovery in India', in M. Svendsen and A. Gulati (eds) *Strategic Change in Indian Irrigation*, Macmillan, India

India, Ministry of Agriculture (1996) *Agricultural Statistics at a Glance*, Ministry of Agriculture, New Delhi

India, Ministry of Agriculture (2002) *Agricultural Statistics at a Glance*, Ministry of Agriculture, New Delhi

India, Ministry of Agriculture (2006) *Agricultural Statistics at a Glance*, Ministry of Agriculture, New Delhi

India, Ministry of Water Resources, Government of India

India Planning Commission (2001) *Tenth Five-Year Plan: 2002–2007*, Government of India

Joshi, P. K. (1997) 'Farmers' investments and government interventions in salt-affected and waterlogged soils', in J. M. Kerr, D. K. Marothia, C. Ramaswamy, K. Singh and W. R. Bentley (eds) *Natural Resource Economics: Theory and Application in India*, Oxford and IBH, New Delhi

Marothia, D. K. (1997) 'Agricultural technology and environmental quality: An institutional perspective', keynote paper, *Indian Journal of Agricultural Economics*, vol 52, pp473–487

Perry, C. (2007) 'Efficient irrigation; inefficient communication; flawed recommendations', *Irrigation and Drainage*, vol 56, pp367–378

Vaidyanathan, A. (1994) 'Agrarian relations in the context of new agricultural technology: An issue paper', *Indian Journal of Agricultural Economics*, vol 49, pp317–329

Vaidyanathan, A. (1999) *Water Resource Management: Institutions and Irrigation Development in India*, Oxford University Press, New Delhi

11
Institutional Analysis of the Performance of Ground-Water Institutions in India

Vasant Gandhi and Ashutosh Roy

Introduction

Ground water has rapidly emerged to occupy a dominant place in India's agriculture and is therefore critical to food security. It has become the main source of growth in irrigation over the past three decades, and now accounts for over 60 per cent of the irrigated area in the country. The development of ground-water irrigation has had only limited government involvement, having arisen gradually through highly decentralized private activity. In many cases these activities have escaped the gaze of policy makers, or have been considered too difficult to monitor in the politico-economic sense at least. Accordingly, it is important to acknowledge at the outset that the institutional ingredients of ground-water activities are likely to differ markedly from those outlined for surface water in the previous chapter, where the state played a major role in water resource development.

Despite its significance, ground-water irrigation is unsustainable in its present form in India and needs urgent understanding and attention. The number of irrigation blocks considered overexploited is increasing at the alarming rate of 5.5 per cent per year (Brisco and Malik, 2006). Official documentation also shows that new ground-water development must be halted in many locations (see for example, India, Central Ground Water Board, 2003) and yet the sinking of wells continues rapidly at enormous private, public and environmental cost.

As has been noted throughout this manuscript, many of the problems that beset irrigation are not of a physical and technical form. Rather, they reflect institutional weaknesses in the allocation and management of the resource. This is perhaps even more the case with ground water where the imperative to bring overexploitation into check remains the major challenge. The way India will manage its ground-water resources in the future will clearly have very serious implications for the future growth and development of the agricultural sector in India, as well as for the alleviation of poverty generally. Accordingly, shedding light on the institutional aspects of contemporary ground-water use provides a useful starting point for policy reform.

This chapter focuses specifically on the operation of ground-water institutions in three states of India: Gujarat, Maharashtra and Andhra Pradesh. The chapter is used to apply the empirical techniques established in Chapter 9 to data collected from a collaborative project sponsored by the Australian Centre for International Agricultural Research (ACIAR).

The chapter is organized into four additional parts. First, we trace the development of ground water as the major source of irrigation over recent decades. In this section we illustrate the magnitude of ground-water development with particular reference to the state of Gujarat. Second, we turn to the empirical analysis of ground-water institutions and offer a synoptic overview of ground-water users in the sample. Here we briefly consider the decision-making processes used by ground-water entities and outline the governance arrangements for partnerships and cooperatives. Third, we consider several empirical relationships, guided by the New Institutional Economics (NIE) and governance literature. This section follows a similar approach to that used in earlier chapters in order to allow readers to draw meaningful comparisons. Importantly, we focus on the internal institutional performance of ground-water organizations leaving discussion of regulation of extraction to later chapters. In the final section we offer some brief concluding remarks.

Growth of ground-water irrigation in India

The growth in irrigated area and the rising contribution of ground water can be seen from the statistics given in Table 11.1. The net irrigated area has increased from 21 million ha in 1950–51 to 56 million ha in 2001–02. The share of ground-water irrigation through wells has risen from 28 per cent to 62 per cent in the same timeframe. The main contribution has come from the rapid growth in tube-well irrigation, having risen from zero in 1950–51 to over 40 per cent by 2001–02.

The green revolution has been a major force driving the growth of ground-water irrigation. Beginning in the mid 1960s, the green revolution was a major turning point in India's agriculture. The adoption of new seeds and fertilizers provided great benefits and the productive benefits of these technologies were at their best under irrigation. As was noted in the previous chapter, substantial investments were simultaneously undertaken in surface water projects to provide irrigation water to large numbers of farmers. However, a number of other relevant and significant changes took place in the late 1960s and 1970s

Table 11.1: *Sources of irrigation in India: 1950–51 to 2001–02 (1000ha)*

Year	*Canal*	*Tanks*	*Tube-wells*	*Other wells*	*Total wells*	*Other sources*	*Total net irrigated area*
1950–51	8295	3613	0	5978	5978	2967	20,853
1960–61	10,370	4561	135	7155	7290	2440	24,661
1970–71	12,838	4112	4461	7426	11,887	2266	31,103
1980–81	15,292	3182	9531	8164	17,695	2551	38,720
1990–91	17,453	2944	14,257	10,437	24,694	2932	48,023
1995–96	17,120	3118	17,894	11,803	29,697	3467	53,402
2000–01	15,710	2518	22,324	11,451	33,775	2831	54,833
2001–02	15,877	2336	22,816	12,020	34,836	2827	55,876
Percentage share of various sources							
1950–51	39.78	17.33	0.00	28.67	28.67	14.23	100
1960–61	42.05	18.49	0.55	29.01	29.56	9.89	100
1970–71	41.28	13.22	14.34	23.88	38.22	7.29	100
1980–81	39.49	8.22	24.62	21.08	45.70	6.59	100
1990–91	36.34	6.13	29.69	21.73	51.42	6.11	100
1995–96	32.06	5.84	33.51	22.10	55.61	6.49	100
2000–01	28.65	4.59	40.71	20.88	61.60	5.16	100
2001–02	28.41	4.18	40.83	21.51	62.35	5.06	100

Source: Gandhi and Namboodiri (2002), based on India, Ministry of Water Resources

(Brisco and Malik, 2006). Electricity supply expanded in rural areas making pumping of ground water relatively easy and economical. New modular well and pumping technologies became widely available. In the surface irrigation and flood-prone areas, water-logging and/or salinity became serious problems, and it was realized that encouragement of ground-water pumping provided an effective mechanism for lowering the water table and reducing the severity of water-logging and salinity problems. Farmers also came to realize that ground water was abundant in many areas, especially in the large alluvial basins. The reach of institutional credit expanded, making finance more widely available for private investment in wells. Farmers also came to appreciate that they could develop and apply water 'just in time' from ground-water sources, something which was not always possible in the institutionally complex and poorly managed canal systems.

The result was a quiet 'revolution' in which ground-water irrigation developed at a very rapid rate (Brisco and Malik, 2006), while tank irrigation declined, and surface water irrigation grew much more slowly than historical norms (see Figure 11.1).

Cheap and unmetered electricity, slow development of surface irrigation and poor management of canal systems further encouraged ground-water

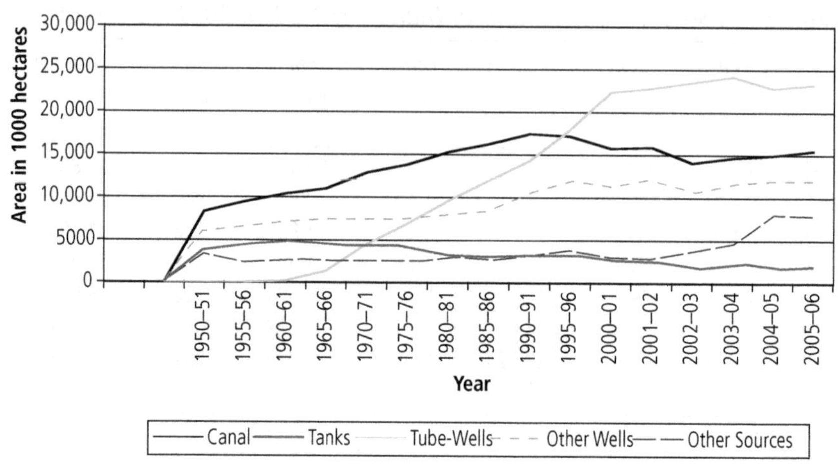

Figure 11.1 *Sources of irrigation in India*

development (Shah, 1993; Brisco and Malik 2006). Over the last two decades, 84 per cent of the total addition to the net irrigated area came from ground water, and only 16 per cent from canals (Brisco and Malik, 2006). Thus, the net area irrigated by private tube-wells grew to about double the area irrigated by canals.

In the early phase of ground-water development in the 1950s, after independence, ground-water extraction was dominated by traditional dug wells with depths generally not exceeding 30 feet (1 metre = 3.281 feet). Labour or animal devices such as Persian wheels were often used to lift the water, constituting over 60 per cent of the irrigation devices at that time. Frequently, there was conjunctive use and the hydrological nexus between well irrigation and tank irrigation was appreciated, if not fully understood (Jeet, 2005). Against this technological backdrop and the existing crop choices, the balance between demand and supply of water could generally be maintained, except during years of very low rainfall. Water use was generally sustainable at this time.

The second phase began in the 1970s and saw considerable growth of dug-cum-bore wells. The depth of the wells increased to about 50–100 feet and the use of centrifugal pumps became common. More water could be lifted which, in turn, encouraged the expansion of the irrigated area and the growing of crops with a greater water requirement. The easing of restrictions on institutional credit during the 1970s further encouraged the development of wells such that there were a substantial number in existence by the end of the decade. On the other hand, most of the tanks became unusable for irrigation due to poor maintenance and this resulted in even greater dependence on ground water.

During the third phase, beginning from the mid 1980s, the extraction technology changed towards submersible pumps and the depth of wells increased to more than 400 feet in many areas. Water extraction increased rapidly, under the influence of subsidized electricity, lack of metering, the availability of credit, and the commercialization of agriculture (Singh, 2003). This led to rapid declines in the water table, a declining quality of water in many cases and an increased frequency of well failure. Similarly costs of well investment and operation have risen exponentially in this latest phase as the expansion of ground-water use has resulted in an accelerated decline in the water table in several parts of the country (Dhawan, 1995; Moench, 1992).

The number of shallow wells doubled roughly every 3.7 years between 1951 and 1991 (Moench, 1996), the total surpassing 18.5 million wells nationwide and accounting for over 50 per cent of the irrigated area at that point. Ground water now provides for about 60–70 per cent of the irrigated area, and about 80 per cent of the domestic water supply. This rapid expansion has resulted in steep declines in the water table, low productivity of wells, intrusion of sea water in many areas and a marked deterioration in ground-water quality. In arid regions such as Rajasthan and Gujarat, ingress of naturally occurring brackish ground water has become a matter of great concern. According to IWMI (2002), the withdrawal rate in India is about twice the recharge rate. Thus, even though ground water is a powerful tool for development and poverty reduction, developing and managing this resource in a sustainable manner is a formidable challenge. Attempts to regulate ground water through restrictions on credit and electric connections have had very little effect and there are serious reservations about other legislative moves, as illustrated by Upadhyay (Chapter 7).

Ground-water scenario in Gujarat

This component of the research has focused on Gujarat, particularly northern Gujarat, which has become well known in the country for the large-scale exploitation of ground water. According to the official statistics presented in Table 11.2, the cumulative number of tube-wells energized in Gujarat by 2001–02 was 3515, the irrigation potential created was 287,670ha, and the potential utilized was 170,111ha. It is evident that the number of new tube-wells created every year has increased dramatically in recent years to about 300 per annum.

Ground water is the main source of irrigation in Gujarat, accounting for 81 per cent of the irrigated area, in a total irrigated area of about 3 million ha (1999–2000). Severe depletion of the aquifers has led to a high number of well failures in North Gujarat (Bunsha, 2002). Some tube-wells have gone to a depth of over 1000 feet. Tube-well irrigation began largely with individual well owners but, due to the depletion of the water table and the rising cost of wells, group irrigation institutions were formed in many parts of North Gujarat (Kumar, 2000). Over the years, it has been shown that local institutions can evolve norms and rules with regard to investment in tube-wells and the use of the sourced ground water (Kumar, 2000). Despite the declining water table, the very high investment cost of tube-wells (about Rs 1 million) and the high uncertainty of success, many water institutions are able to source and use the

Table 11.2 *Number of tube-wells installed, potential created and water courses linked by Gujarat State Water Resources Development Corporation (1995–96 to 2001–02)*

Year	No. of tube-wells completed		No. of tube-wells energized		Potential created (ha)		Potential utilized (ha)	
	During the year	Cum.	During the year	Cum.	During the year	Cum.	During the year	Cum.
1995–96	25	2634	30	2776	840	258,780	420	155,666
1996–97	25	2659	25	2801	490	589,270	245	155,911
1997–98	17	2676	29	2830	1320	260,590	660	156,571
1998–99	29	2705	56	2886	1920	262,510	960	157,531
1999–00	129	2834	364	3250	14,560	277,070	7280	164,811
2000–01	297	3131	242	3492	9680	286,750	4840	169,651
2001–02	350	3481	23	3515	920	287,670	460	170,111

Source: www.Indiastat.com

ground water successfully. They present an interesting subject for study, particularly given the context of the institutional themes explored in this book.

Synopsis of empirical data on ground-water institutions

Approach and data

As indicated above, ground-water irrigation constitutes the major means for irrigation in Gujarat and much of the rural population is heavily dependent on it. In order to study ground-water institutions the district of Mehsana in northern Gujarat was selected. Mehsana district has become well known in the state and the country for exploitation of ground water. It has seen a drastic decline in the water table in recent years. In the face of extremely high capital and operating costs, the major force behind continuing development of ground-water irrigation has been the innovative formation and working of farmer-based ground-water institutions in the area. The overdraft and drastic depletion of ground water have threatened the sustainability, efficiency and equity of water use. The ground-water institutions in this locale are of two main forms: cooperatives, which tend to be larger, and private partnerships, which are usually smaller in scale. The study examined the structure, functioning and performance of a sample of these ground-water institutions in order to understand and derive lessons for better design of new institutions and reorientation of existing institutions. The research attempted to examine these ground-water institutions through the NIE framework and management theor-ies discussed in other chapters. To reiterate, the NIE framework identifies different features of successful institutions. These include clarity in objectives, good interaction, adaptiveness, appropriateness of scale and compliance.

Eight ground-water institutions spread across five villages were selected and studied. Out of these, two were tube-well cooperatives and six were tube-well partnerships. A total of 100 households associated with these eight institutions were surveyed. The survey pertains to the 2004–05 cropping year.

Basic profile

The average landholding in the sample of 100 beneficiary households was 1.86ha (Table 11.3). After taking account of the limited leasing-in and leasing-out activities, the land area operated differed little. The average irrigated area was 1.67ha, indicating 89 per cent of the land area was subject to irrigation. This was relatively less intense than the surface water irrigation discussed in the previous chapter.

Table 11.3 *Land-holding pattern in ha*

Landholding	*N*	*Min*	*Max*	*Mean*	*Std dev*
Land owned	100	0.31	5.00	1.86	1.23
Leased in	6	0.50	2.13	1.02	0.65
Leased out	2	2.50	3.00	2.75	0.35
Land operated	100	0.38	5.00	1.86	1.22
Irrigated area operated	100	0.25	5.00	1.67	1.12

The profile of education (see Table 11.4) shows that 91 per cent of the households had some education and 43 per cent had education to tenth grade and above. This is better in comparison to the average literacy figures for India, suggesting that the members of these institutions are among the more educated on average. About 96 per cent of the respondents are members of tube-well institutions, two were non-members and another two were office bearers. Thus, the respondents were, by and large, ordinary members of the water institutions.

Table 11.4 *Education and membership type*

Education	*%*	*Membership type*	*%*
Illiterate	9	Non-member	2
Std 1–4	14	Member	96
Std 5–9	34	M C member	1
Std 10–12	31	Chairman	0
Below graduate	2	Vice-chairman	0
Graduate	7	Secretary	0
Above graduation	3	Staff	1
Total	100	Total	100

Relationship between the water institution and water resource availability

Table 11.5 indicates that 79 per cent of the households reported very active or active participation in these institutions. Almost all the households have indicated very substantial to substantial reliance on ground-water institutions. This is consistent with the great dependence on ground water for irrigation in Gujarat. Regarding the source of irrigation, 97 per cent of the households indicated that they depended on ground water alone for irrigation. The distribution of the households in the watershed indicates that the sample was evenly distributed with about 40 per cent located in the middle reach.

Table 11.5 also indicates that more than half (61 per cent) of the households regularly faced water scarcity or acute scarcity. Thus, a large number of households in this sample regularly confront the harsh reality of water shortages. Almost 74 per cent of the households indicated that water availability had been declining or sharply declining over time. Two-thirds of the households in the sample indicated that ground-water quality also deteriorated over time. In sum, the data support the view that most households in this sample are in a grim water situation and yet social and economic cohesion remained strong, with 95 per cent of respondents reporting good cohesion in their community.

Water-table depth

Respondents indicated that the water table has descended sharply in recent years and the average reported depth stood at 532 feet in the dry season and 498 feet in the rainy season (Table 11.6). The water table was at about half that depth 20 years ago, and the data suggest that it has been declining at about 10–20 feet per year in the last few years.

Decision making

The findings in Table 11.7 indicate that in ground-water institutions, the government has almost no role in decision making, as you would expect given the genesis of these entities. Investment decisions are made by the ground-water institution, usually jointly among farmers. The release, distribution, pricing and collection of dues are all decided by the institution without reference to superordinate powers. Repairs, maintenance and monitoring of water use are also done jointly by the institution and the farmers. Cropping decisions are made exclusively by farmers.

Governance

As noted earlier, two kinds of ground-water institutions were identified and covered in this survey: namely, tube-well cooperatives and tube-well partnerships. Tube-well cooperatives are typically cooperative organizations formed to take over the operation of formerly government-constructed tube-wells. In essence, this has been the grassroots institutional response to the state handing over public assets to farmers. These institutions are larger, may

Table 11.5 *Participation, reliance, irrigation sources and water availability*

Participation		*Location*	
Participation	%	Location	%
Very active	13	Head end	33
Active	66	Middle end	41
Passive	21	Tail end	26
None	0	Total	100
Total	100		
Reliance		*Water situation*	
Reliance	%	Situation	%
Very substantial	32	Excess water	0
Substantial	68	No scarcity	18
Some	0	Occasional scarcity	21
Very little	0	Scarcity	57
None	0	Acute scarcity	4
Total	100	Total	100
Irrigation sources		*Change in water availability*	
Sources	%	Changes	%
River	0	Increase	0
Open well	1	No change	26
Tube-well	97	Decline	72
Canal	1	Sharp decline	2
Tank	0	Total	100
Rainfed	0		
Total	100		
Water quality		*Social cohesion*	
Current situation	%	Social cohesion	%
Improvement	0	Excellent cohesion	6
No change	33	Good cohesion	94
Deterioration	66	Some conflict	0
Sharp deterioration	1	Several conflicts	0
Total	100	Total	100

Table 11.6 *Average reported water-table level (depth in feet)*

	This year	*Last year*	*3 years ago*	*5 years ago*	*10 years ago*	*20 years ago*
Rainy season	498.08	477.31	447.73	397.73	307.50	242.50
Dry season	532.69	511.92	488.64	450.45	387.50	320.00

Table 11.7 *Decision making of related activities (percentages)*

Decision/activity	*Govt*	*Institution*	*Individual farmers*	*Joint*	*Others*	*Don't know/none*
Planning for capital investment in irrigation structures	0	80	0	20	0	0
Actual capital investment in irrigation structures	0	60	20	0	0	20
Actual release of water	0	100	0	0	0	0
Distribution of water among farmers	0	100	0	0	0	0
Pricing of water distributed to farmers	0	100	0	0	0	0
Collection of dues from farmers	0	100	0	0	0	0
Implementation of maintenance/repair	0	80	0	20	0	0
Monitoring use of water	0	30	50	20	0	0
Stopping misuse/waste	0	0	70	0	0	30
Crops to be grown	0	0	100	0	0	0

not be formally registered, but have a formal governing structure consisting of a general body, management committee, and secretary. Two such institutions, each with a sample of 20 beneficiaries, were covered in this survey (total of 40). Tube-well partnerships, on the other hand, are small new bodies that have sprung up to organize the capital investment and operation of new deep tube-wells, typically on a private share basis. They usually only have a general body and no other formal structure for management. The operational responsibilities are informally distributed among the members, usually on a rotational basis. In this instance, six such institutions were covered in the sample, each with ten members (total of 60). Given these institutional types and sampling processes, the results reveal certain fixed patterns of response compared to the earlier analysis of surface water organizations. The results in Table 11.8 indicate that the general body is active to very active in all institutions. Where a chairman, management committee and secretary exist, they are reported as having been active or very active. The members are generally active and non-members are either very active or have no role at all, depending on their circumstances.[1] There is no material difference between head-reach and tail-reach farmers in their pattern of involvement, but clearly government officials play no role at all.

Most respondents indicated that the procedures for becoming a member of the organization were clear and villagers were well aware of these (see Table 11.9). Farmers' incentives to become members were not social pressure or obligation – rather the likelihood of accruing direct benefits. Most indicated that participation in management decisions was not freely available to all. The respondents, however, indicated that management generally did a good job of running the organization.

Table 11.8 *Governance: Role of the following in the running of the institution (percentages)*

Role of	*Very active*	*Active*	*Passive*	*Don't know/none*
General body	30	70	0	0
Chairman	20	19	1	60
Managing committee	20	19	1	60
Members	20	80	0	0
Non-members	20	0	0	80
Secretary	21	19	0	60
Government officials	0	0	0	100
Small/marginal farmers	30	40	0	30
Head-reach farmers	10	40	20	30
Tail-reach farmers	10	40	20	30

Table 11.9 *Membership and governance quality (percentages)*

Membership and governance quality	*Agree*	*Partially agree/disagree*	*Disagree*
The way to become a member of the institution is clearly documented and widely known	100	0	0
Members participate in the activities of this institution because of social or economic pressure	0	0	100
Members participate in the activities of this institution because it benefits them directly	100	0	0
All members have the opportunity to join management teams/committees	20	0	80
The management does a good job	90	10	0

Empirical testing of New Institutional Economics fundamentals, governance concepts and performance

In the interests of completeness we briefly review the institutional dimensions of these organizations, notwithstanding that the results are heavily influenced by the largely 'private' nature of these entities and limited variation within these data.

Clarity of objective and interaction

Findings in Table 11.10 indicate that the organization had a clear set of objectives, and that these were clear to all the members. There is good interaction between the members and there were regular meetings. However, the calibre of leadership was in some doubt. There is no interaction between the government and the institution, which stands in stark contrast to the lofty legislative ambition for ground-water governance outlined in Chapter 7.

Table 11.10 *Clarity of objectives and interaction quality (percentages)*

Clarity of objectives/purpose	*Agree*	*Partially agree/disagree*	*Disagree*
This organization has a clear set of objectives/purpose	100	0	0
The objectives of this organization are clear to all members of the organization	100	0	0
Good interaction			
There is good interaction between the members of the institution	100	0	0
There is good leadership to facilitate, improve and guide the interaction	2	98	0
There are regular meetings	99	0	1
There is good interaction between the institution and the government	0	0	100

Adaptiveness, scale and compliance

The respondents indicated that there were clear mechanisms in place for changing the rules, if the need arose, and the rules laid down were not excessively rigid in nature (Table 11.11). There were also clear processes for adapting the rules and systems according to needs and setting. The scale in terms of geographic coverage was deemed appropriate for efficient management. The data support the view that management had adequate authority to bring compliance. Overall, respondents perceived that the institution was capable of ensuring fairness and justice. Given the nature of the entities under analysis, the unanimity of opinion on these issues is understandable.

Institutional performance

The critical areas for water resource management in India have been identified earlier and comprise the following: efficiency (addressing scarcity of the resource); equity; environmental stewardship; and financial viability. The performance of these institutions is now examined against these criteria on the basis of a set of items presented in Tables 11.12–11.16.

Table 11.11 *Adaptiveness, scale and compliance (percentages)*

	Agree	*Partially agree/disagree*	*Disagree*
There are clear mechanisms for changing the rules of this organization if the need arises	100	0	0
The rules and systems of the organization are very rigid	0	0	100
There are processes for adapting the rules and systems according to the needs and setting.	100	0	0
The scale of the institution is appropriate for efficient management	100	0	0
Members are aware of and willingly follow the rules set down by this organization	100	0	0
The management has enough powers to bring compliance with institutional objectives and rules	100	0	0
The institution uses its powers to bring compliance.	100	0	0
The institution is able to ensure fairness and justice	100	0	0

Table 11.12 covers the issues relating to scarcity, equity of water distribution, environmental concerns and financial viability. These data indicate that the institutions in question address scarcity inasmuch as there are regular assessments of the quantity of water available every season or year and processes are in place for allocating water to farmers. Quite clearly, there is no institutional interest is using water prices to assist in allocation decisions: the cooperatives or partnerships do not price the water according to its scarcity value or by crop.[2] Overall, institutions in this genre would appear to do well by ensuring equity and having in place a process for equitable distribution. In this context there were mechanisms for guaranteeing proper distribution between large and small farmers, and between head-, middle- and tail-reach farmers. Not withstanding these claims, there would appear to be only limited monitoring or enforcement at the institutional level to back this up. On the environmental front, the responses indicated that the institution was clearly having a negative effect by rapidly depleting the ground-water resource in the village, and the institution was either unaware of or disinterested in monitoring the extent of environmental harm. This is a major weakness of the institution and one which is taken up later in this book by Ananda, Crase and Keeton in Chapter 14. On financial viability, the institution was able to raise payments from the beneficiaries, but the respondents only partially agreed that the institution was financially viable in the longer term.

Some key indicators about the overall impact and performance of these ground-water organizations are detailed in Table 11.13. On the economic efficiency front, the institution would appear to have led to better maintenance of irrigation structures, diversification of the cropping pattern (particularly to

Table 11.12 *Addressing of scarcity, equity, environment and finance (percentages)*

	Strongly agree	*Agree*	*Partially agree/ disagree*	*Disagree*	*Strongly disagree*
The institutions assesses the quantity of water available in a season/year	69	31	0	0	0
The institution has processes for determining the allocation of this water to the farmers	62	38	0	0	0
The institution prices the water according to its scarcity value	4	0	0	65	31
The institution prices the water according to the crop	12	1	0	24	63
The institution has processes for equitable distribution of the water among the farmers	54	46	0	0	0
There is proper distribution of water between small and large farmers	51	48	1	0	0
There is proper distribution of water between head-, middle- and tail-end farmers	53	46	1	0	0
Equitable allocation of water is monitored and enforced	7	34	45	13	1
The activity of the institution is rapidly depleting ground water in the village	36	64	0	0	0
The institution is aware of and monitors such environmental harm/depletion	0	0	1	53	46
The institution is able to raise recurring payments from the beneficiaries	14	86	0	0	0
The institution is financially viable	0	0	100	0	0

high value crops), and reduced the cost of water access and use. It has also led to more equitable distribution of water and fewer disputes and generated a sense of empowerment and ownership among users. However, within each of these dimensions there is some degree of variation.

Table 11.13 *Impact of the institution on efficiency, equity and empowerment (percentages)*

	Highly positive	*Positive*	*No impact*	*Negative*	*Highly negative*
Better maintenance of irrigation structure	60	39	1	0	0
Diversification of cropping pattern	29	66	4	1	0
Change in cropping pattern in favour of high value crops	55	44	0	0	0
Price/cost of water	61	39	0	0	0
Equitable distribution of water	63	37	0	0	0
Resolution of disputes and dealing with offences	24	71	5	0	0
Empowerment of farmers to manage irrigation systems	67	33	0	0	0
Beginning of a sense of ownership by farmers	64	36	0	0	0

In order to gain insights into the individual motivations that culminated in the formation of these institutions and to establish the extent of ongoing institutional challenges respondents were asked a separate series of questions. The results in Table 11.14 indicate that the main problems confronting these institutions include high maintenance costs, the cost of electricity, poor water quality, the depleting water table and non-availability of water at source. However, lack of cooperation from members is not indicated as a problem.

Table 11.14 *Problems faced by institutions and members (percentages)*

	Very major	*Major*	*Light/occasional*	*None/no*
High cost of maintenance	0	100	0	0
Lack of member cooperation	3	0	0	97
Non-availability of water at the source	100	0	0	0
Poor quality of water	96	4	0	0
High cost of electricity	99	0	0	1
Water table receding fast	98	1	0	1

Were there impacts from these institutions at a whole-of-village scale? The farmer respondents indicated that, by and large, the impact on the village had been positive to highly positive, although a few indicated no impact or negative impacts (Table 11.15). The consequences for the poorer groups, such as labourers and wage earners or small and marginal farmers, was also considered positive. There were also suggestions that benefits had accrued to women as a result of the operation of these institutions, although the detail pertaining to these perceptions was patchy. The impact of the organization on large/medium and head-reach farmers was considered less beneficial than for other groups, but was nevertheless positive.

Table 11.15 *Impact of the institution (percentages)*

	Substantially positive	*Positive*	*No impact*	*Negative*	*Substantially negative*
Village as a whole	35	60	2	0	3
Women	51	49	0	0	0
Large/medium farmers	44	56	0	0	0
Small/marginal farmers	41	59	0	0	0
Labour/wage earners	52	48	0	0	0
Head-reach farmers	64	36	0	0	0
Tail-reach farmers	44	55	1	0	0

On the question of overall performance, no respondent rated the institution as very successful, although many (21 per cent) considered it successful or satisfactory (79 per cent). In the context of financial health, none considered the institutions predicament to be very strong or strong, with almost all regarding the financial performance as satisfactory (98 per cent).

Table 11.16 *Overall assessment of the success and financial health of the institution by the respondents (percentages)*

Success/overall performance			*Financial health*		
Success	*Rating*	*%*	*Financial health*	*Rating*	*%*
Very successful	4	0	Very strong	4	0
Successful	3	21	Strong	3	0
Satisfactory	2	79	Satisfactory	2	98
Poor	1	0	Poor	1	2
Total		100	Total		100

Results of bivariate statistical analysis

We now turn to a form of bivariate statistical analysis to examine the significance of selected associations across the study results. As with the format used earlier, this has been done through the familiar analysis of variance (ANOVA) framework. The findings are presented in terms of the mean values of each group and the statistical significance of the difference across the means. Where the institutional performance is involved, this is gauged on the basis of the opinion of the respondents on the overall success of the institution (ranging from 4 to 1 as described above). The results are presented in Tables 11.17–11.24. It should be noted that the sample is relatively small and the variation in many cases is not large. Accordingly, the interpretation of the results is more problematic than that gleaned from data presented in earlier chapters.

Nevertheless, the results are offered to provide a comprehensive basis for comparing across institutional forms.

Table 11.17 examines the relationship between socio-economic cohesion in the village and institutional performance. The F-test indicates there is no significant relationship. This is perhaps because there is very little variation in the data on cohesion, with 94 per cent indicating good cohesion.

Table 11.17 *Relationship between cohesion and institutional performance*

Cohesion	*Excellent cohesion*	*Good cohesion*	*Some conflict*	*Several conflicts*	*Severe conflict*	*F-stat*	*Sig.*
Performance-mean	2.33	2.20	–	–	–	0.58	NS

Note: * Significant at 10%; ** Significant at 5%; *** Significant at 1%, NS Not Significant.

The results in Table 11.18 indicate that participation in the institution has a significant association with performance, with active participation being associated with the highest performance levels.

Table 11.18 *Relationship between participation and institutional performance*

Role	*Very active*	*Active*	*Passive*	*None*	*F-stat*	*Sig.*
Performance-mean	2.02	2.28	–	2.27	2.72	**

Note: * Significant at 10%; ** Significant at 5%; *** Significant at 1%; NS Not Significant.

Results in Table 11.19 indicate that the location of the farmer in the watershed is related to the manner in which they rated institutional performance, with the middle reach indicating the highest performance, but the differences are relatively small.

Table 11.19 *Relationship between location in the watershed and institutional performance*

Location	*Head*	*Middle*	*Tail*	*F-statistic*	*Statistical significance*
Performance-mean	2.09	2.32	2.19	2.93	**

Note: * Significant at 10%; ** Significant at 5%; *** Significant at 1%; NS Not Significant.

A significant association between water availability and the rating of institutional performance was evident. Those with occasional scarcity show the highest performance rating and this is higher than that recorded under no scarcity and acute scarcity.

Table 11.20 *Relationship between water availability and institutional performance*

Water situation	*Excess water*	*No scarcity*	*Occasional scarcity*	*Scarcity*	*Acute scarcity*	*F-stat*	*Sig.*
Performance-mean–	–	2.06	2.38	2.21	2.00	2.54	**

Note: * Significant at 10%; ** Significant at 5%; *** Significant at 1%; NS Not Significant.

The association between change in water availability and institutional performance was not statistically significant. However, where there was no change in water availability, the performance was rated the highest, and where there was a sharp decline, the lowest – as may be expected.

Table 11.21 *Relationship between change in water availability and institutional performance*

Water availability	*Increase*	*No change*	*Decline*	*Sharp decline*	*F-stat*	*Sig.*
Performance-mean	–	2.31	2.18	2.00	1.19	NS

Note: * Significant at 10%; ** Significant at 5%; *** Significant at 1%; NS Not Significant.

Governance and institutional success

The results in Table 11.22 explore the relationship between the governance activities of the organization and institutional performance. The governance structures for most ground-water institutions surveyed are quite simple. Nevertheless, the results indicate that when the chairman, management committee and secretary are active, the performance was better, at statistically significant levels.

Table 11.22 *Analysis of relationship between role-activity and institutional performance*

	None	*Passive*	*Active*	*Very active*	*F-statistic*	*Statistical significance*
Chairman	2.16	2.00	2.44	2.00	2.63	**
Managing committee	2.16	2.00	2.44	2.00	2.63	**
Secretary	2.16	–	2.42	2.00	3.35	***

Note: * Significant at 10%; ** Significant at 5%; *** Significant at 1%; NS Not Significant.

The findings offered in Table 11.23 deal with the relationship between representation by farmers in the management of the organization and institutional performance. These data indicate that adequate representation of farmers, as well as the opportunity to join the management committee, are positively related to institutional performance and are statistically significant.

Table 11.23 *Relationship between representation of farmers in management and institutional performance*

	Strongly agree	Agree	Partially agree	Disagree	Strongly disagree	F-stat	Stat sig
Adequate representation of farmers in management matters							
Performance-mean	–	–	2.40	–	2.16	5.64	***
Members having opportunity to join management committee							
Performance-mean	–	2.40	–	–	2.16	5.64	***

Note: * Significant at 10%; ** Significant at 5%; *** Significant at 1%; NS Not Significant.

In Table 11.24 we examine the relationship between good interaction within the management committee and institutional performance. These results indicate that the association with institutional performance is positive and statistically significant – when there is good interaction, performance is better.

Table 11.24 *Good interaction within the management committee and performance*

	Strongly agree	Agree	Partially agree/ disagree	Disagree	Strongly disagree	F-stat	Stat sig
Performance-mean	–	2.40		–	2.16	5.64	***

Note: * Significant at 10%; ** Significant at 5%; *** Significant at 1%; NS Not Significant.

Results of multivariate analysis

Again, following the analytical approach used to scrutinize other water sources (see Chapters 9 and 10), we adopt a TOBIT modelling technique to simultaneously consider multiple impacts on the performance of ground-water institutions. The usual statistical caveats apply,[3] although an additional cautionary note is also pertinent in this instance. As we highlighted in the introduction to this chapter, the analysis here deals primarily with the internal performance of institutions as perceived by members of tube-well cooperatives and tube-well partnerships. Thus, while respondents may rate the performance highly, this needs to be considered in the context of the objectives set by the entity. Recall that individual farmers have come together in these circumstances ostensibly to increase the effectiveness with which they can mine ground water and to overcome the prohibitive costs of sinking deeper and deeper tube-wells. The longer term efficacy of these measures is not considered in this analysis, other than via our earlier observation that even farmers seem to realize that these institutions are unlikely to be adding to environmental sustainability. In this case success is measured against the perceived necessity of respondents to extract sufficient water to stave off poverty and hunger.

The TOBIT model is used to study the behaviour of institutional performance and identify key determinants. Different measures of institutional performance are used for the dependent variables, including the overall rating of institutional performance, and other dimensions of performance. The models developed employ seven explanatory variables, which were selected on the basis of the theoretical framework, factor and correlation analysis to identify independent factors and the extent of variation in the available data.

The results are given in Table 11.25. The model developed to consider overall institutional performance or success indicates that the expertise of management was the most statistically significant and positive determinant of institutional performance. This shows that the ability of management to deliver rationality, particularly technical rationality, appears to be the most important determinant of success for these ground-water institutions. The importance of delivering on technical rationality in managing the deep tubewell and pump technology for the success of these institutions should come as little surprise.

The model developed to test the determinants of better maintenance of the irrigation infrastructure indicates the importance of the secretary's being active, and the institution pursuing and regularly making plans towards achieving objectives. Once again there appears to be a strong case for technical rationality (typically addressed by the secretary), as well as the need to pursue objectives in a determined fashion to bring success and better performance in this high investment and difficult enterprise.

A similar result appears when the impact on the village as a whole is modelled. More specifically, there is a strong association between the institution pursuing and regularly making plans towards the achievement of objectives and positive impacts of the cooperative/partnership on the village community.

A final model dealing with the impact on labour and wage earners was developed to give some insights into the relationship between poverty alleviation and these institutions. Here the expertise of management shone through as significant, as did good leadership, although the significance for the latter variable is indicative of the multcollinearity problems with these data.

Concluding observations

Ground water now occupies a dominant place in India's agriculture. It has been the main source of growth in irrigation in the recent past and now accounts for over 60 per cent of the irrigated area in the nation. Despite its significance, ground-water irrigation has not been well handled and seems destined for trouble. The number of irrigation blocks (areas) considered overexploited is increasing rapidly and yet the sinking of wells continues unabated and at enormous private, public and environmental cost. The development of

Table 11.25 *TOBIT model: Success of institution as dependent variable*

Parameter	*Success of institutions*	*Better maintenance of the structure*	*Impact on village as a whole*	*Labour and wage earners*
Intercept	2.93***	1.54	−4.49***	4.12***
General body	0.10	0.40	0.01	0.19
Managing committee	0.32	0.28	−0.41	−0.24
Secretary	−0.32	2.81***	0.36	0.48
Management has the expertise to do a good job	0.12***	0.12	−0.01	0.19*
The institution pursues and regularly makes plans towards achievement of these objectives	−0.48	6.23***	7.75***	4.92
There is good leadership to facilitate, improve and guide the interaction	−0.32	−1.54	0.41	−1.82**
The scale of the institution is too large – e.g. for proper control	0.20	0.000	−0.00	−0.08

Note: * Significant at 10%; ** Significant at 5%; *** Significant at 1%.

the institutions required to guide the arrangements necessary for effectively managing the resource has received very little attention. This research has focused on northern Gujarat, which has become well known in the country for the large-scale exploitation of ground water. The region has seen a drastic decline in the water table and in the face of extremely high capital and operating costs the major force behind continuing development of ground-water irrigation has been the innovative formation and workings of ground-water institutions.

Some of these institutions have originated from government devolution of tube-wells and these tend to be larger, formal, cooperative structures. Others, in fact the vast majority in the region, are relatively small private share partnerships with informal general bodies and rotating management. Thus, the survey data was not as rich in variation as occurred with other types of water institutions, limiting the empirical analysis.

Nevertheless, results still indicated that several elements of the NIE framework and management theory of governance were relevant in explaining the performance of these institutions. The activity level of the chairman, management committee and secretary were all found to be significantly related to institutional performance. The representation of the members in management decisions was also an important determinant. The multivariate TOBIT analysis indicates that the ability of the management to deliver rationality, particularly technical rationality, appears to be the most important determinant of success for these ground-water institutions. Invariably, this is tied to the importance of delivering technical rationality when managing a deep tube-well and related pumping technologies. The results on better maintenance of the irrigation structure also bring out the importance of technical rationality, typically addressed by the secretary, as well as the need to pursue objectives in a determined fashion. The impact on the village as a whole is found to be better when the institution pursues and regularly makes plans towards achievement of its objectives, and when management possesses the necessary expertise.

Notwithstanding these insights into the internal mechanics of local ground-water institutions, a major challenge remains. This relates to reining in ground-water extractions to more closely match sustainable yields. The extent to which the incentives for ground-water extraction can be reconfigured along these lines is a major task for higher-order agencies, but one that can be informed by institutional analysis. This is a mission taken up in later chapters in the final section of this book.

Notes

1 Non-members may be actively involved by drawing subsidiary benefits from the entity, say by purchasing water from the institution. The non-members are typically those who did not contribute capital to become members but are given rights to purchase water from the institution if there is a surplus available.

2 Arguably, farmers confront a proxy price for scarcity, as operation and maintenance expenses rise with quantity as water is drawn from deeper aquifers.

3 It is not possible to eliminate multicollinearity, and the results should be interpreted appropriately within these limitations. Some signs may be incorrect and some significances low because of this.

References

Briscoe, J. and Malik, R. P. S. (2006) *India's Water Economy: Bracing for a Turbulent Future*, The World Bank and Oxford University Press, New Delhi

Bunsha, D. (2002) 'Groundwater capitalism in Gujarat', in N. K. Dubashi (ed) *Tubewell Capitalism: Groundwater Development and Agrarian Change in Gujarat*, Oxford University Press

Dhawan, B. D. (1995) *Groundwater Depletion, Land Degradation, and Irrigated Agriculture in India*, Commonwealth Publishers, New Delhi

Gandhi, V. P. and Namboodiri, N. V. (2002) 'Investment and institutions for water management in India's agriculture: Profile and behaviour', in D. Brennan (ed) *Water Policy Reform: Lessons from Asia and Australia*, Australian Centre for International Agricultural Research (ACIAR), Canberra, pp106–130

India, Central Ground Water Board (2003) *Annual Report: 2002–03*

International Water Management Institute (IWMI) (2002) 'Socio-ecology of groundwater in India', *Water Policy Briefing*, IWMI-Tata Water Policy Program, IWMI

Jeet, I. (2005) *Groundwater Resources of India: Occurrence, Utilization and Management*, Mittal Publications, New Delhi

Kumar, D. M. (2000) 'Institutions of efficient and equitable use of groundwater: Irrigation management institutions and water markets in Gujarat, western India', *Asia-Pacific Journal of Rural Development*, vol 10, no 1

Moench, M. (1992) 'Drawing down the buffer', *Economic and Political Weekly*, vol 27, no 13, ppA7–A14

Moench, M. (1996) 'Groundwater policy: Issues and alternatives in India', International Irrigation Management Institute, IIMI Country Paper, India, no. 2, Colombo, Sri Lanka

Shah, T. (1993) *Groundwater Markets and Irrigation Development: Political Economy and Practical Policy*, Oxford University Press, Bombay

Singh, D. (2003) 'Groundwater markets and institutional mechanism in fragile environments', in R. Chopra, C. H. Hanumantha, and R. Sengupta (eds) *Water Resources, Sustainable Livelihoods and Eco-System Services*, Concept Publishing Company, New Delhi, pp311–340

12

Institutional Analysis of the Performance of Rain-Water Harvesting Institutions in India

Vasant Gandhi and Suresh Sharma

Introduction

As noted in the preceding chapter, there has been a rapid expansion of ground-water irrigation in India in the last few decades, such that this now accounts for almost 60 per cent of the irrigated area. The consequent rapid extraction of water has resulted in steep declines in the water tables, low productivity of wells, deteriorating ground-water quality, and even intrusion of sea water in many areas. In addition, large numbers of shallow wells have run dry. Some estimates indicate that the withdrawal rate in India is twice the recharge rate (IWMI, 2002). In response to this, a major grassroots institutional initiative on improving the ground-water availability has been the check dam movement in the Saurashtra region of Gujarat state in India. This revolves around the formation of local village-level institutions to jointly undertake the planning, finance and construction of a system of check dams as well as other rain-water harvesting structures in and around the village. The purpose is to collect and hold the rainwater for a short time so as to recharge the underground aquifers, thereby bringing water to the open wells, most of which have run dry. From the late 1990s, such institutions have been formed in hundreds of villages in the region and the movement appears to have had a significant impact on water availability and agricultural incomes.

In the interests of completeness, we subject these check dam institutions to the same empirical tests as those that were applied to surface and ground-water institutions and report the results in this chapter. Again, the overriding ambition is to establish which components of institutional design are conducive to superior performance. The chapter itself comprises six additional parts. We begin by providing a brief overview of the status and development of the check dam phenomenon, with particular focus on activities in Gujarat, in northwestern India. In section three we describe the empirical sample and deal with some of the generic characteristics of the data. Section four turns to the question of decision making and governance arrangements, before commencing the empirical investigation in section five. Here we consider the concepts drawn from New Institutional Economics (NIE) and test for their support in the data. Section six comprises a bivariate and multivariate analysis of institutional performance before some brief concluding remarks are offered in section seven.

Background

Community-based water harvesting is arguably more important today than ever before. Enthusiasm for community-based rain-water harvesting systems has increased significantly throughout India, but particularly in the northern states, such as Gujarat. Broadly speaking, these types of initiatives fall under a policy suite described as watershed development, but of particular interest in the present context is the expansion of check dams that are used to irrigate crops and meet other household water requirements.

Check dams are small low barriers built across the pathways of rain-water surface flows. The pathways could be natural or manmade, small or large, and may include gullies, old village roads, streams and shallow rivers. In the rainy season, the check dams retain surface water overflows so that water percolates and recharges the water table below. A series of check dams is usually planned along a water flow path so that water flowing over one structure is captured by the next, and so on. In this way, the benefits of ground-water recharge are spread over a large area and potentially impact on a large number of wells. Check dams do not require much technical know-how to construct and the capital investment is generally modest. Construction is often labour-intensive, which facilitates participation by most of the villagers. The involvement of the local people in the planning and implementation appears to have been crucial to make these interventions possible and successful.

The rain-water harvesting movement in the Saurashtra area of Gujarat was inspired primarily by the success in a village called Raj Samadhiyala. Commencing initially as a local initiative, the check dam concept and development have benefited substantially from private voluntary support organized through several organizations, such as the Jal Dhara Trust. The Trust pooled funds from expatriate village residents who had migrated to the city of Surat. Many of these expatriates had done well in diamond-cutting businesses and sought to offer some philanthropic support to their original community. The Trust not only helped organize funds but also supported the initiative with technical know-how and, in some cases, earth-moving equipment. The movement also benefited from active government support. During the year 2000 the government of Gujarat launched the Sardar Patel Participatory Water Conservation Scheme to aid in the construction of check dams. As part of this programme a scheme was devised whereby 60 per cent of the cost of a check dam would be met by the state on condition that villagers contributed the remaining 40 per cent, primarily in the form of labour. However, the village institutions, eager for speedy implementation before the rainy season, often did not wait for government paperwork clearance and went ahead with their own contributions and those sourced from private sources; government funding often followed. According to some reports, 15,000 check dams had been constructed in the state by the year 2002 (*Times of India*, 2002), and according to government statistics given in Table 12.1, over 90,000 check dams had been completed by 2007 (Gujarat, 2007).

Table 12.1 *Number of check dams constructed by various departments in Gujarat, June 2007*

District	*Number of check dams*		
Ahmedabad	629	Amreli	4822
Anand/Kheda	367	Banaskantha	2766
Bharuch	685	Bhavnagar	7290
Dahod	5468	Dang	1678
Gandhinagar	328	Jamnagar	7871
Junagadh	5080	Kuchchh	5804
Mehsana	832	Narmada	1302
Navsari	1234	Panchmahal	7856
Patan	1587	Porbandar	902
Rajkot	14,192	Sabarkantha	8228
Surat	2174	Surendranagar	2493
Vadodara	2684	Valsad	4477
Total	90,648		

Source: Gujarat, 2007

Of the 5600 villages in Saurashtra, 3000 have small and medium check dams while there are 300 large check dams in the region (*DNA Newspaper*, 2008). The outcome has been profound, as evidenced by this comment from Maldebhai Bodar, a farmer from Sevantara village where there are 35 check dams:

> *Earlier it was very difficult getting water for even one crop in a year. Now we have three crops.* (DNA Newspaper, 2008)

Tilala and Shigani (2005) recently undertook a study of the impacts of water harvesting structures on the Raj Samadhiyala village of Saurashtra. This is one of the most admired rain-water harvesting experiments and the study sought to evaluate the impacts on direct beneficiaries and non-beneficiaries. They found that the water harvesting structures had a substantial positive impact on the cropping patterns of farmers, crop yields and farmers' incomes. Similarly, Sikarwar et al (2005) technically evaluated the impact of five small check dams and five marginal check dams constructed by the Gujarat State Land Development Corporation, Bhavnagar (GSLDC) across the river Ambakai between 2002 and 2004. Of interest was the impact of these structures on water-table decline, the cropping pattern employed by farmers, net revenue and the socio-economic status of farmers. In sum, all these variables showed substantial improvement as a result of the check dams.

Sampling and characteristics of respondents

The underlying sampling frame for the study as a whole was described in Chapter 9. In the case of rain-water harvesting institutions, seven institutions were selected from three districts in the Saurastra region of Gujarat, namely Amreli, Bhavnagar and Rajkot. A total of 100 beneficiaries affiliated with check dam institutions made up the sample. The study used both an institutional questionnaire and household questionnaires to collect data and followed a similar format to that described in earlier chapters. It is important to note that check dam institutions differ markedly in their structure and motivation from some of the institutions examined earlier. However, following a standardized approach to analysis has the advantage of drawing useful comparisons with other institutional initiatives.

Basic characteristics of respondents

The average landholding in the sample of 100 households involved with check dam institutions was 4.53ha. This is considerably larger than that reported for the other institutional types, primarily reflecting the relative aridity of the region (Table 12.2). After limited leasing-in and leasing-out activities, the operated land-holding rises slightly to 4.71ha. The average irrigated area operated is 3.59ha indicating about three-quarters of the land area is subjected to irrigation.

Table 12.2 *Land-holding profile (ha)*

Landholding	*N*	*Min*	*Max*	*Mean*	*Std dev*
Owned	100	0.67	13.33	4.53	2.47
Leased in	5	1.67	10.00	4.20	3.74
Leased out	2	2.50	2.50	2.50	0.00
Total	99	0.67	13.33	4.71	2.61
Irrigated operated area	100	0.67	13.33	3.59	2.09

The educational profile of respondents (see Table 12.3) shows that 93 per cent of households had some education, but very few had education beyond the ninth grade and none were advantaged by college qualifications. Thus, the literacy level in these households appears to be relatively poor, especially compared to other institutions sampled, such as those sampled for ground water in the same state. Of the households sampled only three were office bearers so, by and large, ordinary members make up the bulk of the sample.

Table 12.3 Education and membership

Education	*No. of farmers*
Illiterate	7
Std 1–4	36
Std 5–9	51
Std 10–12	6
Below graduate	0
Graduate	0
Above graduate	0
Total	100
Type of membership	*No. of farmers*
Non-member	0
Member	97
Managing committee member	2
Chairman	1
Total	100

Social cohesion and participation in the water institution

Findings in Table 12.4 indicate that in terms of social cohesion, all the respondents reported having good or better cohesion in the community with 19 per cent reporting excellent cohesion. The results in Table 12.4 also indicate that 99 per cent of the households report being active participants in the institution.

Table 12.4 *Social cohesion in the community and participation in the water institution*

Social cohesion		*Participation level*	
Social/economic cohesion	*No. of farmers*	*Participation*	*No. of farmers*
Excellent cohesion	19	Very active	0
Good cohesion	81	Active	99
Some conflict	0	Passive	1
Several conflicts	0	None	0
Total	100	Total	100

Source of irrigation, reliance on institution and water availability
The only source of irrigation for the households was open wells and reliance on the water institution for water access was reported as very high, with 81 per cent indicating it as substantial and 19 per cent as very substantial. About 87 per cent of the households indicated that they face some degree of water scarcity.

Table 12.5 *Sources of irrigation*

Sources	*No. of farmers*
River	0
Open well	100
Tube-well	0
Canal	0
Tank	0
Rainfed	0
Lift from tank	0

Table 12.6 *Reliance on Institutions*

Reliance	*No. of farmers*
Very substantial	19
Substantial	81
Some	0
Very little	0
None	0
Total	100

Table 12.7 *Water availability situation*

Situation	*No. of farmers*
Excess water	0
No scarcity	13
Occasional scarcity	35
Scarcity	52
Acute scarcity	0
Total	100

Decision making

The data in Table 12.8 indicate that in this instance the government has no role in decision making. This confirms the earlier observation about the grassroots nature of these initiatives and the somewhat belated efforts of government to play some role in the development of check dams in this state. The infrastructure planning is done by the whole entity, but the provision of resources and the actual construction was managed jointly by the institution and the farmers. There are no issues pertaining to the release, distribution and pricing of water or the collection of dues, given the nature of this kind of institution. Respondents reported mixed results for the assignment of responsibility for maintenance and repairs – 84 per cent of respondents indicated that this task was vested with the institution, although 16 per cent of respondents reported that repairs and maintenance resided with farmers. Monitoring of water use, stopping misuse and cropping decisions were exclusively left to farmers. Again, these results need to be considered in the context of the unique nature of these institutions.

Table 12.8 *Decision making of water-related activities (percentages)*

Decision/activity	*Govt*	*Institution*	*Individual farmers*	*Joint*	*Others*	*Don't know*
Planning for capital investment in irrigation structures	0	100	0	0	0	0
Providing resources for investment	0	0	0	100	0	0
Actual capital investment in irrigation structures	0	0	0	100	0	0
Decision on maintenance/ repair requirement	0	84	16	0	0	0
Providing resources for maintenance/repair	0	84	16	0	0	0
Implementation of maintenance/repair	0	84	16	0	0	0
Monitoring use of water	0	0	100	0	0	0
Stopping misuse/waste	0	0	100	0	0	0
Crops to be grown	0	0	100	0	0	0

Governance

The data in Table 12.9 indicate that the general body and the members are currently passive. This is because the primary activity of this institution is a one-off event and the demands for ongoing governance and decision making by the general body are modest. However, the chairman, management committee and the secretary are reported to be active by about half the respondents and very active by the other half, indicating some modest variation. Government officials are also indicated as having some active part in the institutional arrangements. The local government of the *Panchayat* and *sarpanch* would appear to show some active involvement but not overly much.

Table 12.9 *Role in running the institutions (percentages)*

Role of	*Very active*	*Active*	*Passive*	*None*
General body	0	0	100	0
Chairman	48	52	0	0
Managing committee	53	46	0	1
Members	7	8	85	0
Secretary	48	52	0	0
Government officials	38	62	0	0
Panchayat	14	86	0	0
Sarpanch	7	93	0	0
Other local institutions	0	0	0	100

There is some lack of clarity whether the institution has been created by the government, perhaps because the government has encouraged the activity and offered some financial support. Nevertheless, the innovation has been largely as a result of local people taking the initiative. The mechanisms for joining such institutions are clear and members participate, not because of social pressure, but because of the benefits that flow from membership. It is generally believed that management has the expertise to do a good job, although there is some variation reported here.

Table 12.10 *Other governance-related issues (percentages)*

	Strongly agree	*Agree*	*Partially agree/disagree*	*Disagree*	*Strongly disagree*
The institution/organization has been created by the government	0	0	100	0	0
The way to become a member of the organization is clearly documented and widely known	44	56	0	0	
Members participate in the activities of this organization because of social or economic pressure	0	0	0	33	67
Members participate in the activities of this organization because it benefits them directly	51	49	0	0	0
Management has the expertise to do a good job	38	46	0	2	14
The management does a good job.	23	76	1	0	0

New Institutional Economics fundamentals

We now turn to some of the conceptual basics drawn from the NIE to assess their relevance in the context of check dams.

Clarity of objective and interaction

The distribution of the responses in Table 12.11 indicates that the organization had a clear set of objectives, and these were clear to the members as a whole. There was good interaction between the members and good interaction between the management and the members. However, there was some variation reported across institutions.

Table 12.11 *Clarity of purpose and good interaction (percentages)*

	Strongly agree	*Agree*	*Partially agree/disagree*	*Disagree*	*Strongly disagree*
This organization has a clear set of objectives/purpose	66	33	0	0	0
The objectives of this organization are clear to all members of the organization	54	45	0	1	0
There is good interaction between the members of the institution	61	39	0	0	0
There is good interaction between the management and the members	68	32	0	0	0

Adaptiveness, scale and compliance

The respondents indicated that there were clear mechanisms for changing the rules if the need arose and the rules laid down were not excessively rigid in nature (Table 12.12). There were apparently clear processes for adapting the rules and systems according to needs and setting and the scale – in terms of geographic coverage – was reported as being appropriate and facilitating efficient management. The data also support the view that compliance with the rules was sufficient but there was no external monitoring or enforcement in place.

Measuring institutional performance

The main criteria for adjudging the performance of water resource management in India have been previously identified as efficiency (addressing scarcity of the resource), equity, environmental stewardship and financial viability. We now turn to each of these factors by considering the basic data solicited from respondents along these lines.

Since the rain-water harvesting institutions are not involved with the distribution or pricing of water, their performance along these lines cannot be readily adjudged. Table 12.13 presents results on the broader perceived impacts of the institution, including the effects on equity. The data indicate that the institution was perceived as having facilitated empowerment and a sense of ownership among the farmers. Moreover, active involvement of all classes was reported. The institution was also perceived as having a substantial positive impact on the whole village, including small/marginal farmers and labourers. Even the impact on the environment was reported to be positive, presumably because local ground-water recharge was conceptualized as benefiting the environment.

Table 12.12 *Adaptiveness, scale/size and compliance (percentages)*

	Strongly agree	Agree	Partially agree/disagree	Disagree	Strongly disagree
There are clear mechanisms for changing the rules of this organization if the need arises	34	65	0	1	0
The rules and systems of the organization are very rigid	0	0	0	67	33
The scale of the institution is appropriate for efficient management	73	27	0	0	0
The compliance with the rules is sufficient	60	40	0	0	0
There is external monitoring and enforcement for compliance	0	0	0	27	73

Table 12.13 *Impact of the institution on the village, different communities and the environment (percentages)*

	Highly positive	Positive	No impact	Negative	Highly negative
Empowerment of farmers to manage irrigation systems	42	58	0	0	0
Beginning of a sense of ownership by farmers	61	39	0	0	0
Active involvement of all classes	30	70	0	0	0
Village as a whole	91	9	0	0	0
Women	71	29	0	0	0
Large/medium farmers	61	38	1	0	0
Small/marginal farmers	67	33	0	0	0
Labour/wage earners	25	74	0	0	1
Environment and natural resources	83	17	0	0	0

The data presented in Table 12.14 show that these institutions were generally financially viable, although there was some variation reported. As a general rule, institutions had little problem raising sufficient funds from the government, donors and the public. Nevertheless, banks were reported as being unwilling to invest in these institutions. This may be explained by the common property characteristics of check dams and the difficulty of articulating the interests involved to the satisfaction of the banks at least.

Table 12.14 *Financial viability (percentages)*

	Strongly agree	*Agree*	*Partially agree/disagree*	*Disagree*	*Strongly disagree*
The institution is financially viable	46	40	14	0	0
The institution is able to raise sufficient funding support from the government	45	55	0	0	0
The institution is able to raise funding from donors and public	63	37	0	0	0
Banking and financial institutions would be willing to invest in the institution	0	0	0	24	76

The data reported in Table 12.15 appear to support the view that government policy had proven helpful for these institutions and that government does not presently pose any threat to institutional performance.

Table 12.15 *Impact of policy (percentages)*

	Strongly agree	*Agree*	*Partially agree/disagree*	*Disagree*	*Strongly disagree*
Membership of this organization has improved because of government policy	69	31	0	0	0
The financial performance of this organization is threatened by government policy	0	0	0	23	77
The activities and services of the organization have improved because of policy	56	44	0	0	0

The overall performance rating for check dam organizations is reported in Table 12.16. About 56 per cent of the respondents considered the institution to be very successful, whereas 44 per cent consider it to be successful. Poignantly, there was no rating below this. All respondents indicated that the financial health of the institutions was strong, in part reflecting the one-off nature of the institution's main tasks and the relatively modest calls on repairs and maintenance expenditures.

Table 12.16 *Performance and financial health of the institution (percentages)*

Performance			*Financial health*	
Success	*Rating*	*No. of farmers*	*Financial health*	*No. of farmers*
Very successful	4	56	Very strong	0
Successful	3	44	Strong	100
Satisfactory	2	0	Satisfactory	0
Poor	1	0	Poor	0
Total	100		Total	100

Understanding institutional performance

Results of bivariate statistical analysis

As with the earlier approach we now turn to a bivariate analysis of important institutional elements. It needs to be noted that the data on check dam institutions contain relatively limited variability, making empirical assessment more challenging. The research here derives from the application of bivariate statistical analysis to examine the statistical significance of selected associations across several of the study results by applying the analysis of variance (ANOVA) framework. The findings are presented in terms of the mean values of each group and the statistical significance of the difference across the means. Where the institutional performance is involved, this is gauged on the basis of the opinion of the respondents on the overall success of the institution (ranging from 4 to 1 as described above). In addition to the complication created by small variations within these data, it must also be acknowledged that the sample is relatively small, thereby making some of the results more opaque than might be preferred.

General observations

The results in Table 12.17 summarize the relationship between socio-economic cohesion in the village and institutional performance. Even though the mean for performance is slightly higher under excellent cohesion, the difference is not statistically significant.

Table 12.17 *Relationship between cohesion and institutional performance*

Cohesion	*Excellent cohesion*	*Good cohesion*	*Some conflict*	*Several conflicts*	*Severe conflict*	*F-statistic*	*Statistical significance*
Performance-mean	3.58	3.56	–	–	–	0.03	NS

Note: *Significant at 10%; ** Significant at 5%; *** Significant at 1%; NS Not Significant.

The reported performance of the institutions had the highest mean under scarcity conditions. However, the differences are not large and proved not to be statistically different (Table 12.18).

Table 12.18 *Relationship between water situation and institutional performance*

Water situation	*Excess water*	*No scarcity*	*Occasional scarcity*	*Scarcity*	*Acute scarcity*	*F-statistic*	*Statistical significance*
Performance-mean	–	3.48	3.63	3.69	–	1.46	NS

Note: *Significant at 10%; ** Significant at 5%; *** Significant at 1%; NS Not Significant.

Governance

According to the results presented in Table 12.19, the more active the secretary and government officials, the higher was performance. Nevertheless, these differences are again small and not statistically significant.

Table 12.19 *Relationship between role-activity and institutional performance*

Role	*Passive*	*Active*	*Very active*	*F-statistic*	*Statistical significance*
Secretary	–	3.62	3.50	1.34	NS
Government officials	–	3.61	3.47	1.85	NS

Note: *Significant at 10%; ** Significant at 5%; *** Significant at 1%; NS Not Significant.

New Institutional Economics

Clear objectives

Results in Table 12.20 indicate that when the institution had a set of clear objectives the performance was better and the difference in this instance was statistically significant.

Table 12.20 *Analysis of relationship between clear objectives and institutional performance*

Objectives	*Strongly agree*	*Agree*	*Partially agree/ disagree*	*Disagree*	*Strongly disagree*	*F-stat*	*Stat sig*
This organization has a clear set of objectives/purpose	3.64	3.41	–	–	–	4.72	***

Note: *Significant at 10%; ** Significant at 5%; *** Significant at 1%; NS Not Significant.

Good interaction

In order to test for the influence of good interaction, several dimensions were assessed. Results in Table 12.21 indicate that performance is generally better under several scenarios: namely when there is good interaction between the management and the members; when there is good interaction between the institution and the government; and when the organization helps members to settle disputes. However, in each case these differences did not prove statistically significant.

Table 12.21 *Analysis of relationship between good interaction and institutional performance*

Interaction	*Strongly agree*	*Agree*	*Partially agree/ disagree*	*Disagree*	*Strongly disagree*	*F-stat*	*Stat sig*
There is good interaction between the members of the institution	3.51	3.59	–	–	–	0.57	NS
There is good interaction between the management and the members	3.59	3.54	–	–	–	0.21	NS
There is good interaction between the institution and the government	–	4.00	3.56	–	–	0.78	NS
There is good leadership to facilitate, improve and guide the interaction	3.55	3.58	–	–	–	0.06	NS
This organization helps members to settle disputes	3.57	3.53	–	–	–	0.13	NS

Note: *Significant at 10%; ** Significant at 5%; *** Significant at 1%; NS Not Significant.

Adaptability

Results in Table 12.22 indicate that when there are clear mechanisms for changing the rules, the performance is generally better, and the difference is statistically significant.

Compliance

Compliance relationships are summarized in Table 12.23. The results support the view that when the members of the entity are aware of and willingly follow the rules set down by the organization then performance is significantly better. In this case the results proved highly significant.

Table 12.22 *Analysis of relationship between adaptability and institutional performance*

Adaptability	*Strongly agree*	*Agree*	*Partially agree/ disagree*	*Disagree*	*Strongly disagree*	*F-stat*	*Stat sig*
There are clear mechanisms for changing the rules of this organization if the need arises	–	4.00	–	3.46	–	3.98	***

Note: *Significant at 10%; ** Significant at 5%; *** Significant at 1%; NS Not Significant.

Table 12.23 *Analysis of relationship between compliance and institutional performance*

Compliance	*Strongly agree*	*Agree*	*Partially agree/ disagree*	*Disagree*	*Strongly disagree*	*F-stat*	*Stat sig*
Members are aware of and willingly follow the rules set down by this organization	3.25	2.57	1.68	1.55	1.37	70.15	***

Note: *Significant at 10%; ** Significant at 5%; *** Significant at 1%; NS Not Significant.

Results of multivariate analysis

The analysis above has used a bivariate approach with one explanatory factor at a time. Next, a multivariate approach was employed to mirror the analyses undertaken of alternative water institutions (Chapters 9 to 11). The TOBIT model is again employed and the same caveats apply – potential multicollinearity particularly.

The TOBIT models are used to shed light on the sensitivity of institutional performance to various influences. Different measures of institutional performance were used as dependent variables, including the overall rating of institutional performance assigned by respondents. The models employ between 7 and 12 explanatory variables, all of which were selected based on the theoretical background and/or factor and correlation analysis. Consideration was also given to the extent of variation in the available data.

The results on overall institutional performance are given in Table 12.24. The model indicates that, where the objectives are clear to the members, management has sound expertise, and management has authority to adapt the rules and systems, then institutional performance is enhanced. In addition, superior performance is promoted when the institution uses its powers to effect compliance. Where government has played an active part in the derivation of rules there would appear to be better performance. This stands in contrast to the results of some of the earlier analyses, but may be explained by the modest influence of government in the overall affairs of these organizations. In addition, good interaction between the members and capable leadership to facilitate interaction increased the chances of better performance. Thus, a wide variety of factors seems to be associated with good performance, but clear objectives and the management's role through expertise, adapting rules and bringing compliance appear to be particularly important.

Table 12.24 *TOBIT regression: Dependent variable – overall performance/success*

Parameters	*Estimate*	*Value*	*Approx. Pr>/t/*
Intercept	–4.68	–1.04	0.3001
Managing committee active	–0.08	–0.44	0.6598
Secretary active	–0.22	–1.07	0.2831
Management has the expertise	0.20***	2.72	0.0066
Rules determined by the government	1.06***	4.24	<.0001
The objectives are clear to the members	0.76***	3.10	0.0019
The institution regularly plans for achievement of objectives	0.01	0.07	0.9469
There is good interaction between the members	0.46**	2.19	0.0282
There is good leadership to facilitate interaction.	0.41*	1.78	0.0746
There are clear mechanisms for changing the rules	0.21	1.14	0.2545
The management has authority to adapt the rules and systems	0.60***	2.77	0.0056
The institution uses its powers to bring compliance	0.78***	2.91	0.0036

Note: *Significant at 10%; ** Significant at 5%; *** Significant at 1%; NS Not Significant.

The model reported in Table 12.25 was developed to examine the determinants of the financial viability of the institution. The results indicate that one important determinant is having an appropriate scale for the institution, and capable leadership and good interaction between members were also conducive to better performance on this front. Again, having the government influence the shape of the rules would appear to be associated with better performance. Other than this, having objectives that are clear to the members would also appear to be an important and positive influence.

The model in Table 12.26 examines the determinants of the broad impact on the whole village. The model uses a shortlist of variables, all of which proved statistical significance. The variables relating to appropriate scale, having higher-level issues appropriately addressed by higher-level institutions, the presence of good interaction between the members, and clarity of objectives in the minds of members were all positive and significantly related to better impacts on the village at large. In addition, when the management committee was active, when there were clear mechanisms for changing the rules, and good leadership was on hand to facilitate interaction, then the overall impacts were superior.

Table 12.25 *TOBIT regression: Dependent variable – financial viability of institutions*

Parameters	*Estimate*	*Value*	*Approx. Pr>/t/*
Intercept	−3.44	−0.81	0.42
Managing committee active	−0.09	−0.44	0.65
Secretary active	−0.24	−1.16	0.24
Management has the expertise	0.12	1.42	0.15
Rules determined by the government	1.10***	4.77	<.00
The objectives are clear to the members	0.48**	2.12	0.03
The institution regularly plans for achievement of objectives	0.28	1.34	0.18
There is good interaction between the members	0.87***	3.65	0.001
There is good leadership to facilitate interaction	0.79***	3.40	0.001
The management has authority to adapt the rules and systems	0.34	1.62	0.10
The scale of the institution is appropriate	0.92***	3.35	0.001
Higher-level issues are addressed by higher-level institutions	0.17	0.69	0.49
The institution uses its powers to bring compliance	0.10	0.45	0.65

Note: *Significant at 10%; ** Significant at 5%; *** Significant at 1%; NS Not Significant.

Table 12.26 *TOBIT regression: Dependent variable – impact on village as a whole*

Parameters	*Estimate*	*Value*	*Approx. Pr>/t/*
Intercept	5.801	55.64	<.0001
Managing committee active	1.65	11.93	<.0001
The objectives are clear to the members	1.83	13.10	<.0001
There is good interaction between the members	2.05	36.64	<.0001
There is good leadership to facilitate interaction	0.176	2.61	0.0089
There are clear mechanisms for changing the rules.	0.409	8.08	<.0001
The scale of the institution is appropriate	3.53	78.22	<.0001
Higher-level issues are addressed by higher-level institutions	3.53	78.22	<.0001

Concluding observations

Rapid extraction of ground water has resulted in steep declines in water tables, low productivity of wells, deterioration of ground-water quality, and even in some instances intrusion of sea water. In response to this, a major grassroots institutional initiative focused on improving the availability of ground water has emerged in the form of the check dam movement. This has proven particularly active in the Saurashtra region of Gujarat in northern India. These institutions revolve around the formation of local village-level groups to jointly undertake the planning, finance and construction of a system of check dams as well as other rain-water harvesting structures in and around the village. Since the late 1990s a large number of these institutions have been formed and they are now commonplace in hundreds of villages in the region. There is also growing evidence that these initiatives have had a major impact on water availability and agricultural incomes. In this instance we sought to unbundle the nature and performance of these institutions to understand their functioning in greater detail. Ideally, this can inform future design principles for such institutions.

In general, these institutions are reported by respondents as being quite successful and as having a positive impact on the whole village. The results indicated that several elements of the NIE framework and management theory of governance were useful in explaining the performance of these institutions. Bivariate statistical analysis indicates the importance of several factors: the active role played by the secretary and government officials; having clarity of objectives; encouraging good interaction between the members; designing mechanisms for changing the rules; and promoting the willingness of members to follow the rules. Multivariate analysis indicates that a similar suite of variables underlies successful performance. These include having appropriate scale, objectives that are clear to the members, management that has the expertise and authority to adapt the rules and systems, and ensuring that the institution uses its powers to bring compliance.

Overall, appropriate scale, clarity on objectives, good interaction and having management with the ability to adapt rules and bring compliance appear to be major determinants of success. The implications of these findings for policy development and decision making are considered in greater detail in subsequent chapters.

References

DNA Newspaper (2008) 08 November

Gujarat (2007) Narmada, Water Resources, Water Supply and Kalpsar Department, Government of Gujarat, available online at http://guj-nwrws.gujarat.gov.in/pdf/checkdam_01.pdf

International Water Management Institute (IWMI) (2002) 'Socio-ecology of groundwater in India', *Water Policy Briefing*, IWMI-Tata Water Policy Program, IWMI

Sikarwar, R. S., Rank, H. D. and Subbaiah, R. (2005) 'Impact assessment of water harvesting structures in Ladudi watershed', in N. C. Patel, R. Subbaiah, P. M. Chauhan, K. C. Patel and J. N. Nandasana (eds) *Sustainable Management of Water Resouces*, Himanshu Publications, Udaipur

Tilala, H. and Shiyani, R. L. (2005) 'Economic impact of water harvesting structures on farmers of north Saurashtra agro-climatic zone', in N. C. Patel, R. Subbaiah, P. M. Chauhan, K. C. Patel and J. N. Nandasana (eds) *Sustainable Management of Water Resouces*, Himanshu Publications, Udaipur

Times of India (2002) Ahmedabad, 8 February

Part 4
Policy Implications of Institutional Analysis

13
Rights Devolution Under Irrigation Management Transfer in Developing Asia: Theoretical Considerations and Empirical Results

Gamini Herath

Introduction

The management of irrigation water in developing countries in Asia has become a critical issue. Since gaining independence, most countries have made heavy investments (under the guise of the 'hydraulic mission') on large-scale irrigation infrastructure and undertaken the responsibilities for the management of irrigation water supplies. At the time of independence in 1946, India had 22.5 million ha under irrigation, of which 9.7 million ha were under major and medium schemes (Gandhi and Namboodiri, 2002). By way of contrast, the potential irrigated area in 2000 exceeded 90.0 million ha (Gandhi et al, 2007). In Sri Lanka, until the 1980s, new irrigation construction accounted for between 20 and 40 per cent of total public investment but operation and maintenance (O&M) accounted for only 5 per cent (Aluvihara and Kikuchi, 1991). Similar investments were observed in Pakistan and Bangladesh and Nepal. However, since the 1980s the emphasis has broadly been on rehabilitation. Schemes such as Gal Oya in Sri Lanka showed good returns to rehabilitation, with the internal rates of return estimated to exceed 26 per cent (Aluvihare and Kikuchi, 1991).

In India, Pakistan and Bangladesh there has been an unprecedented increase in exploitation of ground water since the 1980s (Gandhi et al, 2007).

There are now nearly half a million tube-wells in Pakistan's Punjab province alone, supplying about one-third of the irrigation at the farm gate (Shah et al, 2000). In Bangladesh, minor irrigation through low lift pumps for surface water and shallow tube-wells for ground water spread very rapidly in the 1970s (Ahmed and Sampath, 1992). In Sri Lanka ground-water use has been supported by government subsidies since the 1970s (Kikuchi et al, 2003).

These investments have had dramatic impacts. In the Indian Punjab, agricultural productivity grew by around 6 per cent and by the end of the 1980s, wheat and rice yields doubled. Sri Lanka produced only about 40 per cent of its total rice requirements in 1948, but by 1985, 90 per cent self-sufficiency in rice production was achieved. Between 1951 and 1985, rice production in Sri Lanka increased sixfold at an annual compound growth rate of 5.3 per cent (Aluvihare and Kikuchi, 1991).

However, there were many problems in this era (Gulati and Narayanan, 2002). Sri Lanka spent less than 10 per cent of total expenditure on maintenance between 1950 and 1988 (Aluvihare and Kikuchi, 1991). Cost recovery was also a major failure evident in this period (Gulati et al, 1995; Herath, 2002). In Sri Lanka, India, Pakistan, Bangladesh, the Philippines and Indonesia, irrigation users' fees were collected but lie between 10 and 90 per cent of O&M costs. The World Bank found that in 17 irrigation schemes it examined, less than 30 per cent of the total costs were recovered through pricing or other fees (Sampath, 1992). Some 36.6 per cent of the irrigated areas in Pakistan are also waterlogged. In Pakistan, soil salinity caused a 25 per cent reduction in production of major crops in the saline ground-water areas. In the Sind Province the reduction is around 40–60 per cent in the saline ground-water areas.

Some economists argue that these failures in irrigation management are due to the absence of market incentives and appropriate institutions (Ostrom, 1990). Recent evidence shows a continuing effort by economists to obtain a better understanding of the role of institutions in irrigation water management (Lam, 2005) and the compilation of papers for this volume is representative of that interest. The New Institutional Economics (NIE) provides a flexible framework (Williamson, 1985; North, 1990) and a finer theoretical focus for delineating the forces that generate and distribute income by analysing the nature of transactions. Importantly, NIE also specifically recognizes that the allocation of rights and responsibilities for transactions depends on the nature of the transaction and the costs of monitoring and enforcement.

Since the 1980s, there has been significant effort by most governments in developing countries to introduce major institutional reforms in the irrigation sector. The most significant of these was irrigation management transfer (IMT), introduced on a massive scale in the 1990s. The upshot of this initiative was that management responsibilities were transferred to user groups to achieve efficiency, equity and poverty alleviation. Notwithstanding these efforts, institutional reforms in some jurisdictions remain largely rhetorical (Mollinga et al, 2007).

In this chapter, I examine the performance of new institutional approaches introduced for irrigation water management in Asian developing countries since the 1980s. My main interest lies in IMT in south Asia. A critical study of the historical, economic, social, political and institutional forces behind the evolution and progress in water reforms should provide valuable insights that I hope will assist in the systematic identification of the potential and problems in water reform institutions and management of irrigation. This chapter also provides a useful extension to the empirical work presented in earlier parts of this book, especially Chapter 10. More specifically, it embellishes and develops the observation that the manner in which rights are devolved can have a pervasive influence on the performance of irrigation entities. This chapter examines only three issues, although other matters such as poverty alleviation, environmental challenges and the like are also important. The specific objectives of this chapter are to:

1 briefly revisit the role of institutions and develop relevant theoretical frameworks for considering irrigation investment;
2 assess the performance of institutional change with special reference to IMT from several perspectives; and
3 identify the limitations and policy implications of water user associations (WUAs) to irrigation development.

The chapter itself is organized as follows. Section two provides a brief review of institutions and section three identifies several theoretical frameworks useful for evaluating irrigation management institutions. Section four evaluates the outcomes of recent reforms from several perspectives. Section five identifies some policy implications and offers some brief concluding remarks.

Definitions and nature of institutions

A succinct review of the various definitions of institutions is provided earlier in this volume. Among the most important conclusions from NIE is that economic organizations impose costs because complex contracts are usually incomplete and the future is generally uncertain. Institutions accordingly evolve to reduce these transaction costs, which are the key to the performance of economies.

According to Williamson (1975; 1985), asset specificity, bounded rationality, incomplete information and information asymmetry can lead to opportunistic behaviour (i.e. adverse selection, moral hazard). Institutions evolve in order to minimize opportunistic behaviour and improve economic performance (Williamson, 1985). Under these circumstances, hierarchical approaches may evolve to govern transactions (Simon, 1957; Dequech, 2001). In such cases a critical question arises as to the appropriate level at which rights (i.e. decision-making power) are vested.

Theoretical frameworks

This section briefly reviews some theoretical frameworks relevant to irrigation institutions: namely social capital, the path dependence of institutions, state–society synergy, and public choice theory. Any one of these models cannot alone provide a complete explanation. Market failure, where markets do not provide economically optimal solutions due to the presence of externalities and public or common property characteristics, is well known and hence not discussed here (Varian 1992).

Institutional themes

Social capital and collective action

Collective action approaches are widely used by self-interested individuals to manage common property resources (Runge, 1986; Ostrom, 1990; Bromley, 1992). Rules and endogenous authority systems encourage cooperative strategies because the rules provide certainty about the expected actions of others (Runge, 1981; 1986). There are stronger incentives for collective action by local groups (Olson, 1982; Runge, 1986; Nabli and Nugent, 1989; Ostrom, 1990), with low incomes, critical dependence on a local resource, high uncertainty and a degree of homogeneity within the community. Runge (1986) argues that people will cooperate for their common good without provision of external (state) coercion if they can be assured that a critical mass of users obey a common property arrangement (Moorhead and Lane, 1993).

A society's institutions such as social norms, cultural values, trust and reciprocity and social sanctions can be regarded as social capital (Woolcock, 1998; Rudd, 2000). The trust and reciprocity presented in rural communities increase the success rate for collective action. The farmer-managed irrigation systems of Nepal, Sri Lanka, India (Warabandi) etc. are well managed and rely on local rules and norms to achieve higher cropping intensities and yields than government-sponsored systems. The Warabandi system in India stretches back for more than 125 years. India also had the *ahar-pyne* system in Bihar and the *Phad* system in Maharashtra, managed by farmers (Ballabh, 2005).

Property rights are related to collective action. The absence of clearly defined and well-enforced property rights increases the costs of transactions. Demsetz (1967) and Coase (1960) argue that, in the absence of transaction costs, private property rights are the most efficient system of land use. Property rights lower transaction costs and exclusive rights provide sufficient incentives to encourage development (North and Thomas, 1977). However, if transactions costs are high, private property rights may not be the best (i.e. lowest cost) option.

Path dependence

While interest groups may influence the direction of change, a factor that can determine the rate of change of institutions is path dependence. It means that long-standing networks of political and economic relationships remain unchanged and may shift only in a gradualistic fashion. North (1990) argues that even when a total change of the formal institutions is introduced, say by government decree, the informal institutions have greater survival tenacity and may affect the progress of formal institutional change. During a period of rapid change, such as was witnessed with the mass introduction of IMT in many countries, new institutions are barely in place and existing institutions can be captured by individuals, giving rise to unstable arrangements.

State–society synergy

Institutional innovations will ideally focus on state–society synergy. State–society synergy enhances developmental efforts. A clearer understanding of synergistic relations between government and society is essential to develop well-articulated strategies to maximize returns from policy intervention. The structure of synergistic relations can be analysed by focusing on two concepts: complementarity and embeddedness (Evans, 1996).

Complementarity implies that governments have comparative advantage in delivering certain types of collective goods which complement inputs that are more efficiently delivered by societal actors or groups such as WUAs. Complementarity implies a clear delineation of the role of the state and society in water resources management. Lam (1996) highlights an example from Nepal, where the state kept out of the day-to-day running of irrigation projects but provided inputs that local people could not provide. Moreover, local organizations provided activities within the scope of their portfolio, leading to a clearly defined complementary division of labour between bureaucracy and local people (Evans, 1996; Lam, 1996).

Embeddedness, in contrast, refers to networks and relationships that trespass the public–private divide. Intimate interconnections among public and private actors provide a greater degree of embeddedness and this is reflected in a dense network of social relationships. Embeddedness makes state representatives a part of the communities and the enhanced trust and reciprocity from these arrangements creates an enduring relationship. The social capital created in the interstices between state and society keeps growth on track. Complementarity creates conditions for productive interaction, but without embeddedness the potential for mutual gain is hard to realize (Evans, 1996).

Focusing on synergy is a useful way to understand IMT as a set of public–private relations based upon complementarity and embeddedness. Complementarity exists when rule-based ambience delivers increased efficiency of water management. The state provides the relevant ambience but the irrigation bureaucracy is not directly linked to the WUAs. Synergy can also be constructed, implying that in its absence conditions to enhance synergy can be undertaken (Evans, 1996).

Public choice theory

Public choice theory is the application of economics to political decision making (Mueller, 1989). Public choice theory attempts to explain decision making by voters, bureaucrats and politicians. According to public choice theory, government decision making is subject to various pressures – from interest groups, lobbying, voting behaviour and government self-interest – all ultimately expressed in the 'political market' (Johnson, 1994).

Irrigation management is inherently political because it involves interaction among different actors and interests but some interests are politically more powerful than others. The actors' assessments are mediated by their own interests and position in the social system (Mollinga et al, 2007). Many interest groups are present in most societies, some being highly institutionalized (in the 'Big I' sense of institutions). The success of interest groups depends on their organization, access to information and their knowledge of the political machinery to address particular issues. These interest groups can influence public policy to promote their own interests. These groups can spend large sums of money and time, lobbying politicians to obtain special favours. This is called rent-seeking, which is inefficient inasmuch as it absorbs valuable resources.

According to public choice theory, some bureaucrats have strong links with water lords, elitist farmers and/or rich landowners. Government agencies can support these special individuals or groups by developing policies that also maximize their political opportunities. Mollinga (2001) identifies three levels of political involvement, namely hydropolitics, the politics of water policy and the everyday politics of water use. This chapter focuses mainly on the everyday politics of water use and, to a lesser extent, the politics of water resources policy formulation.

Institutional reforms

Nature of reforms

IMT was arguably the most prominent institutional policy since the 1980s and generally involved partial transfer of decision making. Management control of main water sources was retained by public authority and O&M responsibilities of secondary water sources were shifted to the WUAs (Johnson, 1995). IMT has been further intensified since the 1990s with the aim of reducing the role of government and achieving greater equity and fairness in the distribution of benefits, and purportedly reducing poverty. Most policy makers and experts agree that better management of irrigation water can be achieved if the irrigation systems are distanced from political interference and debureaucratized (Gulati and Narayanan, 2002). However, the design of WUAs in the face of variations in the environment, agrarian structure, and the politico-economic environment is complex and difficult (Herath, 2002). Serious problems have been experienced in most countries adopting the IMT/WUAs model. This experience is analysed in the next section.

Evolution of WUAs

In 1988 the Sri Lankan government adopted IMT for major irrigation schemes. The government irrigation agency was responsible for the head works and the main canal system while WUAs were responsible for the O&M activities below the distributory channel (Samad and Vermillion, 1999). By March 1997, there were 757 WUAs (Saleth and Dinar, 1999). In general, the WUAs were able to formulate rules for the maintenance of irrigation infrastructure, devise procedures for the distribution of water, and impose and collect irrigation fees (Samad, 2002). In 1988 full responsibility for O&M activities of small irrigation schemes was transferred to the farmer organizations (FOs). Prior to the IMT era, the Gal Oya Project in southeast Sri Lanka introduced local FOs in 1980 with considerable success (Uphoff, 1996; Ostrom, 1990). This Gal Oya initiative was amply supported by the Hector Kobbakaduwa Agrarian Research and Training Institute (HARTI), Cornell University in the US, the Sri Lankan government and the farming community.

In India, as noted in earlier chapters, the approach to IMT varied across states. Andhra Pradesh was the first state to initiate large-scale water management reforms, which made WUAs mandatory under the Andra Pradesh Farmers' Management of Irrigation Systems Act 1997 (Reddy and Reddy, 2002). Andhra Pradesh, which recorded a 9 per cent decline in irrigated area, adopted a 'big bang' approach to IMT. In 1997, some 10,292 WUAs were created and elections were held for 9800 WUAs and state-wide training by NGOs was provided. WUAs were also given greater responsibility for irrigation fee collection (Easter, 2000). Nearly 80 per cent of these WUAs were in minor systems.

In Gujarat, IMT was adopted in a step-wise fashion, reflecting the model used in many other Asian countries (Parthasarathy, 2000). In the Pigut Medium Irrigation Project in Gujarat, the WUAs are in charge of water management, setting fees; and they report collecting 100 per cent thereof. The Baldeva Medium Irrigation Project in the state of Orissa adopted a gradual approach in transferring O&M activities to WUAs for the distributaries and minor canals (Easter, 2000). Each WUA manages an area between 300 and 600ha. Farmer participation was to be closely integrated with physical improvements, where written contracts were provided to supply a guaranteed amount of irrigation water.

In 1999, the government of Madhya Pradesh in India adopted IMT through WUAs for all canal networks (Marotia, 2002). The aim was to create autonomous institutions as legal entities and define management areas on a hydraulic basis. Also, some of the schemes were transferred after completing minimum rehabilitation works. The WUAs have functional and administrative autonomy and freedom to raise resources and resolve disputes (Marotia, 2002).

The impact of IMT

Impact of IMT on water saving, crop yields and income

Efficient use of water generally increases yield and income per ha. In the Gal

Oya project in Sri Lanka, the FOs/WUAs were able to bring nearly 25,000ha under cultivation with around 1 acre-foot of water in the 1997 cropping season. All this occurred at a time when the Irrigation Department indicated that not more than 10,800ha could be cultivated. Prior to the FOs being in place, around 2.4–2.7ha-m of water were released in the dry season. In 1985, this had fallen to 1.65ha-m and reached 1.35ha-m in the late 1980s (Herath, 2008). Simultaneously, the average yield of paddy increased by 10 per cent to 4360kg/ha (Uphoff and Wijayaratna, 2000). US$1 million worth of rice was produced during the dry season when water was considered inadequate to grow rice (Uphoff and Wijayaratna, 2000). Amarasinghe et al (1998) estimated that about half the improvement of efficiency in Gal Oya was solely due to the activities of FOs.

Another case study of IMT in Sri Lanka showed that in the pre-IMT period, paddy yields had been declining. But in the post-IMT period, there was an increasing trend in paddy yields where the schemes were rehabilitated and transferred, although cropping intensity did not increase (Samad, 2002). The increase in yield is significant where both rehabilitation and IMT have occurred simultaneously. Results also suggest that rehabilitation prior to transfer is a prerequisite for success in IMT. Those schemes that were transferred but not rehabilitated and those which were rehabilitated but not transferred exhibited no significant increasing or decreasing trend in yield. This implies that there is some degree of complementarity between rehabilitation and IMT. Rehabilitation is capital- and technology-intensive and lies primarily in the domain of the state in developing countries. Thus, rehabilitation before transfers ensures greater complementarity on the sequencing of institutional change. Regrettably, this process was not followed in many countries.

The Rajangana and the Mee Oya, two major irrigation schemes in the North Central and the North Western Provinces respectively of Sri Lanka were managed under WUAs for more than ten years and reflect less successful cases of IMT (Aheer, 1999). In this instance the FOs were relatively weak. There was wastage of irrigation water and exacerbation of environmental problems (Aheer, 1999; Moore, 1989). The poor performance in Rajangana and Mee Oya schemes was due to inadequate commitment of resources by farmers, which constrained the capacity to increase efficiency of water management.

Conjecture about the effectiveness of IMT circumscribes its deployment in Andhra Pradesh. For instance, the irrigated area is claimed to have increased by between 20 and 40 per cent resulting in an extra 200,000ha of irrigation and expanded rice yields worth US$1.53 million (Rao et al, 1999). However, others have noted that these 'successes' coincided with changes in the reporting requirements and do not accurately reflect the status of irrigation efficiency (Raju, 2000). Parthasarathy and Joshi (2001) explored the efficacy of WUAs in three different locations in Andhra Pradesh and revealed no discernable improvement in the performance due to WUAs. The study revealed that 51.5 per cent of the stakeholders were unaware of the WUAs. Only 7 per cent participated in the WUA elections and 13 per cent participated in the annual general meetings. The majority of the tail-end farmers attended meetings, although a greater proportion of the head-end farmers were aware of the existence of WUAs. The irrigation bureaucracy, which had shown only a lukewarm reception towards WUAs, was entrusted with the task of training personnel associated with WUAs. Some training was provided to the presidents of WUAs and this continued until the elections in 2005, but on the ground implementation appeared shaky (Raju, 2000).

Kajisa et al (2007) examined collective action in irrigation tanks in Tamil Nadu. They found that in most inactive villages (villages where collective action had fallen as farmers exited WUAs, choosing instead to use well water), rice yield per ha was 7.6 per cent lower than those achieved in active villages employing collective action. Marotia (2002) found that in the 20 schemes he analysed in Madhya Pradesh, where IMT was adopted, only 5 per cent had adequate water supply and 55 per cent had moderate and scarce water supplies. In the Pigut scheme in Gujarat water used per unit area decreased by 40 per cent following the instigation of WUAs. In contrast, cropping intensity has improved in the Mulla scheme and declined in the Bhima scheme in India (Vermillion and Al-Shyabani, 2004), although IMT had reportedly improved water distribution in these two schemes. Farmers believe that there is a clear improvement in the access to water after IMT. The physical condition of the transferred minors has also improved subsequently. In the Palhi minor district in Nepal where IMT has occurred paddy and wheat production have been increasing over the last three years as a result of these improvements. However, Samad (2002) contends that there has been no significant difference in the aggregate yields between the transferred and the non-transferred schemes. Cropping intensity in the West Gandak in the period between 1992 and 1996 was also reported as being stagnant following IMT.

In sum, the impacts of IMT on water use, cropping and incomes appear mixed. Importantly, and as evidenced by the empirical findings presented in Part 3 of this book, it is often the process by which rights have been devolved that is as significant as the devolution itself. Put differently, it is not simply a matter of handing over infrastructure to farmers – there needs to be adequate capacity within farmer organizations and a willingness on the part of the bureaucracy to support these groups. In addition, handing over degraded irrigation assets does not appear to be a recipe for success.

Water pricing under IMT

Mainstream economists generally champion greater use of market prices for water (Rosegrant and Binswanger, 1994). However, 'market pricing' for irrigation water is far from having a clear, distinct or wholly accepted meaning, even after IMT. Usually an ad hoc flat fee is levied, implying a zero marginal cost for water. In addition, departures from marginal cost pricing do not seem to follow any regular principles. Irrigation fees are consequently not an allocation device but a political signalling device (Kloezen et al, 1997).

The design of incentives to ensure that the full economic costs of irrigation are covered is challenging (Lam, 2001; Saleth and Dinar, 2004). Variations deriving from season, crops, region and climate all create challenges (Sampath, 1992). Difficulties in measuring water deliveries, uncertainty with respect to availability and delivery in gravity-fed systems and the poor status of the infrastructure of the systems all undermine pricing reforms. More generally, market-based approaches may themselves not be appropriate, at least in the short term, because of the common property characteristics of water and potential market failures (Lam, 2001; Saleth and Dinar, 1999). In most countries in Asia, wet rice growing by small-scale farming using gravity-fed irrigation is not conducive to defining property rights to water, at least not in the sense that would support a conventional market (Gandhi et al, 2007). Further, market-based policies are unlikely to achieve efficient use of water unless they are linked to institutions capable of implementing, monitoring and enforcing pricing policies at the local and national levels.[1] Efficient pricing is not simply a market issue but an important political issue.[2]

Many governments have moved away from imposing the full costs upon the users of irrigation because charges are heavily resisted by farmers (Samad, 2005). The political consequences of reallocating water away from agriculture are often considered too high. According to Price (1994, p108), 'In South Asia, the cost of forgone agricultural production, multiplier effects regionally, and the resulting social problems of large pockets of poor rural residents are possible results that are politically unacceptable to governments and present little incentive to promote open water markets.'

The intensely political nature of water pricing is clearly observable in the implementation of the National Water Resources Policy and Institutional Arrangements developed in the year 2000. This proposed policy framework had nine principles. Several of them were related to water ownership, water scarcity, water sharing and water rights. It was also aimed at proper water entitlements and pricing of irrigation water and implementation of IMT (Gunatilake and Gopalakrishnan, 2002; Samad, 2005). Considerable resources were allocated to developing the legal, institutional and political frameworks to introduce an appropriate pricing regime for irrigation water. While the new policy was built on good economic principles, policy implementation stalled because of difficulties in achieving consensus within political circles (Saleth and Dinar, 2004; Gunatilake and Gopalakrishnan, 2002).

One criticism of at least some of the WUAs in India for failing to cover costs is that they focus on farmer participation but not so much on cost recovery and sustainability (Gulati and Narayanana, 2002). The primacy of politics, despite the critical importance of appropriate pricing reforms, led to a greater emphasis on the politically more desirable notion of user participation. User participation facilitates political partisanship being embedded in reforms, which has delivered perverse results.

Nevertheless, moves towards more efficient pricing seem inevitable in the long run and markets could improve as other institutional features are dealt with (Sampath, 1992). Future research could be aimed at investigating the conditions necessary to establish successful water markets in settings such as those found in developing countries. This implies developing better economic incentive systems, including improved property rights, water pricing and water markets, so that users internalize the economic value of water. However, what is more appropriate in the immediate term is state-wide policy to design institutions to suit the physical, technical and socio-political framework of the individual states.

O&M costs and irrigation fee collection

IMT adopted the principle of cost recovery, but as noted above, the conceptualization of cost recovery was often not efficient. The cost to farmers using heavily subsidized canal water is extremely low, varying between 5 and 15 per cent of the canals' actual operating costs. These arrangements created perverse incentives for farmers, bureaucrats and politicians to engage in rent-seeking activities (Lam, 2001; Gulati and Narayananan, 2002).

In Sri Lanka, full recovery of O&M costs from members did not occur and governments frequently subsidize maintenance expenditures (Herath, 2002; Samad, 2002). The financial performance of 50 major irrigation schemes in Sri Lanka evaluated using piecemeal linear regression for the period 1985–90 (before IMT) and 1990–95 (after IMT) (Samad, 2002) showed that IMT had not led to any reduction in government expenditure on O&M. The two detailed studies of Nachchaduwa and Hakwatuna Oya also showed that, in general, water fee collections had not been well developed and only a minority of farmers actually paid any irrigation fees at all. The Rajangana scheme in Sri Lanka had poor fee collection capacity, due to a lack of experience, and this, in turn, created financially weak FOs. Further, there were competing demands for the finances of the FOs, including construction of buildings, purchase of capital equipment, working capital for service provision, and advances for rehabilitation and maintenance (Aheer, 1999).

In a similar vein, the Mulla and Bhima schemes (minor canals) in the state of Maharashtra in India showed that there was no significant reduction of O&M expenditure by the government compared to non-transferred canals (Brewer et al, 1999). In the 22 projects examined in Madhya Pradesh, Marotia (2002) found that 95 per cent of the funds allocated for repair and maintenance had been used by the WUAs, and 62 per cent of the farmers paid their irrigation fees.

In Andhra Pradesh, about 15 per cent of farmer contributions remain uncollected and there was no flexibility in pricing, distribution and enforcement built into the distribution schedules. In Madhya Pradesh, Marotia (2002) found that the voluntary contribution of labour was generally poor. Marotia (2002) attributes these problems to the newness of the WUAs and argued that over time improved performance might be expected.

In this regard the Pigut scheme in India is illustrative that improvements can occur over time – recovery of costs increased from 89 per cent in 1989, in the WUAs' first year, to 100 per cent in 1992–93. In the case of the Mohini project in Gujarat, bulk water was sold on a volumetric basis to the WUA by the irrigation agency and the WUA then collected water charges from the farmers. In Gujarat NGOs and the irrigation officers were also responsible for mobilizing farmers through pilot projects that were more successful than in Andhra Pradesh. These players generated more positive embeddedness, contributing towards better performance of the WUAs. Clearly, some schemes performed relatively better than others on this front.

Reddy and Reddy (2002) found a significant difference between the formal WUAs and the informal association in Karimaddela. In the Erraguntla Scheme farmers received a lower fund allocation from the state, because the scheme was used to cultivate mostly irrigated dryland crops. This reflects a relatively poor performance inasmuch as the 'wet' crops are generally more profitable. As a result, farmers are not paying their dues, reflecting poor integration into the market system. In contrast, the informal Karimaddela scheme shows a very different result. In addition to cost-based contributions, alternative sources of income generation have been used to complement the revenues from irrigation charges. Farmers have apparently paid more than the stipulated irrigation charge despite a threefold increase in irrigation fees. This is attributed to the highly satisfactory service offered by the WUA. This scheme is also well integrated into the market-based approach.

The review above of the costs and fee collection experience reveals that various concerns still remain even after IMT. The performance varies depending upon the degree to which decision-making power has been devolved. Fee collection also depends upon the management skills of the WUAs. Basic skills in budgeting and financial record-keeping at least should be a preliminary necessity for all WUAs so that these do not become a hindrance to the costing and fee collection tasks. Poor fee collection in some schemes may also reflect poor implementation of IMT generally.

Equity in the distribution of benefits

Factors such as wealth inequality, head-end and tail-end differences in irrigation systems, gender, ethnic and cultural heterogeneity can lead to adverse distributional effects within IMT (Bardhan, 1984). Several theories of how heterogeneity can affect collective action have emerged in the literature and these were touched upon earlier.

The impact of IMT on equity is not always observable or reported, as many studies of IMT did not directly focus on this issue per se. However, differential water access to small farmers concentrated at the tail end of irrigation schemes can sometimes lead to iniquitous income distribution. In the Gal Oya project in Sri Lanka, tail-end areas showed the best results in terms of water use, production and productivity. Farmers were able to distribute very limited water effectively, resulting in better-than-normal cropping outputs (Uphoff and Wijayaratna, 2000). The gradualist approach and the many partners involved in a dense network of relationships transcending the public–private boundaries generated greater embeddedness in this case, which presumably led to better performance (Uphoff and Wijayaratna, 2000). However, in Nachchaduwa, a major irrigation project in Sri Lanka, about 33 and 25 per cent of the farmers in the head and tail end respectively reported worsening water supply after IMT. This was largely attributed to poor rehabilitation of infrastructure done before IMT. In Andhra Pradesh poor farmers are generally at the tail end of irrigation systems and are often deprived of access to irrigation water (ADB, 2003).

Kajisa et al (2007) analysed income inequality of paddy farmers in Tamil Nadu and found that the Gini coefficient was higher for the inactive villages (i.e. those where collective action was absent). This would support the view that yield variation is larger in the inactive villages than in the active villages. A similar picture is observed when considering per capita income. Lower incomes and higher inequality were observed for inactive villages. It shows that poverty and inequality for the inactive villages are higher than those for the active villages and the difference is statistically significant.

Bardhan (2000) found that land-holding inequality is significantly and negatively associated with canal maintenance. He established evidence of a U-shaped relationship between the Gini coefficient and this indicator of performance. At low and high levels of inequality there is little intra-village conflict but for inequality in the middle range conflicts are more likely. Khwaja (2000) also found a U-shaped relationship between land-holding inequality and project maintenance in Pakistan. Starting at perfect equality, increasing inequality reduces maintenance effort, while at high inequality levels, maintenance levels rise again. Baker's 1997 study of *kuhl* irrigation systems in Himachal Pradesh found that the *kuhl* irrigates more than one village, the irrigators of the *kuhl* comprise multiple castes, and land distribution is relatively unequal and inequity more significant.

Gender is another factor that leads to inequality among water users. Prevailing stereotypes about gender, including the view that women cannot work with men, and that a woman's involvements should be limited to specific activities, conspire to effectively exclude many women from WUAs. Evidence from Sri Lanka indicates that female participation in WUAs is much lower than for men (Meinzen-Dick and Zwarteveen, 2003; Molen, 2001). Studies in Sri Lanka showed that female participation is not widespread in WUAs and this failure to adequately represent women in WUAs and FOs can exacerbate equity objectives (Molen, 2001).

Reddy and Reddy (2002) examined formal and informal WUAs located at the tail end of the Kurnool–Cuddapath canal. The two villages selected, namely Karimaddela and Erraguntla, were covered by the WUA legislation. They found that there is bias in the membership towards upper classes with better socio-economic status, which clearly can lead to exacerbation of existing income inequality. The formal WUAs could not penetrate the existing inactive community in the Erraguntla village and, since less water-intensive crops dominated the area, the opportunity cost of not being involved in collective action was not significant. In the Karamiddala scheme rent-seeking was minimal, and equity was maintained through rotational irrigation.

In Madhya Pradesh equity was promoted within the structure of the WUAs by introducing the concept of territorial constituencies. Here all landholders in possession of land in an irrigation system have equal voting rights with elections held by secret ballot. The WUAs have a five-year tenure and the association has the right to recall an elected member after one year.

Rent-seeking and elite capture

In Andhra Pradesh there is some evidence of elite capture, especially in large-scale canal irrigation. Bureaucratic apathy, insufficient devolution of power, systematic corruption and lack of incentives to manage the systems for the benefit of the farmers have also been reported (Ballabh, 2005; Bardhan, 2000). Perhaps ironically, a south Indian study provides significant evidence that when rules are crafted by the elite they tend to be more compliant. However, non-compliance is common when the elite do not craft the rules. This manifests in a vicious circle where elitism determines IMT outcomes, primarily in order to retain compliance capacity (Ballabh, 2005).

Rent-seeking is still evident and this has played a major role in slowing down the rate of progress. In 30–40 per cent of the WUAs, the former Irrigation Department contractors became the presidents and there is some evidence that this has been conducive to collusion with the bureaucracy in order to win contracts. Involvement of the Public Works Department (PWD) is positively related to situations where water scarcity is severe, but such involvement has come at a cost – increased violation of water-sharing rules and hence an erosion of cooperative behaviour.

Concluding remarks and policy implications

This chapter shows that IMT in most developing countries falls well short of being proclaimed as an 'unqualified success'. IMT has uncovered some positive achievements but there is scope for considerable improvement. The predominance of bureaucratic power in irrigation, political expediency and a strong interdependence between politicians and other key economic interests tends to undermine synergistic relations between state and society. Institutional reforms are often in the interest of local elites and others extracting sizeable economic rents. These circumstances create weak WUAs with poor skills and knowledge, often unable to enhance the administrative, managerial and financial capacities of participants. Institutional reforms should ideally reconfigure institutions to empower, organize and mobilize local resources but do so in a manner that ensures transparency and accountability on the part of the bureaucracy.

Although social capital can play an important role in the evolution and sustainability of water management institutions (Uphoff and Wijayaratna, 2002; Lam, 2005) governments have all too often failed to promote collective action in the farming community, often due to political expediency. Participatory management should provide greater autonomy to local groups and incorporate social norms and cultural values, but this is easier said than done in the political landscape of irrigation in developing countries.[3]

In general, property rights over water have not been well defined and certainly not in a manner that guarantees farmers water of the desired quality and quantity and at the required time. There is also strong evidence that deficiencies in rights and management are not evenly spread, with the poor and marginal farmers often suffering the most. Governments should ideally ensure that the interests of vulnerable groups (for example, tail-enders and women farmers) are fully incorporated into the decision-making process to guarantee a better distribution of benefits, but this seems a long way off.

Perhaps the most pertinent message from this chapter is that international evidence on the impact of IMT on irrigation performance is extremely variable and subject to many influences. For instance, decentralizing decision making to WUAs when a defunct irrigation infrastructure exists has (perhaps not surprisingly) proven largely unsuccessful. Yet where the infrastructure has been renovated and adequate processes put in place to support and delineate the role of WUAs and the water bureaucracy, then success is more common. Accordingly, the processes by which IMT takes place would appear to be as significant as IMT itself, a finding consistent with the empirical details provided in other parts of this manuscript. Moreover, these empirical insights and lessons should be used to guide future IMT efforts.

Notes

1 Transferable water rights are considered to offer scope for creating efficient water rights. These institutions are not widespread in the developing world. However, various cases can be found. Martin and Yoder (1986) compared two villages in Nepal: Thulo Kulo and Raj Kulo. The irrigators in Thuklo Kulo have transferable water rights. Farmers who want water can purchase it from other farmers. Water goes to the highest bidder. In Raj Kulo, water rights during the monsoon rice season are restricted to individuals who cultivate land in a certain part of the village. Here water rights are tied to particular plots and hence not independently transferred. Water is diverted elsewhere and not to the command area.

2 Privatization and market allocation of water are neither feasible nor desirable in the short term. It is suggested that the government limit itself to the provision of technical and financial assistance and create an environment where farmers and water users can work through WUAs. The government should provide strong institutional support and leadership for water markets to emerge. This means that efforts need to be directed to make WUAs financially autonomous, where the need to obtain fees becomes important and makes the organization cost-conscious. This means that the WUAs should have the ability to set fees and reduce their own administrative costs, and that the fees should reflect the level of management of the scheme.

3 The politics of irrigation reform are also formidable in developed nations, an issue made clear by Crase (Chapter 3) and Pagan, Crase and Gandhi (Chapter 4).

References

ADB (2003) *Water Sector Roadmap Bangladesh: Bangladesh Water Sector Review*, Asian Development Bank, Manila, available online at www.adb.org/water/CFWS/Roadmap-BAN.pdf

Aheer, M. M., (1999) 'Impact of irrigation management policy on environment: Lessons from Sri Lanka', *Asia-Pacific Journal of Rural Development*, vol 9, no 1, pp71–78

Ahmed, A. U. and Sampath, R. K. (1992) 'Effects of irrigation induced technological change in Bangladesh rice production', *American Journal of Agricultural Economics*, vol 74, no 1, pp144–157

Aluvihare, P. B. and Kikuchi, M. (1991) *Irrigation Investment Trends in Sri Lanka: New Construction and Beyond*, IWRI, Colombo, Sri Lanka

Amarasinghe, U. A., Sakthivadivel, R. and Hammond M. (1998) *Impact Assessment of Rehabilitation Intervention in the Gal Oya Left Bank*, IWMI Research Report, no. 18, available at http://dlc.dlib.indiana.edu/archive/00004199/, accessed 20 December 2008

Ballabh, V. (2005) 'Emerging water crisis and political economy of irrigation reforms in India', in G. P. Shivakoti, D.S. Vermillion, W. F. Lam, E. Ostrom, U. Pradhan and R. Yoder (eds) *Asian Irrigation in Transition, Responding to Challenges*, Sage Publications, New Delhi

Baker, J. (1997) 'Common property resource theory and the Kuhl irrigation systems of Himachal Pradesh, India', *Human Organization*, vol 56, no 2, pp199–208

Bardhan, P. (1984) *Land, Labour and Rural Poverty: Essays in Development Economics*, Oxford University Press, Delhi

Bardhan, P. (2000) 'Irrigation and cooperation: An empirical analysis of 48 irrigation communities in south India', *Economic Development and Cultural Change*, vol 48, pp847–868

Brewer, J., Kolavalli, S., Kalro, A. H., Naik, G., Ramnayanan, S., Raju, K. V. and Sakthivadivel, R. (1999) *Irrigation Management Transfer in India*, Oxford & IBH Publishing, New Delhi

Bromley, D. W. (1992) 'The commons, common property and environmental policy', *Environment and Resource Economics*, vol 2, pp10–17

Coase, R. H. (1960) 'The problem of social cost', *Journal of Law and Economics*, vol 3, pp1–44

Demsetz, H. (1967) 'Toward a theory of property rights', *American Economic Review*, vol 57, pp347–359

Dequech, D. (2001) 'Bounded rationality, institutions and uncertainty', *Journal of Economic Issues*, vol 35, pp 911–930

Easter, W. (2000) 'Asia's irrigation management in transition: A paradigm shift faces high transactions costs', *Review of Agricultural Economics*, vol 22, pp370–388

Evans, P. (1996) 'Government action, social capital and development: Reviewing the evidence on synergy', *World Development*, vol 24, pp1119–1132

Gandhi, V. P. and Namboodiri, N. V. (2002) 'Investment and institutions for water management in India's agriculture: Profile and behaviour', in D. Brennan (ed) *Water Policy Reform: Lessons from Asia and Australia*, ACIAR Proceedings No. 106, Canberra

Gandhi, M., Crase, L. and Herath, G. (2007) 'Determinants of institutional success for water in India: Results from a study across three states', paper presented at the 51st Annual Conference of the Australian Society of Agricultural and Resource Economics, February, Queenstown, New Zealand

Gulati, A. and Narayanan, S. (2002) 'Subsidies and reforms in Indian irrigation', in D. Brennan (ed) *Water Policy Reform: Lessons from Asia and Australia*, ACIAR Proceedings No. 106, Canberra

Gulati, A., Svendan, M. and Choudhury, N. R. (1995) 'Capital cost of major and minor irrigation schemes in India', in M. Svendsen and A. Gulati (eds) *Strategic Change in Indian Irrigation*, ICAR, New Delhi, IFPRI, Washington DC and Macmillan, New Delhi

Gunatilake, H. M. and Gopalakrishnan, C. (2002) 'Proposed water policy for Sri Lanka: The policy versus the policy process', *Water Resources Development*, vol 18, no 4, pp545–562

Herath, G. (2002) 'Issues in irrigation and water management in developing countries with special reference to institutions', in D. Brennan (ed) *Water Policy Reform: Lessons from Asia and Australia*, ACIAR Proceedings No. 106, Canberra

Herath, G. (2008) 'Irrigation management: Does bottom up work better than top down in Sri Lanka?', in R. Ghate, N. S. Jodha and P. Mukhopadhyay (eds) *Promise, Trust and Evolution*, Oxford University Press, Oxford

Johnson, R. M. W. (1994) 'The national interest, Westminster, and public choice', *Australian Journal of Agricultural Economics*, vol 38, pp1–30

Johnson, S. H. (1995) 'Selected experiences with irrigation management transfer: Economic implications', *Water Resources Development*, vol 11, no 1, pp61–72

Kajisa, K., Palanisami, K. and Sakurai, T. (2007) 'Effects of poverty and equity on the decline in collective tank irrigation management in Tamil Nadu, India', *Agricultural Economics*, vol 36, pp347–362

Khwaja, A. I. (2000) 'Leadership, rights and project complexity: Determinants of collective action in the maintenance of infrastructural projects in the Himalayas', unpublished paper, Harvard University, Cambridge, MA

Kikuchi, M. P., Weligamage, R., Barker, M., Samad, H., Kono, H. and Somaratne, M. (2003) *Agro-Well and Pump Diffusion in the Dry Zone of Sri Lanka: Past Trends, Present Status and the Future Prospects*, Research Report 66, International Water Management Institute, Colombo, Sri Lanka

Kloezen, W. H., Garces-Retrpo, C. and Johnson, S. H. (1997) *Impact Assessment of Irrigation Management Transfer in the Alto Rio Lerma Irrigation District, Mexico*, Research Report 15, International Water Management Institute, Colombo, Sri Lanka

Lam, W. F. (1996) 'Improving the performance of small scale irrigation systems: The effects of technological investments and governance structure on irrigation performance in Nepal', *World Development*, vol 24, pp1301–1315

Lam, W. F. (2001) 'Coping with change: A study of local irrigation institutions in Taiwan', *World Development*, vol 29, no 9, pp1569–1592

Lam, W. F. (2005) 'Reforming Taiwan's irrigation associations: Getting the nesting institutions right', in G. Sivakoti, D. l. Vermillion, W. F. Lam, E. Ostrom, U. Pradhan and R. Yoder (eds) *Asian Irrigation in Transition: Responding to Challenges,* Sage Publications, New Delhi

Marotia, D. K. (2002) 'Institutions' arrangements for participatory irrigation management: Initial feedback from central India', in D. Brennan (ed) *Water Policy Reform: Lessons from Asia and Australia*, ACIAR Proceedings No. 106, Canberra

Martin, E. and Yoder, R. (1986) 'Water allocation and resource mobilisation for irrigators: A comparison of two systems in Nepal', paper presented to the annual conference of the Nepal Studies Association, 4–6 November, University of Wisconsin, Madison

Meinzen-Dick, R. and Zwarteveen, M. (2003) 'Gendered participation in water management: Issues from water users associations in South Asia', in A. G. Quisumbing (ed) *Household Decisions, Gender and Development*, International Food Policy Research Institute, Washington DC

Molen, I. van der (2001) 'An assessment of female participation in minor irrigation systems in Sri Lanka', Working Paper 8, International Water Management Institute, Colombo, Sri Lanka

Mollinga, P. P. (2001), 'Water and politics: Levels, rational choice and Southern Indian canal irrigation', *Futures*, vol 33, pp733–752

Mollinga, P. P., Meinzen-Dick, R. and Merrey, D. J. (2007) 'Politics, plurality and problemsheds: A strategic approach for reform of agricultural water resource management', *Development Policy Review*, vol 25, pp699–719

Moore, M. (1989) 'The fruits and fallacies of neoliberalism: The case of irrigation policy', *World Development*, vol 17, pp1733–1750

Moorhead, R. and Lane, C. (1993) *New Directions in African Range Management: Natural Resource Tenure and Policy*, International Institute for Environment and Development, London

Mueller, D. C. (1989) *Public Choice*, Cambridge University Press, Cambridge

Nabli, M. K. and Nugent, J. B. (1989) 'The new institutional economics and its applicability to development', *World Development*, vol 17, pp1333–1347

North, D. C. (1990) *Institutions, Institutional Change and Economic Performance*, Cambridge University Press, Cambridge

North, D. C. and Thomas, R. P. (1977) 'The first economic revolution', *Economic History Review*, vol 30, pp229–241

Olson, M. (1982) *The Logic of Collective Action: Public Goods and the Theory of Groups*, Harvard University Press, Cambridge, MA

Ostrom, E. (1990) *Governing the Commons: The Evolution of Collective Action*, Cambridge University Press, Cambridge

Parthasarathy, R. (2000) 'Participatory irrigation management program in Gujarat: Institutional and financial issues', *Economic and Political Weekly*, vol 35, no 35, pp3147–3154

Parthasarathy, R. and Joshi, H. (2001) *Access to Water and Equity Dimensions of Irrigation Management Transfer: A Comparison of Gujarat and Andhra Pradesh, India*, Report for the International Water Management Institute, Colombo, Sri Lanka

Price, W. (1994) 'Water markets in South India', in Le Moigne et al (eds) 'Water policy and water markets', Technical Paper No 249, World Bank, pp107–111

Raju, K. V. (2000) 'Participatory Irrigation Management in Andhra Pradesh: Promise, practice and a way forward', Working Paper 65, Institute for Social and Economic Change (ISEC), Bangalore, India

Rao, H. C., Dhawan, B. D., Gulati, A. (1999) 'Towards reforms in Indian irrigation: Price and institutional policies', unpublished paper presented at the NCAER-IEG-World Bank Workshop on Reforms in Indian Agriculture, 15–16 April, Delhi

Reddy, V. R. and Reddy, P. P. (2002) 'Water institutions: Is formalization the answer? (A study of WUAs in Andhra Pradesh)', *Indian Journal of Agricultural Economics*, vol 57, pp519–535

Rosegrant, M. W. and Binswanger, H. P. (1994) 'Markets in tradeable water rights: Potential for efficiency gains in developing country water resource allocation', *World Development*, vol 22, no 11, pp1613–1625

Rudd, M. A. (2000) 'Live long and prosper: Collective action, social capital and social vision', *Ecological Economics*, vol 34, pp131–144

Runge, C. F. (1981) 'Common property externalities: Isolation, insurance and resource depletion in a traditional grazing context', *American Journal of Agricultural Economics*, vol 63, pp595–606

Runge, C. F. (1986) 'Common property and collective action in economic development', *World Development,* vol 14, pp623–635

Saleth, M. and Dinar, A. (1999) 'Water challenges and institutional response, a cross-country perspective', Policy Research Working Paper 2045, The World Bank, Washington DC

Saleth, M. and Dinar, A. (2004) *The Institutions Economics of Water: A Cross Country Analysis of Institutions and Performance*, Edward Elgar, Cheltenham, UK

Samad, M. (2002) 'Impact of irrigation management transfer on the performance of irrigation systems: A review of selected Asian experiences', in D. Brennan (ed) *Water Policy Reform: Lessons from Asia and Australia,* ACIAR Proceedings No. 106, Canberra

Samad, M. (2005) 'Water institutional reforms in Sri Lanka', *Water Policy*, vol 7, pp125–140

Samad, M. and Vermillion, D. (1999) *Assessment of Participatory Management of Irrigation Schemes in Sri Lanka: Partial Reforms, Partial Benefits*, IWMI Research Report, 34, available at www.lk.iwmi.org/pubs/pub034/Report34.pdf, accessed 19 December 2008

Sampath, R. K. (1992) 'Issues in irrigation pricing in developing countries', *World Development*, vol 20, pp967–977

Shah, T., Hussain, I. and Rehman, S. (2000) 'Irrigation management in Pakistan and India: Comparing notes on institutions and policies', Working Paper No. 4, International Water Management Institute, Colombo, Sri Lanka

Simon, H. (1957) *Administrative Behaviour*, 2nd edition, Macmillan, New York

Uphoff, N. (1996) *Learning from Gal Oya: Possibilities for Participatory Development and Post-Newtonian Social Science*, Intermediate Technology Publications, London

Uphoff, N. and Wijayaratna, C. M. (2000) 'Demonstrated benefits from social capital: The productivity of farmer organizations in Gal Oya, Sri Lanka', *World Development*, vol 28, pp1875–1890

Varian, H. R. (1992) *Intermediate Microeconomics*, W. W. Norton, New York

Vermillion, D. L. and Al-Shyabani, S. (2004) *Small Dams and Social Capital in Yemen: How Assistance Strategies Affect Local Investment and Institutions*, Research Report 76, IWMI

Williamson, O. E. (1975) *Markets and Hierarchies: Analysis and Antitrust Implications*, Free Press, New York

Williamson, O. E. (1985) *The Economics Institutions of Capitalism*, Free Press, New York

Woolcock, M. (1998) 'Social capital and economic development: Toward a theoretical synthesis and policy framework', *Theoretical Sociology*, vol 27, pp151–208

14
The Role of Information and Decision-Making Capacity in a Hierarchical Process

Jayanath Ananda, Lin Crase and William Keeton

Introduction

In an earlier part of this volume, colleagues explored the relationship between institutional performance and the characteristics of 'good institutions' proffered by Pagan (Chapter 2) and others. The upshot of this analysis was that institutional performance varied markedly in different settings. Moreover, the components of an institutional design were observed to fluctuate in their relative impact on performance. However, even highly successful institutions can produce outcomes that are less than optimal in a global sense. For example, the performance of ground-water partnerships and cooperatives was highly rated on performance grounds when viewed through the eyes of participating farmers. After all, without these institutional innovations farmers would not have been able to assemble the necessary capital and operational resources to access ever-decreasing water tables. Yet the very success of these institutions arguably manifests in increased extraction of ground water, often in areas where withdrawals already exceed sustainable yields. Similarly, the performance of some rain-water harvesting institutions was categorized as being 'successful' although the impacts of this 'success' on downstream users was not captured in the analysis. The ability of check dams to retard water in one location presumably has impacts on others and there is no way of using the extant analysis to adjudge the broader efficacy of these arrangements.

Another important finding to date has been that devolving decision making to lower-order bodies with a stake in water can bring both benefits and costs. On the one hand, successfully devolved decision making was tied to improved operation and maintenance, greater compliance and overall performance in surface water irrigation. And yet in other settings this has been less successful and the existence of a water user association (WUAs) had delivered only modest benefits. Important in this context was the capacity of the entity to make informed decisions and to lead and foster cooperation. More specifically, it was noted that the presence of a skilled management committee or an active secretary or skilled chairman was a critical determinant when WUAs had been given authority to make decisions.

Put simply, the data analysed in the empirical section of this book shows that it is not enough to simply shift decision-making responsibility to farmers and farmer groups. Successful water resource management hinges on the capacity of decision makers to reach a preferred decision and the calibre of the information on hand to shape that decision.

These are important elements that have been largely underexplored to date. In addition, they constitute significant policy constraints. For instance, Upadhyay (Chapter 7) noted that there is a trend in India towards devolving responsibility for ground-water management and enforcement to the *Gram Sabha* and the village community. One of the apparent motivations for this trend has been the intractable nature of the problem of reining in ground-water extraction and the inability of state agencies to bring compliance on the scale that is urgently required. Clearly, the likelihood of devolved decision making actually producing an improvement in the status of ground-water management will depend in no small measure on two key issues – the information available to local decision makers and the capacity of those decision makers to harness those data into an optimal institutional regime.

It is the purpose of this chapter to consider these two dimensions of decision making in greater detail. More specifically, we use this chapter to explore the theoretical and practical consideration that should be taken into account when deciding on the extent of decentralized decision making. The remainder of the chapter is organized into six additional parts. In the second section we consider, in general terms, the benefits and costs that attend differing levels of decentralized decision making. Here we explore the usefulness and yet alluringly deceptive subsidiarity principle. Subsequently, we turn to the detailed mechanics of the decision-making process and provide a synoptic overview of competing theoretical models in this field. This is followed by an examination of the components of decision-making capacity. We specifically consider the role of leadership in this context. The fifth section is constructed around the concept of information and the scale at which information needs to be available to enhance decision making in a hierarchical framework. A series of illustrative examples taken from Indian irrigation is then used to map some general guidelines for integrating the information and capacity dimensions of decision making into policy formulae. Finally, we offer some brief concluding remarks.

Decentralized decision making

Several authors in this text have observed a trend towards decentralized decision making in water resource management. For instance, Naramboodiri and Gandhi (Chapter 10) described the formation of WUAs where policy makers saw this as a panacea for dealing with dysfunctional, monolithic, state-controlled water agencies. A similar trend was noted in the Australian context where reforms have focused heavily on enhancing the clarity of individual water use and access rights, particularly in the context of communal irrigation schemes that were once operated by state governments (see Crase and Gandhi, Chapter 1). The compelling logic of this approach can, in part, be traced to generic principles of communal decision making frequently articulated in such concepts as the subsidiarity principle.

The subsidiarity principle argues that any communal function should be performed by the smallest organizational unit possible. Most commonly espoused in the context of the federal governance literature, the principle is frequently invoked when considering the appropriate level of government to deliver a particular public good or social function. The logic of the subsidiarity principle resides in such seminal work as Arrow's (1954) impossibility theorem which, under reasonably plausible assumptions, showed that there is no rational way for devising a social welfare function that adequately captures the preferences of the community at large. The upshot of this state of affairs is that any communal decision will necessarily involve some degree of coercion, since the level of service provided by a 'shared' good is unlikely to perfectly match all consumers' preferences. Thus, the larger the group the more implausible that the level of service (and its related costs) matches individual preferences and the more likely that coercion will be required to maintain order.

Against this background, the subsidiarity principle reduces to:

> *making sure that decisions are taken at the most appropriate level; for example, by those most directly affected, by those best informed and by those best placed to deal with the consequences.* (Guerin, 2002, p1)

For instance, consider the case where an irrigation network requires upgrading to remain functional. If responsibility for this decision rests with the state then several potential problems emerge. First, the state agency needs to know what will be the impact of a given level of infrastructure investment in order to justify the expenditure. After all, a rational agency (what Simon (1960) would call 'rational administrative man') should only increase public expenditure to the point where the marginal costs of that expenditure match the marginal gains. Since farmers are those most likely to be aware of the productive benefits of a change to irrigation functionality, there are information asymmetries that might ultimately be exploited by one party or the other – say by the agency pursuing a 'gold-plated' refurbishment, should it be dominated by technocrats rewarded from building 'bigger projects' rather than optimal ones. Second, the motivation for the agency to become adequately informed about the preferences of end users is weakened by the cost of assembling this knowledge. In effect, this is a potential cost of having the decision made at a higher level in the decision-making hierarchy. Third, these arrangements embody flaws that erode the incentives to deliver an optimal service/level of expenditure. If the state undertakes to fund the refurbishment, then farmers have an inducement to overstate the benefits, since ultimately they do not pay the full cost. Alternatively, if farmers are to pay for the infrastructure, but it is delivered by the state agency, then there is no innate mechanism to limit construction expenditures, shirking or corruption by state officials.

Now contrast this with a situation where a small group of farmers (or even an individual farmer) faces the same investment choice. Clearly, there are incentives to match the benefits of the expenditure with the costs, since the group who has the information about potential benefits will also bear the costs that attend the work. Moreover, if the group is reasonably small then the likelihood of homogeneity increases and the difficulty (i.e. cost) of sharing information about preferences is also much lower. In addition, there are strong incentives to constrain expenditure to the minimum and to guard against cost overruns. Finally, should the project fail or prove to be even more profitable than predicted, the decision makers can then deal directly and promptly with the consequences.

Oates (1968; 1972) invokes this form of logic when analysing the distribution of functions under a model of fiscal federalism. While not explicitly related to irrigation, this form of reasoning still essentially holds and argues that the appropriate jurisdiction for any public good[1] is defined by the set of individuals who consume that good, as this group is likely to internalize the benefits and costs of provision.

There are, nevertheless, two important caveats offered by Oates (1972, p54) and these relate to potential scale efficiencies gained through provision by a centralized authority and the possibility of interjurisdictional effects. In the case of the former, there may be instances where a communal good can be provided at lower cost simply because of mass consumption. The provision of telephony services is likely to be more efficiently delivered at a national level than by smaller villages or communities, for example. Here the optimal size of the decision-making group 'involves a trade off between the increased cost-saving from joint consumption in larger groups versus the greater welfare from more responsive levels of consumption in smaller groups' (Oates, 1972, pp41–42). The second caveat relates to the potential for spillover benefits or costs to attend an activity such that the appropriate jurisdiction for capturing these is the state or national government. For example, leaving responsibility for the immunization of children to be managed solely at the local level may lead to an underinvestment in this task. Poorer communities may not fully immunize children, choosing instead to invest in increased food consumption.

However, higher levels of immunization bestow benefits on neighbouring communities and the only feasible means of capturing these benefits and increasing the level of immunization is through intervention by a state or national agency, for example through subsidies for immunization programmes.

Taken together, the subsidiarity argument and its attendant caveats would appear to provide a clear prescription for the choice between centralized and decentralized decision making. Dollery, Crase and Johnson (2006, p45) have adapted the typology of Brady (2002) to provide a summary of this dichotomy and this is detailed in Table 14.1.

Table 14.1 *Factors implying decentralization of a function*

Factors in favour of centralized decision making
Decisions can be based on non-transferable central knowledge, system-wide knowledge, knowledge of unrelated organizations, and knowledge of externalities
Where accountability for judgements must rest with the democratically elected body
Where economies of scale can be achieved
Where economies of scope can be achieved
Where there is a need for coherence and coordination across the public sector
Where there is a need for uniform national standards
Where it is difficult to contract out or subordinate government objectives
Factors in favour of decentralized decision making
Decisions can be based on non-transferable local knowledge
Where there is need for community involvement, local empowerment and local participation
Where there is need to avoid concentration of power and risk of absence of power
Where there is need for customization, innovation and flexibility

Source: Adapted from Dollery et al, 2006, p45

Notwithstanding the usefulness of this approach for reflecting on the appropriateness of devolving water management decisions to local communities, WUAs or the like, this technique runs the risk of oversimplifying the decision-making process itself. For example, in Table 14.1 among the benefits of decentralized decision making are listed the advantages of 'community involvement', 'local empowerment' and 'local participation'. Regrettably, this sheds relatively little light upon how a decision is actually made in a given context, the information that constrains that decision, and the part played by various actors in a 'local' or communal decision environment. These are important elements and yet standard neoclassical economics has been reluctant to explore this area in more detail.

At the extreme of neoclassical thinking is the view that all individuals possess stable utility functions, fully understand their preferences and can instantaneously reach a decision without cost. This 'black box' view of individual decision making belies the expansive literature on consumer decision-making behaviour. Some of this literature is devoted to illustrating the many and varying influences over the most trivial expenditures, such as personal toiletries, and the complex psychological and social forces at play (see, for example, Blackwell et al, 2006). To apply the same 'black box' approach to demanding communal decision making would surely be 'one assumption too many' and we use the following section to consider alternative approaches to this problem.

Decision-making processes

In an effort to unravel some of the complexity of the communal decision-making process we borrow heavily from Hogwood and Gunn's (1984) characterization of policy-making models. This approach suggests that there is a continuum of decision-making processes. At one end of the spectrum Herbert Simon's seminal works (1947; 1957a; 1957b; 1960; 1983) form the reference point. At the other end of the spectrum lies the approach described by Lindblom (1959) as 'muddling through'. Here we focus primarily on Simon's 'rational administrative man' but in order to fully appreciate the scope of these alternatives, we first briefly define the decision-making process itself.

Typologies of decision making are relatively common in the behavioural literature and, as we noted earlier, the consumer behaviour literature provides a useful contrast to the standard neoclassical 'black box' treatment of consumers as decision makers. For instance, Blackwell et al (2006) offer a seven-stage process model that can be used 'to analyse how individuals sort through facts and influences to make logical and consistent decisions' (p70). First, consumers are required to recognize that there is a need for a purchase. This ostensibly hinges on recognition that there is sufficient divergence between the desired state and the preferred state to motivate further action. Second, the consumer undertakes a search for information. This stage may involve a search for new information or simply rely on recall from existing memory. Third, the consumer undertakes some form of pre-purchase evaluation. This can require considerable cognitive effort where various attributes are measured, assigned weights and traded off. Next, the consumer embarks on stage four, the purchase proper. Consumption occupies the fifth component of the process, which precedes post-consumption evaluation and divestment of the good/service.

Students of consumer behaviour soon realize that individual consumer decision making is far more complex than the characterization of consumption by the neoclassic economics literature. A consumer decision process model can also be complicated by the changing environment that circumscribes the decision – what prima facie appears as a linear process can quickly become iterative with stages being compressed or extended as required. Nevertheless, a model of this form has the advantage of helping to make sense of a range of consumer behaviours and reactions, whether they are related to weighty purchases, such as houses or retirement funds, or strategies for purchasing a piece of fruit from a local store. Most decision-making models of this genre acknowledge the role of group influences on the individual's choices. But what of collective, group or communal decisions per se?

There is remarkable similarity between the consumer decision-making process model described above and those dealing with communal decision making or policy formulation generally. Hogwood and Gunn (1984, p4) offer a ninefold typology for the formulation of policy decisions as follows:

1 Deciding to decide (issues search or agenda setting);
2 Deciding how to decide (or issue filtration);
3 Issue definition;
4 Forecasting;
5 Setting objectives and priorities;
6 Options analysis;
7 Policy implementation, monitoring and control;
8 Evaluation and review;
9 Policy maintenance, succession, or termination.

As with the behavioural models developed to analyse consumers, this should not be taken as a prescription for a preferred mode of decision making in all instances; rather, the model offers a conceptual framework for reflecting on how decisions might be made, how they are actually made, and for tracing the impact of various forces within the decision-making process. In the present context we invoke this type of model primarily as a vehicle for considering the efficacy of devolving water management decisions to local authorities or communities.

In simple terms decision-making models provide a mechanism for studying complex choice processes and cover three broad approaches. First, there is the 'ideal' approach that offers a conceptually ideal way of undertaking the decision-making function. In the parlance of Hogwood and Gunn (1984, p44) this is not ideal, in the sense that it is 'preferable to all other', rather it is idealized to provide insights into what might occur when certain stylized conditions hold. This provides a starting point for considering how deviations from the idealized state can give rise to particular real-world phenomena. The familiar model of the idealized perfectly competitive market is a case in point, where economists use this stylized version of a market to scrutinize the probable outcome when competition is less than 'perfect'. The second approach is to use descriptive models of what is seen in the real world. This approach appears relatively straightforward but is no simple task – no two individuals are likely to see the real world through the same lens. Nevertheless, the descriptive model becomes an important step for mapping deviations from the idealized state and, if appropriate, advocating prescriptions for change – these steps form the third approach. A prescriptive model is normative in nature and sets about combining idealized and descriptive components. In essence, a prescriptive model compares the idealized conditions with real-world constraints and sets about analysing the mechanisms for 'improving' on the status quo.

Among the most enduring concepts in this context are those that stem from the writings of Simon (1947; 1957a; 1957b; 1960; 1983). Simon's idealized rational model of policy making and administration suggests that the task of reaching a public decision comprises five main components, commencing with intelligence gathering and concluding with choosing a preferred option.[2] The important feature of this idealized state is that the decision maker or decision-making body accesses the complete set of information and choices. For instance, in the case of 'assessing the consequences of options' the fully rational policy maker 'would identify *all* the costs and benefits of *all* his policy options' (Hogwood and Gunn, 1984, p45 – emphasis added).

Simon's descriptive approach notes that the real world was far more likely to be typified by 'bounded rationality' and 'satisficing behaviour' emerges. Simon traces these conditions to a range of human 'limitations' (such as cognitive constraints for processing and gathering information), organizational limitations, cost limitations and situational limitations. Unperturbed by these elements of the descriptive model, Simon (1960) offers a prescription for enhancing decision making.

In this regard Simon (1960) divides decision making into two broad categories; 'programmed' and 'non-programmed' decisions. As the nomenclature would suggest, programmed decisions are characterized by a level of routine and repetition that allows for the development of a definitive response to the problem at hand. Simon (1960) contends that decisions in this category lend themselves to improvements in systems analysis or similar approaches. Moreover, even without complete information programmed decisions can be improved by applying heuristics to problem solving and ensuring that systems are in place to facilitate learning by doing.

By way of contrast, non-programmed decisions are more novel and unstructured in form and require different resources. Since the problems in this genre are new, complex and potentially intractable, the organization must 'fall back on whatever general capacity it has for intelligent, adaptive, problem-oriented action' (Simon, 1960, pp5–6). This capacity is relatively expensive and this gives rise to important implications for the distribution of decision making in a hierarchical framework where resources are limited. With this in mind we briefly turn to the issue of 'leadership' before dealing specifically with hierarchical decision making in water resource management.

Leadership

Several important themes flow through this chapter. First, making decisions is no simple task, particularly community-based decisions, although it is often assumed that this 'just happens' once responsibility is devolved. Second, information is important as it helps shape better decisions. However, information is not free and is often incomplete. Third, having assembled information (albeit incomplete) there needs to be capacity to undertake a decision-making process, regardless of what that process is. Again, such capacity is not boundless and needs consideration.

The extent to which such rudimentary issues as these are adequately incorporated when designing water policy is questionable and yet, when policy failures arise, this is all too often characterized as simply a failure of leadership[3] (see, for instance, Independent Evaluation Group, World Bank 2001). In addition to the empirical analyses offered in Chapters 9 to 12, there are numerous studies in the development and management literature that highlight the role of indigenous leadership (see, for example, Kiggundu et al, 1983). However, since it is not always feasible to 'create leaders' it is likely to be more useful, in a policy sense, to consider precisely the role played by leadership in the decision-making process.

In the previous section we described Simon's (1960) rational administrative man and the idealized decision-making process that accords rational behaviour. We noted that, in crude terms, Simon's model traces five basic steps and these can be loosely described as: (1) intelligence gathering; (2) identifying options; (3) assessing the consequences of options; (4) relating consequences to values; and (5) choosing the preferred option (Hogwood and Gunn, 1984, pp45–46). It is important to note that there are numerous real-world challenges to invoking this model but perhaps the greatest difficulty relates to the articulation of values and establishing how these are to be incorporated into the process, say at steps (4) and (5) above. Others (see, for instance, Lindblom, 1959) rate the 'values' component of the decision-making process more overtly and place it at the beginning of the decision-making process. Nevertheless, this does not reduce the intellectual difficulty of establishing what (or whose) values count, and how these values are to be traded off in the real world.

We contend that it is here that leadership can play a major part in facilitating the decision-making process, particularly at the community level. Viewed in this light leadership is a resource that can help shape communal values so that a decision can then be mapped against the available information. Arguably, leadership can also play a role in providing a short cut to establishing heuristics for programmable decisions when information is incomplete. However, leadership is not a perfect substitute for complete information and a proper decision-making process, as illustrated by numerous public policy failures led by successful political leaders in developing and developed nations.

Information, scale and hierarchies

To date we have attempted to establish that:

- There is a theoretical and practical case for having some decentralized decision making.
- It is not enough to resort to the intuition that some decisions are better handled by local authorities or communities on the grounds that these groups are 'better placed' to make the decision.
- Understanding the intricacies of how decisions are made needs to be included in the analysis.

- Decision making requires resources (capacity) and information, both of which are in finite supply.
- Leadership can usually lubricate decision making but it cannot make it costless or guarantee a better decision.
- Improvements in decision making are feasible if consideration is given to the type of decision required, and to who has the resources and access to information to make the best decision.

Much of this earlier discussion has been couched in terms of a single decision taken by a single entity (a village or WUA, for example). However, this approach is deceptively simplistic, particularly in the context of water. Almost without exception, water allocation decisions are nested in a hierarchy of decision making. Put simply, a decision by a community (or WUA, or ground-water cooperative) is itself constrained by the decisions that have (or have not) been taken by superordinate groups or individuals.[4] Much of the thinking along these lines can be traced to the seminal work of Eleanor Ostrom and her institutional analysis and development framework.

The institutional analysis and development (IAD) framework (Ostrom, 1986; 1990) also provides a useful theoretical structure to explore the role of information and expertise in water management. This framework combines an actor-based perspective with attention to institutional rules and inter-governmental relations. The institutional framework envisages individual actions as a function of both the attributes of the individual (values and resources) and the decision-making situation (Kiser and Ostrom, 1982). The decision-making situation is a product of institutional rules, the nature of the relevant good, and the attributes of the community (Kiser and Ostrom, 1982). Ostrom (1986) defines institutional arrangements as a rule set that directs or constrains actions at multiple, nested levels (see Figure 14.1). Institutional rules determine who and what are included in decision-making situations, how information is structured, what actions can be taken, in what sequence and how individual actions will be aggregated into collective decisions.

Ostrom's institutional analysis has been expanded by defining three levels of policy action: the operational level (e.g. water user level), the collective choice level (e.g. the statute governing the water agency) and constitutional level (e.g. the constitution governing the legislature) (Ciriacy-Wantrup, 1971; Kiser and Ostrom, 1982; Sabatier, 1991). Policy outcomes at each level can be conceptualized using the IAD framework depicted in Figure 14.1. The three functional tiers of institutions are governed by corresponding rules (Paavola, 2007). More often than not, the functional tiers are organized as nested structures. Put differently, the decisions made at each level of the institutional hierarchy are bound by the institutional rule set of the superordinate level. For instance, state institutional mechanisms determine the regional and local-level institutional design while federal institutions determine the state institutional arrangements. Decisions at the regional and local level determine individual actions and resource use patterns at the grassroots level. Nested governance is

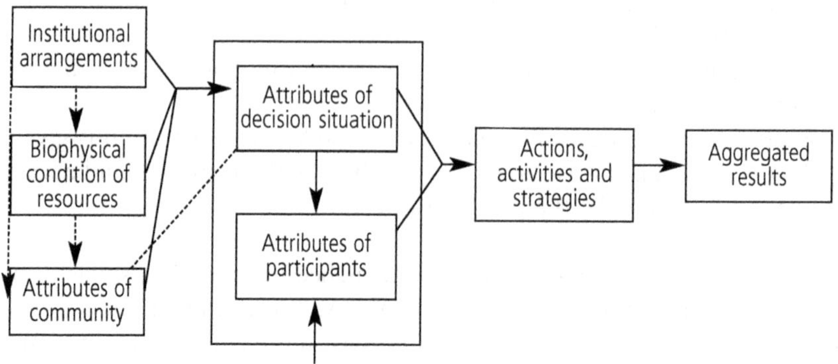

Figure 14.1 *Institutional analysis and development framework*

Source: Kiser and Ostrom, 1982

seen as a logical solution to large-scale common pool resource problems from several theoretical fronts, including collective action and a 'robustness' perspective[5] (Marshall, 2008). Ostrom (1999) highlighted the merits of decentralized decision making in managing large-scale common property resources. They include enhanced access to local knowledge, the ability to harness informal institutional arrangements to exclude untrustworthy elements, the ability to capture feedback on the performance of institutional rules, lower enforcement costs, and the reduced possibility of failure in institutional rules for an entire region (Ostrom, 1999).

Scale of decentralization and assigning governance functions

Mapping various governance functions across multiple entities within a decision hierarchy is a challenging task. Undoubtedly, the success of decentralization largely depends on this task's assignment and execution.[6] Therefore, identifying tasks or governance functions becomes the first step of any decentralization process. The task selection for decentralization can be approached from four main perspectives: constitutional, economic, managerial and social (Dollery et al, 2006).

As we noted earlier, the subsidiarity principle provides some limited guidance in this regard. Notwithstanding external resources, two variables are pivotal for mapping tasks to governance structures. First, the capacity of the entity to carry out a given function is critical. The term 'capacity' encompasses several dimensions, including financial, physical, human and social capacities – including leadership. Hence, executing a task satisfactorily at a given level partly depends on sufficient access at that level to all dimensions of capacity. Moreover, although problematic, representation of all relevant actors who have an interest in the task also generally contributes to the successful execution of a given task (Marshall, 2008).

Attempts have been made to develop a generalized model for allocating governance functions across a decision-making hierarchy but these have not always proven successful. Hurwicz (1973) elaborates a related problem of designing informationally decentralized systems thus:

> *Two difficulties make the problem non-trivial: calculation and information transfer. First, consider the calculation of the maximising values for the variables of the problem. Assuming even that all the relevant information concerning the parameters of the problem is in the hands of the computing agency, this agency needs a well-defined computational procedure (algorithm) to find solutions. Even when there is an algorithm ... it may be that the information processing capacity of any agency is inadequate.* (Hurwicz, 1973, pp4–5)

Not surprisingly, solving for an efficient optimal solution in this context usually proves too complex, if not impossible.

Information is critical to the subject of decentralization as numerous definitions of decentralization are based on information economics. A major thrust in the information literature is about the dispersion of information among numerous economic agents. It is also at the core of explaining the failure of central planning (Hurwicz, 1960). Moreover, there is a lack of incentives for economic agents to share their information truthfully with others, especially with governments, which is also referred to as the incentive compatibility problem (Hurwicz, 1972). In fact, Hurwicz showed that even with compatible incentives, an optimal outcome cannot be guaranteed because of private (asymmetric) information.

The theory of mechanism design (Hurwicz, 1960; Maskin, 1999; Myerson, 1979) tackles this problem by selecting a 'mechanism' 'rules of the game' which defines the – who decides what, communicates with whom, in what fashion, and how eventually allocations are made to a prescribed normative standard (Mookherjee, 2008). The revelation principle (Myerson, 1979) simplifies this allocation problem by calculating the most efficient rule of the game for getting people to reveal their private information truthfully (Chak, 2008). According to the revelation principle, the central government could design optimal contracts to extract locally available information (Greco, 2003). The implicit assumption here is that local and central governments share the same objectives and have no conflicts. Hence there is no reason for local governments not to fully and truthfully reveal their information to the centre. However, self-interest and the political economy of governments and their subordinate organizations cloud this argument.

The application of these concepts to water decision making in India is used to illustrate these general principles.

A decision-making hierarchy for the canal-water sector in India

The institutional structure for canal-water management in India can be conceptualized as a hierarchical nested model (Figure 14.2). Within the hierarchy, the responsibility for developing and managing the water resources has been distributed among national, state, district and local governments, as noted earlier by Upadhyay (Chapter 7) and others. At the national level (see Figure 14.2), the Ministry of Water Resources (MoWR) is the apex body charged with overall planning, policy formulation, coordination, development and regulation of the water resources in the country. Under the MoWR, there are several subordinate units including the Central Water Commission, which is the premier technical organization with respect to managing water resources, the National Water Development Agency (interbasin water transfers), and the Central Groundwater Board which is responsible for management of groundwater resources.

At the next level of the decision hierarchy, and in accordance with the constitutional provisions, states formulate laws and policies relating to water management and projects, particularly medium and minor irrigation projects. Within states, Departments of Irrigation or Water Resource Management are in charge of developing and maintaining irrigation projects as well as groundwater development. The District Irrigation Advisory Committee, chaired by a District Collector is then charged with decisions related to irrigation activities at the district level (Mandal and Rao, 2007). At the village level, *Gram Panchayats* (village local governments) are responsible for coordinating irrigation activities with numerous WUAs.

The type of information required for the smooth functioning of institutions largely depends on the scale and functional aspects of the water institution. For instance, a river basin institution may formulate basin-wide policy and regulations. In order to be effective in this particular function, it needs basin-wide data on hydro-meteorological information, sectoral water allocation, details of inter-organizational agreements, information on WUAs and the like. At the lowest level of the decision-making hierarchy, individual irrigators may face twofold information deficiency, that is about their own preferences and about others' preferences (Crase and Dollery, 2006). In addition, the irrigator needs to be cognisant of information on the initial stock of resources, current use patterns and future trends, current production technology, and maximum sustainable yields.

Local knowledge acquired through stakeholder engagement at various levels of the decision-making hierarchy is thought to be an important input at various stages of irrigation, water management and planning. Since water resource management encompasses a wide range of information-gathering activities (e.g. hydrological monitoring, water quality and effluent discharge monitoring, bio-monitoring, water abstraction, water accounting, etc.), transfer of all the above information to water stakeholders is difficult. Moreover, the flow and timing of information transfer are equally imperative to support decisions at various levels.

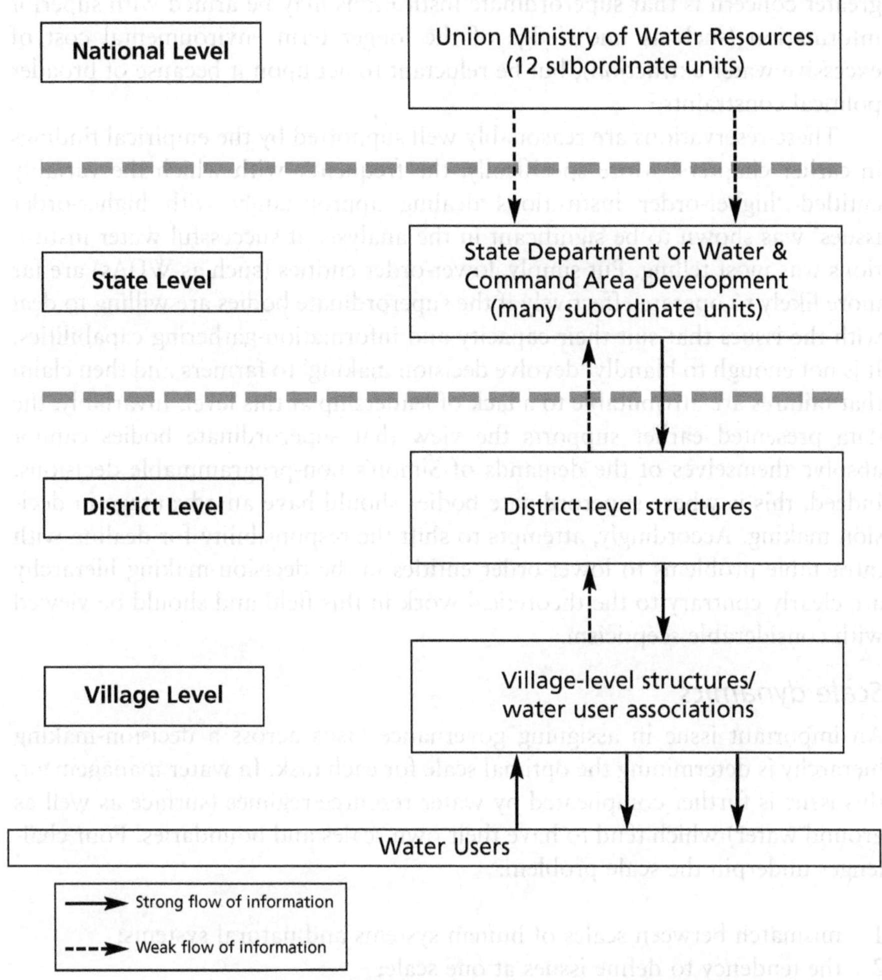

Figure 14.2 *Institutional arrangements (simplified) for canal-water planning and decision making in India*

Misallocation of resources is the end result of information deficiencies and hence an imposition of constraints on the resource use from a superordinate institution is justified. However, a somewhat questionable presumption here is that the superordinate institution has access to superior information than that available to lower-level actors and that superordinate institutions have the will to act upon that information (Crase and Dollery, 2006). For instance, inefficient water pricing due to imperfect information at a superordinate level can transmit an incorrect message to the lower levels of the hierarchy. Perhaps of greater concern is that superordinate institutions may be armed with superior information (such as knowledge of the longer term environmental cost of excessive water extraction), but be reluctant to act upon it because of broader political constraints.[7]

These reservations are reasonably well supported by the empirical findings in earlier chapters. More specifically, the frequency with which the variably entitled 'higher-order institutions dealing appropriately with higher-order issues' was shown to be significant in the analysis of successful water institutions was most telling. Put simply, lower-order entities (such as WUAs) are far more likely to operate effectively if the superordinate bodies are willing to deal with the issues that suit their capacity and information-gathering capabilities. It is not enough to blandly 'devolve decision making' to farmers and then claim that failures are attributable to a lack of leadership at this level. Invariably, the data presented earlier supports the view that superordinate bodies cannot absolve themselves of the demands of Simon's non-programmable decisions. Indeed, this is where superordinate bodies should have an advantage in decision making. Accordingly, attempts to shift the responsibility for dealing with intractable problems to lower-order entities in the decision-making hierarchy are clearly contrary to the theoretical work in this field and should be viewed with considerable scepticism.

Scale dynamics

An important issue in assigning governance tasks across a decision-making hierarchy is determining the optimal scale for each task. In water management, this issue is further complicated by water resource regimes (surface as well as ground water) which tend to have their own scales and boundaries. Four challenges underpin the scale problem:

1 mismatch between scales of human systems and natural systems;
2 the tendency to define issues at one scale;
3 mismatch between scales of knowledge and scales of management; and
4 ignoring linkages (Cash et al, 2004).

Interstate river water disputes in India are typical of the mismatch between human and natural scales. In such cases, the authority or jurisdiction of the management does not coincide with the scale required by the resource either in space or time. Sharing of river water in irrigation and river valley projects and dams and command area development projects often has interjurisdictional implications. In fact, these factors provided an impetus for establishing more decentralized systems, particularly empowering *Panchayats* and WUAs. A related challenge is the appropriate scale at which the problem is defined. Framing water problems purely as a 'global' problem or a 'local' problem may lead to failure (Cash et al, 2004).

Different information is required to carry out specific governance functions in a nested decision hierarchy. Ostrom (1990) lists generic governance functions for nested enterprises. They include appropriation, provision, monitoring, enforcement and conflict resolution. At the operational level, individuals make choices within the constraints of operational rules. For instance, an irrigator in a canal system has to decide on the extent of irrigation and the cropping pattern. This decision entails information on water availability, labour availability, producer prices and marketing arrangements. At the field level, the individual irrigators may have to negotiate with one another regarding clearing the canal system to access irrigation water. However, the timing of irrigation for a cropping season may be decided collectively at a higher level of the decision-making hierarchy, for example at the level of the WUA. In this case, the scale of the governance problem is limited and homogeneity and social capital within the WUA may further reduce transaction costs and foster collective action. WUAs make decisions within the constraints of collective choice rules, such as the assigning of O&M responsibilities, dispute resolution, rules to implement a *warabandi* schedule, etc.

Current ground-water management in India epitomizes the mismatch between scales of knowledge and scales of actions, and this was reflected in the reservations expressed by Upadhyay (Chapter 7) and others. As the state legislation on ground-water extraction is still being developed, various changes to the Environment (Protection) Act 1986 have been proposed. One such proposal advocates state-level monitoring of ground-water levels through scientific methods under the advisory guidance of the Central Ground Water Board (Ministry of Water Resources Planning Commission, 2007). The enforcement for the regulation is made at a much lower level through the involvement of *Panchayats*. To be effective, state-level ground-water monitoring should transfer information to lower levels of the decision-making hierarchy in an efficient manner. This information transfer may be inefficient due to various transaction costs caused by poor linkages between state and local levels as well political economy constraints. In the case of surface irrigation, too, there is a mismatch between hydrologic units and the administrative units of village and district, which form the basis for *Panchayats* (Gulati et al, 2005). The clear implication is that if *Panchayats* are given irrigation responsibilities, water users from other villages in the command area can be excluded from the decision-making process.

Poor institutional linkages or completely ignoring linkages can become a scale problem to the extent that the issue is scale-dependent and has cross-interactions with other issues. Devolving management responsibilities to *Panchayat* and *Gram Sabhas* has created institutional competition among entities within the decision-making hierarchy. For example, the Panchayati Raj Amendment to the Indian Constitution charged the local governing bodies with a wide range of tasks including health, education and welfare functions in addition to water management. Hence there is a considerable overlap and potential for competition between local *Panchayats* and WUAs. In fact, in some cases, WUAs are referred to as *'pani (water) Panchayats'* (Gulati et al, 2005). Both surface water and ground-water management display cross-level institutional interplay. The horizontal interactions between WUAs and *Panchayats* are equally as important as the vertical interplay between WUAs and their superordinate district-level structure (see Figure 14.2). The horizontal institutional interplay is further complicated by the tendency of state departments and donor-funded projects to create their own associations and committees.

The extent of decentralization and capacity appraisal of some governance functions in the Indian water sector are presented in Table 14.2. Undoubtedly, certain functions, such as constitutional reforms and interstate water disputes, need to be carried out at the national level. In other words, the nature of the function itself may constrain the extent of decentralization. Ground-water management is almost entirely controlled by private institutions, while some regulatory powers have been assigned at the national level. However, the inability of the superordinate structures to monitor the behaviour at the user level, due to information and capacity constraints, makes it logical to decentralize the ground-water resource monitoring and enforcement functions to lower levels. The question remains, however, as to whether these lower-order entities are likely to be adequately supported by the information-gathering capacity and intellectual might of the state and national agencies. There are some grounds for questioning whether this may simply result in a 'problem shifting' exercise rather than a 'problem solving' outcome.

Table 14.2 *The capacity and degree of centralized and decentralized decision making in the Indian water context*

Level of decision making	*Interstate river water decisions*	*Ground-water regulation*	*Ground-water monitoring*	*Surface water allocation decisions*	*Surface water pricing*
National	**** ↑	*	↓		↑
State	**	***	**		*
District		****	*****	****** ↓	****
Village			******	*******	****
Water user					

Notes: ⟶ Direction of centralization or decentralization.
* capacity (the greater number of stars indicates a greater capacity).

Concluding remarks

Decision making is a complex process, far more complicated than that envisaged by the neoclassical literature. Our understanding of the detailed mechanics of communal decisions is improving, but our knowledge is far from complete. Nevertheless, this has not stood in the way of numerous policies premised on greater involvement of communities and lower-order stakeholders in decision making, particularly in the context of the management of water resources. This policy direction has manifested itself in the notion of participatory irrigation management which gave rise to a large number of WUAs in countries like India.

We have argued in this chapter that embracing participatory approaches on the grounds that 'decentralized decision making provides a means of engaging with communities' is an inadequate rationale for policy choice. Moreover, we have contended that there is much to be gained by drilling down to the intricacies of the decision at hand before resorting to a decentralized decision-making process as a matter of course. In this context we specifically advocate that greater consideration be given to exploring the role of information and decision-making capacity at different levels in a hierarchical decision model.

The empirical research presented in earlier chapters supports the view that decentralized decision making has the potential to bring benefits but this falls short of a guaranteed formula for success. Poignantly, the same data also show the pivotal role of higher-order organizations dealing appropriately with complex issues that lie within their jurisdiction. This implies that devolving responsibility for water management to smaller groups can only yield benefits if accompanied by thoughtful rules to ensure that information and decision-making capacity are used to their optimum across the decision-making spectrum. Shifting responsibility for intractable problems to farmer groups is unlikely to resolve those problems unless accompanied by other policy measures. Regrettably, there are no signs that this subtle but important message is being heeded by policy makers at this time.

Notes

1 Here we contend that communal irrigation infrastructure holds some of the characteristics of a public good, or are at least quasi public goods. In any case, the general insights offered by Oates are a useful starting point for considering the provision of communal infrastructure.

2 In many respects, this is simply a more condensed version of the ninefold typology of Hogwood and Gunn (1984).

3 A comprehensive definition of leadership is beyond the scope of this chapter. Here we take the term leadership to imply a capacity to successfully influence others – after all, by definition a leader must have followers. For a more detailed treatment of these issues see, for instance, Rausch (2005) and Vroom (2003).

4 In the property rights literature this is usually referred to as attenuation of rights. For an illustration of how this operates in the context of water, see, for example, Crase and Dollery (2006).

5 A socio-ecological system is said to be robust if it prevents the ecological system upon which it relies from moving into a domain that cannot support human population (Anderies et al, 2004).

6 The decentralization process can be conceptualized as a cycle: (i) identifying governance functions that need to be decentralized; (ii) mapping governance functions with governance structures; (iii) implementation; (iv) evaluation; (v) capacity building.

7 Proponents of democratic decision-making processes would contend that such political influences are simply another form of information. The authors, nevertheless, hold a more jaundiced view of the politics of water.

References

Anderies, J. M., Janssen, M. A. and Ostrom, E. (2004) 'A framework to analyse the robustness of social-ecological systems from an institutional perspective', *Ecology and Society,* vol 9, no 1, pp18

Arrow, K. J. (1954) *Social Choice and Individual Values*, Wiley, New York

Blackwell, R., Miniard, P. and Engel, J. (2006) *Consumer Behaviour*, 10th edition, Thompson Publishing, Mason, CH

Brady, N. (2002) 'Striking a balance: Centralized and decentralized decisions in government', New Zealand Treasury Working Paper, 01/15, NZ Treasury, Wellington

Cash, D. W., Adger, W. N., Berkes, F., Garden, P., Lebel, L., Olsson, P., Pritchard, L. and Young, O. (2004) 'Scale and cross-scale dynamics: Governance and information in a multi-level world', paper presented at the Millennium Ecosystem Assessment Bridging Scales and Epistemologies Conference, Alexandria, Egypt, 17–20 March

Chak, M. (2008) 'The 2007 Nobel prize in economics: Mechanism design theory', *Czech Journal of Economics and Finance,* vol 58, nos 1–2, pp82–89

Ciriacy-Wantrup, S.-V. (1971) 'The economics of environmental policy', *Land Economics*, vol 47, pp41–42

Crase, L. and Dollery, B. (2006) 'Water rights: A comparison of the impacts of urban and irrigation reforms in Australia', *Australian Journal of Agricultural and Resources Economics,* vol 50, pp451–462

Dollery, B., Crase, L. and Johnson, A. (2006) *Australian Local Government Economics*, UNSW Press, Sydney

Greco, L. G. (2003) 'Oate's decentralization theorem and public governance', paper presented at the XV Conference on Economic Analysis and Law, University of Pavia, Pavia, Italy, 3–4 October

Guerin, K. (2002) 'Subsidiarity: Implications for New Zealand', New Zealand Treasury Working Paper, 02/03, New Zealand Treasury, Wellington

Gulati, A., Meinzen-Dick, R. and Raju, K. V. (2005) *Institutional Reforms in Indian Irrigation,* International Food Policy Research Institute, Sage Publications, New Delhi

Hogwood, B. and Gunn, L. (1984) *Policy Analysis for the Real World*, Oxford University Press, New York

Hurwicz, L. (1960) 'Optimality and information efficiency in resource allocation process', in K. Arrow, S. Karlin, P. Suppes (eds) *Mathematical Methods in Social Sciences*, Stanford University Press, Stanford, CA

Hurwicz, L. (1972) 'On informationally decentralized systems', in R. Radner and C. McGuire (eds) *Decision and Organization,* North Holland, Amsterdam, pp297–336

Hurwicz, L. (1973) 'The design of mechanisms for resource allocation', *American Economic Review,* vol 63, pp1–30

Independent Evaluation Group, World Bank (2001) 'Paddy irrigation and water management in Southeast Asia', available at http://lnweb90.worldbank.org/oed/oeddoclib.nsf/DocUNIDViewForJavaSearch/6962AEEB6DBD3E8E852567F5005D8DA8#top, accessed 8 December 2008

Kiggundu, M., Jorgensen, J. and Hafsi, T. (1983) 'Administrative theory and practice in developing countries: A synthesis', *Administrative Quarterly,* vol 28, no 1, pp66–84

Kiser, L. and Ostrom, E. (1982) 'The three worlds of action', in E. Ostrom (ed)

Strategies of Political Inquiry, Sage, Beverly Hills, pp179–222
Lindblom, C. (1959) 'The science of muddling through', *Public Administration Review*, vol 19, pp79–88
Mandal, S. and Rao, M. G. (2007) 'Overlapping fiscal domains and the effectiveness of environmental policy in India', in A. Breton, G. Brosio, S. Dalmazzone and G. Garrone (eds) *Environmental Governance and Decentralization*, Edward Elgar, Cheltenham, UK
Marshall, G. R. (2008) 'Nesting, subsidiarity and community-based environmental governance beyond the local level', *International Journal of the Commons*, vol 2, no 1, pp75–97
Maskin, E. (1999) 'Nash equilibrium and welfare optimality', *Review of Economic Studies*, vol 66, no 1, pp23–38
Ministry of Water Resources Planning Commission (2007) *Report of the Expert Group on Ground Water Management and Ownership*, Planning Commission, Government of India, New Delhi
Mookherjee, D. (2008) 'The 2007 Nobel prize in Mechanism Design Theory', *Scandanavian Journal of Economics*, vol 110, no 2, pp327–260
Myerson, R. (1979) 'Incentive compatibility and the bargaining problem', *Econometrica*, vol 47, pp61–73
Oates, W. E. (1968) 'The theory of public finance in a federal system', *Canadian Journal of Economics*, vol 1 (February), pp37–54
Oates, W. E. (1972) *Fiscal Federalism*, Brace and Jovanovich, Harcourt, London
Ostrom, E. (1986) 'An agenda for the study of institutions', *Public Choice*, vol 48, no 1, pp3–25
Ostrom, E. (1990) *Governing the Commons*, Cambridge University Press, Cambridge
Ostrom, E. (1999) 'Coping with the tragedies of the commons', *Annual Review of Political Science*, vol 2, pp493–535
Paavola, J. (2007) 'Institutions and environmental governance: A reconceptualization', *Ecological Economics*, vol 63, pp93–103
Rausch, E. (2005) 'A practical focus on leadership in management: For research, education and management development', *Management Decision*, vol 43, nos 7–8, pp988–1000
Sabatier, P. A. (1991) 'Toward better theories of policy process', *Political Science and Politics*, vol 24, no 2, pp147–156
Simon, H. (1947) *Administrative Behaviour*, 1st edition, Macmillan, London
Simon, H. (1957a) *Administrative Behaviour*, 2nd edition, Macmillan, London
Simon, H. (1957b) *Models of Man*, John Wiley, London
Simon, H. (1960) *The New Science of Management Decision*, Prentice Hall, Englewood Cliffs, NJ
Simon, H. (1983) *Reason in Human Affairs*, Blackwell, Oxford
Vroom, V. H. (2003) 'Educating managers for decision making and leadership', *Management Decision*, vol 41, no 10, pp968–978

15
Water Institutions and their Relationship to Poverty Alleviation

Vasant Gandhi and Vaibhav Bhamoriya

Introduction

A major motivation driving India's efforts to develop water resources and improve the management of the resources relates to enhancing livelihoods and incomes, particularly in rural India, where poverty constitutes a vast problem. About 72 per cent of the people in India reside in the rural areas and this mass largely depends on agriculture for their livelihood. Strikingly, the India Planning Commission (2008a) estimates that about 73 per cent of those who were living below the poverty line in 2004–05 were resident in rural areas. Thus, addressing the issue of rural poverty has assumed great importance for national planning and policy, notwithstanding its international significance in the context of the millennium goals for development (World Bank, 2008).

Nevertheless, relatively little attention has been paid to the impact of irrigation development on poverty alleviation. Moreover, relatively little is known of the explicit role of water institutions and their effect on poverty via enhanced agricultural production. This chapter attempts to make some progress on this front and considers the broader policy objective of poverty alleviation and its links with irrigation development and agricultural performance. Accordingly, we use this chapter to attempt to shed light on agricultural livelihoods, and the potential benefits bestowed on the poor by improving irrigation institutions generally. The chapter is also used to explore the distributional impacts of water reform and indicate mechanisms for improving both the efficiency and equity of irrigation in India.

The chapter itself is divided into six additional parts. The next section deals primarily with the extant knowledge on poverty in India. Here we briefly focus on existing studies in the field, consider the status of poverty, and reflect on past efforts to reduce poverty. The third section is used to probe a number of poignant relationships, especially the nexus between poverty, agriculture and irrigation. Distributional considerations are dealt with in the fourth section, including a review of the mechanisms for dealing with equity within water institutions, as highlighted by the empirical components in this text. In the fourth section we briefly consider the role of technology in the alleviation of poverty before offering some concluding observations in section seven.

Poverty in India

Extant studies

A large number of studies have sought to measure and analyse poverty in India. These includes studies which have dealt with measurement of poverty levels (see, for instance, Dandekar and Rath, 1971a,; 1971b; Bardhan, 1973; Rath, 1996) and others which have dealt primarily with factors determining the incidence of poverty (see, for example, Ahluwalia, 1978; Sundaram and Tendulkar, 1988; Kakwani and Subbarao, 1990; Nayyar, 1991; Ghosh, 1996; Dasgupta, 1995; Vyas and Bhargava, 1995; Sharma, 1995; Datt and Ravallion, 1996). Ahluwalia (1978) is representative among the first serious attempts to explain the determinants of variation in rural poverty. Narayanamoorthy (2000) subsequently reviewed these studies and has argued that the work in this field has identified some broad relationships on the incidence of poverty. First, several studies have determined an inverse relationship between agricultural growth and the incidence of rural poverty (such as Ahluwalia, 1978). Second, it was found that studies often focused on macro growth and how development should reduce poverty, although there are substantial reservations about the trickle-down effect of the development process to the poor in India (such as Bardhan, 1986). Third, they find that it is often very difficult to achieve a sustained reduction in the level of rural poverty through anti-poverty programmes alone (Rath, 1985). This leads to a more sanguine view of agricultural development and its impact on livelihoods and poverty inasmuch as it offers more potential as an enduring influence on livelihoods. In this regard Narayanamoorthy (2000) argues that irrigation should be considered an important explanatory variable of the incidence of poverty because irrigation, through its production-augmenting and wage-enhancing effects, substantially improves the flow of income. Notwithstanding the dichotomy in the explanatory literature, there is little doubt on the political economy front that agriculture, and the role of irrigation as part of agriculture, are ostensibly seen as panaceas for alleviating poverty in India.

Status of poverty in India

There are various estimates of the incidence of poverty in India. According to official data assembled by the Planning Commission of India (India, Planning

Commission, 2008a), the proportion of the population considered 'poor' stood at 54.9 per cent in 1973–74, with 321.3 million souls making up this group. Of these, 81.3 per cent were classified as rural (see Table 15.1). By way of contrast, by 2004–05 the proportion categorized as 'poor' had dropped to 27.5 per cent; however, in nominal terms this remained largely unchanged with some 301.7 million people still falling into this category. Again, a substantial portion of this cohort lived in rural areas – some 73.2 per cent. Alternative estimates for 2004–05 (see Table 15.1) put the proportion of the population considered poor at about 21.8 per cent, or 238.5 million persons. Nevertheless, the dominance by rural residents remained similar, with 71.4 per cent of the poor being classified as living in rural areas.

Table 15.1 *Percentage and number of poor in India – based on National Poverty Line*

Year	*Poverty ratio*			*Number of poor*			
	Rural	*Urban*	*Total*	*Rural*	*Urban*	*Total*	*Rural*
	(%)	*(%)*	*(%)*	*(million)*	*(million)*	*(million)*	*(%)*
1973–74	56.4	49.0	54.9	261.3	60.0	321.3	81.3
1977–78	53.1	45.2	51.3	264.3	64.6	328.9	80.4
1983	45.6	40.8	44.5	252.0	70.9	322.9	78.0
1987–88	39.1	38.2	38.9	231.9	75.2	307.0	75.5
1993–94	37.3	32.4	36.0	244.0	76.3	320.4	76.2
1999–2000	27.1	23.6	26.1	193.2	67.0	260.2	74.3
2004–05 (1)	28.3	25.7	27.5	220.9	80.8	301.7	73.2
2004–05 (2)	21.8	21.7	21.8	170.3	68.2	238.5	71.4

Notes: (1) Uniform reference period comparable with 1993–94 estimates.
(2) Mixed reference period comparable with 1999–2000 estimates.
Source: India, Planning Commission, 2008a[1]

Other estimates made by the World Bank (World Bank, 2008) are based on notional international poverty lines. These data indicate that in 2004–05, 34.3 per cent of the people in India earned less than US$1 per day. Adjusting the benchmark to US$2 per day sees about 80 per cent of the population falling short.

Table 15.2 *Percentage of poor in India – based on International Poverty Lines*

Population below US$1 per day	34.3
Population below US$2 per day	80.4

Source: World Bank, 2008

Figure 15.1 shows the trend of the incidence of poverty in India since 1973. It indicates that there has been considerable progress in alleviating poverty, although there is some suggestion in these data that the trend is slowing recently.

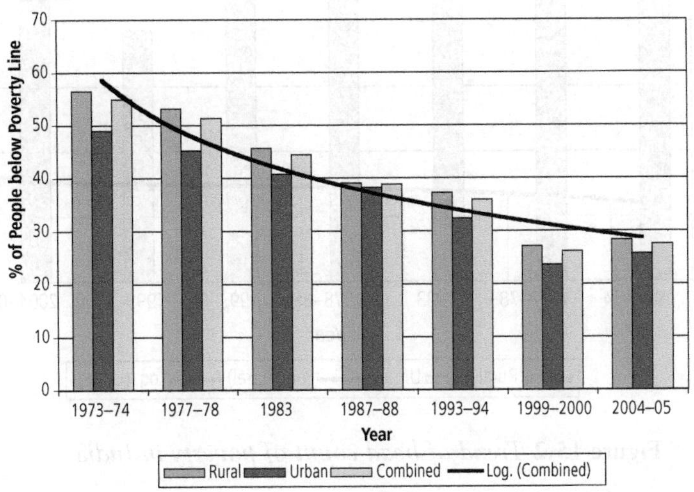

Figure 15.1 *Trend of poverty incidence in India*

Source: India, Planning Commission (2008a)

By way of contrast, Figure 15.2 is used to illustrate the trend in absolute numbers of people below the poverty line in urban and rural areas. Clearly, the absolute number of poor people is much larger in the rural areas as compared to urban areas. Figure 15.2 also shows that the number of poor in the rural areas has not declined a great deal, although a negative trend is evident from the logarithmic curve. The number of poor in the urban areas appears to be showing an increase, although there is a slight fall in the absolute number of poor evident in the last year for which data are readily available.

Poverty reduction experience in India

In the 1960s and 1970s the introduction of semi-dwarf high-yielding varieties of wheat and rice as part of the green revolution led to dramatic increases in agricultural production and raised farmers' incomes, especially in northwest India (World Bank, 2008). Rural poverty fell from 64 per cent in 1967 to 50 per cent in 1977 and subsequently to 34 per cent by 1986. A large share of the gains came directly from an increase in real wages and a decline in real grain prices and accordingly growth in the agricultural sector reduced poverty in both urban and rural settings. Land reform, rural credit and education policies also played a substantial role in the 1970s and 1980s, but industrial growth failed to reduce poverty in its own right (World Bank, 2008). Beginning in 1991, India instituted decisive economic and trade reforms that spurred

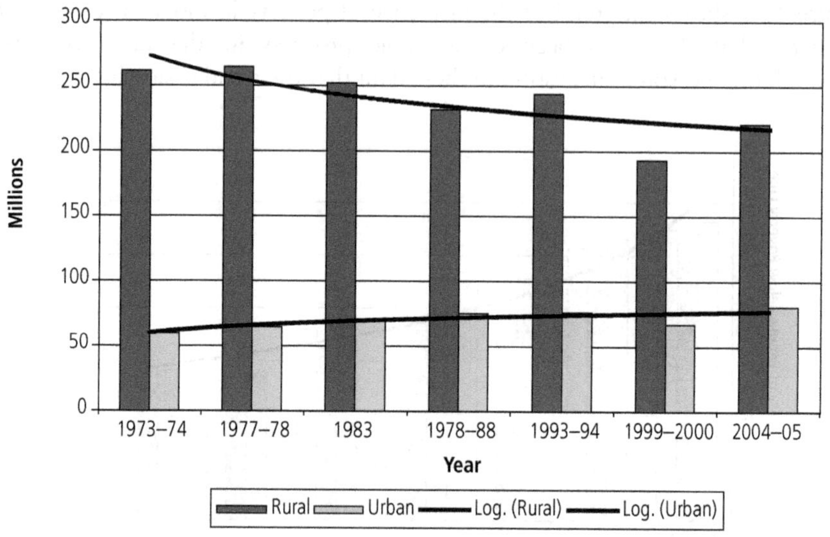

Figure 15.2 *Trend of head count of poverty in India*

impressive growth in manufacturing and especially in services. Poverty data for 2004, compared to the 1993 figures, show a continuing downward trend in poverty that largely reflects the influence of this more recent policy episode.

Although there is a consistent poverty-reducing pattern across almost all Indian states, success is far from even. From 1980 to 2004 initially poorer states grew more slowly, resulting in income divergence in both absolute and relative terms (World Bank, 2008). The rapid trade liberalization of the 1990s has sharpened differentiated regional impacts. Rural districts with a higher concentration of industries disadvantaged by trade liberalization have experienced slower progress in reducing poverty, in part because of limited mobility of labour across regions and industries.

Urban incomes and expenditures have also increased faster than rural incomes, resulting in a steady increase in the ratio of rural-to-urban mean real consumption from just below 1:1.4 in 1983 to about 1:1.7 in 2000 (World Bank, 2008). Notwithstanding these differences, India has experienced relatively modest income inequality for much of its recent history and there has been impressive growth and poverty reduction in the 1990s. Yet India's recent reforms, unlike China's, were not directed at agriculture per se. However, there is a renewed policy focus on agriculture in India, because many believe that the full benefits of poverty reduction via the potential of agriculture have not yet been fully realized (Von Braun et al, 2005; India, Planning Commission, 2008b).

The poverty, agriculture, irrigation nexus

We now briefly turn to some of the poignant relationships in the context of the empirical work reported in earlier chapters. More specifically, we are concerned with the relationship between agriculture and poverty, the link between irrigation and agriculture, and the connection between improved irrigation management and poverty alleviation. We address each of these relationships separately below.

Poverty and agriculture

Information from the National Sample Survey (NSS) quinquennial data collection in 1999–2000 (India, NSSO, 2001) indicates that 38 per cent of the rural population in India was self-employed in agriculture. In addition, FAO (2008) estimates that 31 per cent of the rural population were engaged as agricultural labourers. Put differently, as much as 69 per cent of the rural population could be dependent directly on agriculture for their livelihood. Moreover, a substantial number were engaged in other agro-based occupations and agro-based industries and were therefore indirectly dependent on the sector. Clearly, agriculture has no small stake in alleviating poverty in rural India.

According to the World Bank (2008, p26) three out of four poor people in the developing countries of the world live in the rural areas (883 million in 2002), and most directly or indirectly depend on agriculture for their livelihoods. As a general premise then, more dynamic and inclusive agriculture can dramatically reduce rural poverty and hunger.

China's rapid growth in agriculture has been largely responsible for the decline in rural poverty from 53 per cent in 1981 to 8 per cent in 2001. Agricultural growth in China was the precursor to the acceleration of industrial growth, very much as the agricultural revolution predated the industrial revolution that spread across the temperate world from England in the mid 18th century to Japan in the late 19th century (World Bank, 2008, p26).

However, parallel to these successes are numerous failures in stimulating agricultural advancement, the most striking being the still unsatisfactory performance of agriculture in sub-Saharan Africa. This is especially the case when contrasted with the green revolution in south Asia, where yields have increased by more than 50 per cent and poverty has declined by 30 per cent (World Bank, 2008, p26).

Where growth in the nonagricultural sectors has accelerated, such as in Asia, the reallocation of labour out of agriculture is lagging, thereby concentrating poverty in rural areas and widening rural–urban income disparities. This has also become a major source of political tension and insecurity. Agriculture is a major user (and regrettably a frequent abuser) of natural resources. By making better use of water and land and providing environmental services, such as the management of watersheds, agriculture has the potential to make growth more environmentally sustainable and therefore more palatable at the political level.

There is a large and persistent gap between the share of agriculture in GDP and the share of agriculture in the labour force in most of Asia and this is borne out in India. As a general rule when GDP per capita rises, agriculture's share declines. This occurs while agricultural output simultaneously increases in absolute value, because the nonagricultural sector is usually growing more rapidly. The large and persistent gap between agriculture's share in GDP and its employment status suggests that poverty is concentrated in agriculture and rural areas. In addition, as nonagricultural growth accelerates, many of the rural poor remain poor, in relative terms at least (World Bank, 2008, p28). That the incidence of poverty among agricultural and rural households persists at the macro level is confirmed by the micro evidence from numerous country poverty studies undertaken by the World Bank. The persistent concentration of poverty in rural areas illustrates the difficulty of redistributing income generated outside agriculture and the deep inertia in people's occupational transformation as economies restructure. Broad-based growth in the rural economy appears essential for reducing poverty in both absolute and relative terms (World Bank, 2008, p29).

From a simple decomposition, 81 per cent of the worldwide reduction in rural poverty between 1993 and 2002 can be ascribed to improved conditions in rural areas (migration accounted for only 19 per cent of the reduction) (World Bank, 2008, p29). The comparative advantage of agricultural growth in reducing poverty is also supported by econometric studies: cross-country econometric evidence indicates that GDP growth generated in agriculture has large benefits for the poor and is at least twice as effective in reducing poverty as growth generated by other sectors (World Bank, 2008, p29).

Agriculture and irrigation

The most direct impact of irrigation on agricultural is through increased productivity of land. Instances of this are widely documented and need no repetition here (see, for instance, World Bank Independent Evaluation Group, 2008; Huang et al, 2006; Lipton et al, 2003). Irrigation is reported to raise yields by one-third to one-half as compared to yields in rainfed areas (Dhawan, 1995). Irrigation is also widely acknowledged as bringing stability to agricultural output as it protects the farmer from the seasonality and vagaries of weather, at least to some degree. This also has a direct impact on poverty alleviation.

We document just a few recently published studies to illustrate these points. In a recent study by Palanichamy et al (2008) in Tamil Nadu it was found that cropping intensity and yield were significantly enhanced by access to irrigation, as presented in the Table 15.3. It is worth noting that tail-end farmers without access to pumping technologies were observed to have yields almost 20 per cent below those of their neighbours with pumps and close to 30 per cent less than head-end farmers with assured access to irrigation.

Similarly, FAO reports developed on the basis of Indian data show that irrigated crops produce much more than rainfed crops (see Figure 15.3). About

Table 15.3 *Cropping intensities and yields by location and water availability*

Season	*Location along branch canal*			
	Head reach	*Tail reach*		
		All farms	*With pumps*	*Without pumps*
Summer	124	122	128	80
Monsoon	120	110	109	100
Annual	244	232	237	180

Expected maize yields on farms by location based on water availability

Location		*Expected maize yield/ha*
Head reach		59.60Q
Tail reach	With pumps	50.70Q
	Without pumps	42.70Q

Note: Q = quintals.
Source: Palanichamy et al, 2008

56 per cent of total agricultural production comes from irrigated agriculture, which is approximately 35 per cent of the net sown area. Furthermore, the spread of irrigation has also enabled crop diversification (FAO, 1997).

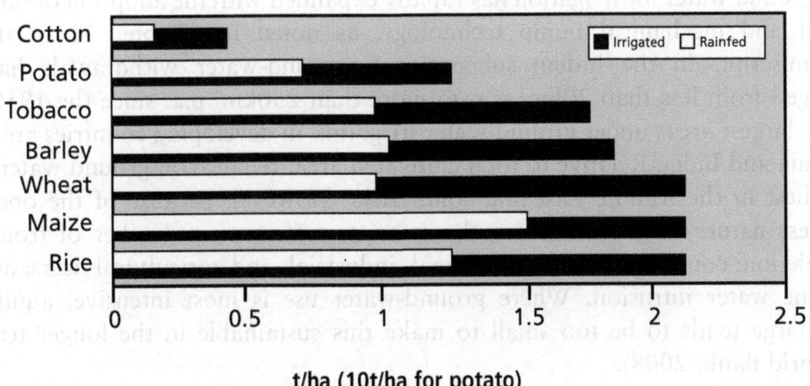

Figure 15.3 *Influence of irrigation on crop yields*

Source: FAO, 1997

In a similar vein Phansalkar (2007) reports that cattle-rearing activities benefited significantly from irrigation as it facilitates the cultivation of green fodder and water supplies that remain critical for good animal husbandry. Thus, in arid locations where irrigation is available there are additional indirect benefits reported that may have non-trivial impacts on the landless. We have already established that access to water and irrigation is a major determinant of land productivity and the stability of yields. To reiterate, in many instances irrigated land productivity is more than double that of rainfed land (World Bank, 2008). In south Asia 39 per cent of the area in production is under irrigation compared with only 4 per cent in sub-Saharan Africa. It is worth noting that if climate change leads to rising uncertainties in rainfed agriculture, investment in water storage will be increasingly critical. There may be many opportunities to enhance productivity by revamping existing irrigation schemes and expanding small-scale schemes and water harvesting, even under growing water scarcity and the rising costs of large-scale irrigation schemes.

Agriculture currently uses 85 per cent of water consumed in developing countries, mainly for irrigation. Even though irrigated farming accounts for only about 18 per cent of the cultivated area in the developing world, it produces about 40 per cent of the value of agricultural output (World Bank, 2008).

Maintaining and bolstering the productivity of irrigated land is a critical component for meeting the challenge of feeding much of the developing world. However, many countries are experiencing serious and worsening water scarcities. In many river basins, freshwater supplies are already fully used, and urban, industrial and environmental demands for water are escalating, increasing the water stress. Globally, about 15–35 per cent of total water withdrawals for irrigated agriculture are estimated to be unsustainable – in simple terms the use of water exceeds the renewable supply (World Bank, 2008). Intensive use of ground water for irrigation has rapidly expanded with the adoption of tube-well and mechanical pump technology, as noted in Chapter 11 of this manuscript. In the Indian subcontinent, ground-water withdrawals have surged from less than 20km^3 p.a. to more than 250km^3 p.a. since the 1950s. The largest areas under ground-water irrigation in developing countries are in China and India. Relative to total cultivated area, reliance on ground water is highest in the Middle East and south Asia. However, because of the open-access nature of ground water, the resource suffers on a number of fronts: depletion; contamination by municipal, industrial, and agricultural users; and saline water intrusion. Where ground-water use is most intensive, aquifer recharge tends to be too small to make this sustainable in the longer term (World Bank, 2008).

Ground-water resources are being overdrawn to such an extent that water tables in many aquifers have fallen to levels that make pumping difficult and very costly. Small farmers with little access to expensive pumps and often insecure water rights are most affected (World Bank, 2008). Saline intrusion is the most common form of ground-water pollution and is directly related to excessive extraction. Ultimately, this leads to the loss of large tracts of agricultural land, affecting both rich and poor.

Water is a critical constraint to raising agricultural productivity, and much of the success of the green revolution came from improved productivity in areas where assured irrigation was provided through canals or through ground-water irrigation (Ahluwalia, 2005). Against this background the view that irrigation is a major driver for increasing productivity and growth in agriculture is easily supported. Since irrigation is a major contributor to agricultural growth, and agricultural growth is closely associated with poverty reduction, it might be reasonably inferred that access to irrigation would have a strong impact on poverty alleviation (Shah and Singh, 2003).

Poverty and irrigation

Irrigation is known to create employment benefits. It increases the area under cultivation, and correspondingly increases the demand for activities such as weeding and harvesting, both of which are labour-intensive in the developing world. In this regard, the complementary demand for labour and water in irrigation are well established. The estimated employment potential through irrigation for the duration of the Eleventh Five-Year Plan in India (2007–12) is given in Table 15.4. Importantly, the major beneficiaries in this case are landless and marginal farmers who work as farm labourers and are among the poorest in rural areas. Some have also argued that the longer term impact on poverty will be greater than the immediate impact, because irrigation has the potential to end the cycle of negative income and debt that undermines efforts to accumulate assets (World Bank Independent Evaluation Group, 2008). The longer term impact of irrigation on poverty includes the emancipation of vulnerable households from the uncertainty of rainfall fluctuation, thereby enabling them to avoid the economic torture that periodic shocks inflict on them by undermining their asset base (World Bank Independent Evaluation Group, 2008). The impact of shielding against rainfall fluctuations accrues regardless of whether surface or ground water is employed.

Table 15.4 *Employment potential in the Eleventh Five-Year Plan (million person years)*

	Direct employment	*Indirect employment*
Major and medium irrigation	2.1	10.1
Minor irrigation	5	1.05
Flood control	2.5	–
Total	9.6	11.15

Source: India, Planning Commission, 2008b

Most of the indirect benefits of irrigation are known to be non-scale neutral. The impact analysis of the Andhra Pradesh irrigation projects by the World Bank reveals that in the first year of receiving canal water poverty was reduced by about a quarter. Analysis also showed that, even though the larger farmers gain more in absolute terms, the greatest income growth in proportionate terms accrues further down the income distribution, due largely to the increase in wage employment.

Irrigation also raises the cropping intensity and this is particularly the case for smaller farms. Small farmers can harvest a full crop with less water as there is a smaller area to be irrigated. In addition, smaller farmers are not constrained by the necessity to access additional complementary labour, at least not to the same extent as larger farmers. Hence the benefits of increased cropping intensity also seem to pass more evenly among various landholding classes (Huang et al, 2006). The impact of irrigation on animal husbandry is also relatively evenly spread – even on a small plot of land fodder is made available throughout the year with limited irrigation facilities (Phansalkar, 2007).

There are additional benefits that accompany ground-water irrigation relative to those that attend canal- or surface water irrigation. Ground water is more suitable for the application of modern agricultural techniques, such as drip and sprinkler irrigation, precision irrigation and fertigation. Ground water generally delivers better results because of the precision with which water can be delivered in India, and this extends to dairying (Kumar et al, 2004). Accordingly, the benefits accruing to various landholding classes depend also on the type of irrigation and the quality of irrigation provided or made available to farmers. Even the landless can benefit from the right irrigation initiatives (Lipton, 2007).

Narayanamoorthy (2000) has attempted to analyse the role played by irrigation in reducing the level of rural poverty in India. This was undertaken using cross-sectional data from 14 major states. The data were also longitudinal in the sense that they were taken at four points in time. Employing correlation and regression analyses he finds a significant inverse relationship between the incidence of rural poverty and the irrigated area per thousand of the rural population. This relationship held across the four reference points as illustrated in Table 15.5.

Table 15.5 *Correlation of rural poverty percentages with different measures of irrigation across 14 major states in India*

	1972–73	*1977–78*	*1983–84*	*1987–88*
Gross irrigated area percentage	–0.62	–0.69	–0.58	–0.55
Irrigated area per thousand rural population	–0.85	–0.86	–0.77	–0.69

Source: Narayanamoorthy (2000)

Rath (1996) follows a similar line by arguing that policies for alleviating rural poverty should first and foremost extend irrigation in farming areas since this would have the most significant impact on productive employment.

Equity considerations

Distributional inequity of irrigated vs unirrigated land

In a land-based activity such as agriculture, a major determinant of the distribution of wealth and income is the ownership of the major asset – land. It is believed that inequity in land-holding is at the root of inequality and poverty in most rural areas and this is the basis of land reforms in many developing countries. In this light, it would be interesting to compare the distribution of land-holdings for irrigated land with that of unirrigated land. Is irrigated land more equally distributed than unirrigated land or vice versa? We approach this task by invoking standard methodologies for measuring inequity, such as the familiar Lorenz curve and Gini coefficient.

The analysis has been undertaken by employing official data of 2000–01 from the Agricultural Census (India, Ministry of Agriculture, 2008). In Figure 15.4 the Lorenz curve for the irrigated area is closer to the diagonal than that generated for the total arable area, and even more so than that of the unirrigated area. This supports the view that the assets associated with irrigated land are more equitably distributed than those related to unirrigated land. This is confirmed by the Gini coefficients generated from this analysis and reported in Table 15.5. The Gini coefficient for unirrigated land was 0.579 whereas that for irrigated land was 0.479. On the basis of these data it would appear that the benefits of irrigated land would be more equally distributed than those of unirrigated land. The expansion of irrigation would tend to reduce the inequality of wealth and income, other things being equal, of course.

Table 15.6 *Gini coefficients of total, irrigated and unirrigated land-holdings*

	Gini coefficient
Total land	0.5534
Unirrigated land	0.5792
Irrigated land	0.4794

Source: Developed from India, Ministry of Agriculture, 2008

What is the pattern of inequity in irrigated land across different types of irrigation: canal, tank, traditional open wells, and tube-wells? Again, these phenomena are examined using Lorenz curves in Figure 15.5, using 2000–01 data accessed from the Indian Ministry of Agriculture (2008). The figure shows that traditional open-well irrigated land is the most inequitably distributed. This is followed by land subject to canal irrigation. Tube-well irrigated land is more equally distributed than both canal and open-well irrigated land – indicating that despite the high capital investment required for tube-wells, the benefits of this form of irrigation may be more equally distributed than that of open wells or canals. Tank irrigated land is the most equally distributed of all. The Gini coefficients given in Table 15.7 confirm the relative inequities in this distribution. The Gini coefficient for traditional open-well irrigated land is as high as 0.6008, whereas that for tube-wells is 0.4516 and that for tanks is 0.2767.

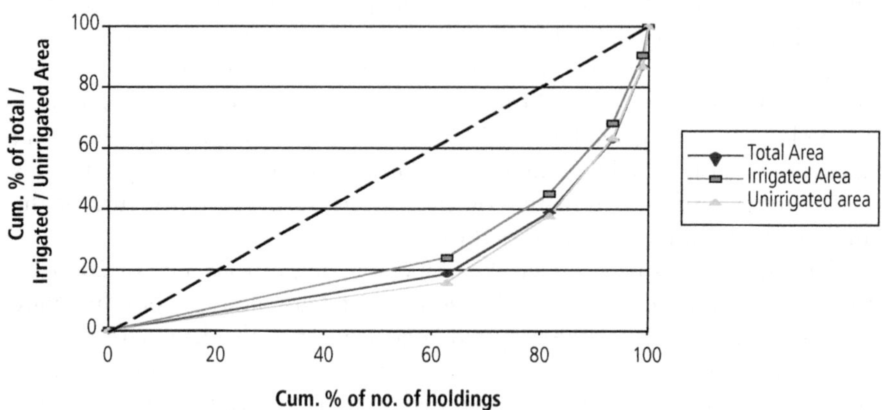

Figure 15.4 *Lorenz curves for total/irrigated/unirrigated area*

Source: Developed from India, Ministry of Agriculture, 2008

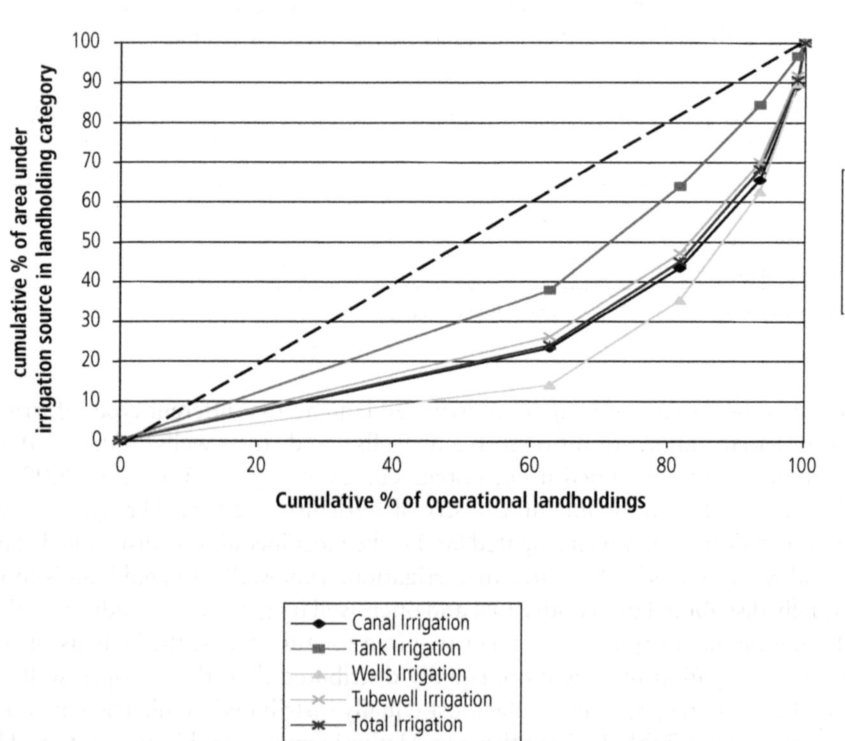

Figure 15.5 *Lorenz curves for irrigated land by source of irrigation*

Source: Developed from India, Ministry of Agriculture, 2008

Table 15.7 *Gini coefficients for land-holdings under various irrigation types*

	Gini coefficient
Wells irrigated land	0.6008
Canal irrigated land	0.4950
Tube-well irrigated land	0.4516
Tank irrigated land	0.2767
Total irrigated land	0.4794

Source: Developed from India, Ministry of Agriculture, 2008

Place of equity in water institutions

It has been shown in other chapters that for effective management of the water resource, institutions are essential and the lack of adequate attention to institutional development is a major cause of the concern in water resource management in India. However, proper consideration of the design of institutions is essential if they are to effectively address scarcity, equity, environmental and financial concerns (Gandhi et al, 2007).

From the point of view of poverty alleviation, addressing scarcity and equity appear particularly important. Deliberately addressing scarcity by measures to improve water-use efficiency can greatly impact on crop intensity, production and incomes, thereby making possible a substantial impact on poverty alleviation. However, focusing solely on this dimension and assuming that there will be positive outcomes for the poor would be naive.

Equity is being increasingly recognized as an important concern of water institutions. Livingston (2004) indicates that evaluating the performance of water institutions in a positive way requires consistency between social goals and institutional structure. In water institutions, equity is expected to be delivered through achieving equitable distribution of water and this may be related to equal representation of interests and opinions, equity in processes, status, authority, participation and decision making.

Equity is addressed in a limited way in the current water laws in India. The Andhra Pradesh Farmers Management of Irrigation Systems Act (1997, amended 1999) (Andhra Pradesh Irrigation and Command Area Development Department, 2003) clause 3.2 states that every water user's area should be divided into territorial constituencies – 6 in minor irrigation systems and 12 in major and medium irrigation systems, for management and representation. The rules espoused in clause 4.3 of this Act state that one of the specific objects of the farmer organizations shall be to make water available to tail-end areas. In clause 6.3 it also states that it is the responsibility of the farmers' organization to supply water to all members in the command area as per the approved terms. Similarly, clause 7.3 indicates that every member has the right to receive water as per the specified quota for use. Clause 7.6 states that every member has the right to participate in the general body meeting and receive annual reports while clause 7.7 indicates that every member has the right to receive equitable benefits from the activities of the organization. Equitable responsibilities are assigned to the extent that clause 8.3 stipulates that every water user has the responsibility to adhere to the water delivery schedules. Clause 16.6 of these rules also mandates that the function of every managing committee is to ensure equitable distribution of water among various water users. The rules also establish processes for a social audit of the WUA with clause 20(ii) used to stipulate that such audits shall cover equity in water distribution.

To give effect to these conditions, the *Election Manual for Farmers Organizations* under Andhra Pradesh Farmers Management of Irrigation Systems Act (1997) notes in clause 14.2 that

> *for equitable distribution of water within the Water Users Association, it is necessary to have the two important functionaries, namely the President and the Vice-President, elected from two different reaches of the Water Users Association. To achieve the above objective:*
> *(a) the District Collector after delineating the Territorial Constituencies based on hydraulic basis shall also demarcate half of them as the Territorial Constituencies of lower reach, based on their proximity to the water source and notify them accordingly*
> *(b) the Election Officer shall invite nominations for the post of Vice-President from the lower reach if the president is from the upper reaches and vice versa.*

Naik and Kalro (1998), in a case study of WUAs in irrigation management in Maharashtra, report that, after irrigation management transfer to WUAs, a more equitable water distribution was achieved with fewer conflicts and greater goodwill in the community generally. This was largely because the WUAs devised and adopted water distribution rules most suitable to local conditions, and the rules were pragmatic and ensured equity. These findings are broadly consistent with the theme throughout this chapter. More specifically, attention to the detail of the rules embodied in WUAs and the like is a critical determinant of the overall success of devolved decision making. This would appear to hold for equity considerations as well as efficiency of water use.

Results presented in Chapter 9 from a sample of 450 beneficiaries associated with 29 water institutions across the three states of Gujarat, Maharashtra and Andhra Pradesh indicate that the institutions vary substantially in their treatment of equity considerations (see Table 15.8). A large number have in place processes for addressing equity, but many do not. While proper distribution between small and large farmers is addressed in most cases, this is somewhat less so between the head-, middle- and tail-end farmers. Monitoring and enforcement of equitable allocation was also inadequate in many cases.

The same survey indicates that about 60 per cent of the respondents found that the institutions have had a positive impact on equitable distribution of

Table 15.8 *Treatment of equity by water institutions*

Particulars	*Strongly agree (Yes)*	*Agree*	*Partially agree/disagree*	*Disagree*	*Strongly disagree (No)*
	5	4	3	2	1
Institution has processes for equitable distribution of water among farmers	23.8	37.1	6.0	8.4	24.7
Proper distribution of water between small and large farmers	27.3	34.2	10.4	3.6	24.4
Proper distribution of water between head-, middle-, and tail-end farmers	27.1	26.7	9.8	5.3	31.1
Equitable allocation of water is monitored and enforced	4.9	23.8	28.7	7.3	34.9

Table15.9 *What has been the impact of the institution on the following? (percentages)*

Particulars	*Highly positive*	*Positive*	*No impact*	*Negative*	*Highly negative*
	5	4	3	2	1
Equity					
Equitable distribution of water	27.1	32.9	39.3	0.4	0.2
Empowerment of farmers to manage irrigation systems	32.7	37.6	20.4	6.7	2.7

Table 15.10 *Has the institution contributed directly or indirectly to the development of the following? (percentages)*

Type	*Impact of the institution*				
	Substantially positive	*Positive*	*No impact*	*Negative*	*Substantially negative*
	5	4	3	2	1
Poor	18.0	28.7	53.3	0.0	0.0
Small/marginal farmers	27.3	48.9	22.9	0.9	0.0
Labourers/wage earners	23.3	53.6	22.7	0.0	0.2
Tail-reach farmers	16.2	38.7	12.4	6.0	4.4

water but in about 40 per cent of cases there was no discernable change, as illustrated in Table 15.9.

About 53 per cent of the respondents in the same survey indicated that there was no impact on the poor (see Table 15.10) that could be traced to the activities of the water institution, whereas 47 per cent found a positive impact. Over 70 per cent reported a positive impact on small/marginal farmers and labourers/wage earners, but about 10 per cent indicate a negative impact on tail-reach farmers.

In addition to the empirical findings presented in earlier chapters dealing with the issue of equity, there are other examples where equity dimensions have been highlighted in the context of irrigation and watershed projects. The success of the innovative project in the village of Sukhomajri, Haryana, which was completed in the early 1980s, shows how landless people can also benefit. In this project, the community designed a system that paid equal attention to the needs of landed and landless people. The rights to impounded water in the three local check dams were equally shared between the landed and the landless, and the benefits of rain-water harvesting were distributed by ensuring that a portion of the incremental gain (from improved crop harvests) was ploughed back into a fund for community development. The landless subsequently benefited by selling their share of water to landowners (Sharma, 2003).

WUAs are often perceived as the flag bearers for participatory irrigation management (PIM) in irrigation management transfer (IMT). This is because WUAs purportedly try to create a platform where all farmer members can interact and participate in decision making and planning. A critical element for the success of these arrangements is the control and management of the WUA and its decision-making capability and autonomy.[2]

Poverty and irrigation technology

The sophistication and cost of technology can sometimes act as a barrier to poverty alleviation via irrigation. Nevertheless, there are many irrigation technologies which are pro-poor and have helped to bring the benefits of irrigation to poor smallholders. The efforts of one organization, the International Development Enterprises (IDE), are notable in that regard. This organization has been able to promote three technologies in India that are reportedly very effective. The human-powered treadle pumps for small and marginal farms under the brand name of *Krishak Bandhu* are reported to be a major success in south Asia, where over a million were sold by 1998. There have also been reports of women using these pumps at night to avoid the social stigma associated with such work, but significant benefits are reported to have been delivered to the poor farmers through this simple and effective technology.

The second technology from IDE is the kitchen-yard drip irrigation kits for vegetable cultivation. Originally launched in Nepal, these kits have become popular in many parts of India, particularly the tribal areas. In Nepal, women and families are known to have benefited substantially from these gravity-based ultra small kits that cost around Rs1500 per acre. The benefits derive from the additional and regular income associated with the use of the technology.

The third technology launched by IDE is the drip-tape. This is a low-cost innovation that reduces the capital cost of drip irrigation while extending the durability and life of the drip pipes. It can be used for two to three years at one-eighth the cost of conventional drip irrigation equipment.

There are also numerous other pro-poor irrigation technologies. For example, lift irrigation schemes being implemented through simple technologies by PRADAN, an NGO in the eastern part of the country, helped raise yields for tribal farmers in some of the poorest states, such as Jharkhand, Bihar and Orissa (Bhamoriya and Mahapatra, 2002). Simple and effective *Jal-kunds* or storage devices enabled the Wadi Project of DHRUVA-BAIF in South Gujarat to benefit numerous small and impoverished farmers. These are small structures creating a modest pond with a capacity of about 4000 litres. This is sufficient for three to four protective irrigations for crops such as cashew and mango during summer dry spells. The use of neem oil (a layer is applied to the surface of the water) and knitted covers further reduces evaporation by 75 per cent in these humble storages. *Jal-kunds* utilize water from a variety of water sources and have substantially helped poor tribal people (Bhamoriya, 2004).

Concluding observations

Poverty is a serious problem in India and its alleviation is a national and international priority. Based on national estimates, India has over 300 million poor people (even more by international estimates) and 73 per cent of them reside in the rural areas, depending primarily on agriculture. Various studies in India and elsewhere have demonstrated that one of the most effective ways of reducing poverty is to drive agricultural growth. This philosophy has been largely responsible for a reduction in poverty from an estimated 55 per cent in 1973–74 to 27 per cent in 2004–05.

Irrigation is a major driver of agricultural growth and also helps to stabilize agricultural incomes. Irrigation development is found to be closely and negatively linked to poverty levels across states in India. However, water resource management is suffering immensely from poor institutional development in India. In overcoming these institutional deficiencies, it is very important to remain cognisant of equity considerations so as to maximize the impact of irrigation development on poverty itself. This should include incorporation of equity considerations into the laws, rules, structures and processes of water institutions.

The empirical data reported in earlier chapters reveals substantial variation in the treatment of equity within entities charged with managing water resources in India. This should be of concern to policy makers since studies in this field have invariably found that where equity considerations are deliberately incorporated into institutions, the equity and poverty alleviation outcomes are significantly better.

Notes

1 These estimates are based on the national poverty line estimate and data from the latest large sample consumption expenditure survey of 2004–05.
2 These issues were discussed in greater detail by Ananda, Crase and Keeton in Chapter 14.

References

Ahluwalia, M. S. (1978) 'Rural poverty and agricultural performance in India', *Journal of Developmental Studies*, vol 14, no 2, pp298–323

Ahluwalia, M. S. (2005) *Reducing Poverty and Hunger in India: The Role of Agriculture*, IFPRI 2004–2005 Annual Report Essay, IFPRI, Washington DC

Andhra Pradesh Irrigation and Command Area Development Department (2003) Govt of Andhra Pradesh, April

Bardhan, P. K. (1973) 'On the incidence of poverty in rural India of the Sixties', *Economic and Political Weekly*, vol 8, nos 4, 5 and 6, Annual Number, pp245–254

Bardhan, P. K. (1986) 'Poverty and trickle-down in rural India: A quantitative analysis', in J. W. Mellor and G. M. Desai (eds) (1986) *Agricultural Change and Rural Poverty: Variations on a Theme by Dharm Narain*, Oxford University Press, Delhi

Bhamoriya, V. (2004) 'A case study of poverty', IWMI internal publication for the Central India Initiative

Bhamoriya, V. and Mahapatra, S. (2002) 'Where is the demand?', IWMI internal publication for the Central India Initiative

Dandekar, V. M. and Rath. N. (1971a) 'Poverty in India – I: Dimensions and trends', *Economic and Political Weekly*, vol 6, no 1, pp25–48

Dandekar, V. M. and Rath, N. (1971b) 'Poverty in India – II: Policies and programmes', *Economic and Political Weekly*, vol 6, no 2, pp106–145

Dasgupta, B. (1995) 'Institutional reforms and poverty alleviation in West Bengal', *Economic and Political Weekly*, vol 30, nos 41 and 42, pp2691–2702

Datt, G. and Ravallion, M. (1996) 'Why have some Indian states done better than others at reducing rural poverty?', Policy Research Working Paper No. 1594, Policy Research Department, Poverty and Human Resources Division, World Bank, Washington DC

Dhawan, B. D. (1995) *Groundwater Depletion, Land Degradation and Irrigated Agriculture in India,* Commonwealth Publishers, New Delhi

FAO (1997) Aquastat country profile for India, available at www.fao.org/nr/water/aquastat/countries/india/index.stm)

FAO (2008) website, 'Country profile for India', www.faorap-apcas.org/india.html, accessed 14 December 2008

Gandhi, V., Crase, L. and Herath, G. (2007) 'Determinants of institutional success for water in India: Results from a study across three states', paper presented at the 51st Annual Conference of the Australian Agricultural and Resource Economics Society (AARES), 13–16 February, Queenstown, New Zealand

Ghosh, M. (1996) 'Agricultural development and rural poverty in India', *Indian Journal of Agricultural Economics*, vol 51, no 3, pp374–380

Huang, Q., Rozelle, S., Lohmar, B., Huang, J. and Wang, J. (2006) 'Irrigation, agricultural performance and poverty reduction in China', *Food Policy,* vol 31, pp31–52

India, Ministry of Agriculture (2008) *Agricultural Statistics at a Glance 2008*, Government of India

India, National Sample Survey Organization (NSSO) (2001) Ministry of Planning, Government of India, New Delhi

India, Planning Commission (2008a) Databook for Deputy Chairman (Planning Commission website), Planning Commission, October

India, Planning Commission (2008b) *Eleventh Five-Year Plan 2007–12*, vol 3, ch 2, Government of India, Oxford University Press, New Delhi

Kakwani, N. and Subbarao, K. (1990) 'Rural poverty in India, 1973–86', vol 1, Policy Research Working Paper No. 526, World Bank, Washington DC

Kumar, M. D., Singhal, L. and Rath, P. (2004) 'Value of groundwater: Case studies in Banaskantha', *Economic and Political Weekly*, 31 July

Lipton, M. (2007) 'Farm water and rural poverty reduction in developing Asia', *Irrigation and Drainage*, vol 56, pp127–146

Lipton, M., Litchfield, J. and Faurès, J. (2003) *Preliminary Review of the Impact of Irrigation on Poverty with Special Emphasis on Asia*, FAO, Rome

Livingston, M. L. (2004) *Proceedings of the Universities Council on Water Resources - UCOWR 2004*, Southern Illinois University, Carbondale, IL

Naik, G and Kalro, A. H. (1998) 'Two case studies on the role of water users associations in irrigation management in Maharashtra, India', received by the World Bank's WBI CBNRM Initiative

Narayanamoorthy, A. (2000) 'Irrigation and rural poverty nexus: A statewise analysis', *Indian Journal of Agricultural Economics*, vol 56, no 1

Nayyar, R. (1991) *Rural Poverty in India: An Analysis of Inter-State Differences*, Oxford University Press, Bombay

Palanichamy, N. V., Paramsivam, P. and Palanisami, K. (2008) 'Economic analysis of canal water distribution in Parambikulam Aliyar Project Area of Tamil Nadu', in K. Palanisami, C. Ramasamy and C. Umetsu (eds) *Groundwater Management and Policies*, Macmillan India, New Delhi

Phansalkar, S. J. (2007) 'The poor and their livestock: Meeting the challenge of water scarcity', *International Journal of Rural Management*, vol 3, no 1, pp1–25

Rath, N. (1985) 'Garibi Hatao: Can IRDP do it?', *Economic and Political Weekly*, 9 February

Rath, N. (1996) 'Poverty in India revisited', *Indian Journal of Agricultural Economics*, vol 51, nos 1 and 2, pp76–108

Shah, T. and Singh, O. P. (2003) 'Can irrigation eradicate rural poverty in Gujarat?' Research Highlight no. 10, IWMI-Tata Publication, Anand

Sharma, A. N. (1995) 'Political economy of poverty in India', *Economic and Political Weekly*', vol 30, nos 41 and 42, pp2587–2602

Sharma, S. (2003) 'Rethinking watershed development in India: Strategy for the twenty-first century', Chapter 6, Proceedings of the Asian Regional Workshop on Watershed Management, Nepal

Sundaram, K. and Tendulkar, S. D. (1988) 'Towards an explanation of interregional variation in poverty and unemployment in rural India', in T. N. Srinivasan and P. K. Bardhan (eds), *Rural Poverty in South Asia*, Oxford University Press, Delhi, pp316–362

Von Braun, J., Gulati, A. and Fan, S. (2005) *Agricultural and Economic Development Strategies and the Transformation of China and India*, IFPRI, Washington DC

Vyas, V. S. and Bhargava, P. (1995) 'Public intervention for poverty alleviation: An overview', *Economic and Political Weekly*, vol 30, nos 41 and 42, pp22559–2572

World Bank (2008) *World Development Report (2008)*, World Bank, Washington DC

World Bank Independent Evaluation Group (2008) *An Impact Evaluation of India's Second and Third Andhra Pradesh Irrigation Projects: A Case of Poverty Reduction with Low Economic Returns*, World Bank, Washington DC

16
Institutions and Irrigation in India – Concluding Lessons and the Way Forward

Lin Crase and Vasant Gandhi

Introduction

In this book we have argued that improving the performance of irrigation in India hinges substantially on appropriate institutional design – engineering solutions by themselves are unable to provide the panacea for addressing water resource management in this country. In order to support this argument we have collectively undertaken two main tasks. First, an extensive and rigorous theoretical framework was developed around concepts pertaining to institutional design. Second, the theoretical framework was deployed to gain empirical information about the performance of different irrigation entities in India. An outcome from this approach has been a series of significant policy lessons for how irrigation should be managed in India. The study also provides important potential implications beyond this setting.

In order to sharpen our focus we initially posed five main questions in Chapter 1. Namely:

1 What theoretical and conceptual insights would be useful for the institutional analysis of water resource management?
2 What is the magnitude and contour of the extant water resource management in India?
3 What empirical methods can be harnessed from the theoretical insights offered by New Institutional Economics and related disciplines, and how might these assist in guiding policy and institutional reform?

4 What does empirical analysis tell us about institutional performance?
5 What lessons might be derived for policy makers?

These questions are now revisited in order to assemble key findings and reflect upon general themes that we hope will resonate with policy makers.

What theoretical and conceptual insights would be useful for the institutional analysis of water resource management?

The theoretical underpinning of much of this work rests with New Institutional Economics. Core concepts employed include the notion of 'institutions', defined as the set of rules by which human behaviour is governed. In some instances throughout this manuscript authors have referred to institutions as organizations that embody those rules. However, the key issue revolves around understanding the defining nature of 'good' institutions or rules, regardless of the extent to which they are ultimately amalgamated into an organizational entity.

The literature on New Institutional Economics provides useful guidance in this regard by specifying with some precision the notion of transaction costs. Here we have opted to employ a fairly broad definition and have conceptualized transaction costs as all costs associated with the creation, use and change of an institution (i.e. a set of informal and/or formal rules) (Pagan, Chapter 2). The basic premise of good institutional design is that transaction costs should be minimized as this will raise the welfare of those parties involved with exchanging and using resources. However, the intellectual appeal of transaction costs must be necessarily balanced against other constraints. For example, transaction costs are notoriously difficult to measure, as demonstrated by Pagan (Chapter 2), and understanding their pervasive form is no simple task. In that regard, it has also been acknowledged that some of the recent thinking in this field has drawn a link between transaction and transformation costs, since the technology of production is, in many cases, inextricably linked to the institutional environment that circumscribes it. Another important refinement has been the conceptual bifurcation between static and dynamic elements. In this context it soon becomes clear that the institutional and technological choices of today have potential costs for the future and any assessment of 'good institutional design' should make allowance for these events.

On the basis of this literature five generic characteristics were identified as being congruent with good institutions. First, having clear objectives was highlighted as pivotal. This feature was expected to provide shared clarity of purpose and also to articulate the mechanisms for adjustment. Second, good institutional design takes into account the necessity to link formal and informal rules through good interaction. Where formal rules are not well aligned with informal rules it was anticipated that cohesion among individual members would be weak and the costs of gaining acceptance and compliance would be higher. Third, a generic feature of good institutions was that of adaptability or adaptiveness. While potentially conflicting with the first institutional feature, adaptability implies a structured approach to recognizing and dealing with variation and uncertainty. This is particularly relevant when the institutional setting is in natural resources, such as water. Fourth, good institutions are characterized by an appropriate scale for dealing with an issue or set of issues. The spatial definition of institutions is particularly important in the context of water where institutional hierarchies are common and hydrological linkages necessarily lead to downstream impacts. Fifth, the ability to bring compliance is another defining feature of good institutions. Maintaining compliance is itself costly, as is the absence of compliance, since lower rates of compliance reduce the meaningfulness of the institutions. However the burden of those costs will differ substantially and, as a general principle, better compliance rates are consistent with better institutional performance.

In order to refine these generic principles and relate them specifically to irrigation and water resource management, Crase (Chapter 3) and Pagan, Crase and Gandhi (Chapter 4) set about scrutinizing irrigation and water reform in Australia. The intent was to use a setting removed from the pressing social and political milieu of India and yet still allow us to hone our understanding of institutional design in a real-life setting. While the Australian setting differs in many ways from India, there are sufficient political and hydrological similarities to draw some higher-order messages about institutional design and policy reform generally.

Among the most pertinent of these observations relates to the hierarchical nature of decision making and the reality that community preferences change over time (see Crase, Chapter 3). Surface water resources in Australia and India are both vested in the states with federal governments holding some superordinate control. In the Murray-Darling Basin in Australia the federal government has sought to expand its influence over decision making; first, through its suasive financial powers and second via legislative modifications. These changes highlight that the weight of decision making over water resources can move up and down an institutional hierarchy as priorities change. Importantly, it also serves to remind us that transaction and transformation costs potentially arise at each level of the decision-making hierarchy and between institutional levels. In the case of modifications to water rules in Australia, Crase (Chapter 3) argues that many of the much-heralded early water reforms were consistent with the institutional criteria identified by Pagan (Chapter 2), although he expresses some disquiet about recent policy episodes. Nevertheless, these recent policy changes also serve a useful role in helping understand institutional dynamics – in order to achieve good institutional outcomes at the lowest level of water management, it is necessary to resolve higher-order dilemmas at the superordinate level. Put simply, it is not enough to simply devolve an intractable problem to a lower-order entity because of the perceived costs of dealing with it at a state or national level. If the problem exists at a basin or inter-basin level, then simply asking states or irrigation communities to deliver a solution is hardly adequate. This observation supports Pagan's (Chapter 2) claim that attention needs to be given to scale when designing good institutions, but also overtly acknowledges that the rights of all water users are invariably attenuated by decisions made at higher levels of governance.

The mechanics of decision making within water agencies located within an institutional hierarchy was specifically dealt with by Pagan, Crase and Gandhi in Chapter 4. Reflecting on the reluctance of various bureaucracies to sanction interstate water trade between the Australian Capital Territory and New South Wales, Pagan, Crase and Gandhi demonstrated that the internal machinations of each decision-making body are critical in shaping the final outcome. More specifically, how agents within organizations perceive their responsibilities can ultimately influence the course of major policy reforms. On this basis, it was considered important to broaden the generic characteristics of good institutional design in an effort to capture some of the internal dynamics and operations of organizations. Drawing directly from the management science literature, three additional conceptual components were advocated to balance the five generic principles derived from and supported by the New Institutional Economics. More specifically, technical rationality, organizational rationality and political rationality were proffered as useful additional constructs since these would provide additional explanation into the internal effectiveness of organizations not specifically captured by those elements emanating from the New Institutional Economics.

In sum, eight conceptual components were seen as being critical to good institutional design and measuring and articulating these was expected to substantially explain institutional performance in irrigation. Five of these elements were directly related to the New Institutional Economics: clear institutional objectives; harmonization of informal and formal rules; adaptiveness; appropriateness of scale; and an ability to bring compliance. The remaining three elements related to the internal operation of organizations: technical rationality; organizational rationality; and political rationality. The challenge was to explore whether these elements were empirically significant in a consequential context and there are few more pressing settings than those that circumscribe irrigated agriculture in one of the most populous nations on Earth – India.

What is the magnitude and contour of extant water resource management in India?

Having delineated a generic framework for adjudging the performance of irrigation institutions it was important to establish the context for any empirical work. This was accomplished over the following four chapters (5–8). Herath (Chapter 5) commenced this process by drawing attention to the role of social capital and collective action which are often considered important in developing countries. There are important linkages between human and natural systems in rural communities in developing countries that are often less obvious in the irrigation landscape of developed nations. Notably, there is an interrelationship between institutional dynamics and the rate of environmental degradation in most developing countries like India. The presence of weak institutions invariably accelerates degradation and a vicious cycle can result. Herath noted that this is not always the case and there are numerous instances of institutional success that contrast with the many notable failures. He also reviewed the extant empirical work undertaken in south Asia and finds that there is considerable scope for improvement and opportunity to provide greater insights into institutional dynamics.

Substantial institutional change has characterized water resource management in India in recent decades and the key arrangements that attend the status quo were described in considerable detail by Ananda (Chapter 6). Ananda concluded that 'Indian water institutions portray a complex mosaic of socio-economic, cultural and political realities in concert with numerous environmental challenges.' Unravelling this mosaic to uncover the elements of success was therefore likely to prove to be a formidable task. However, the rewards of 'getting things right' are also non-trivial.

Ananda observed that large irrigation schemes that have been historically managed by the state are 'faced with continued physical deterioration, siltation of dams, lack of O&M, poor cost recovery and disintegration of institutions'. However, irrigation is not confined to large surface water schemes and ground water has emerged as the most extensive form. Ananda attempted to rationalize the institutional hierarchy for managing water resources in India and observed that a range of local, state and federal authorities exist within a nested framework. These cover a range of irrigation types, including tanks, canals and ground-water entities. The performance of each irrigation type was provisionally assessed against Pagan's (Chapter 2) performance framework. Ananda found that, by and large, the ground-water institutions aligned more closely with the generic characteristics of good institutional design than did the other forms of irrigation. Importantly, this was viewed primarily from the perspective of the beneficiaries of these arrangements and did not specifically account for the fact that ground-water extractions in many cases clearly exceed sustainable yields. Moreover, these problems are arguably a manifestation of the inability of superordinate agencies to set reasonable bounds for resource management.

Another important element of Ananda's review of Indian water institutions related to his assessment of water user associations and the concept of participatory irrigation management. The origins of water user associations vary. In some instances, collective associations have managed water use at a local level for thousands of years. This was also noted by Herath (Chapter 5). Ananda contended that these entities 'have shown a high resilience to various adverse conditions and managed to survive'. By way of contrast, a large number of associations were developed quite recently in response to policy enthusiasm for participatory irrigation management. Often this emanated from the general view that local farmers would do a better job of maintaining infrastructure if they were given a greater say in its use. Interestingly, Ananda summarizes the correlation between these two forms of water user association (i.e. farmer-induced versus government-induced) and the generic institutional design criteria of Pagan and found marked differences. More specifically, he argued that there was a prima facie case for believing that the farmer-induced associations would perform better than those induced by government decree. This issue was given close attention in the empirical work that followed.

A more detailed analysis of the legal dimensions of water institutions in India was also provided to ground the subsequent empirical work. Upadhyay (Chapter 7) offered a synoptic account of water law in India, with close attention given to the most prolific form of irrigation – ground water. Consistent with the observations of Ananda (Chapter 6), Upadhyay noted the general policy enthusiasm for devolving responsibility for water management to local decision makers, which he loosely described as 'people-oriented, decentralized and demand-driven water programmes'. Importantly, Upadhyay noted that states have retained constitutional power over water resources, although they have tended to endow *Panchayats* with responsibility for 'Water Management', 'Minor Irrigation' and 'Watershed Development'. This is consistent with the principles of nested decision making highlighted by others.

Perhaps the thorniest issue raised by Upadhyay relates to the challenge of controlling ground-water extraction. While water resources are generally vested in the states in India, there persists a view that ground water is an easement attached to overlying land. There is some basis for querying the absolute nature of these arrangements and Upadhyay established a strong case for revisiting these conventions by systematically analysing the course of a 'model bill' designed by the government of India to bring ground-water extractions into check. Notwithstanding these noble attempts, relatively little real progress is evident. Upadhyay traced legal developments in Andhra Pradesh and Maharashtra against this backdrop and found that frequently the rhetoric was not matched by appropriate action. In some instances this was due to a lack of technical expertise but overall he appeared sceptical that 'uncomfortable' regulations would ever be invoked, regardless of the perils of unfettered ground-water extraction. The review of the legal arrangements also raised additional questions about the efficacy of devolving responsibility for resource management. Put simply, Upadhyay raised serious doubts about the extent to which ground water can be adequately managed at local level when it is so difficult to meaningfully monitor the status of the resource at this scale.

The status of ground water in India was also given attention by Gandhi and Namboodiri (Chapter 8). Utilizable ground-water resources reportedly stand at about 432km^3 in India while surface water resources amount to 690km^3. Notwithstanding their magnitude, the highly variable nature of these water resources in temporal and spatial terms makes management problematic. Water resource management is critical for India due to skewed rainfall, growing food demand, and the large dependence on agriculture for livelihoods. The historical response to these circumstances has been active government sponsorship of irrigated agriculture. British rule left India with over 20 million ha of irrigated land by the time of independence, almost half being major and medium surface water irrigation schemes. Enthusiasm for irrigation development continued after independence and by 1985 more than three times this irrigation potential had been created in the form of major, medium and minor projects. However, serious concerns about unsatisfactory management, delivery and utilization of water at the farm level have emerged.

Gandhi and Namboodiri (Chapter 8) bemoaned the growing gap between the potential created for irrigation and the area actually irrigated. Among the more notable tends in irrigation in India in recent times is the expansion of ground-water extraction. Whereas technical solutions are known and implemented, serious institutional deficiencies exist. Many analysts argue that water resource management in India is heading for a crisis unless policies and institutions are radically transformed. The major challenge for India is to design institutions that can deliver on the efficient use of the scarce resource, offer equity in its benefits, reduce environmental harm, and achieve financial viability.

What empirical methods can be harnessed from the theoretical insights offered by New Institutional Economics and related disciplines, and how might these assist in guiding policy and institutional reform?

The ambition of this project was to establish the extent to which the characteristics of good institutional design impacted on irrigation institution performance in India. This investigation commenced in earnest with the work reported by Gandhi, Crase and Roy in Chapter 9. The setting for this empirical component was the states of Gujarat, Maharashtra and Andhra Pradesh – all water-scarce jurisdictions with differing institutional responses to the problems at hand. In addition, the empirical work was based on a variety of irrigation entities covering surface water, ground-water and rain-water irrigation. This approach was adopted to allow for comparisons across jurisdictions and across resource types.

The data set that underpinned this work comprised household surveys of farmers, where respondents provided extensive details of their productive activities and their perceptions of institutional performance. The latter proved particularly vexing, inasmuch as performance has many dimensions, ranging from strictly short-term productive considerations to broader notions of equity and long-term environmental sustainability. Nevertheless, the sample of 450 respondents provided the basis for undertaking some useful empirical tests.

In this preliminary stage a bivariate approach was employed which involved scrutiny of potential relationships using the familiar analysis of variance (AVOVA) framework. The need to address technical, organizational and political rationality emerged as important determinants of institutional performance. The importance of the secretary and the staff being active, and the necessity to have well-trained personnel with the right expertise, indicates the importance of addressing technical rationality. In addition, the management committee being active and having the necessary skills supports the view that it is critically important to address coordination and organizational rationality. The importance of the general body along with the elected chairman being active indicates that, without adequately addressing political rationality, the water institutions cannot be successful. The results indicate that successful institutional design extends beyond leadership – what is required is the correct institutional design with the required structure, active processes and effective systems.

Given the richness and extent of the data set, an additional series of factor analyses and cleansing techniques were required to establish meaningful measures for the theoretical constructs developed in earlier chapters. Importantly, seven key factors were evident and these are repeated here for convenience:

Factor 1: Managing committee (active), secretary (active), management has expertise, management has authority to adapt rules, compliance is sufficient.
Factor 2: Organization created by government (negative), rules of organization determined by government (negative), objectives are clear, clear mechanism for changing rules, scale is appropriate, organization uses its powers.
Factor 3: Good interaction between members of the institution, good interaction between management and members.
Factor 4: General body active, institution regularly plans and pursues objectives.
Factor 5: Higher-level issues are appropriately addressed by higher-level institutions.
Factor 6: Good leadership to facilitate interaction.
Factor 7: Management has the expertise.

Subsequently, a process was adopted to test the veracity of important relationships against the dimensions of institutional success. This second stage involved multivariate analysis and, in this case, raised particular empirical challenges. The first of these problems arose from the categorical nature of much of the data. After several pre-tests it was clear that the cognitive burden on respondents could only feasibly be contained by using a categorical format for some questions. Consequently, the data collected for this exercise were not always continuous, and respondents provided information in an ordered format – e.g. rating performance from 1 to 5. Accordingly, assumptions that accompany conventional regression techniques would be violated, were empirical analysis of these data to proceed along the lines of standard linear regression. To account for this the multivariate approach adopted a TOBIT framework capable of dealing with this constraint.

A second major challenge related to dealing with multicollinearity in the empirical models. Given that good institutions probably embody more than one attribute from the theoretical framework, it might be expected that explanatory variables would be correlated. The development of factors went some way to dealing with this problem but it is not possible to completely account for multicollinearity within these data.

Given these constraints, perhaps the most meaningful insights were derived from the analysis of the data set as whole, and this was reported by Gandhi, Crase and Roy (Chapter 9). The comprehensive data set has the advantage of including greater variability and, by including the maximum observations, increases the potential for establishing statistically significant relationships. The bivariate analysis revealed important relationships in the data but the deployment of the multivariate TOBIT technique offers more poignant lessons. Regardless of whether performance was specified in efficiency, equity or envir-onmental terms, there was clear evidence that the theoretical attributes developed in earlier chapters were influential in determining success across jurisdictions and irrigation types. The New Institutional Economics fundamentals were found to be very important, particularly in indicating ways of reducing transaction costs and promoting cooperative solutions. The results showed that problems of institutional failure in water resource institutions in India can be overcome in many cases by using the cogent features of institutional design emerging from New Institutional Economics. In addition, the necessity of incorporating components suggested by management theories of good governance is also clear in this research. Successful institutions invariably embody these features.

What does empirical analysis tell us about institutional performance with different water sources?

To shed additional light on institutional performance an empirical analysis was undertaken for each of the irrigation types – surface water, ground water and rain water (check dams).

Surface water

Namboodiri and Gandhi (Chapter 10) considered the performance of surface water institutions along similar lines to those applied to the data set as a whole. The bivariate analysis revealed that the performance of canal cooperatives was generally superior to that of water user associations. This was consistent with Ananda's (Chapter 6) prediction that the government-induced nature of some water user associations would limit their overall success. Other general findings in the context of surface water were that tail-end users rated institutional performance somewhat lower than their upstream neighbours and stronger social cohesion in a village was positively and significantly associated with better performance.

The multivariate analysis offered additional insights particularly as it allowed for the specification of performance in different ways. When modelled against overall performance, important internal elements of the organization proved positive and significant. These included having an active general membership body and a capable and energetic management committee. In addition, the capacity to undertake systematic planning and having a strong compliance culture were conducive to better overall performance. By way of contrast, overall performance was rated lower when the entity was created by government, again supporting the view by Ananda that such arrangements can prove to be suboptimal.

Denoting performance primarily along economic lines, for instance, by gauging the extent to which prices are used to reflect scarcity, provides alternative insights. Here the experience of staff members, capable leadership, strong compliance and sound interaction between members were shown to be significant drivers. In the context of enhanced operation and maintenance activities, New Institutional variables such as clarity of objectives and structured planning to facilitate adjustment were shown to be significant, as were several concepts from the management science perspective – particularly, the presence of experienced and capable staff able to deal with technical rationality. Poignantly, the model of maintenance activities also reveals that the role of higher-order decision-making bodies remains significant – when superordinate bodies deal appropriately with pressing issues then subordinate agents function more effectively.

Testing for performance along environmental and financial sustainability lines produced results that were broadly consistent with earlier models. The role of the internal decision mechanisms, personified in the capabilities of office bearers and managers, and good interaction between members and experienced staff proved to be positive influences. Similar observations could be made about the wider welfare effects on the village community, with the presence of capable staff members and regular planning proving important. Planning processes were also shown to be significant promoters of better financial performance, as was the necessity to have higher-order decision-making entities dealing with systemic or basin-wide problems.

Ground-water

Ground-water now forms the largest single source of irrigation in India and this has largely resulted from the widespread use of tube-wells and the simultaneous expansion of the electricity grid to the rural population. Several institutional forms can be found in the context of ground water, including large formal institutions arising from the devolution of state-controlled wells. However, the majority of the ground water is extracted from private tube-wells, tube-well partnerships and relatively informal tube-well cooperatives.

In order to better understand the functioning of ground-water organizations, Gandhi and Roy (Chapter 11) analysed the data drawn from irrigation farmers in northern Gujarat. One of the distinguishing characteristics of Gujarat irrigation is its heavy reliance on ground water, which constitutes over 80 per cent of the irrigated area in the state. Given the limited variation in institutional types in this context it was anticipated that the empirical analysis would not produce the same level of clarity as that offered by the earlier investigations (i.e. the analyses of the whole data set and surface water irrigation). Nevertheless, there was clear evidence, even in this more limited context, that elements of the New Institutional Economics and management theory of governance played important roles.

The bivariate approach that was used in the other settings again showed the necessity for good internal decision-making mechanisms with the activity level of the chairman, the managing committee and secretary all proving to be significantly and positively correlated to institutional performance. Similar support was found in the multivariate models. Modelling the overall success of the entity indicated that technical rationality, delivered via good management practices, was paramount in this regard. The model developed around main-ten-ance activities also illustrated the importance of technical elements where the role of the secretary was significant. In this model the capacity to undertake planning significantly improved performance, as it did in the model designed to scrutinize the impact on the overall welfare of the village community. Welfare in the village was also likely to be enhanced when the ground-water organizations had better management expertise.

Notwithstanding these findings, there is an important cautionary note that applies to local ground-water organizations in this setting. Ground-water cooperatives and partnerships are usually held together by strong individual incentives to maximize the benefits that accrue to the members of those entities. For example, tube-well partnerships in the study region often emerged as a direct response to the failure of shallow wells and the necessity for individual farmers to pool resources to extract water from greater depths. Arguably, the very success of these institutions on some fronts spells disaster on others. The skilled management to extract water from greater depths and the ingenious institutional arrangements to support these endeavours need to be considered in the context of the long-term sustainability of extractions. It is somewhat ironical that stronger institutional performance in this case may simply accelerate the depletion of scarce resources and worsen the long-term outcome.

This issue assumes even greater importance when combined with the earlier insights offered by Upadhyay (Chapter 7). Recall that Upadhyay expresses some reservation about the apparent enthusiasm among policy makers for devolving responsibility for compliance and monitoring of ground-water extraction to local authorities. Throughout this volume we have sought to expose the folly of this simplistic approach to decision making. Moreover, we have emphasized the necessity for policy makers to reflect on the principles of good institutional design suggested by New Institutional Economics and organizational theories drawn from management science. In the context of ground-water, having superordinate bodies dealing with problems suited to the scale of their operation, such as basin-wide over-extraction, would seem to hold much more promise than an approach that simply shifts the problem and costs to local authorities. This was considered in greater detail by Ananda, Crase and Keeton (Chapter 14), but remains one of the most significant challenges for water management in India.

Rainwater institutions – check dams

At a practical level many local institutions in India have produced marked and useful impacts on water resource management. Arguably, one such initiative is the check dam movement which was described in some detail by Gandhi and Sharma (Chapter 12). Check dams have arisen as a localized effort to enhance ground-water recharge and usually centre on the development of a structure (or series of structures) designed to retard runoff during the wetter months of the year. The upshot has been improved ground-water recharge in many villages, particularly in Gujarat, where the movement has attracted greatest attention.

The institutions required to accompany these initiatives are relatively uncomplicated compared to those that attend ongoing work, as would occur with a canal cooperative, for example. Nevertheless, some degree of organization and rule-setting is required to bring even singular check dam projects to fruition. For instance, as a minimum the village community needs to establish mechanisms for planning, financing and construction.

In the interests of completeness a similar empirical analysis to that used to scrutinize other water sources was applied to these entities. The objective was to establish the veracity of the conceptual framework in this setting. Overall, the performance of check dam organizations was rated quite highly by those affected and the bivariate and multivariate results point to the importance of several constructs. More specifically, Gandhi and Sharma observe that 'overall, appropriate scale, clarity of objectives, good interaction, and having management with the ability to adapt rules and bring compliance appear to be major determinants of success'.

There is one caveat that needs to be added to these results. Check dams, by definition, positively impact on the hydrology in a local area. However, it may not always be possible to modify local hydrology without impacting on others. Thus what is missing from the analysis of check dams is an understanding and appreciation of their overall impact on hydrology and other potential water users. Again, this points to the necessity for superordinate bodies to develop and maintain an adequate understanding of the wider impacts of water use at a local scale – not because such entities will do a better job of micro-managing water, but because broad-scale issues are more appropriately dealt with by institutions with jurisdictions that match that scale.

What lessons might be derived for policy makers?

Having developed a robust theoretical framework and tested its empirical significance in a range of settings, it is now important to reflect on what this means for policy formulation. Clearly, we have already introduced several elements of this, but three specific areas of interest were given attention in Chapters 13 to 15.

First, Herath (Chapter 13) considered the relevance of the mechanisms for devolving responsibility for irrigation to farmers and farmer groups. He did so by recounting the events of irrigation management transfer (IMT) and the associated development of water user associations, which were also subjected to scrutiny as part of the empirical analysis by Namhoodiri and Gandhi (Chapter 10). Poignantly, Herath finds that, 'IMT has shown some positive achievements but there is scope for considerable improvement'. This is supported by the earlier empirical work which found substantial variations in the performance of surface water entities and specifically tied this to elements of the conceptual framework, such as having clear objectives or having capable management able to facilitate decision making. Herath further contends that, all too often, the results from establishing water user associations fall short because the reforms that occur 'are often in the interest of local elites and others extracting sizeable economic rents. These events created weak WUAs with poor skills and knowledge to enhance administrative, managerial, and financial capacities of participants.'

Combined with the empirical work on surface water organizations, there is a resounding message for policy makers. It is not enough to simply absolve higher-order agencies of responsibility for surface water management on the grounds that local communities possess inherent qualities that lead to a better job. Clearly defined rights must accompany this devolution; otherwise cost and blame-shifting between levels of the decision-making hierarchy will become the norm.

A similar message emerged from Chapter 14 where Ananda, Crase and Keeton considered the conundrums that arise from the dispersion of information and varying capacities to make decisions. In this instance, the theoretical literature on decentralized decision making offered some useful guidance but, as the authors pointed out, this same literature runs the risk of treating decision-making processes as a 'black box'. Rather, what is required is a more detailed appreciation of decision making itself. By focusing on the bifurcation between routine and non-routine decisions, it quickly becomes evident that the structure of the decision-making hierarchy and the capacity at different levels of that hierarchy are important components of the institutional design landscape.

Useful insights are available from the institutional literature and these were summarized in Chapter 14. However, one message continues to resonate from this review – the imperative to match scale and recognize linkages. This has several components. First, it is necessary to match the scale of human activity with the scale of natural systems. This should not be taken to imply that all socio-political boundaries need to be realigned with natural hydrology or ecosystems. Rather, what are required are low-cost mechanisms for dealing with hydrological or ecosystem spillover effects when jurisdictions are founded on different criteria. Second, it is important to have in place institutions that recognize that variations in scale usually attend water-related decisions and this requires differing responses. For instance, in many cases check dams may have trivial downstream effects and the benefits and costs of these structures will be largely internalized by the communities that develop them. This will be the case where water evaporates quickly or enters a saline sink if not first intercepted. However, in other instances check dams (or other watershed development works) may have a wider impact on the availability of water resources to other users. These differing impacts demand differing institutional responses and at different scales. Moreover, failing to understand these nuances will lead to suboptimal outcomes; either uncompensated spillover effects will persist or users' rights will be unnecessarily attenuated, thereby stifling local initiative. Third, there needs to be an acknowledgement that the scale of knowledge must at least approximate the scale of decision making. This theme has arisen several times throughout this volume and needs little more elucidation, other than to emphasize that decentralized decision making counts for nought when the subordinate decision maker lacks knowledge or capacity. Finally, it is important not to overlook institutional linkages. The property rights literature makes it quite clear that rights are not exclusive in the sense that stronger rights for some imply less say in decisions by others. For example, stronger rights for farmers or farmer groups must intrinsically be associated with less say on the part of the state. Ironically, however, this also requires greater effort by the state to ensure that lower-order rights are validated and respected. In simple terms, it is not a matter of state management versus community or individual management; regardless of which entity is assigned authority, this can only operate effectively as long as other groups consciously choose to embrace institutions that recognize that authority.

In concluding this volume an effort was made to move to the most pressing justification for this work. As Gandhi and Bhamoriya (Chapter 15) observe, national estimates place the number of poor people in India at over 300 million, with almost three-quarters of these living in rural areas and being heavily dependent on agriculture for their livelihood. The rationale for investing resources in improving irrigation institutions hinges on the fact that increased productivity in agriculture has been shown to substantially reduce poverty in India and the productivity of agriculture is inextricably linked to irrigation. In simple terms, irrigation development is closely and negatively linked to poverty levels across states in India.

A systematic process of overcoming institutional deficiencies holds great promise in the fight against poverty. However, it is also important to include equity considerations in the institutional design criteria so as to maximize their benefits. Gandhi and Bhamoriya (Chapter 15) argued that there should be a purposeful inclusion of equity considerations in the laws, rules, structures and processes of water institutions. The data analysed in this volume and other studies in this field find substantial variation in the extent to which equity is dealt with in local water institutions in India. Poignantly, there is strong evidence that where equity considerations are deliberately addressed, the overall impacts on equity and poverty alleviation are significantly better.

As we have shown, the returns from improved institutional design can be substantial. The empirical work reported in this volume indicates that attention to the details of institutions is critical, but this need not require substantive calls on the public purse. Changing institutions is not costless, neither does it require large foreign reserves or sophisticated transfers of capital. Yet the rudiments of good institutional design are not always evident in irrigation in India. It is to be hoped that the lessons we have identified can be combined with adequate motivation and political resolve to address these issues while there is still opportunity and scope to avert a crisis.

Index